The Enlargement of the European Union and NATO
Ordering from the Menu in Central Europe

By 2004 the European Union and NATO had each added several new member states, most from the postcommunist countries of Eastern and Central Europe. In order to prepare for membership, these countries had to make many thousands of institutional and legal adjustments. Indeed, they often tried to implement in just a few years practices that evolved over many decades in Western Europe. This book emphasizes the way that policy elites in Central and Eastern Europe often "ordered from the menu" of established Western practices. When did this emulation of Western practices result in more effective and efficient institutions. When did it cause more problems than it solved? Professor Jacoby examines empirical cases in agriculture, regional policy, consumer protection, health care, civilian control of the military, and military professionalism from Hungary, the Czech Republic, Poland, Bulgaria, and Ukraine. The book addresses debates in institutionalist theory, including conditionality, Europeanization, and external influences on democratic and market transitions.

Wade Jacoby is associate professor of political science and director of the Center for the Study of Europe at Brigham Young University in Provo, Utah. His first book, *Imitation and Politics: Redesigning Modern Germany*, was a Choice Outstanding Academic Book for 2000, and he has published in many journals, including *Comparative Political Studies, Politics and Society, Review of International Political Economy, East European Constitutional Review, WSI-Mitteilungen, Governance, German Politics and Society*, and the *British Journal of Industrial Relations*. Jacoby received the Carl Friedrich Prize of the American Political Science Association and was a German Marshall Fund visiting scholar at both the Center for German and European Studies and the Center for Slavic and East European Studies at the University of California, Berkeley.

Praise continued . . .

"Wade Jacoby is one of the leading experts of the processes of transnationalization in the Central European countries. In the extremely boring literature on globalization and the spreading of supra (trans)-national norms, his work is like a breath of fresh air: it is concrete, rich in empirical details and thought provoking conceptual formulations. His book will provoke fruitful and intense debate among the students of European integration, and, very likely, also among the students of transnationalization and globalization."

Laszlo Bruszt, Central European University

"This book makes an intelligent contribution to the debate on European enlargement. In particular it will help students of Europe understand in what ways the European Union and NATO shaped political and economic outcomes in the post-communist world. Jacoby paints a picture of international organizations as neither all powerful nor as epiphenomenal; he tells us when they matter and when they do not."

Jeffrey Kopstein, University of Toronto

The Enlargement of the European Union and NATO

Ordering from the Menu in Central Europe

WADE JACOBY
Brigham Young University

CAMBRIDGE
UNIVERSITY PRESS

CAMBRIDGE UNIVERSITY PRESS
Cambridge, New York, Melbourne, Madrid, Cape Town, Singapore, São Paulo

Cambridge University Press
32 Avenue of the Americas, New York, NY 10013–2473, USA

www.cambridge.org
Information on this title:www.cambridge.org/9780521833592

First published 2004
First paperback edition 2006
Reprinted 2006

Printed in the United States of America

A catalogue record for this book is available from the British Library.

Library of Congress Cataloging in Publication Data
Jacoby, Wade.
The enlargement of the European Union and NATO. Ordering from the Menu
in Central Europe / Wade Jacoby.
p.   cm.
Includes bibliographical references and index.
ISBN 0-521-83358-0
1. Public administration — Europe, Central.   2. Public administration — Europe,
Easter.   3. European Union, — Europe, Central.   4. European Union — Europe,
Eastern.   5. Europe — Economic integration.   6. North Atlantic Treaty
Organization.   I. Title.
JN96.A58133   2004
341.242 2 0943 —dc22   2003069727

ISBN-13   978-0-521-83359-2 hardback
ISBN-10   0-521-83359-0 hardback

ISBN-13   978-0-521-68208-4 paperback
ISBN-10   0-521-68208-8 paperback

For my girls

Contents

Tables, Graph, and Figures

GRAPH

FIGURES

Preface and Acknowledgments

> A simple transfer of Western habits, norms, and laws to Eastern Europe cannot but produce a disaster.
>
> (Ekiert and Zielonka 2003: 23)

A "simple transfer" implies a superficial and mechanical act. Anyone who has studied political and economic change in Central and Eastern Europe (CEE) in the postcommunist era has become well acquainted with superficial and mechanical transfers. Though I will argue that there is a lot more going on in the region – much of it positive – the analogy of a "simple transfer" is worth a moment's reflection. Like all analogies, this one simplifies some aspects of a complicated reality in order to crystallize an essential point or a key trend. In this case, the point is that simply admiring and adopting Western practices is likely to cause more problems than it solves – indeed, to cause "disaster."

In the long process of writing this book, I have cited several analogies about the transformation of Eastern Europe. One favorite is the aria competition, an old story that Martin Krygier (2002) has applied to CEE. The analogy is based on an aria competition with two entrants. After the first singer finishes, the judges immediately award first place to the second singer, figuring there was no way she could be as bad as the first. Krygier goes on to note that CEE citizens thought communism was so bad that postcommunism simply had to be better. But might not CEE citizens, Krygier asks, have tried harder to better understand the alternative to communism? Similarly, the many journalistic comments that likened CEE preparations for EU membership to a kind of beauty contest also implied a certain superficiality.

Another striking analogy is András Sajo's notion of missionaries and savages (1997). With this image, Sajo captures both the sense of moral superiority that often accompanied Western "missionary" efforts to promote reform in CEE. Of course, the notion of the missionary is laden with different meanings in different communities, but the addition of "savages" leaves little doubt about Sajo's critical stance toward the sense of inferiority and gratitude that CEE officials were often obliged to display.

As I wrote, I often played around with other analogies of my own. I did so mostly in order to get some kind of conceptual handle on processes that were maddeningly complex and dynamic. The use of analogies seemed to me at the time (and still does) a reasonable way to impose some intellectual order on processes in a constant state of flux. I framed one early journal article around the image of tutors and pupils, where I showed how the European Union (EU) had constructed routines in which some kind of structured social learning was possible for CEE elites (Jacoby 2001). In many ways, it was an audacious move on the part of the EU – trying to use essentially pedagogical techniques to compress into a few years some processes that had taken many decades in Western Europe.

But in other moments that same process began to look much less pedagogical and much more openly shaped by power relationships. I wrote an article called "*Priest* and *Penitent*," in which I argued that CEE states in 1999–2000 faced a difficult dilemma: The precondition for receiving targeted help from the EU to fix their institutional deficits was to "confess" in great detail their institutional sins to the priestly power of the EU (Jacoby 1999). To do so was dangerous in an environment in which many Western opponents of enlargement were looking for confirmation that CEE states would not make good EU members. In other words, in order to get tactical help, CEE states had to make themselves strategically vulnerable.

In time, the EU took a number of steps to reassure CEE elites and citizens that some kind of enlargement would occur, as it already had for the North Atlantic Treaty Organization (NATO) in 1999. If this softened the priest–penitent dilemma, I argued that CEE states still had to contend with a cross-country race in which the exertion of turning 80,000 pages of EU rules into national law was starting to show (Jacoby 2002a). Moreover, despite generic assurance that enlargement would occur, the EU was long unwilling to set a firm timetable. It is difficult, I noted, to perform optimally in a race whose endpoint is not known in advance but seems to shift over time.

Not all of the helpful analogies are limited to EU examples. Celeste Wallander compares NATO, after the addition of the Czech Republic, Hungary, and Poland, to a soccer team that holds tryouts to select players "but then can never cut delinquent ones from the roster if they break training and lose their skills and conditioning." She argues that NATO "needs a credible mechanism to bench, and ultimately drop, flabby members" (2002: 3).

This book, which is concerned with both the EU and NATO, is subtitled *Ordering from the Menu*. It makes occasional use of the image of CEE states as restaurant patrons. The central idea is that one major aspect of "returning to Europe" has been the effort to leave communism behind by emulating existing institutions and policy designs either directly from specific international organizations like the EU or NATO, or from their individual member states. I use this ordering analogy to underscore that CEE states have institutional choices, but that those choices usually are constrained by the available menu.

I would stick by the sum of these analogies even now: It has been a long and difficult process, generally positive for the CEE states but also risky. At times it felt degrading, even for the participants who got in to the EU and NATO, let alone those who did not. Those who joined were relieved and exhausted once membership was finally achieved. In short, these analogies are often surprisingly reliable in revealing some of the basic contours of enlargement.

But of course, even when applied to one case, analogies miss as much as they reveal. They are the kind of radically simplifying heuristic one uses to make sense of an extremely complex situation because they help fix one's gaze on a few central points of reference. Ultimately, though, we cannot rest with analogies, which, at their best, are helpfully misleading. This book has two purposes, then. First, it explains institutional change in CEE during the years when reforming and pretending to reform often ran side by side. Second, it seeks to move beyond partial analogies and link the process of change to a synthesis of major institutional theory traditions.

For help on the book's conception and research design, I would like to thank Ian Bache, Michael Baun, Suzanne Berger, József Böröcz, Robert Cox, David Dolowitz, John Glenn, David Good, Robert Grey, Anna Grzymała-Busse, Peter Hall, Marc Morjé Howard, Andrew Janos, Ken Jowitt, Peter Katzenstein, Mills Kelly, Jonah Levy, Andrew Moravcsik, Conor O'Dwyer, Ed Page, Richard Samuels, Wayne Sandholtz, Frank Schimmelfennig, Ulrich Sedelmeier, Milada Vachudova, Helen Wallace, and John Zysman.

For help on individual chapters, I would like to thank Wendy Asbeek Brusse, Dirk Bezemer, Brack Brown, Pavel Černoch, Antoaneta Dimitrova, Christopher Donnelly, Rachel Epstein, Wyn Grant, Bélá Greskovits, Brad Gutierrez, David Kirkham, Ann-Christina Knudsen, Jana Luhanová, Martin Mckee, Eva Orosz, Dragan Pasovsky, Denisa Provazníková, Jeffrey Simon, Beate Sissenich, Brian Taylor, Gunnar Trumball, and Peter Weingarten. For research assistance, I thank Mark Champoux, Jenny Champoux, Daniel Burton, Rachel Ligairi, Benjamin Miller, Steven Page, and Christy Watkins at Brigham Young University. Special thanks to my superb BYU colleagues Scott Cooper, Darren Hawkins, and Daniel Nielson. Also at BYU, David Magleby, Kelly Patterson, and the David M. Kennedy Center for International Studies helped make this research possible. I also wish to acknowledge additional support from Grinnell College and the University of California, Berkeley. Research grants from the German Marshall Fund and the National Council for Eurasian and East European Research also furthered this work.

Introduction

Ordering from the Menu in Central Europe

> So when *does* an idea's time come? The answer lies in the match between idea and moment. An idea's time arrives not simply because the idea is compelling on its own terms, but because opportune political circumstances favor it.
>
> (Lieberman 2002: 709)

In 1989–90, the communist regimes of Eastern Europe fell. In a few countries, social movements had challenged and eroded communism; in other places, the regimes seemed to collapse of their own weight. In either case, however, the notion of becoming a normal European state was an idea whose time had come. Almost all the new governments that emerged looked to distance themselves from many communist-era practices and institutions. Elites and citizens generally thought of these changes as part of a "return to Europe." Even those who argued that one could not "return" to a place (Europe) that one had never left still acknowledged the need for radical changes. Within a few years, elites and citizens also came to a broad consensus that their states should aspire to join the European Union (EU) and the North Atlantic Treaty Organization (NATO), and many subsequent institutional changes were pursued with these goals in mind.

This book analyzes Central and Eastern European (CEE) states' efforts to return to Europe by trying to become members of the EU and NATO. Unlike available accounts of the "dual enlargement," it pays particular attention to the proclivity of CEE elites to emulate existing institutions from Western Europe. As the subtitle puts it, these elites often "order from the menu" as opposed to creating their own new practices entirely from scratch. The menu is composed of institutions and practices used by the EU and NATO or by their member states. Emulation, defined more fully below, includes a variety of related processes that have in common the fact that elites in one country use formal institutions and practices from abroad to refashion their own rules or organizations.[1] The elites in question are members of the CEE governments, along with top parliamentarians and civil servants, all of whom play key roles in such emulation as they draft the reform plans of the government and its individual ministries.

Emulation is a curious and understudied phenomenon: Why do the attractions of foreign designs sometimes outweigh the attractions of indigenous innovation? In the case at hand, how faithfully have CEE elites attempted to reproduce Western European designs in their own societies? How much have EU and NATO external pressures or incentives shaped their choices? Finally, to what extent have institutions and practices adopted from Western Europe promoted democratic or market-oriented practices in CEE? The answers to these questions have rich implications for scholars of globalization, regionalization, development, international organizations, and institutional change in a variety of policy areas.

The book also contributes to the debate about the extent to which outsiders can assist processes of reform occurring in other countries. This issue has a central place in several social science disciplines and is a regular topic of public discussion on reforming states in the wake of regime collapse or transition. A host of important studies look at the effect of foreign aid, trade, and foreign direct investment on both economic growth and, though to a lesser extent, on political reforms as well. On the more overtly political side, a large historical literature covers military occupations and a smaller one treats the use of institutional conditionality, mostly in Latin America and Africa. With some exceptions, this literature tends to emphasize the limits of external coercion in promoting reform.

Too often, however, we lack evidence on crucial questions. For example, proponents of the 2003 military invasion of Iraq downplayed or ignored the limits just noted – limits that soon seemed all too real. When

---

[1] In principle, this book uses the distinction between institutions as rules and organizations as groups of formally constituted individual actors who pursue some common purpose (Stone Sweet, Fligstein, and Sandholtz 2001: 6; Hall and Taylor 1996; North 1990). In practice, it is sometimes hard to tell when emulation is of rules and when it is of organizational structures (often delimited by rules). In such cases, *institutions* is sometimes used in a more generic sense. In any case, however, the focus is on both organizational structures and the formal norms and laws propagated through such structures. I do not include uncodified norms, routines, and mentalities.

are institutions "foreign" enough to promote real change and yet not so foreign as to be unacceptable? We have too few studies of a crucial dimension of external assistance: the use of foreign institutional models to change the legal architecture – constitutional and statuatory – of the reforming state. True, there are literatures on both diffusion and policy borrowing. But while the former pays little attention to the ways institutions change as they spread from one setting to another, the latter squashes a large number of contrasting motives and strategies into one overstuffed concept. So what happens when international actors promote particular institutional changes in the context of a massive shift in domestic structures? Or what happens when these reforming states are simply intrigued by an apparently better practice somewhere else? Both situations have been ubiquitous in CEE since 1990.

Policy makers should care about these issues. Regardless of whether they are internal reformers, external occupiers, or ostensibly neutral consultants, such reformers ask many of the same questions: Does what works in one place tell us anything about what might work in another? Are there lessons that one country's leaders can learn from another? If so, is it better to learn by taking explicit advice, or is it better to observe from a distance? Should lessons lead to rapid change, or is real learning best achieved gradually? If local conditions differ – and they always do – should we try to change the practices or change the local conditions? Running through all of these questions are the crucial issues of external imposition versus domestic choice and superficial and cosmetic changes versus real and enduring ones.

The intense and sustained use of emulation in CEE thus offers a unique research opportunity, with links to several broader problems. For example, while the International Monetary Fund (IMF) and World Bank often give leveraged policy advice to borrower nations, it is not clear how and when international organizations can best promote model institutional structures and formal rules. The reconstruction and occupation of post-conflict states has also stimulated debates about the possibilities and limits of institutional change by design. The importance of sustained and systematic attention to institutional redesign under the influence of foreign models is nowhere more apparent than in the Europe of the last years of the twentieth century and the first years of the twenty-first. Nowhere have the conditions been more propitious for emulation, as the East Europeans have had the idea, the opportunity, and the incentives to pursue this course for close to a decade.

The questions answered in this book also fill a widely acknowledged gap in the literature on CEE. A decade and a half after the collapse of communist regimes, the time is ripe for a reappraisal of the sources of institutional design in CEE and, in particular, of the role of outsiders. The early, almost exclusive focus on forces internal to the region has been augmented by a steadily growing interest in the external influences on, or even the external governance of, the various political and economic transformations of the region (Schimmelfennig and Sedelmeier 2004; Grabbe 2004; Lieven and Trenin 2003; Pravda and Zielonka 2001; Carothers 1999; Dawisha 1997; Grey 1997; Pridham et al. 1997). This writing on external influences describes a range of Western actions to promote change, though much of it still leaves us quite far from understanding how those Western policies are taken up by the weak states of CEE. It shows that external influence is a multistranded process and not a discrete variable. As a result, authors who begin by setting up external pressures or international imperatives as alternatives to domestic explanations of economic and political change in CEE usually abandon the claim that these are real alternatives (Crawford and Lijphart 1995: 194–6; Stark and Bruszt 1998: 5–8). A sustained focus on both domestic and external pressures will be needed to replace the mostly atheoretical concepts in the literature on external influences.[2]

CEE elites have used emulation very extensively. For example, in Hungary's June 1999 parliamentary session, of the 180 laws passed, 152 were not subject to any debate simply because they were part of the EU *acquis communautaire*, which is the set of treaties, rules, standards, principles, and policies that acceding countries are required to adopt (Kopstein and Reilly 2000: 27; *Magyar Nemzet* [Budapest], June 19, 1999). This observation, which could be replicated many times across the region, raises some real puzzles. Given the common expectation that states will jealously guard their sovereignty, why would states just freed from Soviet domination willingly subject themselves to invasive reform demands from Western Europe? Given the importance of control of the national legislative agenda, why would elected officials surrender agenda-setting power to the EU or NATO? The outcomes are as puzzling as the motives. If international organizations (IOs) – especially the EU – really wield significant

---

[2] On the chronologically prior but related issue of the purported "diffusion" of neoliberal economic policies of the early 1990s to postcommunist states, see Bockman and Eyal (2002). These authors do successfully cast historical networks as an alternative explanation to a crude version of "imitation." This book shares both the skepticism about diffusion and the focus on the historical underpinnings of CEE enthusiasm for Western models, though it treats choices that come later and are made by actors who were not part of the actor-network identified by Bockman and Eyal.

power, why does the kind of emulation attempted and the outcomes that result vary so greatly? Finally, if CEE elites are simply pretending to reform, how do we explain the extraordinary changes that have occurred in some policy areas? To unravel most of these puzzles, we must first appreciate the great variation in the choices for and results of emulation.

EXPLAINING MODES AND OUTCOMES OF EMULATION

This book explains two patterns: the kinds of emulation CEE elites attempt and the outcomes of reform that follow from these efforts. Both patterns encompass significant variation, and the empirical chapters of the book discuss this variation in great detail. For now, it is sufficient to sketch only the main outlines of the causal relationships.

The first outcome to be explained is what I call the emulation "mode." How have CEE elites tried to emulate Western European institutions? I argue that what appears to be one messy complex of borrowing Western structures is better understood as four different, but related modes (see Table 1). The typology in Table 1 follows from two factors whose combination generates these different modes: the degree of pressure brought to bear externally and the degree of faithfulness in replication (Dolowitz and Marsh 1996; Powell and DiMaggio 1991; Kopstein and Reilly 1999: 20–1). In any given case, EU and NATO officials largely determine the first value (coded in simple binary fashion in Table 1 as "more voluntary or less voluntary"), and CEE national governments largely determine the second (coded as "faithful or approximate"). Crucially, modes of emulation are often the result of the constrained choices of CEE elites; elite preferences for faithful versus approximate emulation – or their refusal to emulate at all – underscore their room to fashion a response to these constraints.[3] The combination of these two factors – what we might call pressure and precision – marks a pattern that is richer than the crude notions that CEE states either do exactly what the powerful IOs demand or that they merely pretend to do so as a way to gain membership. Depending upon the policy area being considered, CEE states often do some of each and, as the discussion below will indicate, several other things in addition.[4]

The four modes of emulation are as follows: The upper-left cell of Table 1 comes straight from a well-established literature. Scholars of

---

[3] I thank Robert Cox and Wayne Sandholtz for help in clarifying this point.
[4] Thus, the unit of analysis and comparison in this book will be the policy area. This choice is defended below in the section on cases, methods, and data.

TABLE 1. *Different Uses of Emulation in the Design of Postcommunist Institutions*

	More Voluntary	Less Voluntary
Faithful	Copies	Patches
Approximate	Templates	Thresholds

"diffusion" and "policy borrowing" have long tried to understand the macrosociological and network factors that promote the voluntary and reasonably faithful spread of institutions from one place to another (for reviews, see Jacoby 2000: 4–12; De Jong, Lalenis, and Mamadouh 2003; Strang and Soule 1998). Such cases, labeled copies for shorthand, did exist in CEE, but this book argues that they were rather rare.[5]

Much more common were three other modes that occurred alongside simple copying. The first alternative mode I call templates. As communism collapsed, some CEE elites voluntarily looked to Western Europe for general templates in which they used the West European model more as a loose approximation than a detailed blueprint. In some cases, CEE states took their inspiration or sought advice directly from EU and NATO officials, but in many other cases they were able to use national templates from those organizations' member states. In some cases, CEE experts had fairly intimate familiarity with Western practices, either from careful study, extended exchange visits, or years in exile in the West. A large number of Western experts also visited the region, armed with advice that ran the spectrum from well-conceived to obviously ludicrous. In many cases, this form of emulation was blended in the same policy sector with institutional reforms that were entirely indigenous. As a result, a common pattern was that CEE elites often tried to make significant local adaptations of the foreign template.

The second alternative mode I call thresholds. In these cases, the EU and NATO set minimum standards for policy and institutional changes. But typically, these standards were rough and approximate – that is, "We can't tell nonmembers how to design their institutions ..." – and also less voluntary – "... but if you eventually want to join, you'll need to make the following reforms...." Thus, pressure was high, but precision could be low. Both the EU and NATO long tried to minimize mandates of precise institutional outcomes. At times, this reluctance reflected a lack of internal

---

[5] The policy borrowing literature does sometimes refer to the likelihood that copies will not be exact. Here, the most extensive typology is Rose (1991: 21–2).

consensus among members or deference to the sovereignty of CEE states. In part, however, IO officials also were wary of a checklist approach, because for several years, each IO had an internal consensus against a rapid enlargement. Some officials worried that if they gave precise targets to CEE reformers, they would come under more pressure to admit CEE states if those targets were met. In other cases, NATO and EU officials claimed to see value in letting CEE states discover appropriate structures without undue outside pressure. Yet as membership drew nearer, both organizations began to articulate certain minimal conditions. In many cases, we will see that these thresholds remained vague; as in Justice Potter Stewart's famous assessment of pornography, EU and NATO officials often claimed to know what was acceptable or unacceptable when they saw it. Once the IO in question articulated such thresholds, CEE elites could, by definition, no longer make use of the two voluntary modes (copies and templates), at least not in response to that particular threshold.

The third alternative mode to copying is located in the upper-right cell of Table 1. As CEE states' membership has drawn nearer, both organizations sometimes have required mandatory and faithful patches. This mode allowed CEE elites the least discretion of all, for these patches have been quite explicit, often involving specific legal texts to be incorporated en bloc into national law.[6] While such patches have been more common in EU accession as a result of the detailed and demanding *acquis communautaire*, NATO accession has also generated CEE patches, especially in the last-minute defense legislation that attempted to meet specific NATO Target Force Goals (TFGs). In some cases, CEE elites inserted patches into policy domains where their existing structures were quite thin. In other cases, they used patches to fix what NATO and the EU had deemed to be holes in more developed legislative practices or administrative capacities. As we will see, policy areas that had once been marked by the industrious if voluntaristic use of templates came later to be the site of a mad rush to patch what was still deemed incompatible with prevailing IO practices. Indeed, one of the virtues of patches was the speed with which they could be implemented. Some policy areas subject to EU and NATO thresholds were patched when the threshold could clearly have been met by some form of indigenous reform that owed no debt to specific Western models. Yet since both the conceptual and political demands

---

[6] Patches were most common in response to the EU, whose number of regulations, directives, and legal acts grew from 1,947 in 1973 to 24,130 by 1997 (Grzymała-Busse 2004: 25).

of developing indigenous reforms can be quite high, off-the-shelf patches were often the preferred response to pressure from the IO.

In short, not all emulation is the same. We should be skeptical of accounts that characterize emulation as homogenous, usually by noting the futility of isolated acts of "mindless imitation" or "mimicry."[7] Different modes of emulation are the result of different mixes of IO constraints and CEE elite choices, and this section provides a terminology adequate to the complexity of the issues. We should also be skeptical of accounts that do not explicitly recognize the dynamism of modes of emulation. Over the course of the 1990s, the CEE states went through several ups and downs on the road to membership in the EU and NATO. The shifting domestic political moods interacted with the shifting policies of the IOs themselves. Table 1, therefore, distinguishes between degrees of voluntarism on the part of the CEE elites.[8] The basic pattern is that early in the 1990s, CEE reforms were very lightly constrained, if at all, by the IOs. As first NATO and then the EU announced forthcoming enlargements and began to inventory CEE practices, the degree of voluntarism fell off markedly. The NATO case then suggests that after membership is achieved, the scope for voluntaristic reforms rises once again.

But modes of emulation are only half of the story. Just as there is a range of variation in ways to emulate existing Western practices, so too is there a range of outcomes that result. In some cases, we will see emulation feeding into a robust "politics as usual," while in other cases emulation will create policy areas almost *de novo*. As in Table 1, a necessary initial step is to provide labels for these outcomes, the pattern of which the empirical chapters then explain. I use four such labels, which I shall define below: struggle, scaffolding, homesteading, and learning. Two of these labels – struggle and learning – reflect fairly common and well-studied kinds of outcomes. The two others – scaffolding and homesteading – are less familiar, though hopefully still intuitive once explained. All four, however, are meant as short descriptions of the range of the kinds of politics that

---

[7] This trope is remarkably common in journalistic accounts of institutional reform, but it also appears widely in academic accounts, often under the guise of an "alternative explanation." Chapter 8 will take up this issue in more detail, but one common root of this disparagement of emulation as a source of institutional change is that it is much easier to recognize when it fails than when it succeeds. This disparity generates a major selection bias because we are much more likely to study emulation that fails.

[8] Excellent accounts of the temporal dimension in postcommunist reforms can be found in Fish (1998b) and Grzymała-Busse (2002). More generally, arguments that emphasize historical "sequencing" have been used to explain both stasis (e.g., Pierson 2000a, 2000b) and change (e.g., Blyth 2002).

result when elites try to or are obliged to emulate policies and institutions that exist elsewhere. A key aim of the book is to describe and explain this full range of variation.

As in the case of Table 1, I use two broad factors to map this variation as it has existed across a range of policy areas in postcommunist CEE. Again, I highlight one factor at the international level and one factor at the domestic level. At the international level, we need to know about the nature of the demands emanating from the IO. Are they many and detailed? Few and vague? I capture this dimension by use of the concept of "rule density," by which I mean the extent of IO demands.[9] This book looks at five policy areas, the selection of which is discussed below. In three of them – agriculture, regional policy, and civilian control of the military – the IO rules were dense. In two others, health care and consumer protection, they clearly were not.

The other dimension is the density of policy sector actors present at communism's collapse. The intuition is that emulation proceeds differently where state and social actors are well developed than in policy sectors that are new.[10] Of the five policy areas, there are three where actors

[9] In discussing the EU, this book often refers to *acquis* density, rather than rule density, since the EU's rules are known collectively as the *acquis communautaire*. There is an existing literature on the "legal transposition" of EU directives (binding EU legislation that each member state uses its own "form and method" (Art. 249) to achieve), but I do not rely on it in this book for two reasons. First, (as that literature recognizes) current EU member states shape directives in directions that they know they can later transpose – indeed, in many cases the directive effectively codifies the rules of some subset of existing member states. This is not possible in CEE, because they have not been members in the period considered here and have had to transpose directives that they have had no role in shaping and that take no account of their own national traditions. Thus, transposition is likely to be a much harder task for CEE states than for member states even when one excludes the obvious fact that existing member states have far superior systems of public administration (Dyson and Goetz 2003). The second reason not to rely on the transposition literature is that the book includes NATO cases that do not fit the presumptions of that literature. Chapters 4 and 5 do, however, argue that NATO also has a kind of *acquis*, much of which it has first tried to codify during the recent enlargements. For a detailed discussion of rule density as applied to CEE cases, see Schimmelfennig and Sedelmeier (2004) and Schwellnuss (2004).

[10] The obvious alternative specification would be "actor preferences." I use actor preferences very extensively in the case studies. But for mapping the range of variation, this factor is less useful because of the broad consensus across postcommunist societies that gaining entry into the EU and NATO was important. Choosing cases based on variation on this dimension would have meant giving undue prominence to the fairly small numbers of extreme right and left actors opposed to IO membership and blurring the differences between more mainstream actors who almost all, at least officially, have supported their country's efforts to gain membership in these IOs.

were dense and two where they were thin. In health care, agricultural policy, and civilian control of the military, reform proponents faced powerful actors from the start of the postcommunist era. In each case, some of the actors were nonstate interest groups, while others were part of the state apparatus itself, often ministries or factions within ministries. These actors have contested the adoption of some Western models and significantly reshaped others.

TABLE 2. *Outcomes of Efforts at Emulation Through Copies, Templates, Thresholds, and Patches*

	Low Density of Actors	High Density of Actors
Low Density of Rules	Homesteading (consumer protection)	Continuous Learning (health care)
High Density of Rules	Scaffolding (regional policy)	Open Struggle (agriculture, civilian control of the military)

Table 2 sketches the range of variation. The right column of the table shows the dominant pattern when actors were well established. In those cases where the IO placed heavy demands on these powerful actors (i.e., rule density was high), emulation led to high-profile "struggles." In the agriculture case, emulation was a precondition for Common Agricultural Policy (CAP) support, and the struggles revolved around the extent of financial support that would flow to farmers after the emulated structures and policies were in place. In the military case, meeting certain thresholds of civilian control was a precondition for membership, yet this provoked fights between civilians and certain factions of their militaries. By contrast, when those demands were light, well-established actors could use emulation to engage in relatively unpressured "learning." This is the outcome in health care in both countries studied, as both the Ministries of Health and the major interest groups paid close attention to specific health care models from Western Europe and even the United States.

Regional economic development and consumer protection are two areas in which CEE interests were much less organized in 1989–90 and thus constituted far less of a brake on reform initiatives. These cases are on the left side of Table 2. In regional policy, a dense set of EU rules (though not so dense as in agriculture) provide a "scaffolding" around which previously latent or unorganized interests have congealed. In consumer protection, where the density of EU rules is quite modest, the rules have been sufficient only to encourage new groups to "homestead" this policy domain and have generated only a few isolated pioneers to push forward this new policy area.

Tables 1 and 2 do different kinds of work in this book. Table 1 indicates that four kinds of emulation have been occurring in CEE. Table 2 describes the central tendencies that should result from any given effort at emulation, whether through highly voluntaristic copies or highly constrained patches. In Table 1, the observations about elite pursuit of different modes of emulation were premised on significant room for strategic choice; that is, the IO officials choose the stringency of their own institutional standards, and CEE elites choose whether to use emulation faithfully or approximately. Of course, neither of those choices is unconstrained: The IOs are often constrained by their member states, and the CEE elites are clearly constrained by the rules of the IO they wish to join, as well as by domestic politics. Even so, the outcomes shown in Table 2 clearly are more structural and less contingent than those in Table 1, because neither rule density nor actor density is easily manipulable.[11]

The Table 2 outcomes follow from the two factors identified earlier – the density of the existing IO rules and the density of state and social interests in the various policy areas of CEE societies.[12] Put differently, there is no direct causal link between Table 1 and Table 2. In part, the two tables are not wholly independent. For example, the density of actors often influences elite choices about the modes of emulation to pursue. In general, high actor density pushes elites toward more approximate forms of emulation that might capture the virtues of foreign models while still shaping them to local conditions. A strong causal link between the tables also is hard to demonstrate, because CEE states often drew on several modes of emulation in each of the policy domains identified in Table 2. In many cases, elites began the postcommunist period attempting to use a rough template of an existing Western European institutional model, only to be confronted by an IO in the mid-1990s with a much more specific threshold in the same policy area, and then confronted, within a few more

---

[11] That said, the EU and, to a lesser extent, NATO have learned to manipulate the size and scope of their rules. Several examples are given below.

[12] This summary stresses deterministic factors, but the case studies add contingency. For example, while Table 2 is premised on high variation across policy domains – in part because of the "most similar cases" design described in the next section – the case narratives indicate where national peculiarities play key roles in shaping outcomes. As we will see, these contingent factors are key in explaining which CEE states will actually be able to use the institutions and implement the policies that they have emulated.

years, the demand that very specific patches be employed if membership negotiations were to proceed. As a result, it turns out that most modes of emulation are empirically linked to most of the possible outcomes.[13] Thus, we have two somewhat distinct patterns to explain and two different sets of causal logics to explain them.

All that said, there is an indirect causal link between modes of emulation and outcomes. Since both the EU and NATO have made non-negotiable demands on CEE states that wish to join, the states have had to adopt certain institutions and practices irrespective of whether the result was an uncontroversial "modernization" or a bitter struggle. For the issue of getting such institutions "on the books," the mode of emulation simply is not a decisive factor. But when we ask whether these new institutions and policies will actually make a difference in the CEE states – whether they will be used and come to find public acceptance – modes do matter. In short, even where the destination is fixed by the IO, it turns out to matter what road is taken to get there. For example, one of the findings stressed below is that emulation works least precisely where it is used most – in policy sectors with heavy external demands and few domestic precursors. There, elites have often scrambled to get the right policies "on the books" but lack the actors who could make such policies have the effects the EU and NATO have intended.

CASES, METHODS, AND DATA

As noted, this book draws on Table 2 by using at least one policy case from each of the four cells. The book's unit of analysis is thus the national policy area, and the primary empirical basis encompasses the Czech and Hungarian preparations for joining the EU and NATO. This provides ten initial cases – five in each of two states. Its secondary basis employs briefer case studies of select policy areas in three other postcommunist states (Poland, Bulgaria, and Ukraine) and also one non-postcommunist case (Sweden).

---

[13] There are some logical exclusions. While copying could logically lead to any of the four outcomes, the other modes cannot. States should rarely employ voluntaristic templates in cases where interest constellations lead them to expect large struggles. For example, this logic is consistent with the fact that U.S. President Bill Clinton clearly did not use the "Canadian health care model" as a template for U.S. reforms, though it may explain why it was useful for opponents to claim that he did. Because both thresholds and patches respond to IO demands, they cannot lead to the learning outcome, which in this book presupposes elites free to explore foreign models and their applicability to their own national context absent any IO demands to do so.

The Czech–Hungarian comparison constitutes a "most-similar cases, most-likely cases" research design (Mill 1970; Snyder 2001). The states share several important features that previous research has linked to emulation by diffusion. Most important, both have had long experience with broader European institutional developments and have relatively high levels of economic development.[14] They are thus likely to be relatively privileged in pursuing institutional change through emulation relative to distant and underdeveloped states such as Ukraine. Both are de facto unitary states with long-term integration into the Germanic law subfamily of civil law traditions. Both have had alternations of government between the center right and center left inside parliamentary regimes with broadly similar party spectrums and electoral thresholds.[15] Both developed an early domestic consensus that joining the EU and NATO were central foreign policy goals. This means that, unlike Bulgaria, Romania, and Slovakia, we can observe differences between voluntary emulation and that which is driven by the IOs (Vachudova 2004). The countries are about the same size (with populations around 10 million), and inside CEE, both were among the early front-runners for EU and NATO membership. If there is any place in CEE where conditions for comparing emulation are propitious, it is here.[16]

Like all methods, this choice privileges some questions at the expense of others. I build on "most similar" cases because they help us focus on the importance of a few key variables at the IO and policy levels and exclude a host of complicating factors in the poorer and more distant areas of the postcommunist world.[17] Further, I try to maximize observations on different policy areas rather than on the largest range of postcommunist countries. Even if modest, these controls are important because as many commentators have noted, CEE is a region where many things are changing

---

[14] The classic study on geographic and fiscal influences on diffusion rates is Walker (1969).
[15] But Hungary has had a stronger consensus on EU and NATO membership and has not had a party dominate its national agenda for as long as the ODS (Civic Democratic Party) did in the Czech Republic.
[16] In comparative political studies of the CEE, familiarity often breeds contempt. There is a tendency for case studies of the CEE to skewer the country that is studied closely and to laud the efforts of some alternative CEE case where things supposedly have been done much better. This book acknowledges that there has been lots of progress in both countries and that both still have glaring problems to overcome.
[17] Variation is highest across policy cases. It is modest across IOs. It is lowest across the two country cases. While chapter 8 gives evidence from less-reformed postcommunist cases (Bulgaria, Ukraine), the low variation across country cases is consistent with research on compliance rates in Western Europe as well. See Börzel, Hofmann, and Sprungk (2003) and Lowi (1972).

TABLE 3. *Central Tendencies in Modes and Outcomes*

Mode	Agriculture	Regional Policy	Consumer Protection	Health	Civilian Control/ Military Professionalism
Modes	Thresholds	Thresholds	Patches	Templates	Thresholds
Outcome	Struggle	Scaffolding	Homesteading	Learning	Struggle

simultaneously. Bunce, for example, states that "virtually everything that can be in transition is in transition in Eastern Europe," and this fact underscores the importance of picking cases that share as many features as possible (1997: 175).

The Czech and Hungarian cases are "most likely" cases in that they are "close" to Western Europe, whether one measured this in terms of history, geography, or the political race for membership. This contrast will become more clear in chapter 8, when the Ukrainian and Bulgarian cases are considered. Focusing on most likely cases is useful because emulation is often difficult to disentangle from indigenous reform, so it helps to focus first on cases where the trend is clearest and strongest. The benefit of this research design is to highlight significant within-country variation; the evidence will show, for example, that "most likely" does not always mean "most successful." The cost of this research strategy is that we will be unable to read diffusion rates off of factors like GDP, FDI levels, or literacy rates. We will see that while the resulting argument is generalizable, it has very high data requirements.

Table 3 summarizes both outcomes just discussed in each of the five policy areas, indicating both a dominant mode of emulation and the broad outcome. For summary purposes, the chart ignores country differences that will be covered extensively in the empirical chapters. It focuses instead on the central themes of the chapters to come, leaving caveats for later. The importance of the "less voluntary" end of the spectrum stands out, for only in the case of health care – where the EU has little leverage – has one of the voluntary modes of emulation been dominant. In all other cases, thresholds and patches have been the main device, though again, the empirical cases will show that voluntary templates did play some role in both the civilian control and regional policy cases. Moreover, in no case are voluntary and faithful copies the dominant mode of emulation. This implies that the mode that is at the center of the dominant social science approach to understanding emulation – for example, the diffusion literature – is much rarer than the other modes discussed in this book. If that is true, we have been thinking about the wrong thing – voluntaristic and faithful copying – in the wrong way, for example, primarily as a consequence of developmental indicators.

In addition to the structured Czech–Hungarian comparison that runs through each of the four empirical chapters (two on the EU and two on NATO), the final chapter reviews more briefly the evidence from four other cases. This chapter checks the findings against cases that vary from the two main cases in ways that are most likely to matter for broader comparative research. Briefly, the Polish case is obviously important in gauging the effects of its much larger population and economy, which, for these reasons, does not lend itself to sustained structured comparison with the two other "front-runner" cases. Especially in the crucial case of agriculture, how does this enormous size affect modes and outcomes of emulation? The case on Sweden, which joined the EU in 1995, allows us to check hypotheses about non-postcommunist countries that seek closer ties to Western organizations. Especially intriguing here is the case in which new members have to lower their institutional standards in order to become members of an IO rather than raise them. The Bulgarian case – using a country from the Ottoman rather than Habsburg Empire – lets us explore the relevance of particular legacies of state formation for efforts to join these Western clubs. Ottoman territories had fundamentally different traditions of public administration than did Roman law countries. Does this difference matter in policy domains that depend heavily on administrative competence?[18] Finally, the Ukrainian case provides something of a null hypothesis: What kinds of institutional changes occur when a state shows little interest in joining Western clubs from which it is, in any case, far distant?

Data sources include EU and NATO documents, quantitative data on programs promoting institutional emulation, such as the EU's Phare program and NATO's Partnership for Peace, third-party evaluations of such programs, and about 100 interviews over five years with EU, NATO, Czech, and Hungarian officials. In addition, the book builds on scholarly case studies of institutional reform in all of the policy sectors noted above. Many policy specialists have commented on the importance of emulation, and this book tries to situate and cross-check many such observations in the light of other forms of qualitative and quantitative data.

---

[18] For a discussion of the historical proclivity of Europeans to dismiss Ottoman administration as beyond the boundaries of the "standard of civilization," see Silvia and Sampson (2003); see also Kitschelt et al. (1999).

STRUCTURE OF THE BOOK

The rest of the book contains eight chapters. Chapter 1 explains emulation as a result of "embedded rationality." It situates a theory of emulation at the junction of three widely used bodies of institutionalist theory – rational choice, historical, and sociological. It draws selectively on the different traditions to identify the most pertinent factors to explain the modes and outcomes of emulation. Using these factors, it then shows that emulation occurs when three potential "motors" of emulation are stronger than three other kinds of potential "brakes."[19] Those less interested in institutional theory can see the general argument summarized in Figures 1 and 2 on pages 35 and 36.

Chapter 2 discusses modes and outcomes in two policy areas – health care and consumer protection – in which the EU *acquis* density is low. In health care, the *acquis* is very small, and this left CEE states free to pick and choose (or ignore) prevailing Western models. What did CEE elites make of the bewildering diversity of Western health care institutions? Which ones might help CEE elites manage health care spending, maintain the broad provision of services that citizens of the region expect from the state, and keep pace with new epidemiological trends that come with new lifestyles? I show that CEE states have used templates to try to go "back to Bismarck" and reconnect to the insurance-based systems of health care that characterize several Western European states. The main outcome has been a slow but steady learning process, interrupted along the way by some emulation that did not work.

Consumer protection is another policy area in which the EU has relatively low rule density. The difference from health care, however, is the almost total lack of any institutional predecessor in this domain. Obviously, Marxist societies performed interest representation primarily around producer groups. Moreover, in economies where the supply of consumer goods was already highly constrained, the main struggle was one against scarcity, not fraud. By and large, one took what one could find. In a policy domain notorious for its collective action problems, those consumer-oriented policies that did exist – especially subsidized prices – were highly dependent upon Communist Party institutions that quickly went defunct. With no significant interest constellations available to identify and modify attractive templates, emulation revolved around a fairly hasty and

[19] I borrow the motors–brakes idea from Stanley Hoffmann, who characterized the French Third Republic as "all brakes and no motor" (1962).

technocratic set of patches implemented in the late 1990s. As for outcomes, this part of chapter 2 shows the gradual "homesteading" of an
almost totally new policy domain in CEE.

Chapter 3 then looks at two policy areas in which the EU's rule density is much higher: agriculture and regional economic development. The
chapter emphasizes thresholds and patches, because these were two areas
where changes were clearly demanded by the IO. Since the EU spends
the dominant portion of its budget here, elites also had very strong incentives to avoid missing out on important sources of funding. Access to
such funds was predicated on enduring a sustained "screening" of CEE
laws by the EU Commission.[20] From Brussels, the screening of Czech and
Hungarian legislation between 1998 and 2002 looked like a systematic
way to modernize that corpus while harmonizing it with EU expectations
through formal negotiations between 2000–2. There is no gainsaying
the remarkable changes that have come about in both policy areas. The
chapters show these changes both in terms of new rules and procedures
and in terms of newly created administrative structures. These chapters
also show, however, that the imperative to transpose the 800,000 page
acquis into national law sometimes gives rise to "Potemkin institutions"
that are more façade than fact.[21] Because current members often also fail
to meet some of their EU commitments, however, compliance problems
are not prima facie evidence that CEE states will be bad members (Iankova
and Katzenstein 2003; Börzel et al. 2003).

This third chapter emphasizes EU efforts to articulate thresholds of
institutional reform in both cases. In the agriculture case, the outcome was
a high-profile struggle, as agricultural interest groups and their patrons
tried to maximize the benefits of EU agricultural spending in CEE. In
regional policy, by contrast, the EU thresholds and technical regulations
functioned as a kind of scaffolding for the thinly organized interests that
might benefit from such funding. The final funding deals are both large
enough to make a real difference in each policy domain yet small enough
to fuel resentment that CEE states are being embraced only as "second-
class members."

There are also two chapters on NATO enlargement. The first focuses on
institutions for civilian control of the military. NATO states worried about
CEE civilian controls in the new situation where party and state were no

---

[20] Useful brief overviews of the enlargement process include Ekiert and Zielonka (2003)
and Cameron (2003).
[21] For related trends in the 1920s in Romania and Bulgaria, see Stokes (1991).

longer fused.[22] Since 1990, there have been several showdowns in CEE, over which officials would have constitutional power over the military establishment. Chapter 4 goes through several uses of NATO thresholds and patches. The outcome is that while the principle of civilian control has been widely embraced at an abstract level, long-running political battles have been required to put it into practice.

The second NATO chapter (chapter 5) takes up the promotion of military professionalism. Compared to civilian control, a related concept, professionalism is more behavioral – emphasizing military effectiveness and efficiency – but still has a large institutional component. The testing ground for the level of military professionalism in CEE are the war in Kosovo and what is widely called the war on terrorism. The former provided an immediate test of new military institutions, the latter an ongoing challenge for the new members (and an opportunity to impress the United States). Hungary's geographic importance to NATO's combined arms operations and the Czech Republic's rather close ties to Serbia meant that both nations played behind-the-scenes roles in the Kosovo confrontation, both sparked intra-NATO disputes with their behavior, and both saw the war widen cleavages in their own societies. Each also has since failed to meet important NATO commitments, and each now faces real challenges in promoting military professionalization.

These problems carry over into the war on terrorism. The Czech and Hungarian militaries are in such difficult shape that they are proposing to specialize in particular activities in which they might have enough capability to make a positive contribution. This specialization is relatively congenial to the United States – since it hopes to be able to draw upon specific European capabilities in an ad hoc way – but is of great concern to many of NATO's European allies. These tensions came spectacularly to a head in February and March 2003.

Chapter 6 relates the evidence in the cases to three prominent strands of institutionalist theory, namely, rational, historical, and sociological. This large body of theory tries to understand both the causes of institutions and also the role of institutions as causes of other outcomes. Though most followers of one school or another stress the competition of those theories, chapter 6 demonstrates that they are not always incompatible. It uses the

---

[22] Most of the violence in postcommunist Eastern Europe happened in states whose militaries had not been subject to Soviet-style command-and-control systems (Bunce 1999). Nevertheless, as the Russian military's role in the Chechen wars has made amply clear, civil–military relations in post-Soviet states cannot simply be assumed to be unproblematic (Taylor 2001).

concept of embedded rationality (introduced in chapter 1) to chart one kind of synthesis. Chapter 7 then takes up a second form of synthesis. Where chapter 6 uses the case data to inform theory building, chapter 7 shows that we can use theory in selected pairs to draw more richness from the cases. The analytical tools are situational in that after they produce new insights, the pairs can easily revert to their constituent parts. Together, these chapters eschew both a "horse race" approach of parsimonious but competing institutional theories and an "everything matters" approach to institutions. They show two complementary ways to synthesize rationalist, sociological, and historical perspectives on institutions by stressing their different weights in a sequential process. By extension, they sidestep theory battles whose marginal utility is now shrinking and point instead to better ways of integrating perspectives most scholars already know to be valuable.

The concluding chapter checks the argument developed through the study of two medium-sized front-runners for EU and NATO membership, with selected shorter cases from around the region. In so doing, it focuses on potential alternative explanations emphasized in other theories. The Polish case helps check for the effects of size, the Bulgarian case for the long-term effects of prior location in the Ottoman rather than Habsburg empire, the Ukrainian case for location on the periphery of EU and NATO influence, and the non-postcommunist Swedish case for the effects of policy achievements that are "higher" than the EU standards rather than "lower." The chapter then returns to the notion that rejoining Europe was an idea whose time appeared to have come. This book does not claim that the idea of returning to Europe had direct causal significance (e.g., Hall 1993; Blyth 2002). Rather, it shows that this idea's realization came to be a lot less romantic and a lot more technocratic with the passage of time. This trajectory, in turn, has important implications for students of outsiders' influences on market reforms and democratization and speaks also to the growing literatures on postcommunist reform, conditionality, and Europeanization.

I

Emulation as Embedded Rationalism

> The sensible, but difficult, question [about CEE] is...What can be done about what works badly here? That is often translated, particularly by Western missionaries and advisors in the region, as: What works well at home, or in "normal" countries, or in the West?
>
> (Krygier 2002: 63)

Why would politicians so recently freed from Soviet constraints and with memories of the earlier imposition of foreign practices under the Habsburg Empire now be willing to order from Western Europe's menu of institutions and rules? In part, as the epigraph indicates, they were advised to do so. But this answer is obviously incomplete, and a fuller answer depends upon additional factors that include communism's collapse and the subsequent opportunity to embrace Western practices, the political benefits that accrued to CEE politicians through modernizing rapidly, and these elites' desires to demonstrate to outsiders and to voters that they embrace needed reforms. That is, once external constraints were lifted by the Soviet Union, a new set of incentives for institutional change generally overpowered the remaining constraints of historical structures and conservative actors. More prosaically, the motors of change became stronger than the brakes of constraint.

CEE elites acted rationally in the face of two kinds of broadly material incentives: from their voters and from the IOs themselves. But their rationality was embedded – as the chapter's title indicates – in two ways. First, the material incentives often pointed in a general direction, but elites often also faced a detailed normative framework urging them to chart a specific

reform agenda.[1] Second, the constraints of historical structures and conservative actors often deflected the reform course charted by elites. The
rest of this chapter lays out these arguments in detail.

As noted, full sovereignty meant the easing of constraint on CEE governments – the end of any remaining obligation to pursue the policies of
the imperialist Soviet power and an opportunity to chart a new course. For
two reasons, emulation was part of this course. First, high-profile Western
IOs like the EU and NATO had created an environment in which the current institutions of their member states provided organizational models
that sometimes appealed to reforming elites in CEE. Second, CEE state
elites (in both the executive and the legislature) often faced specific incentives to adopt some of the institutions and practices of foreign powers.

The electoral benefits of pro-EU membership and pro-NATO membership policies have been more impressive than one might think when
looking only at public opinion figures in CEE (Cichowski 2000; Cameron
2003). The party political consensus on joining the EU and NATO has
been strong in CEE, and much more stable than among the citizenry,
whose support has fluctuated over time.[2] In some states (Poland, Hungary, and the Czech Republic), elite opposition to their country joining
these IOs has been concentrated in the radical fringe.[3] In other states
in which conservative elites initially opposed EU membership (Bulgaria,
Slovakia, and Romania), subsequent elections returned pro-EU coalitions
(Vachudova 2004). Other elite incentives came through the IOs themselves, which found ways to bear some of the countries' adjustment costs.[4]

Beyond responding to material incentives, CEE elites also seemed eager
in some cases to demonstrate that they could guide their societies from
the failed institutional models of communism toward the "normal" and

[1] By "normative," I mean simply that both the EU and NATO have had very concrete
expectations that CEE governments would meet a variety of IO norms; in some cases,
CEE elites also embraced the values embodied in these rules and practices, but they were
expected to adopt the rules and practices whether or not they had intrinsic appeal.

[2] During most of the period covered here, the "real" costs and benefits of enlargement have
been almost impossible for key actors to ascertain with any certainty. Good summaries
of the optimistic view are Grabbe (2001b) for the EU and Epstein (2004) for NATO.
Justifications for more pessimistic views can be found in Reiter (2000) for NATO and
Ellison and Hussain (2003) for the EU.

[3] Though individual politicians – such as the Czech Republic's Václav Klaus – have expressed
forms of Euroskepticism, these states have had no governments that did not make EU entry
a high priority (Gryzmała-Busse and Jones Luong 2002).

[4] And as in Western Europe, CEE politicians also could sometimes use the EU as an alibi
for unpopular reforms (see Hay and Rosamond 2002).

apparently successful institutions of Western Europe. For now, it is worth noting that these three factors – constraints, incentives, and normative models – operate on different levels and with different logics.

The diversity of these three factors gives us a clue as to why emulation defies easy theorization as a mode of institutional change. Normal processes of domestic politics are made more complex by the addition of ideas and incentives that emanate from foreign practices. No doubt this combination of novelty and complexity helps explain why theories of emulation – often couched as lesson drawing, policy and institutional transfer, diffusion, demonstration effects, or conditionality – usually have been "stand alone" explanations that are not tightly linked to broader institutional theories.[5] To be sure, some case studies of emulation have attempted to adjudicate between such broader theories.[6] But single cases are a difficult basis upon which to falsify or support broad and abstract theories. As a result, the call to articulate theories of emulation with larger theoretical traditions has been difficult to answer (Dolowitz and Marsh 1996).

Initially, the dominant theoretical discussions in works on institutional change in CEE turned on theories of transitions, democratization, consolidation, and market reform. Increasingly, however, scholars also have turned to a rich theoretical literature on new institutionalism, and several have begun to apply new institutionalist theories to specific cases in CEE (Schimmelfennig 2004; Vachudova 2004; Gryzmała-Busse 2002; Martens et al. 2002; Benoit and Schiemann 2001; Epstein 2001; Smith and Remington 2001; Wallander 2000; Tökés 1999; Elster, Offe, and Preuss 1998; Stark and Bruszt 1998; Colomer 1995; Geddes 1995). This book is in this broadly institutionalist tradition, and the purpose of this chapter is to cast the various modes and outcomes of emulation in CEE in light of general institutional theories.

THREE INSTITUTIONALISMS

I follow Hall and Taylor (1996) in dividing the burgeoning field of new institutionalism along historical, rational, and sociological lines. This choice links the study of emulation to widely known and discussed theory traditions. Three premises shape this chapter. The first is that the new

---

[5] An impressive exception is Beissinger (2002), who embeds a theory of demonstration effects inside existing social movement theories.

[6] A particularly good example is Westney (1987).

institutionalist literature is reaching a stage of theoretical sophistication and conceptual richness where the task is to find some way to actually use and at least partially integrate what is already available. The second · premise is that emulation is complex enough to need this richness. If we stylize emulation as always mindless, superficial, or coerced, then its relevance is lost for a set of big debates on globalization, regionalization, Europeanization, development, and international organizations. If we analyze emulation carefully, however, then it can tell us a lot about those debates. The third premise is that rather than holding yet another competition between institutionalist theories, this book can make its contribution by pragmatically integrating or synthesizing rational, historical, and sociological lines of institutional analysis.

Though difficult, such efforts at synthesis are well under way. Several scholars have emphasized the virtues of various combinations of two of these theory traditions at once. This trend is popular in research on European integration (Jupille, Caporaso, and Checkel 2003; Peterson and Bomberg 1999). For example, Bulmer and Burch (2001) combine historical and sociological institutionalism together in one explanation of German and British reactions to EU integration, while Pierson (1996) combines rationalist and historical institutionalism to explain the emergence of persistent "gaps" in member state control of the European Commission. As in this book, the usual objective is less to generate brittle and exclusive point predictions than to better understand an overall process.

Before attempting any synthesis, we need a brief description of its constituent parts. Because these institutionalisms are so well established in the literature, a brief summary of the major heuristic devices of each and their application to debates about EU and NATO will suffice here.[7] I emphasize those aspects of each theory that are particularly useful in the CEE context. And in keeping with the overall theme of embedded rationality, I also emphasize those aspects of historical and sociological institutionalism that are broadly compatible with rational behavior, however circumscribed by other factors.

Historical Institutionalism

Scholars of historical institutionalism (HI) emphasize the way existing institutional arrangements shape which political possibilities are open at

---

[7] Excellent recent overviews of institutional theory focused on Europe include Jupille et al. 2003; Aspinwall and Schnieder 2001; Green Cowles, Caporaso, and Risse 2001; Stone Sweet, Sandholtz, and Fligstein 2001.

any given time (Steinmo, Thelen, and Longstreth 1992). HI is particularly adept at showing how institutions often codify a particular political bias and how that bias might stubbornly endure in the face of considerable change in the conditions that produced it. Four HI heuristics and themes are alternately affirmed and criticized in this book. First, institutional stickiness and path dependency result from the influence of settled historical facts on later choices. HI models stress the way that actors adapt to institutions and invest in the ability to work within the rules and procedures of given structures. These investments act as a brake on change, which some actors may be well-placed to resist. Despite breathtaking institutional changes, many facets of CEE politics can only be understood in light of historical antecedents (Stark and Bruszt 1998; Kitschelt et al. 1999; Jowitt 1992). Which antecedents matter most (precommunist, communist era, the extrication from communism) may well vary by issue, but history matters here insofar as simply agreeing to a set of institutional changes is hardly a sufficient basis for the ability to implement those changes.

Second, HI models of change emphasize the potential for a mismatch between prevailing institutions and problem sets at any given time and use this mismatch as a potential motive force for institutional change (Knill 2001; Bulmer and Burch 2001; Pierson 2000b; Thelen 1999). In a related way, HI scholars have also emphasized the way in which effective institutions may well have antecedents that were ineffective. A commonly invoked example is the European Monetary Union, built upon several less than satisfying antecedent institutions yet still shaped in important ways by this past. This means that history is not exclusively a constraint but can also provide a capacity for future change.

Third, as in RI theory (see below), HI scholars of European integration have emphasized the importance of agenda setting, but they do so by looking also at informal rules of conduct, rather than exclusively at treaty-based prerogatives. An example here is Schmidt's emphasis on informal rule-making in the European Council (2001). Finally, HI suggests that whatever motives states may have for full control of the IOs they create, they may, over time, come to have great difficulty reining in certain types of well-endowed IO "agents." Gaps may thus appear in state control of IOs (Pierson 1996).[8]

---

[8] This book does not pursue HI theorizing into organizational culture (cf. Armstrong and Bulmer 1997), nor does it pursue the influence of historical factors that predate the communist era. Both options would be attractive but would make very different data demands,

Rational Institutionalism

As with other variants of rational choice research, rational institution-alism (RI) in European integration begins from the proposition that all actors behave strategically in order to maximize their preferred outcomes (Aspinwall and Schneider 2001: 7). Like HI, this is a complex and multi-faceted literature, and this book will draw upon five of its key propositions developed specifically in terms of IOs. As with HI, rather than pledging allegiance to these propositions, I will use them to guide my questions about the available evidence. First, elites pursue material interests, which, in electoral democracies, can often be assumed to crystallize in a strong reelection motive. Second, states seek integration when those domestic interests who may benefit from it overcome both their own collective ac-tion problems and the opposition of those who might be hurt (Moravcsik 1998). Such opposition is often characterized as "veto positions," though that language is not exclusive to the RI approach (e.g., Immergut 1992; see also Tsebelis 2002; Haverland 2000).

Third, the elite decision to integrate their state into an IO often can be conceived as one where a "principal" (the state) "delegates" cer-tain of its authorities to an IO "agent" (e.g., the European Commission or the North Atlantic Council; Pollack 1997, 2003; Franchino 2001; Majone 2001; Bergman 2000). In the EU case, however, the member states are not individual principals but rather members of a collective principal. This collective principal retains residual privileges over its agents that allow it to recontract with agents as unforeseen circumstances arise. This approach is especially promising in suggesting that member states need to coordinate with other members of the collective principal in order to rewrite such contracts with agents (Nielson, Tierney, and Lyne 2003).[9]

Fourth, decision rules and agenda-setting abilities may matter as much as or more than the raw power of actors in determining outcomes (Steunenberg 1997; Schneider 1995). Thus, elites facing similar external incentives may choose differently as a consequence of differences among domestic institutions, especially if those institutions strongly affect their reelection chances (Nielson 2003).

some incompatible with the rest of the book. The best recent book in this tradition is Janos 2000, especially chapter 7.

[9] An important theoretical and empirical debate is whether some IO agents, especially the European Commission, have become so powerful that they have essentially escaped most state controls of the now nominal "principals." See Sandholtz and Stone Sweet (1998).

Finally, RI emphasizes equilibrium outcomes, though it also underscores the way external shocks force actors to reconstitute such stability (Levi 1997). In the cases at hand, for example, the weak states of CEE experienced the 1990s as a decade of shocks they could do little to control – the Soviet coup attempt, a massive economic decline, the disappointingly one-sided Europe Agreements with the EU, the almost constant war in Yugoslavia, and the threat of wider instability. Each of these events forced CEE actors to rethink fundamental aspects of reform strategy.[10]

Sociological Institutionalism

In much of this book, institutions are outcomes – often the result of elite efforts to reshape domestic structures by different combinations of indigenous reform and reference to models in Western Europe. But one key feature of sociological institutionalism (SI) is to suggest that institutions are also causal variables, shaping the preferences of CEE elites.

This book draws upon SI heuristics in three ways. First, the SI concept of the "institutional environment" – in simplest form, the idea that all organizations must interact with other organizations – sheds light on key behaviors of CEE elites (Powell and DiMaggio 1986). Much of the actual work of the EU and NATO enlargements has consisted of trying to reform national institutions to fit these institutional environments. While some versions of SI stress the way that socialization constructs interests, CEE states are not, in fact, always "persuaded" that the reforms required by the EU and NATO are intrinsically valuable. Thus, I use a "thin" version of SI (Jupille et al. 2003; Ruggie 1998) to also cover those cases where CEE states adopt practices and organizations of the states they wish to join, not because they are persuaded or because their interests are specifically aligned to do so, but because they simply want to be one of the club. This focus on motive forces emanating from the institutional environment is especially useful in explaining significant change where interest groups are thin or even nonexistent.[11]

---

[10] As with HI, other aspects of RI theory on European integration receive short shrift here. These include the complexities of multilevel governance (Scharpf 1985, 1988) and spatial analyses of the decision procedures among the key EU institutions (Tsebelis 1994; Moser 1997; Schneider 1994), themes that are more appropriate to the analysis of member states rather than those aspiring to join.

[11] A rationalist specification of the institutional environment is in Lewis (2003).

Second, the SI literature has a well-developed conceptual language for the diffusion of norms, and some of these concepts work equally well for the diffusion of institutional practices. Especially helpful in this regard are the scope conditions for social learning (Checkel 2003, 2001a; Epstein 2001; Greskovits 1998). "Social learning" is said to be more likely when groups share common professional backgrounds, are faced with clear evidence of policy failure, have a high density of interaction, and are insulated from direct political pressure (Checkel 2001a: 26). Relatedly, the congruence of Western norms with local ones is a factor highlighted by the SI approach, and we will see that the EU and NATO differ on these dimensions.

Third, the SI concept of organizational dualism is useful in understanding the reaction of CEE elites to EU and NATO efforts to monitor their behavior (Meyer and Rowan 1991; Jacoby 2002b). When particular institutional environments favor certain ways of doing things over others, any actor who works in that environment may have an incentive to follow this norm even if it finds conformity to that norm does little to actually boost its performance. In many cases, leaders may rationally construct one part of the organization to conform to appearances and another to maximize production (whatever that might entail in the given case). At the extreme, two organizations emerge – one to be officially monitored and one to do the work. Each is essential to the continued health of the organization. Such outcomes would not be unprecedented in a region famous for "dissembling" in the face of Soviet demands. Both the EU's "screening" process and NATO's Defense Policy Questionnaires and Strategic Reviews provide incentives for both strategic action *and* learning.[12]

A PRAGMATIC SYNTHESIS

As can already be seen, each theory tradition has generated heuristics and concepts that can illuminate processes of change in CEE. Yet as stand-alone theories, each tradition also has significant problems. For example, rationalist approaches get CEE promises right – their elites do promise

---

[12] As with HI and RI, this book uses a truncated version of SI theory. Specifically, it eschews a focus on the way in which institutions and practices are constitutive of actor identity (Adler 1997). Because of the high number of cases, it is unable to pursue what might be called the meaning of the new institutional practices into the cultural repertoires of CEE citizens (Swidler 2001).

to do virtually whatever is asked of them by powerful IOs as long as significant interests are not badly hurt by the effort – but generally leave exogenous both the demands of the IOs and the prospects for real implementation.[13] Moreover, the interest groups that drive intergovernmentalist versions of RI approaches are second-tier players in much of this story, adapting to what state elites have already agreed in Brussels to emulate, often without their knowledge or participation. SI approaches have a robust explanation of IO demands and at least a partial explanation of state responses – in the form of organizational dualism – but they have little to say about implementation (beyond that it is likely to be a big problem). HI approaches are essential for coherent accounts of the unevenness of implementation, and yet a theory built on the weight of the past is bound to be incomplete when change has been so substantial. These problems are ones that proponents of all three traditions might readily note, and they hardly amount to disconfirmations or falsifications of theory. Rather, they point to the fact that each theory has moments it illuminates and moments it neglects.

As noted, this book draws inspiration from all three approaches. Each tradition has certain comparative advantages.[14] Such an effort is unusual, but it is hardly unprecedented. For example, in the field of social movement research, McAdam, Tarrow, and Tilly argue that "an emphasis on political process can provide a terrain for [the] integration" of competing perspectives (1997: 151). Moreover, they insist that "we cannot identify one set of variables with one phase of the process and then move on to the next set of variables for the next set...," and they go on to show the interaction of what they call structural, rationalist, and cultural variables in the rise and fall of the U.S. civil rights movement (163). In the same authors' 2001 book, *Dynamics of Contention*, they argue that it is "useless" to choose among the same three approaches (305).[15]

---

[13] The EU and NATO enlargements have some features of a "single-play game," where RI theory is most indeterminate because there is little chance for feedback and clarification.

[14] It is an open question whether one or another theory tradition could stretch to explain phenomena that other traditions currently explain better. Such efforts at "subsumption" should run parallel to this effort at synthesis.

[15] In a closely related policy case, Lieberman (2002) argues that a synthesis of ideas and institutions – both of which pointed toward stasis – can explain the great changes associated with the rise of U.S. affirmative action policies. Mary Douglas's *How Institutions Think* (1986) works precisely by delimiting certain rationalist, culturalist, and structuralist principles and then by applying those more circumscribed versions to important questions about institutions. Katzenstein and Sil (2004) synthesize realist,

A similar orientation on process characterizes this book. Though the span of time, from the late 1980s to the first postcommunist EU and second NATO enlargements in 2004, is somewhat shorter than that studied by McAdam, Tarrow, and Tilly, three consistent influences on institutional choice and behavior run through this period: the historical reality of poor institutional performance in most of the policy sectors under investigation, the rational incentives for elected officials in CEE to win favor by promoting reform, and the sociological weight of NATO and the EU as institutional environments. I do not offer an "integrated paradigm" as an alternative to existing research traditions. Rather, I show how insights from the different traditions can be synthesized for a specific conceptual purpose and I explain why these theory traditions can sometimes complement one another. The specific synthesis employed below is useful for this book's cases, but it should also be appropriate whenever weak states must engage well-endowed IOs backed by powerful states.

The embedded rationality model avoids simply tossing together the most diverse parts of available institutionalist theories.[16] Rather, it highlights and synthesizes those aspects of theory traditions that, for all their differences, share a core proposition that rationalism plays a central role in political life. To illustrate, the institutional models developed by the different EU and NATO member states and by the IOs themselves represent a flood of new "ideas" about how to organize a vast array of policy domains in the CEE states. But of course the models also represent real material opportunities for CEE elites – to cash in both with voters and with potential patrons inside the IOs. It would, it seems, be reasonable for CEE elites to recognize opportunity here and to pursue it. Yet how should we characterize this use of reason? Some versions of rational choice theory give the impression that the alternative to assuming that actors are

---

liberal, and constructivist positions in debates about security in Asia. Jupille et al. (2003: 20–4) sketch three possible kinds of "synthesis": specifying different domains of application for each theory, sequencing theories chronologically, and incorporating one theory as a special case of a broader theory. This book comes closest to the second approach, though it often uses two or even all three traditions in a given part of the sequence.

[16] To underscore my pragmatic aims, I often speak of the "juxtaposition" of theory traditions when describing situations in which these traditions complement each other. For a good recent summary of the epistemological difficulties with theory synthesis projects, see Checkel 2004.

rational is to assume that they are irrational. By contrast, I show that in these cases the generation of elite reason is highly contingent upon normative models that specify much of the institutional design elites pursue. Put differently, even though it was broadly rational for elites to assent to almost anything the IOs demand, the substance of what they assented to should also be a matter of investigation.

The argument also emphasizes that the pursuit of reason is often constrained by historical factors. When history is present in our analysis, it limits the range of what is possible, rather than merely assuming, for example, that German best practices can be made to work in Hungary. In short, the usual rational choice concession that there are cases in which RI analysis is difficult – because of extreme information problems or the novelty of particular situations – will not do. Pure rationalist approaches radically underdetermine the outcomes sketched in the introduction. But neither will it do to throw out rationality or, even worse, to assume that CEE elites are too inexperienced to think strategically without IO bureaucrats coaching them. Thus, rather than apologizing for rationality or downplaying its effects, we should embed it in the two contexts we clearly see operating in CEE: norms and history.

At this point, it may help to return to the issue of elite motives for emulation introduced at the start of this chapter. What role can institutionalist theories of IOs play in this discussion? To start, all three bodies of theory – RI, HI, and SI – contain both motors and brakes. That is, they each have some mechanism to explain both institutional change and institutional continuity. Moreover, both the motors and the brakes can vary over time or across cases. For example, the motor of emulation for RI is the opportunity for CEE elites to garner electoral support from their voters, and, in some cases, material resources from the IOs that they can distribute. The brakes come in the form of either outright veto positions of major interest groups in their society or the ability of such groups to significantly reshape original elite designs and deflect the plans for emulation. Both these factors can vary widely. The motor from an SI perspective is the very dense institutional environments represented by the *acquis communautaire* of the EU and by the (more modest) institutional demands NATO makes on its member states. For SI, the brakes come in the form of low salience in some issue areas. Some institutional reform projects are much more legitimate than others because the population may accept a pressing need for reform or see the beneficiaries of potential reform as deserving. Finally, from the HI view, the main motor is the existing capacities of CEE states that provide a foundation for emulation.[17] The brakes are the sunk costs and lock-in patterns of existing practices, which, again, vary across place and policy area.

Each theory is plausible, but partial.[18] If we use each alone, it either underdetermines the pattern of attempts at emulation (usually RI) or has an overcommitment to its motor (usually SI) or its brakes (usually HI), such that it fits some cases well and others poorly. The key then, is the interaction of factors emphasized by different theory traditions. How do these factors interact? The basic idea is that emulation efforts are most pronounced when the motors are stronger than the brakes in all three ways just identified. By contrast, elites emulate least when the three kinds of brakes are stronger than the three kinds of motors. The motors–brakes metaphor thus leads to different hypotheses. Most broadly, RI suggests that elites attempt emulation when it brings the promise of voter acclaim and IO resources. SI suggests that elites attempt emulation when the institutional environment is dense. HI suggests that elites attempt emulation when they see a plausible chance to build on existing state capacity.

THE ARGUMENT IN BRIEF: EXPLAINING MODES AND OUTCOMES

As noted in the introduction, the argument is organized around two questions: modes and outcomes. The first question is, Through which processes do elites attempt emulation? Answering this question is one of the book's major contributions, as none of the institutionalist theories alone provides a convincing explanation. The different modes of emulation already introduced flow, in part, from the fact that the EU and NATO enlargements have proceeded very differently. Indeed, the EU's eastern enlargement occured at about the same time as the second round of NATO enlargement. The styles, moreover, have differed even more than the schedules. The European Commission has warned prospective member states that they would have to perform as full members right from the outset of membership.[19] Preparation, therefore, has meant getting the institutions right.

---

[17] In principle, capacity could also lie within CEE societies, but the best recent work on this subject largely confirms earlier pessimistic views on the vibrancy of civil society in CEE (Howard 2003). For the partial exception of Poland, see Ekiert and Kubik (1999).

[18] For extended discussions of each theory's difficulty in explaining the overall patterns, see chapters 6 and 7.

[19] The influence of the European Commission vis-à-vis CEE states is a persistent theme of this book. More generally, debates rage about the power of the Commission in more

This demand is somewhat surprising. Historically, the EU has allowed new members long transitions, letting them develop their capacities gradually. In part, this gradualism fit the smaller and looser *acquis* of the pre–single market period. But when the EU admitted Greece, Spain, and Portugal, it also limited its preaccession demands because member states had decided to use EU membership to solidify postauthoritarian democracies (Glenn 2003; Iankova and Katzenstein 2003). But in the early 1990s, the member states determined not to allow rapid CEE membership in hopes of consolidating new democracies from inside the EU. Instead, the EU made prospective membership difficult. Late in the decade, policy shifted to move toward enlargement, but the EU warned it would insist on a high degree of performance from day one. The EU's demand for immediate performance thus raised the bar for membership over some previous enlargements and generated enormous efforts to change CEE institutions and practices.

The NATO case was different. NATO began the 1990s in a very cautious embrace of the new democracies, and, like the EU, it implied that institutional and material deficiencies left prospective membership a long way off. Like the EU, NATO created a number of programs to promote reforms and perhaps prepare some nations for eventual membership. Once the Clinton administration got solidly behind NATO enlargement, however, the institutional bar was lowered rather than raised. Other geopolitical and domestic aims took priority over concerns about military readiness, and NATO allowed three states (Poland, the Czech Republic, and Hungary) to join in advance of anything close to full military readiness. These differences led to differences in the amount and the timing of IO pressure on CEE states, which, in turn, helped drive the four analytically distinct modes noted in Table 1.

The second question is, What outcomes result from CEE efforts to emulate the West? It is one thing for state elites to agree to emulate – whether faithfully or in more approximate form – prevailing EU or NATO institutions or those of their member states. It is another thing altogether to evaluate how those new or reformed institutions actually function. To do so, we must pay attention to implementation. Just as the initial democratization literature has been followed up by a burgeoning consolidation literature (e.g., Bernhard, Nordstrom, and Reenock 2003), so, too, must any coherent theory of emulation talk not just about the rules on

routinized settings; for recent accounts, see Crombez 2001; Héritier 2001a; Hooghe 2001; Moravcsik 1998.

the books but also about practices in the field. This book explains key postcommunist institutional choices and follows those choices for several years – long enough to evaluate medium-term outcomes. Some outcomes were intended; others were not. Reformist elites have reshaped old institutions, built new ones from scratch, and even created entirely new sets of actors. Less expectedly, EU and NATO demands for immediate performance not only generated enormous efforts to change CEE institutions, but have also led to some distorted institutional patterns when elites tried to move too far too fast. How well can this messy pattern be accounted for by the three bodies of institutionalist theory?

The RI perspective leads us to expect institutional outcomes that are the vector sum of the influences of key actors on CEE elites (once information problems and interaction effects are taken into account). Three sets of pressures are of particular importance: the leverage wielded by the IO in question, the costs and benefits to key domestic interests groups, and the preferences of voters. In the cases in this book, given the priority elites have placed on attaining membership, I assume that IO demands generally trump those of domestic interest groups, who, in turn, trump unorganized voters.[20] RI emphasizes shocks as a motor of change, and while several exogenous shocks occurred – for example, the Bosnian War arguably was a key impetus for the first NATO enlargement – this book presumes that such shocks are processed through one of these channels. Two important hypotheses follow. First, CEE elites implement emulation more where IOs have more leverage over them. Second, CEE elites implement emulation more where they face fewer domestic veto players.

As with RI, the SI perspective on institutional outcomes is initially very similar to its perspective on institutional choice. The hypothesis is that dense institutional environments promote implementation much more than do lean or barely specified ones.[21] Dense institutional environments provide a host of interlocking actors and organizations that are familiar with the workings of and demands of the particular IO. These networks act as formal and informal checks on backsliding or reneging on commitments. Yet just as RI approaches can explain the lack of implementation by reference to low interest on the part of voters, interest groups, or the IO itself, SI approaches can also explain why implementation

---

[20] To be sure, few IOs have as much leverage as the EU and NATO have had.

[21] Börzel et al. (2003) show that both the specificity of rules and their embeddedness in the legal order (which promotes litigation) promote rule compliance in current member states. Density is meant to capture these features of rules along with the obvious focus on the number of rules.

might be halting or indifferent. The SI explanation is that norms embedded in the structures that have been emulated are incongruous with prevailing norms in society. Recall that late in the EU negotiating period, CEE elites often adopted wholesale patches to their national legislation by taking language verbatim from EU directives (binding EU legislation that each member state is supposed to use its own "form and method" [Art. 249] to achieve) or from existing member state legal codes. Such forms of legal transposition appear entirely technocratic until the point at which merely following "the EU way" collides with de facto and/or de jure CEE practices.[22] The resulting hypotheses are that CEE elites implement emulation more when the institutional environment is dense and when norm congruence is high.

Finally, the HI perspective most obliges us to look not just at the *will* to emulate and implement, but the *capacity* to take on new institutional forms. From this perspective, such capacity need not be fully realized and functioning at a high level – if it did, there would likely be much less impetus for radical change through emulation – but it must be present in some form. Such capacity generally resides in one of two places: in the policy area where emulation is occurring (including both the statutory basis and the public administration), or within civil society, which, especially in weak states, may sometimes have capabilities that the state lacks (Stiles 2002). HI expectations are that CEE elites implement emulation more when both state actors and civil society actors already possess some ability to do the tasks required by the new institution.

PUTTING IT ALL TOGETHER

The three theory traditions thus generate hypotheses that can be grouped into primarily external factors (IO leverage and the density of the institutional environment) and primarily domestic ones (veto players,

---

[22] The common claim that emulated institutions must "fit" prevailing practices often misses the fact that for some proponents of institutional change, the objective is not at all to adapt institutions to the "culture," but rather to use institutions to *change* the culture. Though institutions that fit too badly are likely to be irrelevant because they are too confusing and strange for people to embrace, institutions that fit too well may be just as irrelevant. For more on the "fit" debate, see Börzel (1999); Dimitrova (2004); Schimmelfennig and Sedelmeier (2004); Schwellnuss (2004); Dyson and Goetz (2003); Green Cowles et al. (2001); Kohler-Koch (2000); Radaelli (2000); Knill and Lehmkuhl (1999). A similar insight from the "ideas" literature is found in Blyth (2002: 22).

norm congruence, state capacity, and societal capacity). The pattern of modes and outcomes is jointly determined by these external and domestic factors.

If CEE states have had both the motive and opportunity to use emulation as one path to institutional reform, the resulting argument has two stages, each with a set of central tendencies (Katznelson 1997). In the first stage, CEE elites may well wish to accelerate their country's embrace of successful Western ways, but, as noted, they also have to cope with very specific norms propagated by IOs and with their own reading of any domestic constraints they may face. Thus, the actual mode of emulation in any particular case reflects both the amount of pressure brought to bear by the IO in question *and* the degree of faithfulness that CEE governments select in order to accommodate existing practices and actors (see Figure 1). CEE elites must respond to the IOs' institutional demands, but they also must take account of existing national capacities and interests, which will obviously condition their choices about faithful versus approximate emulation. As indicated earlier in Table 1 and in Figure 1 here, this results in four modes, rather than just one undifferentiated process, whether known as diffusion, policy borrowing, or copying.

FIGURE 1. Varieties of modes of emulation.

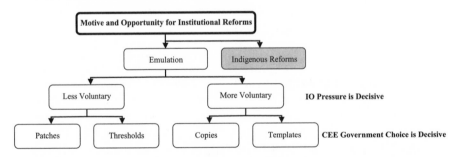

In the argument's second stage, we must understand the range of outcomes that result from emulation in CEE. Figure 2 summarizes these claims. Elites might initially choose any of the four modes of emulation, but they may find it hard to predict the outcomes of their strategies because, once again, their choices are affected by two key factors, neither of which is easy to manipulate. The first factor is the density of the existing IO rules, for the institutional environment continues to set standards against which CEE institutions will be measured.[23] For example, an IO's dense rules can render obsolete a CEE government's efforts to use loose templates. The second structural factor is the density of interests in the policy sector in question. For example, high IO thresholds can be relatively easy for CEE governments to agree to (at least formally) when interests are sparsely organized; by contrast, they can spark mayhem where interests are already densely organized. As Table 2 indicated in the introduction, four central tendencies result: scaffolding, struggle, homesteading, and learning. The key is that in both the first stage (the choice of one mode of emulation) and the second (the outcomes of a given mode of emulation), rational interests are worked out subject to both SI and HI factors. These factors can be constraining, but, as already noted, they can also be enabling.

FIGURE 2. Varieties of outcomes.

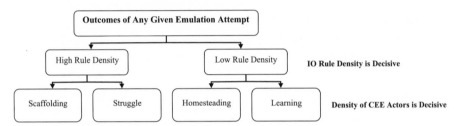

ALTERNATIVE EXPLANATIONS AND FALSIFIABILITY

This two-stage argument summarizes the book's embedded rationality model. Its basic structure builds on the rationalism in all three basic paradigms.[24] The synthetic theory is only necessary if there is real and enduring variation in the modes of attempted emulation and in their outcomes. We will see that all CEE elites do not emulate the same way with the same results, irrespective of the specific national institutional configurations, policy domains, or IOs. If the variation exists as this book describes it, then the argument could be falsified in two ways: First, if variation in the modes of institutional emulation is not tightly linked

[23] Both IOs do raise and lower these barriers to a certain extent, but their member states were determined to impose at least some conditions for membership.
[24] In chapter 7, a number of other insights will follow from three other more limited syntheses of combinations of any two of the research traditions. See also Lupia, McCubbins, and Popkin (2000).

to variation in degrees of faithfulness and voluntarism (with the results summarized in Figure 1), then the argument is wrong. It would also be falsified if outcomes are not primarily the result of the twin variables of the density of the IO body of law and the density of policy sector actors evident at the end of communism (with the results summarized in Figure 2). Such falsification would be most likely if medium-N data sets on postcommunism were able to show that various structural factors largely determined whom states emulated, how they did so, and with what results – the classic approach of many diffusion studies.

The best current quantitative research, however, suggests that such factors, with one key exception, have no such deterministic weight. Research on the determinants of democratic and economic policy reforms (not emulation of specific institutions) provides the closest proxy in terms of a dependent variable. M. Steven Fish (1998b) first showed a strong relationship between the results of a country's first postcommunist election and subsequent economic reforms. Where voters made a clean break, communist-era elites had no time to entrench themselves, and subsequent economic reforms promoted the creation of new constituencies, which further solidified liberal reforms.[25] Jeffrey Kopstein and David Reilly (1999, 2000), using more extensive data, refine and extend the insight about the importance of the first election to political reforms as well as economic ones. Together, these two papers suggest that several initially plausible variables – including foreign debt levels, gross domestic product (GDP) starting points, presidential versus parliamentary systems, and religion – have little purchase in explaining broader patterns of reform. By extension, they seem less promising as explanations for patterns of emulation.

Instead, the key factors seem to be reformers' early choices along with one structural factor: geography. Geographic proximity to Western Europe – variously operationalized as distance from Berlin, Vienna, or Brussels – is strongly and significantly related to both economic and political reforms, even when controlling for the first elections (the other consistently significant factor). Geographic proximity is, of course, one persistent facilitating factor in the diffusion literature, and as Kopstein and Reilly put it, "the countries bordering on Western Europe are strongly influenced, in a positive direction, by their Western neighbors" (2000: 24). Kopstein and Reilly, who use the term "spatial diffusion" to talk about emulation, show that postcommunist states vary significantly in their openness to the "flow" of ideas and practices about liberalization

---

[25] See also Hellman (1998) and Gryzmała-Busse (2002).

and vary in the extent to which they face coherent "neighborhood effects" from bordering states.[26] Thus, location is important insofar as it serves as a proxy for underlying causal processes.[27]

This book follows on these quantitative studies by specifying mechanisms for both causal patterns they have emphasized: early reformers who look to break decisively with the past (sometimes through the voluntary emulation of Western practices) and those powerfully shaped by the practices of their immediate neighbors (and often obliged to emulate as a condition of joining Western clubs). By extension, if the variables these authors have eliminated – or others they have not tested – later prove to be more important determinants of economic and political reforms, then this book's theory will be weakened since it would no longer have the same tie to the dominant explanations of reform across the postcommunist region.

Until and unless such alternative variables prove important, the explanation here takes an important step in going beyond the obvious recognition that external factors have played very important roles in CEE transformations. Why is it unsatisfying merely to recognize that postcommunist transitions have been subject to unusual amounts of "external influences"? Mainly because a radically simplified account would have to blend out a lot of interesting variation. In the mode and outcome questions, three sources of variation stand out and in ways highlighted by the theory traditions. The first variation is cross-national. Historically, Hungary began drawing on Western European designs well before the collapse of communism, while Czechoslovakia, because it had an orthodox and hard-line party, waited until after the end of communism. Rationally, cross-national differences in veto points helped shape elites' response to specific incentives. The most important differences to emerge in the case studies are a somewhat stronger Hungarian executive (Stark and Bruszt 1998: 167, 187) and a much more activist constitutional court in Hungary (Ágh 1995). Sociologically, the key cross-national difference is the gap between the more solid pro-European consensus in Hungary and the persistent Euro-skepticism of an important segment of the Czech elite,

[26] On flows, Kopstein and Reilly's composite index (2000: 14–15) ranks countries by the number of television sets per household, density of international communications, number of tourists hosted, total FDI as a percentage of GDP, and international trade. These avenues provide channels for diffusion beyond the EU and NATO effects emphasized in this book, though they clearly also are useful as channels for EU and NATO effects, as the authors underscore (2000: 24–9).

[27] I am indebted to Robert Cox for underscoring this distinction.

most notably Václav Klaus, the longtime Prime Minister and, since early 2003, the President.[28]

The second compelling variation is across policy areas, already sketched in some detail. Historically, state institutional and bureaucratic capacities vary across policy domains. Moreover, the historical institutionalist focus on "gaps" in EU-member-state control specifically emphasizes variation by policy area (Pierson 1996). Rationally, elites emulate very differently in domains with strong preexisting actors than in domains where actors are weak or nonexistent. Again, the logic is one of veto points, although such actors might also be willing to assume from elites some of the burdens of implementation. Sociologically, one can expect policy domains traditionally seen as essential to national sovereignty – for example, military reforms – to be ones where emulation of others is particularly difficult to legitimize. More generally, variations in policy salience among voters should affect attempts to emulate.

The third variation is across the two Western organizations. Historically, the EU and NATO vary in the extent to which they can draw on Czech and Hungarian experiences in supranational cooperation. While supranational cooperation is new for the EU policy domains, the Czechs and Hungarians do have long experience in supranational military cooperation by virtue of their Warsaw Pact experiences. Rationally, as noted above, the two organizations have set different membership requirements that, in turn, shaped incentives for Czech and Hungarian elites to emulate their institutional practices or those of their member states. Sociologically, for both countries, the challenge of building and sustaining citizen support for membership is quite different in the NATO case than in the EU case. In the former, relatively early entry was quite popular but has also diminished the acceptability of hard choices after membership was attained. One must go back centuries to find the last time either military won a war on behalf of their state, and this also plays a role in the limited public support each military enjoys. As a result, we will see that sustained

---

[28] The pattern is summed up in the useful dichotomy between states in which one party established early dominance (e.g., the Czech Republic) and those in which this did not occur (e.g., Hungary). This dichotomy is even sharper if one uses CEE cases such as Poland (with very high early turnover) and Bulgaria (very low); see Vachudova (2003). The causal logic is that low initial turnover strengthens elite incentives to create "winner take all" institutions that, other things being equal, may then be used to resist reforms – including many suggested by the EU and NATO – that might undercut such sources of power. For illustrations in the areas of civil service reform, local government reform, and oversight of public finance, see Gryzmała-Busse (2003). For the case of regional policy, see chapter 3.

military modernization occurs only where it is most visible: among those forces specifically committed to NATO use. The result is showcase institutions that mask a two-tiered military. In the EU case, a sense that CEE countries were being "strung along" eroded citizen support for EU membership (especially in the Czech Republic) without, however, really diminishing the leverage of the EU in calling for hard changes. Here, the problem is less showcase institutions (as in the NATO case), but rather a major implementation gap across the entire policy area. It is to these three sources of variation that we now turn in chapters 2 through 5.

2

Emulation as Rapid Modernization

Health Care and Consumer Protection

> The "return to Europe" was to mean, in domestic terms, the establishment of "normal," understood as West European-style institutions: a pluralist liberal-democratic political system and a market economy which could offer both consumer affluence and a developed welfare state.
>
> (Batt 1997: 161)

To focus on emulation, we must first clear up some misconceptions about CEE institutional change. Some see emulation as a straightforward tool for well-informed elites to quickly set up the right institutions following prevailing "best practices" (Memmelaar 1990). Others characterize it as the mindless and unreflective mimicry of those new elites who lack their own institution-building capacities (Krygier 2002). Still others emphasize precisely the robust institutional visions of the CEE opposition leaders who emerged from the communist era and deny that these elites had any use for emulation at all (Greskovits 1998). Misconceptions about timing also vary. For some observers, emulation was used only in a brief flurry after 1989, while others take roughly the opposite approach and suggest it was not used until NATO or EU conditionality forced the CEE states to adopt their practices. These are misconceptions not because they are simply wrong – for all are partially true – but because they cannot capture the range of things going on under the deceptively simple cover of "emulation."

This chapter focuses on two areas in which the EU had little leverage. In one case, health care, it is thus relatively easier to establish a crude null hypothesis in terms of how institutional reforms occur absent IO pressure for reforms. In the second case, consumer protection, the influence of the

EU already becomes apparent – and this is so despite a modest *acquis* in this policy area.[1] In turn, chapter 3 will cover cases of emulation under even less voluntary conditions.[2] Thus, chapter 2 focuses more on efforts at rapid modernization, while chapter 3 underscores the political contingencies of emulation. In order to focus on emulation efforts, it will be necessary to say less about parallel indigenous reforms. My account is a probe of one particular category of reform – emulation – rather than an overall picture of all reforms in these two policy sectors. Before turning to the policy cases, however, we need a brief description of EU enlargement as a process.[3]

The High Politics of Enlargement: A Summary

In the early 1990s, the EU held the aspirant members in CEE at arm's length and avoided giving them firm membership targets. EU member states were divided over enlargement, and the only early consensus was to invite Poland, Hungary, and the Czech Republic to begin negotiating "Europe Agreements" with the Commission. These were concluded in November 1991, but the CEE states soon discovered that these association agreements contained neither the robust trade opening nor the link to accession that they had anticipated (Baun 2000: 30–7). Both goals were achieved only quite slowly over the second half of the decade as the EU moved toward accepting the idea of some kind of Eastern enlargement. The 1993 Copenhagen European Council accepted enlargement in principle and underscored three broad conditions: political democracy, market economy, and the ability to take on the obligations of the *acquis*. For purposes of exposition, however, this book divides the process around the 1995 EU White Paper issued in the wake of the Essen summit meeting. The White Paper obliged aspirant members to transpose the roughly one thousand directives at the heart of the internal market. Before 1995, then,

[1] I will refer to *acquis* in the broad sense that it "denotes the whole range of principles, policies, laws, practices, obligations, and objectives that have been agreed or that have been developed within the EU" (Bainbridge 2002: 4).
[2] Other intermediate cases underscore the theme that international leverage is mediated through domestic politics. For example, Rachel Epstein shows that while international financial institutions had some leverage over central bank reforms in Poland up to about 1994, Polish officials continued to learn from international norms even after the formal conditions lapsed. These norms helped certain Polish actors "depoliticize" institutional reforms in this policy area (2004). See also Brusis (2004); Grabbe (2004).
[3] Outstanding overviews of this process include Mayhew (1998), Baun (2000), and Glenn (2003).

emulation was generally voluntary for the CEE states. After that date, an important note of "conditionality" began to enter the calculus (Grabbe 1999b; Schimmelfennig and Sedelmeier 2004; Vachudova 2000).

The Commission warned the CEE states that they would have to perform as full members right from the date of accession (which turned out to be May 1, 2004). Preparation, therefore, has required getting the institutions right. Historically, the EU allowed new members long transitions, letting them develop their capacities gradually. As noted, when the EU admitted Greece, Spain, and Portugal, it limited its preaccession demands. But in the early 1990s, the member states emphasized the prospective costs of taking on states that were not ready. After Essen (and then only slowly), policy shifted to move toward enlargement, but the EU warned it would insist on a high degree of performance from day one. The EU's demand for immediate performance thus raised the bar for membership and generated enormous efforts to change CEE institutions and practices. These efforts came in various guises, such as the Europe Agreements, the White Paper, the Pre-accession Strategy, Phare, National Programs for the Adoption of the *acquis*, annual Commission reports, screening, and negotiations.

Most important, the "transposition" of the EU's 80,000-page *acquis communautaire* became the formal target for aspirant member states.[4] Commission policies slowly changed to reflect this shift. For example, by 1998–9, the Commission's Phare program, which coordinates EU aid to the region, stopped referring to its institution building programs as "demand driven" and began talking of a "preaccession" strategy. While demand-driven programming had meant that Phare was to respond to the priorities set by the governing elites in CEE states, Commission officials in the region began to underscore that "the CEE states are joining us; we are not joining them."[5]

A key part of the EU strategy of readying CEE states for membership was a detailed check on their existing structures and procedures. Some of this was accomplished in national applications (1994–6) and associated Commission opinions (*avis*; 1997) on those applications. But much work was left for the so-called screening process involving ten countries

---

4 Select parts of the *acquis* had long constituted informal targets for many ministerial elites in the region, and some governments (e.g., Hungary) had long had procedures for checking the compatibility of new laws with the *acquis*. For an argument that situates the *acquis* in the context of the older "standards of civilization" debate, see Silvia and Sampson (2003).
5 The Commission's Hans van den Broeck reportedly said this to Czech Prime Minister Václav Klaus.

designated by the EU at the London Council meeting in March 1998. The Commission assigned "task forces" to each country with the job of exploring both existing legislation and the implementation capacity in all areas covered by the primary and secondary legislation of the EU. The task force staff was joined by sectoral experts from each CEE nation for meetings on each sector under scrutiny. The Commission designated thirty-one discrete "chapters" for screening in a process that began in April 1998 and ran through much of 2002. Coterminous with the last two years of screening, the EU also conducted negotiations with the foreign ministry of each country. Satisfactory screening and negotiation led to the provisional closure of chapters, and final negotiations were concluded in December 2002. On April 16–17, 2003, the Accession Treaty was signed at the Athens Summit. Following ratification of the treaty by all current and future members, enlargement officially occured on May 1, 2004.

EU Instruments of Preparation and Channels for Emulation

Since the screening period plays such a pivotal role in this chapter and the next, it is useful to look at it in more detail, for surface appearances could be quite deceiving. In principle, screening could generate both promises from or problems for CEE ministerial elites. That is, wherever their existing structures were inadequate, elites could promise to approximate Western legal structures, fix the problems without using any emulation, or acknowledge that, at least in the short run, they would have problems with that area. In the vast majority of cases, they sought to avoid the latter route, which the EU calls derogations. As a result, promises greatly outnumbered acknowledged problems. In order to keep track of all these promises, the Commission developed the harmonogram, a complicated grid listing for each area to be screened, the relevant EU directives, and the applicant country's existing legislation pertaining to each directive. Depending on the gap between the two, the harmonogram then listed a set of legislative and institutional tasks needed to meet the directive fully, noted the ministry personnel tasked with completing this action, and specified a date for completion.

In response to these demands, the candidate countries had to create new state organizations to cope with EU expectations. For example, the Czech Republic established such structures on at least three different levels: the Government Council for Integration (an advisory body that included ten ministers and the prime minister), the subordinate working committee of the Council (which was staffed at the level of deputy ministerial chiefs), and twenty-two separate working groups (which took responsibility for functional areas like transportation or health care). Some of these structures (e.g., the Council) were self-contained, while the working groups added to the complexity of existing organizations. As the complexity of the enterprise grew, it became more and more of a challenge for the Commission and the CEE governments to monitor the countries' progress.

The Commission also had to create its own new structures. In addition to the Phare program, the Commission established in 1996 a Technical Assistance Information Exchange Office (TAIEX). TAIEX began the harmonogram by compiling for each policy area a so-called A-list of relevant EU legislation. CEE representatives then noted their existing and pending legislation. The harmonograms were discussion agendas during screening, but they subsequently became tools for CEE ministerial actors to coordinate their reforms and announce them as answers to identified legislative deficits. Commission experts from the relevant directorates general (DGs) also gained access to CEE domestic deliberations insofar as they were allowed to critique the ministries' self-grading process, sometimes disputing judgments that existing structures represented "full" or "partial" compliance.[6]

In 2000, the Commission created a "twinning" program that helped overcome the fact that there is no identifiable "EU model" in some areas, but only different national applications of broad EU directives. In order to promote Euroconform structures, Phare paid for personnel transfers between national ministries in current members and counterpart ministries in CEE.[7] The twinning program's role was clearly to reinforce the Commission message that laws must be implemented as well as passed (Martens interview; Černoch interview).

INSTITUTIONAL EMULATION IN HEALTH CARE

We begin the empirical part of the book with health care reforms, where CEE elites have looked to Western models, yet the EU has played a relatively minor role. Here, emulation has been mostly voluntary and almost exclusively approximate, rather than faithful. The diversity of

---

[6] The Commission has twenty-five directorates general, which are roughly analogous to functional ministries.

[7] A certain amount of this had already taken place in the context of ad hoc bilateral aid programs and through Western academics who had done sabbatical projects in the public administrations of CEE states.

institutional practices in Western Europe and the obvious struggles the various national systems have in controlling costs have meant that no one model has been an unambiguous favorite.[8] Further complicating the use of Western templates has been the incommensurability of advice on broad social policy given by a range of international organizations, including the World Bank, International Labor Office, International Monetary Fund, the Organisation for Economic Co-operation and Development (OECD), the Council of Europe, and the EU (Deacon and Hulse 1997).

Some have asserted that the reform of the Hungarian, Czech, and other CEE health care systems made the move "back to Bismarck." That is, these states had insurance-based health care systems until the Soviets imposed their model through the national communist parties. Today, these states seek to implement models based on contemporary Bismarckian models (Marrée and Groenewegen 1997). This general image serves as a very useful starting point (see also Kornai and Eggleston 2001). Alongside the emulation of insurance-based systems, the chapter also considers CEE emulation of different provider-payment mechanisms.

This chapter on institutional change in health care systems does not purport to explain changes in health trends in the region, the determinants of which are extraordinarily complex. It is important to note, however, that Hungary and the Czech Republic have not seen the precipitous drops in public health that plague some postcommunist states, including Russia (Walberg et al. 1998; Nolte et al. 2002). Rather, institutional reform has gone hand in hand with a general increase in health (longer life span, lower incidence of disease, lower infant mortality rates). On the other hand, there has been an actual increase in the incidence of some diseases (e.g.,

---

[8] See Strnad and Gladkij (2001). In 2001, the WHO report ranked the health care systems of 191 countries and included data on the following systems:

Ranking of Health Care Systems: Selected Countries[a]

	Overall	Health	Fairness	Cost
France	1	4	26	4
UK	18	24	8	26
Germany	25	41	6	3
U.S.A.	37	72	54	1
Czech Republic	48	81	71	40
Poland	50	89	150	58
Hungary	66	105	105	59
Russia	130	127	185	75

[a] Based on 1997 data for 191 countries. Highest = 1.
Source: WHO (2001).

TABLE 4. *Comparison of Incidences of Disease and Causes of Death, 1991–99*

	Czech Republic	Hungary
Life expectancy at birth in years	72.06 ('91)	69.46 ('91)
	74.94 ('99)	70.75 ('99)
Infant mortality rate per 1,000 live births	10.38 ('91)	15.64 ('91)
	4.62 ('99)	8.43 ('99)
Tuberculosis incidence, all forms per 1,000	20.17 ('91)	35.36 ('91)
	15.61 ('99)	25.08 ('99)
Viral hepatitis incidence per 1,000	20.74 ('91)	22.68 ('91)
	22.39 ('99)	13.52 ('99)
Cancer prevalence percentage	1.79 ('91)	NA
	3.09 ('99)	NA
Diabetes prevalence percentage	4.76 ('91)	NA
	6.07 ('99)	NA
Standardized death rate, disease of circulatory system per 100,000	615.65 ('91)	638.17 ('91)
	487.17 ('99)	588.45 ('99)

Note: NA = not available.
Source: World Health Organization: 2001. *European Health for All Database*, 25 February 2002: 5.

cancer and diabetes), and Hungary lags behind the Czech Republic in all indicators shown except viral hepatitis (see Table 4).[9] In fact, Hungary has the lowest life expectancy in Western and Central Europe for most adult age–sex categories (European Observatory on Health Care Systems 1999: 8). And in 1995, Hungary had the OECD's highest rates of respiratory cancers, heart disease, and cirrhosis of the liver (Orosz and Burns 2000: 18). Of course, these morbidity figures are affected by many factors, of which the institutional features of health care are only one cluster.[10]

The Hungarian Case: A Brief Overview

The Hungarian health care system has long reflected the urban–rural divides in Hungarian society. Though coverage of industrial workers in insurance funds was mandatory by 1891, access to insurance and services lagged far behind for the rural population. Traditionally, Hungarian

[9] For comprehensive data on both countries, see World Health Organization (2000, 2001).
[10] To take just one example, sharp drops in industrial pollution throughout the CEE states have played a major role in improved public health.

health insurance funds employed their own medical personnel and actually delivered services to their subscribers. These funds and indeed most private health care provisions were ended by the Communist Party in the late 1940s and early 1950s. The Soviet Semashko model provided for the state allocation of all health care services and coverage through a centralized Ministry of Health (MoH). Thus, the same organization both funded health care and provided it.[11] The Semashko systems' weaknesses were evident throughout the 1970s and 1980s (Szalai and Orosz 1992). Long before the collapse of communism, Hungarian officials had to confront the declining health of the population, poor quality of health care, and shortages of financial means (Marrée and Groenewegen 1997: 84; Nelson 2001: 254–5).

To be sure, problems in the health care system were only one of the causes of increased morbidity and mortality (Chenet et al. 1996). Nevertheless, the late 1980s and early 1990s saw a series of reforms, the most important of which replaced the old central state health budget with an insurance-based system funded primarily by a levy on wages (Orosz, Ellena, and Jakab 1998; Orosz and Burns 2000).[12] This compulsory National Health Insurance Fund (HIF) has its roots in the reform communist era (1988–9) and inherited much of its initial personnel and practices from the MoH Finance Department. This choice meant there was no clean break from the old system, a choice that mediated subsequent attempts to move toward a Western-style insurance system. The government's 1990 *Programme for the Nation's Renewal* noted that "we will establish a Hungarian health care system that functions on the insurance principle..." and went on to speak of its desire to change other health institutions "in the way accepted throughout Europe" (15). Hungary's turn "back to Bismarck" rests on this decision to recreate an insurance-based system (Marrée and Groenewegen 1997; Cox 1993). Many CEE states have made a similar choice, though Hungary went farther toward the German model by also placing major social groups, including unions and employers, into top management positions in the HIF (see below).

Hungarian health care is supervised by the central state but provided by local governments to whom the state transferred ownership of most health care facilities in 1990. Providers in county- and city-owned facilities now provide the vast majority of medical services, and they are reimbursed by the HIF. The HIF covers 99% of Hungarians, and it accounted for 70% of all medical payments in 1996. The state regulates the HIF, covers

---

[11] This feature is also true of American Health Maintenance Organizations.
[12] Employers pay 11%, and employees pay 3%.

most capital investment, and regulates public health. During the 1990s, Hungary spent around 7% of its GDP on health care, which is well under the EU average of 8.5% (European Observatory on Health Care Systems 1999: 9–12, 26, 33–4).

The European Observatory on Health Care Systems notes that Hungary's Health Reform Secretariat, founded in 1988, was the center of debates about the utility of models from other Western countries, including the American use of diagnosis related groups (DRGs) as a financing and controlling model and the British patient capitation payments for family physicians (1999: 71). Hungarian academics such as Julia Nagy, Éva Belicza, and András Javor had done preliminary work on DRGs in the 1980s, and they were frequent participants in European discussions about DRGs.[13] Other Western models appealed to Hungarians in their efforts to decrease the portion of health care that takes place in hospitals.

Voluntary emulation changed structures far faster than it changed outcomes. We will see below that since 1990, both DRG and capitation payments have been introduced, but efforts to emphasize primary care have been frustrated. A 2000 OECD study concluded that further reform of the Hungarian health care system remains badly needed. The study notes that the system is "broadly in line with that of other OECD countries," but that it "remains in serious need of reform."[14] Hungarians have the OECD's lowest life expectancy, and "the effectiveness of the nearly universal national health insurance system is greatly reduced by systemic inefficiency, perverse incentive structures, and perennial overspending in pharmaceutical expenditures." The report goes on to suggest that Hungary has an "excess supply of specialists" that results in an "excessively hospital-centric and specialist-based pattern of treatment." The study also noted that difficulties plague the payment systems for inpatient (DRG) and outpatient hospital (points) care. As we shall see, both systems owe something to the inspiration of specific Western models.

The Czech Case: A Brief Overview

Like the Hungarians, the Czechs had a Bismarckian insurance-based system in the interwar period and came ultimately to shift to a socialist centralized system by the 1950s. Unlike Hungary, however, there was no real period of experimentation with the health care system in the 1980s, and

---

[13] Javor then went on to become state secretary in the first postcommunist government. I thank Martin McKee for this information.

[14] All quotations in this paragraph are from Orosz and Burns 2000.

Czechs entered the postcommunist period with little in the way of usable reform antecedents. Yet beginning around 1992, the Czech reforms have been substantial and have opened up a variety of insurance funds as opposed to the single fund in Hungary. After the demise of Czechoslovakia, the Klaus government allowed some facilities to become legally and financially independent. It also permitted patients a broad choice of providers. As in Hungary, most provider facilities are owned by local government entities, and private-practice physicians (rather than salaried physicians) who rent space in these facilities provide the bulk of primary care. (Over 90% of family physicians, dentists, and pharmacies are in private practice.) In the Czech Republic, unlike Hungary, outpatient specialists are also predominantly in private practice. Scheffler and Duitch noted that the Czech reforms have been designed

to achieve solidarity, decentralisation, and privatisation through three major elements: (i) mandatory health insurance for all citizens, financed by a national health insurance fund to which the government and, via a payroll tax, workers and employers contribute; (ii) creation and promotion of competition among non-profit, employment-based health insurance plans in the private sector; and (iii) movement of physicians and other health care workers into private practice and the transfer of some hospitals to decentralised private control. (2000: 5)

Czech reformers have succeeded on the first and last points far better than on the second. In January 1992, a General Health Insurance Fund (CVZP) was formed. In 1993, the CVZP became autonomous in a way analogous to the German funds, though the formal tripartite structure (state, employers, and unions) was thinly rooted. Subsequently, several other autonomous insurance funds (e.g., Škoda–Volkswagen) were formed. For reasons explored below, by 1995, most of these privatized insurance funds faced severe financial difficulties, and CVZP took over many of them. From as many as twenty-seven funds, there remained only nine by 2000 (European Observatory on Health Care Systems 2000: 11; Klener interview). These funds, together with providers and professional chambers, negotiate reimbursement rates, which are then codified by the state. The funds must accept any applicant and provide uniform minimum benefits.

About 80% of Czech health care expenses come from the insurance funds, with taxes covering 11% and out-of-pocket expenses constituting the rest. Czech spending as a percentage of GDP is slightly above the Hungarian level, but the larger GDP means that per capita expenditures on a basis of purchasing power parity reached $943 in 1997 (versus $642 for Hungary and $1,771 for the EU. European Observatory on Health Care Systems 2000: 24–8). Over the 1990s, however, the gap between Czech and EU spending averages converged, while the Hungarian–EU gap actually grew slightly wider. More generally, Kornai and McHale's comparison of CEE health care spending with data from twenty-five OECD and eighty-one developing countries suggests that total spending is actually higher than predicted by their GDP levels (2000: 393–4).

Dense Actors, Thin *Acquis*

This book's premise is that we should see the least EU-mandated emulation in cases where the preexisting networks of interested actors are most dense *and* where the substance of the *acquis* is lightest. The former proposition speaks to veto positions of established actors, and the latter proposition highlights the role of EU leverage. Health care reforms do broadly fit this pattern, for the many interest associations make it far from a tabula rasa, while the EU's very sparse health policy *acquis* provides the EU little leverage.[15] To be sure, one feature of socialist health care was that some interests had privileged access to policy making, while others had comparatively little. As socialism eroded and then collapsed, reconstructing sectoral interest associations was necessary. The medical profession itself refurbished some self-governing bodies and trade unions while inventing some new forms (Lawson and Nemec 2003). Ministerial lines of authority were redrawn, and both local governments and civil society received new warrants for public action.

Notwithstanding a certain amount of flux, however, this multiplicity of actors has made health reforms quite complex. The World Bank has noted the "highly fragmented nature of health policy in the Czech Republic" (1999: 227). In Hungary, health reforms have been hindered by "endemic conflict" between the MoH and the Ministry of Finance (MoF), which have had "overlapping responsibilities in the financing, policy preparation, and administration of health care. A major challenge will be to introduce reforms in a way that reduces these tensions and increases cooperation between agencies" (Orosz and Burns 2000: 43). Also, since the communist system relied on high numbers of specialists, interest representation of health care workers is also highly fragmented (e.g., primary care versus specialized care, doctors versus other health care workers,

---

[15] For a comprehensive overview of EU health programs, see European Commission (2000a).

private practice versus public-sector employment; Nelson 2001: 257). In both countries, moreover, democratization affects reforms. As Nelson argues, citizens will accept top-down decision making in some areas more than others: "On the issues they believe they understand in greater degree, and where there is no obvious reason for rapid action, citizens in democracies are much more likely to expect open debate and consultation. Social-sector issues in general fit this description" (2001: 262).

Phase 1: Voluntary Emulation

This section focuses on voluntary emulation of insurance funds and provider payment systems.[16] Presumably, CEE leaders wish to implement health care reforms that reflect the interests and values of their people. To reach this end, states may occasionally emulate parts of other health care systems, but a critical starting point for emulation is that "there is no 'model country' to represent the 'developed West,' whose example might be followed without hesitation. . . . Policy-makers would be well advised to consider adopting different aspects from different systems to construct a coherent whole most appropriate for their own country" (Kornai and Eggleston 2001: 111).

Yet such mixing and matching is politically contentious. Nelson notes that in health care, "the division of responsibilities among public (national and subnational) agencies, private for-profit agents, voluntary organizations, households, and individuals is highly flexible and immensely controversial." As a result, "It is difficult to reduce the trade-offs among groups and goals to a common denominator" (2001: 259–61). Thus, even if there were a clear model, health sector politics would complicate its pursuit. Moreover, CEE citizens have come to expect virtually free and universal health care. Thus, socialist health care "can only be transformed; it cannot and must not be torn asunder before an alternative system can evolve to take its place" (Kornai and Eggleston 2001: 111). Ultimately, then, we should expect elements of path dependency, an outcome that is overdetermined by the confluence of well-entrenched traditional structures (HI), many veto players (RI), and a weak consensus around international norms for effective health care institutions (SI).

---

[16] Western models of health education were also used. For Palacky University's (Czech Republic) use of the "template" of Virginia Commonwealth University's Graduate Healthcare Management Program, see Ozcan and Gladkij (1997); on Czech use of Western health management models, see Prymula, Pavlicek, and Petrakova (1997).

The Insurance Model

Though the perceived problems of social democratic welfare states in Western Europe makes the wholesale emulation of those models unlikely, early in the decade, the German and Austrian models were a significant point of reference for CEE reformers (Cox 1993). Many elites found the insurance model politically attractive, because they thought it might insulate the health sector from the decline of state revenues by tapping wage and nonwage employer contributions as new sources of finance. On the heels of over a decade of stagnation in communist-era health care spending, insurance systems seemed to promise a more stable financial basis. Crucially, the insurance model was also attractive to health care providers, who earned low salaries compared to other professions in CEE states and compared to providers in Western Europe (European Observatory on Health Care Systems 2000: 19).[17]

Kornai and Eggleston date the more general shift toward the German model to 1991 in Hungary and 1992 in the Czech Republic (2001: 145–6). Both Hungary and the Czech Republic used templates in that they voluntarily approximated characteristics of the German model. The chosen mechanism for the two states drew on the German model in two ways. First, the social insurance fund for health care received its own source of revenue that lies outside the general fund; second, the fund purchases services from health providers, from whom it is institutionally distinct (Kornai and Eggleston 2001: 145, 148). In Hungary, an additional feature of the insurance model was that oversight of these new funds was not given to the MoH but was moved to a neo-corporatist structure dominated by employer and especially by labor unions. As one of the Hungarian Roundtable participants on the committee charged with health policy has recalled, the idea of neo-corporatist oversight "just conquered brains. It was in the air" (Csaba interview).

Yet if emulation was approximate, the omissions were revealing. In Hungary, the HIF, unlike the German and most other Western systems, lacks the ability to negotiate with providers as a purchaser of health services. Instead, it is obligated to buy services from all existing providers. This limitation reflects a deep dispute in Hungarian politics, expressed here in the impotence of the HIF. On one side are those who dismiss the

---

[17] Czech doctors make about twice the average annual Czech salary and specialists about four times as much (European Observatory on Health Care Systems 2000: 43). In Hungary, doctors make just a bit more than secretaries and bus drivers and significantly less than mechanical engineers (European Observatory on Health Care Systems 1999: 66).

utility of insurance-based systems and wish for a "national health system" financed by the state budget. On the other side are those convinced that an insurance-based system can work if it is not held hostage to political rivalry but instead is given a more solid financial basis and real authority (Orosz, Ellena, and Jakab 1998: 232–48). While the latter group "won" enough to achieve the HIF, it failed to secure an HIF right to discipline providers and consolidate sectoral overcapacity. Subsequently, the HIF has been a political football kicked between the MoH, trade unions, prime minister, and the MoF. The initial plan to put the social partners in charge of the HIF was overturned by the Fidesz government in 1998. In turn, the effort to run the HIF through a secretariat controlled by the prime minister failed, and oversight was moved to the MoF in 1999, and in 2001 to the MoH.[18] Thus, some institutional changes inspired by Western models – for example, the basic insurance system – have endured, while others – for example, corporatist oversight of the funds – have not.

Czech reformers also took a keen interest in Western health care models. According to Dr. Martin Bojar, who served in the Czechoslovak government from 1990–2, several Western models appeared in the Czech reform debate. Some appeared episodically or in superficial ways, while others were considered much more carefully. The 1990 reforms were based on materials prepared by a group of doctors who had assembled in the Civic Forum under the guidance of Dr. Martin Potůček. These drew on recommendations of the Charter 77 medical experts, who, according to Bojar, were "definitely inspired by the experience of German-speaking countries, the Benelux, and a number of EU member states."[19] During 1990–1, "the general attitude was to follow trends and recommendation by the World Health Organization (WHO) and the EC [EU] in order to understand underlying trends in Western European heath care." EU accession was "immaterial at the time – the prime focus was reform along the lines of general health care reforms in Europe." In 1991, British and Dutch experts consulted on internal management reforms in the MoH. Belgian government experts were helpful in "providing details for the development of health insurance companies and the shift away from financing health care from the state budget to the launch of private sector health care operators." Several such experts worked directly in the MoH departments responsible for institutional reform. These experts were largely

---

[18] Another case of Fidesz efforts to assert direct control over ministries will be detailed in the case of defense reforms. See chapter 4 below.

[19] All quotes in this paragraph are drawn from the Bojar interview.

from EU member states – Sweden was an exception – but were acting as national experts and had their largest effect in the first few years of the reform debate.

In 1992, Czechoslovakia created the CVZP, with the state as the dominant shareholder. But unlike in Hungary, the single insurer system proved unstable. In part, as Olga Výborná has argued, a state monopoly was hard to justify as a "natural" one when cost calculations were so unclear. For reasons we will discuss next, costs soared, and the resulting criticism opened space for some Czech parliamentarians to further invoke Western models to suggest that a competition of health insurance companies would be key to dampening cost pressures (Výborná 1995). Within a year, the Czech parliament allowed a plurality of private insurers, though, as we saw above, there was a proliferation of new funds followed by substantial consolidation back to nine funds.

CEE experience with insurance-based health systems reveals a consistent pattern of what might be called "attenuated emulation." Certain features of Western models appealed to important reform constituencies. Many politicians saw the models as ways to capitalize on public support by breaking out of the straightjacket of limited socialist spending on health care, while providers saw the models as a way to increase their income and prestige. The CVZP, the design of which was heavily influenced by the Czech medical establishment, actually drove up Czech health care spending by 50% in just two years (Massaro, Nemec, and Kalman 1994: 1871). As we will see below, the Czechs left key cost containment mechanisms out of the insurance system. In other words, those features of the model that appealed to powerful constituencies were taken over, while other aspects of the model were downplayed or not emulated at all. But even such politically contingent and approximate emulation could not guarantee stable outcomes, for we have seen that both Hungarian oversight mechanisms and Czech insurance providers have been quite unstable. In the Hungarian case, oversight has changed three times since 1998. In the Czech case, though one initial rationale for multiple funds was to promote competition, thin financial footings left many funds unable to cover even basic services. In 1997, the Czechs then abolished competition on the basis of supplemental benefits (European Observatory on Health Care Systems 2000: 21).

Today, insurance systems remain in place in both states, and while periodic fiscal crises sometimes generate elite nostalgia for state authority to rein in spending, the basic insurance principle seems to have won fairly broad acceptance among elites. In the population more generally,

support is more ambivalent. While there is no available data on support
for the insurance system per se, a rough proxy might be found in attitudes
about whether taxation and welfare state spending more generally seem in
appropriate balance. As Table 5, indicates, Czech respondents are much
more likely to voice broad support for the current balance between taxes
and welfare state expenditures than either Hungarians or Poles, 43% and
60% of whom (respectively) would like to see taxes cut "even if that
means a reduction in welfare spending."

TABLE 5. *Attitudes on the Trade-off Between Welfare Spending and
Lower Taxes*

Responses	Hungary	Czech Republic	Poland
Taxes should be raised in order to generate resources for extra welfare spending.	8	14	2
No changes are necessary; the level of taxes and welfare spending should remain as they are.	32	47	36
Taxes should be cut, even if that means a reduction in welfare spending.	43	19	60
Don't know	17	20	2
TOTAL	100%	100%	100%

Note: Respondents were asked, "The volume of budgetary expenditure by the state depends on its revenues from taxation. If the government had to choose between cutting taxes
or raising welfare spending, what do you think it should do?" The survey was taken in
September 1999.
Source: Kornai and Eggleston 2001: 331.

Provider Payment Systems
The shift to insurance-based systems that might boost health care revenues raised the related question of how to allocate these revenues to
health care providers. Elites used Western models selectively to move away
from allocating budgets on the basis of political negotiations and move toward allocating spending based upon services actually performed.[20] Here,
too, attenuated emulation and institutional turbulence went hand in hand
as the states introduced new payment mechanisms for family doctors, outpatient specialists, and inpatient hospital care. All payment systems affect

---

[20] For a summary of the bewildering array of new payment systems introduced across CEE,
see Kornai and Eggleston (2001: 287–8).

provider behavior, and all can be manipulated to increase or decrease provider payments. At the most basic level, capitation payments provide a fixed fee per patient. Physicians have an incentive to sign up many patients, and superficial care is thus a major risk. Fee-for-service (FFS) systems reimburse providers by assigning points for each medical procedure they perform. FFS systems often need a cap to guard against provider incentives to "overtreat." Finally, "diagnosis-related groups" (DRGs) are an increasingly common payment mechanism for hospitals. First developed at Yale University in the mid-1970s, DRGs have become widely used in the United States, especially in Medicare and Medicaid, but versions are also used in Norway, Sweden, Portugal, Australia, and Austria.[21] DRGs determine insurance fund payments to hospitals by classifying patients into groups based on diagnoses, procedures performed, age, and gender. Here, providers have incentives to "overcode" any given ailment to receive a larger reimbursement.

Because postsocialist states have many more inpatient hospital beds per capita than do Western European states, the most important financial reforms were in inpatient care, the main focus of this section. Under the first postsocialist government, Hungary adopted and then heavily adapted American DRGs for hospital services. For many MoH officials, DRGs were attractive because they were supposed to promote competition among hospitals, as some would respond to the new financial incentive to raise their efficiency and quality, while others would fail. Sectoral overcapacity thus would shrink. Hungarian doctors anticipated that DRGs would boost their official salaries, but they also expected that the incentives to treat more patients as quickly as possible would increase the number of unofficial "gratuities" Hungarian doctors typically received from patients (Orosz and Holló 2001: 22). DRGs had been introduced on a very limited administrative basis in 1987, but the MoH introduced DRGs to all Hungarian hospitals in 1993.

As with the insurance system more generally, this emulation was not entirely faithful. The American DRG system was adapted to reflect major contextual differences. First, account had to be taken of the much higher use of technology in U.S. hospitals than in Hungary. Second, Hungarian

---

[21] Though German health consultants often promoted DRGs in Hungary, Germany introduced DRGs only in its "Health Reform 2000" program. Here, too, the presence of existing foreign models was so obvious that German lawmakers prescribed that the corporatist social partners who run the German health system build on an "internationally recognized model." After deliberating on eight foreign models, the key actors settled on the Australian DRG system, which was adapted and first introduced during 2003.

hospitals had to build into the DRGs the employment costs of doctors, since those charges are typically billed separately in U.S. hospitals, where doctors often have privileges without being employees. Third, DRGs were adapted to take into account different epidemiological patterns in Hungary. The DRG system did, as one would expect, cut the average hospital stay, since the hospitals had incentives to discharge patients as early as possible (and since no quality-assurance programs were introduced alongside the DRG reforms). On the other hand, hospital admittances rose (Orosz and Holló 2001: 23). Also, overuse reached remarkable proportions as some obstetrics departments performed Caesarian sections on over half of their deliveries, while other units invited males 20–25 years of age for annual screenings for prostate specific antigen (PSA), despite widespread doubts about the effectiveness of such screening even in much older men (Kahan and Gulácsi 2000: 2).[22]

Since DRGs can invite overcoding, there is an incentive for politicians to cap DRG payments. Here, again, Western models were plentiful.[23] The German state of Bavaria has used a capped fund for physician fees in an FFS system so that as use rises in a particular category, average reimbursement rates fall. But what was a regional FFS system for physician fees in Bavaria has been used as the national DRG model for Hungary, and it has made some contribution to cost-control problems faced by the HIF (Csaba interview; Kincses 1995). On the other hand, the cap then changes the nature of the DRG system to "an allocation mechanism among hospitals rather than a reward for performance" (Orosz et al. 1998: 240). Neither could DRGs avoid the political bargaining long endemic to the sector. MoH officials protected some inefficient hospitals by assigning them higher "cost coefficients" for several years. When this system, which undercut the incentives for consolidation, ended, the special favors were preserved through a host of exceptions. Thus, the DRGs did introduce a new financial dynamic, but they were also attenuated to protect important constituencies of the MoH. As Orosz et al. summarize it, there was "a compromise between performance-related finance and the old input-related finance due to fear of hospital bankruptcies" (1998: 240).

[22] The American Cancer Society recommends annual PSA tests for men over 50.
[23] In outpatient specialist care, the Hungarian MoH introduced the German point system as the basis for an FFS model, but an important limitation also attenuated its effectiveness: a low cap on outpatient spending meant providers had very strong incentives to treat people on an inpatient basis. For some treatments, the difference in their remuneration was up to 1,000% (Orosz et al. 1998: 239–40).

The Czechs also made significant modifications when they adopted an FFS system for inpatient procedures.[24] The Czech point system drew closely on the German model (Marrée and Groenewegen 1997: 63; Scheffler and Duitch 2000: 6). Unlike in most existing FFS systems, however, the Czechs made no initial provisions for either a cap or copayments. Insurance companies thus lost important cost-control levers, and health care costs soared by 40% in the first two years as providers rushed to maximize their number of points and fees (Kornai and Eggleston 2001: 289).[25] When the FFS system was capped in 1997, costs did fall, but the value of individual points fell as well. This development fed back to undercut the insurance-based principle: where the expectation of liberal Czech reformers was that funds would compete by negotiating reduced rates with providers, inflation in the point system removed the providers' room for maneuver. The result was the failures of many funds and the subsequent consolidation noted earlier (Scheffler and Duitch 2000: 6).[26] Thus, emulation in one area undercut emulation in another. Just as in the Hungarian case, then, Western-inspired payment mechanisms required almost constant reform in order to find politically sustainable balances between providers' desires for income and autonomy and the funds' financial solvency. Observers of cost-control efforts in OECD countries may find this dilemma familiar.

If Western models had familiar vulnerabilities to market dynamics, they were also vulnerable to established CEE traditions. Perhaps the most fascinating case is the Hungarian tradition of *halapenz* or "gratitude money." Such payments were already well-established in the early communist period in Hungary, and they consisted of a "voluntary" payment by a patient to health care providers. The purpose of the payment is described in various ways – to secure better and/or faster treatment, or as a "placebo" to reassure patients in a time of real anxiety (Nelson 2001; Kornai 2001;

---

[24] Compared to Hungary, the Czech Republic has been cautious about DRGs, and only in 2000 did the MoH approve an experiment to use them in nineteen Czech hospitals (European Observatory on Health Care Systems 2000: 55). As in the Hungarian case, the Czechs needed to adapt the system they chose (known as Grouper-AP-DRG-3M) to Czech conditions (Busse, Petrakova, and Prymula 2001: 31).

[25] In some ways, the Hungarian experience with copayments was even worse: the MoH first introduced copayments during the 1995 austerity program so that citizens had additional health costs just at the time of more generalized economic deflation. The resulting protests eventually resulted in temporarily shelving the scheme (Kornai and Eggleston 2001: 215).

[26] The funds were also hurt by falling contributions as unemployment and legal and illegal means of avoiding health contributions rose. These problems, however, are those faced by all insurance-based systems, including those that manage to remain solvent.

Kornai and Eggleston 2001; Kosztolanyi 1999). The practice continues to supplement the modest incomes of Hungarian health care workers (and to dampen pressure on the state to increase health care funding). The intersection of this traditional practice with Western models came with the recognition that the DRG system chronically underpays Hungarian hospitals, which then cut back even further on wages and benefits for their workers. Some observers feel this dynamic may actually have increased the importance of *halapenz*. These payments amounted in 1999 to an estimated $120 million, or about $345 per month for each of the country's 30,000 doctors. Moreover, this tradition has taken on new forms in postcommunist Hungary, creating incentives for providers to horde access to new technologies, creating extra (unpaid) work within some doctors' own "feudal" networks of health care assistants, and accentuating a two-tier health system (Kosztolanyi 1999).[27]

This is ironic insofar as one of the government's original justifications for moving to an insurance system in the first place was "the elimination of the 'gratuities,' this disgrace to our health care system" (Government of Hungary 1990: 16). Yet while the new insurance funds kept the formal commitment to universal health care, *halapenz* endured and undercut universalism by promoting a two-tier system. Beneficiaries of traditional practices may thus be able to use such practices to attenuate (if not capture) new institutions based on foreign models.

Phase II: The EU's Modest Role in Health Care

The previous section sketched cases in which Czech and Hungarian officials relied on voluntary emulation of Western models for specific health reforms. These reforms usually merely approximated Western structures and thus used templates. Copies were less common. Even fairly technocratic policy measures, such as systems for the payment of provider fees, had to be substantially adapted in most cases. And even then, many of the adaptations could not avoid giving incentives for providers to "game" the system, by overproviding or underproviding health care. While a great deal of reform advice was available, CEE states were perfectly free to take that advice or leave it.

---

[27] For discussions of unofficial payments to physicians in the Czech Republic and Poland, see Lawson and Nemec (2003), O'Dwyer (2003), and Fallenbuchl (1991). These payments are much more widespread in Poland and Hungary than in the Czech Republic.

But late in the decade, the EU began to play some role. The Commission often comments on the sustainability of health-sector institutions. Documents from the late 1990s expressed worry about "the lack of clear, modern public health policies equal to the challenges facing the health system and the relatively low priority given to this sector."[28] The Commission recognized the multiplicity of demands on state budgets, saw that some aspects of current systems were financially unsustainable, and noted the "growing gap between the professionally possible and affordable health services." As a result, the Pre-Accession Strategy stresses "the importance of institution building, especially related to public accountability and budgetary control." The Commission underscored the need for institution building to help transition away from the "vertical" system of socialist medicine, in which hierarchy obviated the need for strong legal regulation: "Most of the Candidate Countries have now taken Member States' systems as their models and move in their reform to less vertically integrated systems in line with the basic elements common to many EU health care systems. This involves the creation of regulatory systems and a strong institutional capacity . . ." (2001b: 6; see also Békési et al. 2001: 703).

The Commission has a thin foothold in health policy and uses two main tools: first, the "health spillover" from other policy areas where the Commission had an active agenda; second, a small *acquis* in the area of public health (Mossialos and McKee 2002). Spillover effects in health care are generated by the Common Agricultural Policy (CAP), food safety, environmental protection, and employment and social policy (Szilágyi 2001: 81; Rath interview). The Commission also has used the *acquis* to weigh in on communicable diseases, declines in vaccination coverage, increased drug use, the need for better emergency facilities, the low social and economic status of health professionals, the relative lack of involvement of the civil society in health issues, and poor environmental conditions. It has called for improved surveillance of communicable disease and better integration of CEE health professionals into European networks. Both the Czech and Hungarian public health systems made substantial progress against communicable disease during the communist period, and their immunization rates are among the highest in Europe (European Observatory on Health Care Systems 1999, 2000). But the Semashko model did less well in preventing noncommunicable diseases (Szilágyi 2001: 80). While

---

[28] The quotations are from the EU Health and Consumer Protection Directorate General (1999: 1–2, 12–13).

the EU would like to see such capacities strengthened, its reports worry
that the transition to insurance-based health care may leave the old public health instruments orphaned or underfunded (European Commission
2001b: 7).

The Commission does most of this through a combination of public
nagging and quiet diplomacy. Unlike in other policy areas we will see,
the Commission has few tools to promote specific changes. Its authority is further limited by fragmentation, since health systems are covered
by DG Social Affairs, but pharmaceuticals by DG Industry, and health
care professionals by DG Internal Market (McKee, Mossialos, and Baeten
2002). Keenly aware that existing member states guard their prerogatives
in health and social policy, the Commission must be cautious as it tries
to squeeze maximum leverage from a minimal health *acquis*. While the
Commission talked of "health issues which are relevant to accession," it
did not explicitly define steps that states must take to reform their health
care systems prior to EU accession (European Commission 2001b: 3). Accordingly, the Commission's regular reports contained few specifics about
health.[29] In response, the Czech 1999 *Position Paper of the Czech Republic on the Commission Opinion of 1998* did not even mention health in
the chapter on consumers and health, but focused entirely on consumer
issues.

Absent detailed leverage, the EU is left to emphasize that if reforms
do not take place, the CEE states' fiscal situation might deteriorate (e.g.,
World Bank 1999: 219). The Commission has little formal role in health
care, and what prerogatives it does have are highly fragmented and often
contested by actors in the very diverse health systems of the current member states. The case is thus representative of the areas in which the "open
method of coordination" may become dominant (Mosher and Trubek
2003).

Summary of the Health Care Case: Emulation as Continuous Learning

Well-entrenched traditional structures (HI), many veto players (RI), and
weak consensus around international norms for effective health care institutions (SI) have meant that there is much continuity in CEE health

---

[29] The 2001 Czech Report mentioned MoH disarray and problems with fiscal surveillance
(European Commission 2001c: 69), while the report on Hungary complained of "major
shortcomings" and worried about the fiscal demands of health care and the overreliance
on hospital stays (European Commission 2001d: 32).

systems. But for all that has changed very little – the continued dominance of public spending and inpatient facilities over private spending and primary care, as well as the endurance of soft budget constraints for institutions and gratuities for physicians – some things have indeed changed. Such changes include those in ownership structures, technology, insurance, and payment systems.

This chapter has emphasized the efforts at change as a way to focus attention on voluntary forms of emulation. This emphasis reveals that CEE elites used emulation to make substantial reforms in an important policy area. We have seen that the shape of both insurance and provider payment systems owes significant debts to elite engagement with existing Western models. Though precommunist insurance systems that had once covered parts of the Czech and Hungarian populations left a "usable past" at the very broadest level, subsequent decades entrenched the idea of universal health care in CEE while Western insurance systems changed radically during the rapid growth of the welfare state. As they grew, Western insurance models generated new kinds of provider payment systems. Elites used their initial postcommunist embrace of selected Western health care models as a way to reject those state command aspects of the communist system that had constrained overall health care spending, produced much antiquated equipment, and often confronted providers with a choice between low salaries and taking bribes. Needing to replace this system rather than merely destroy it, they could essentially choose between an attempt to return to their own precommunist past, some kind of purely authentic indigenous design, or substantial reliance on existing foreign models.

Given this broad choice between nostalgia, heroic innovation, or emulation, CEE states relied heavily, though not exclusively, on the latter. But if the health care case shows that CEE elites have ordered key items from the menu in Western Europe (and even the United States to a certain extent), this chapter has emphasized that emulation in the health sector has been selective and iterative – a process of continuously negotiated learning. Both CEE states were selective in their emulation. Recall, for example, that the Czechs and Hungarians both drew explicitly on German practices for provider payments. But provider payments in Germany are a very complex matter; there is no one "German model" because the system is regionally differentiated and also has many different insurance funds. Thus, while the Hungarians were attracted to a variant of the FFS payment cap system, the Czechs used a variant of the German point system (without caps). Both could legitimately claim to have been informed by "modern practices" – though Germany's per capita health costs are the highest in the EU – and yet each focused on a different part of the German system. Even in the details of payment mechanisms, CEE states selected some features and rejected others, such as the initial Czech rejection of copayments and caps on fee-for-service payments.

Emulation was also iterative. The lack of EU leverage meant that CEE politicians were free to emulate Western models absent any external compulsion to do so. Openness to Western advice was highest early in the 1990s. In subsequent years, elites then tried to adjust and sustain their major initial reforms. Here, too, Western models were sometimes quite helpful. The Czechs tried a number of different ways to slow the explosion of health care spending throughout the mid-1990s, and many of these institutional fixes used different Western financing mechanisms (Kornai and Eggleston 2001). When the Czech MoH put forward a major reform proposal in 1997, health care experts from the United States and a number of European countries – including the UK, Germany, the Netherlands, Belgium, Austria, and Switzerland – had consulted on the reforms (Bojar interview). But if the engagement of an epistemic community of policy professionals seems clear, direct emulation had become a tool for reform at the margins by the middle of the decade. In sharp contrast to the policy area we shall see next, emulation late in the decade was much less important than it had been early in the decade.

INSTITUTIONAL EMULATION IN CONSUMER PROTECTION

Consumer law has, until very recently, been national law, and in Central Europe this is no exception. Hungary and the Czech lands have both seen the historical development of provisions for contract enforcement and modest instruments to protect consumer interests. For example, Hungarian traditions of quality assurance were built around the guild system until late in the industrial age. After the 1872 Act of Industry cancelled the guilds and noted that agreements that "exclude free competition serving the consumer interests shall be considered invalid," subsequent steps in 1883 and 1931 established much of the precommunist legal foundation for consumer protection. EU consumer protection law is quite modest. Fligstein and Stone Sweet's data show that only 1.6% of EC secondary legislation between 1958–69 was in the area of environmental and consumer protection, compared to 4.3% between 1970–85 and 5.7% between 1985–96 (2001: 45).[30] Given these two facts (the dominance of

---

[30] Much of this was environmental, making consumer protection an even smaller legislative domain.

national law in consumer protection and the relative modesty of the EU *acquis* there), it is a paradox that this policy area came to be dominated by CEE efforts to comply with EU norms starting late in the 1990s. How can we understand this puzzle?

Consumer protection is a policy area that took off in the 1970s and 1980s (Trumbull 2002), when Hungary and the Czech lands were part of the Soviet empire. In Marxist theory, consumer protection enjoyed no independent status as a separate legal domain. Citizens were far more likely to be represented in their interests as producers – especially as farmers and workers – than in their capacity as consumers. In addition, the party's organizational monopoly, especially in Czechoslovakia, made the existence of independent consumer advocacy groups difficult if not impossible for much of the socialist period. In short, while various individual laws did give some consumer protections under socialism, the roots of consumer advocacy and protection were quite thin at the end of the socialist period. Thus, while the policy area is not a tabula rasa, any emulation that occurs should be relatively uncomplicated by the existence of well-organized societal interests or well-entrenched state bureaucracies.

For its part, the EU's consumer protection *acquis* can be summarized as modest and fragmented. It is modest, in part, because consumer protection got a late start relative to some policy areas explored below (agriculture), though it has also been around at least as long as others (regional policy). In 1975, the European Parliament proclaimed a set of basic consumer rights, and the International Organization of Consumers Unions (now Consumers International) was founded. In 1985, the European Council unified the system for product liability, and the subsequent decade saw a host of new directives. The main directives include general requirements about having a lead agency for consumer protection and involving non-governmental consumer organizations in making consumer policy. Additional substantive directives include those in product safety, product guarantees, unfair contract terms, misleading and comparative advertising, consumer credit, doorstep selling, distance selling, package travel, time shares, and injunctions.

That the consumer protection *acquis* is also fragmented is no accident. The EU is a union of producers much more than one of consumers. The consumer *acquis* is fairly broad in its sweep, touching on a very wide variety of business practices, but it is not particularly intrusive in its challenge to existing national laws. Since this *acquis* developed over time, it also lacks a unifying text and consequently is difficult for member states to interpret (Pritchard 2000a: 37). The Treaty of Amsterdam did, however, insist that consumer protection be integrated into a wide range of Community policies, and some subsequent directives have that intent. More recently, the "mad cow" and dioxin scandals gave increased impetus for consumer protection in food safety. Also, the scandals of the Santer Commission opened the door for Commission reform, including a reformed Directorate General for Health and Consumer Protection enjoying some increase of powers over the old DG XXIV.

Many EU consumer directives (e.g., on product guarantees) oblige "minimal harmonization," which allows member states to set or keep in place national standards that give consumers even higher levels of protection. Indeed, there are cases in which the levels of protection afforded to Czech and Hungarian citizens go above the minimum levels demanded by the *acquis*. In legislative terms, the screening A-list for consumer protection listed twenty texts, fifteen of them council directives[31] and five of them Commission decisions. Of course, each CEE state ultimately had to transpose other directives into national law, but in point of fact, neither Hungary nor the Czech Republic endured many difficulties during negotiations of this policy area. In administrative terms, market surveillance is the key to effective consumer protection, and it is also where the state is most actively involved. Each state has notable deficiencies in market surveillance, but none of them were large enough to warrant large concern by the EU. In short, given the nonnegotiable EU demands, variation in legal outcomes matters less than variation in the timing and quality of the responses that we see in the Czech Republic and Hungary.

The Czech Case: A Brief Overview

The first postcommunist Czech government professed economic liberalism and, in conjunction with its rhetoric on economic policy, argued that overt state action on behalf of consumers was inappropriate. The Czechs resisted pursuing a formal consumer policy for the early years of the transition. Even when the government changed, no new impetus for consumer protection resulted. This legislative malaise extended up to as late as 1998–9. After that, the Czechs reversed their position that consumer protection should only be the result of market forces and did begin to implement both legislative and administrative changes. Yet they did so without establishing any independent state consumer office. Instead,

---

[31] Since 1994, these are referred to as directives of the European Parliament and the European Council.

since late 1998, the Czechs have used the Consumer Protection Department, housed within the Ministry of Trade and Industry (MTI) (Consumers International 2000: 29). In addition, at least four other ministries and several supervising bodies also compete for oversight of consumer issues, so this is at once a neglected and fragmented policy arena. The fragmentation eventually resulted in the creation of the multiministry Working Group on Consumer Policy, headed by the MTI.

The significance of historical paths has been clear. Socialist-era legislation continues to play a significant role in the area of product guarantees, which still reflect the Marxist presumption that consumer protection was not a separate area of lawmaking per se, but rather was implicitly a matter for the general civil code. Czech laws in the area of guarantees still presume that the state must act on behalf of the consumer, and they therefore resist the notion that consumers are parties to a contract and thus have rights as a contracting partner (Howells and Micklitz 2000: 90, 99).

Since about 1998, however, neither liberal ideology nor socialist legacies have been the chief influences in this policy area. Rather, the Czech government has been hurrying to catch up with other CEE countries to transpose the *acquis*. They had a long way to go, for, as one expert commented in mid-2000, the Czech "catalog of non-transposition of EU consumer directives is almost without parallel in any other applicant country" (Pritchard 2000a: 211). The Czechs also scrambled to build the administrative capacity to enforce the *acquis*. The principal enforcement agency – though again, this is fragmented in the Czech Republic – is the Trade Inspection, which, like the Consumer Protection Department, is located within the MTI. The Trade Inspection has seventeen regional offices and is the main market surveillance instrument in the country, especially since receiving a strengthened legal basis in 2000 (Pritchard 2000a: 39–40).

In the end, the Czechs made enough progress to avoid asking for any derogations in the accession negotiations. One series of expert reports noted four substantial areas that, as of mid-2000, were not yet transposed in the Czech Republic, though they were in Hungary (doorstep selling, distance selling, time shares, and injunctions) (Pritchard 2000a, 2000b). By 2003, subsequent amendments to the civil code had fixed all but the injunctions issue, though these patches came very late in the process (Luhanová interview). EU observers note that other CEE countries that began to develop institutional frameworks at an earlier date have had time to adapt according to practical experience (Pritchard 2000a: 44). As a result, while these countries have emulated as widely as the Czechs, they have had more opportunity to spread awareness, develop market surveillance mechanisms, and test cases through the judiciary.

The Hungarian Case: A Brief Overview

Unlike the Czech Republic, Hungary has transposed all of the EU directives, most in ways that gave EU officials little concern about the legislative standards. Act CLV (1997) is the key legislative platform for consumer protection in Hungary. It is a major framework law incorporating health and safety, consumer credit, information, prices, packaging, dispute resolution, the structure of state consumer protection institutions, and, to some extent, civil groups engaged in consumer protection (Consumers International 2000: 47). On the administrative side, the Hungarians also have emphasized enforcement of consumer legislation and coordination between relevant actors. The EU encouraged Hungarian legislators to see consumer protection as an integrated basket of policies and thus bring together a range of regulations that might otherwise have been kept quite separate. Thus, while several Hungarian consumer protection instruments predate efforts for EU membership, it is clear that efforts to secure membership meant previously unrelated laws were endowed with better administrative capacity and enforcement. In these coordination measures – both between consumer protection bodies and in relation to other areas of law – the Hungarians stand out in CEE (Pritchard 2000b: 226–7).

Institutionally, Hungary has a reasonable base for such coordination. To ensure proper application and enforcement of consumer protection measures, the Ministry of Economic Affairs (MEA) is responsible for preparing policy and legislation, while the General Inspectorate for Consumer Protection (GICP) is responsible for enforcement. In addition, the GICP emphasizes improving coordination and cooperation with other actors. In general, Hungary experiences good cooperation between the GICP and other state bodies, which strengthens Hungarian market surveillance (Pritchard 2000c: 224–6). On the other hand, such oversight remains at a preliminary level, as GICP officials themselves have noted (General Inspectorate for Consumer Protection 2002).

The GICP established and continues to maintain the Central Market Surveillance Information System (KPIR). The system helped prepare Hungary to join the EU's own market surveillance system (RAPEX). In the meantime, the GICP was home to the "transitional" version known as TRAPEX. Since 2001, Hungarian officials can mark products that have been inspected for "consumer friendliness" with a CE (for

European Community). The CE "is a declaration towards the market surveillance authorities that the product complies with the requirements set out by the New Approach Directive, and the authorities are entitled to check its verification" (Huszay 2002). Unfortunately, the CE stamp of quality has been easy to counterfeit. But the fragmentation of enforcement so evident in the Czech case is not so pronounced in Hungary. If it remains the case that local authorities have monitoring tasks well beyond their resources, Hungarian consumer protection is still both legislatively and administratively closer to conformity with the *acquis* than is the Czech situation.

Phase I: Voluntary Emulation

Unlike the health policy case, neither state gave consumer protection any sustained early attention. Yet in the general spirit of building a policy sector that seemed quite underdeveloped, each state made a few attempts to copy – voluntarily and faithfully – several existing bodies of law. The Czech Consumer Protection Act of December 1992 transposed EU Directive 92/59/EEC on general product safety (Maniet 2000: 70–4). The legislation ostensibly aimed to promote safety, quality, and honesty of sale, and to prevent consumer deception (Kočová interview; Tržický interview). The 1990 Act on Prices was based on an EU directive, and advertising regulation was based upon Directive 84/450/EEC (Luhanová interview). Why did the Czech government pass these laws long before the EU asked them to do so and at a time when it was hostile to consumer protection? Interviews suggest that the answer lies in the way that a sense of competition with other candidate states helped convince the government to at least look at emulating the formal structures of other European models. Most such copies remained at very superficial levels in this period. There was almost no effort to create administrative structures that could actually implement these laws, and the majority of early Czech policy making in this sector was the transfer of the Czechoslovakian laws to the new Czech Republic.

Hungarian elites also took some initial steps toward EU compatibility in the early 1990s. The hodgepodge of laws that made up Hungarian consumer protection could build on a firmer communist-era legal basis than could those in the Czech Republic (Tatham 1997). At least three cases of consumer protection legislation that passed during this period stand out as largely unforced copies of existing Western models: Act XLV of 1991 on weighing instruments (corresponding to EEC Directive 9c/384),

Act X of 1993 on product liability (Directive 85/374), and Act XC of 1995 on foodstuffs (several directives on the labeling, analysis, and monitoring of foodstuffs). Yet after the early 1990s, a significant lull set in. In part, this delay was due to disputes about whether Hungary should take a piecemeal approach to the policy area, integrate new consumer provisions into the existing general code, or build a wholly new domain of consumer law. With the adoption of Act CLV on consumer protection in 1997, Hungary chose the latter course and has since showed a clear commitment to adopting a comprehensive consumer policy in line with EU demands (see Pritchard 2000b: 226).

The targets of emulation in both the Czech and Hungarian cases were almost exclusively at the EU level, and neither state attempted much use of approximations of existing national laws (templates), which we saw was much more common in health care. As in the health care case, there was plenty of Western advice to be had. Some EU governments – especially Germany and the UK, along with the Nordic Council – were particularly active in giving advice around the region in the area of consumer protection (Consumers International 2000: 6). Also active was the German umbrella organization Arbeitsgemeinschaft der Verbraucherverbände. But unlike in health care, there was no strong demand for reforms in this policy sector. From an elite perspective, the virtues of EU copies were that, because they were both declatory and voluntary, there was no need to demonstrate any actual institutional capacity nor offend any interests that might suffer from tighter restrictions on their business practices. Diffuse consumer interests remained latent. After the EU began to push its preaccession agenda, however, it provided a strong functional substitute for domestic reform demand.

Phase II: The EU Enters the Picture

My argument emphasizes two less voluntary forms of emulation: thresholds, in which the EU sets minimum legislative or administrative standards that CEE states must meet; and patches, in which CEE states try to directly copy some EU or national legal language. The two forms often go hand in hand; thus, in some cases in which the EU set thresholds, the CEE states responded by adopting specific patches. There is strong evidence that the run-up to membership negotiations sparked a qualitative shift in lawmaking in consumer policy. Consider the frequency distribution of the new Hungarian consumer protection laws contained in Table 6. Some EU directives were addressed by several pieces of legislation and are thus counted more than once, but the overall pattern is clear: 1997

TABLE 6. *Frequency Distribution of Directives in Consumer Protection Addressed by the Hungarian Legislature, 1991–2001*

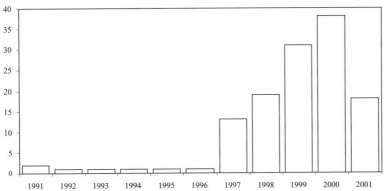

Note: Some directives were addressed by several different legal acts.

marks a clear break where consumer policy moves from a legislative back-water into an area of concern for Hungary. A similar story could be told for the Czech Republic, with the difference that 1997 and even much of 1998 continued to be relatively quiet, leaving a huge legislative agenda for a relatively short period before accession.

To see how EU thresholds work, take the example of unfair contract terms. European states typically have rich, if diverse, national legal traditions in this area. The key EU directive is 93/13/EC, and it contains both an injunction for each state to list unfair contract terms[32] – a German tradition – *and* an acknowledgment of some need for state power on be-half of consumers to counter built-in advantages of producers – a key tenet of French law (Karsten 2000a: 106–8; Trumbull 2002). Hungary's main consumer protection legislation, Act CLV of 1997, did not prohibit unfair contract terms. The Hungarian Civil Code contained provisions that resembled the general principles governing the matter of unfair contract terms, but they dealt more with the conclusion of contracts and not with the prohibition of unfair contract terms per se. Thus, in 2000, the legislation was not yet in line with the *acquis*. Consultants hired by the European Commission to monitor the CEE states argued that in order to be aligned to EU directives, the following changes were required:

- A general notion of fairness and unfairness must be defined.
- A list of unfair terms provided in the annex to the directive must be transposed.

---

[32] Often called a gray list of unfair terms. "Black lists" outlaw certain provisions outright.

- Contract terms need to be required by the civil code as mandated by the directive.
- The directive requires that consumers, not courts, be allowed to initiate unfairness proceedings. (Karsten 2000b: 109–14)

While it is clear that these expectations have a certain level of specificity, it is also plausible to see in them some room for maneuver. Thresholds like these do not specify exactly how legal lacunae are to be filled, though their constraints are often very detailed. The Czech case was similar, in that isolated provisions on unfair contract terms contained in the 1964 civil code, the 1992 Consumer Protection Act, and the 1991 Competition Act on monopolies were clearly inadequate to the demands of Directive 93/13/EC. Again, key thresholds had not been met, among them the lack of a general standard for unfair terms that applied to consumers and not just to business-to-business contracting, a list of unfair terms, and concrete control procedures (Karsten 2000a: 113–15). In response, the Czech government agreed to promulgate a list of unfair contract terms in January 2001 (Luhanová interview).

Another threshold, first articulated in the 1995 White Paper, was the demand for an adequate institutional structure for consumer affairs that designated one authority responsible for pushing consumer initiatives and coordinating actions in the field.[33] Cutting against integration elsewhere, EU thresholds obliged the Hungarian government in 1999 to separate the previously conjoined functions of market surveillance and product testing. Here, the EU enforced its view of the need for functional barriers between different parts of an organization that had previously been integrated (Consumers International 2000: 48). The EU also used thresholds to push for dedicated systems of market surveillance, and the Czechs passed such legislation in 1998.

But thresholds can be tendentious, so it is a mistake to see them merely as technocratic quick fixes. An illuminating example is the product liability standard, which ensures that producers are not overburdened by low-stakes claims by consumers. The EU floor is 500 euros, which means that only products priced above this level fall under the EU regulations. But Hungary remains a poor country, and ministerial officials there argued that consumer protection laws might draw more citizen interest if they

---

[33] Left open was the choice of whether to house this coordinating function in an individual ministry, within an existing ministry, or through the creation of a special office for consumer protection.

protected consumers in a more realistic range of prices. Thus, they initially attempted to set a floor of 50 euros, based on the lower living standard in Hungary. The Hungarian government initially hoped to request a derogation period of five years for the economy and living standards to rise high enough for the 500 euro threshold to become a meaningful one. However, the Hungarians withdrew their request since, according to one official, Commission officials warned them that such a change would be resisted by producer interests in the member states. The Hungarians felt little confidence in winning a contest in which wealthy multinational auto companies would be among the litigants (Boda interview). Thus, it can be difficult for CEE states to adapt EU directives to their own situations.

The screening process forced these thresholds onto the agendas of CEE legislatures and executives. But if screening was a time in which EU thresholds became clearer, it was also a time in which CEE officials often looked to quick patches in order to plug legislative and administrative holes. Take, for example, the Hungarian approach to the Distance Selling Directive (97/7/EC). This directive deals with marketing methods whose characteristics are that "the seller/supplier and the consumer are physically absent when the contract is negotiated and concluded," and "the consumer lacks the possibility to physically check the goods or the services provided before the actual performance of the contract" (DeNayer and Karsten 2000: 161). The directive has been implemented in Hungarian legislation through Government Decree No. 17/1999 (II.5) and was entered into force in May 1999. The decree follows "quasi-literally" the text of the directive. Hungarian legislators adopted this method to maintain separation from rules applicable to other contracts. In essence, it appears that a quasi-literal reading of European law was a way to draw a clear line around a new area of lawmaking and prevent concepts developed there from spreading into other areas (DeNayer and Karsten 2000: 176).

In the flood of legislation unleashed after 1997, Hungary also used patches to respond to legal deficits revealed by screening in the areas of doorstep selling, time shares, package travel, credit institutions, trademark protections, medicinal product safety and advertising, chemical safety, dangerous substances, price indications on foodstuffs and nonfood products, telecommunication, construction products, toy safety, personal information protection (first as a government decree, then as a parliamentary legislation), footwear labeling, machinery safety, and the labeling of mineral water. Many of these new laws were passed so quickly that the Hungarian Parliament had virtually no time to discuss their implications.

For example, the law on child-resistant fittings (Hungarian Governmental Decree No. 8/1998 [II.4]) reads almost word for word like the EU directive it emulates (Council Directive 90/35/EEC). This implies that in extreme cases, EU directives actually function like regulations with direct effects, rather than as guidelines for transposition.

Summary of the Consumer Protection Case: Emulation as Institutional Homesteading

In the health care case, Czech and Hungarian elites had strong incentives to renovate a significant policy area and replace its communist-era practices. They ordered several things from the Western menu, though they did so in a selective and iterative manner. The consumer protection case was different in both ways underscored in the last chapter: there were virtually no previously established actors at the state or societal level, and the EU did have about twenty directives that had to be transposed into national law. This amount of law has been sufficient to create a sparse group of pioneering actors at both the state and societal levels, but nothing more.

One persistent finding of the comparative politics literature on CEE has been that civil society remains relatively weak in comparison to those in most of Western Europe, and this generalization certainly is accurate for the area of consumer protection (Howard 2003). Yet the EU *acquis*, modest though it may be in comparison to agriculture or regional policy, does presuppose a significant level of activity by nonstate consumer organizations. Thus, the 1995 White Paper set out three consumer protection thresholds for CEE states that called for an activist consumer interest sector: consultative procedures that represent consumer interests and include consumers in decision making; granting consumers effective redress mechanisms; and promoting nongovernmental consumer organizations. These thresholds have played a significant role in state policy toward consumer nongovernmental organizations (NGOs). To be sure, it would be too extreme to say that CEE consumer organizations are simply the creations of outside actors. Rather, the EU directives have served as the foundation for homesteading this policy sector.[34]

---

[34] The homesteading notion refers back to the U.S. government act allotting free land to those willing to establish (and improve) farms in the interior and western areas of the United States.

Many pioneers can only survive with outside support. For example, the Czech Centre for Business Consumer Relations and Protection of Consumers was founded in 1992 as a consumer advice center by local authorities in the Moravian town of Trebic. This pioneer eventually drew the attention of outside actors. Its ability to offer training for other consumer organizations in at least twenty-four municipalities throughout the country was clearly a result of financing from the MTI, Phare, and AdV (the main German consumer organization) (Consumers International 2000: 35). Similarly, the Czech Consumers Defense Association, established in 1993, had by 2000 a mere 270 members paying fees of only 50 cents each, while well over 90% of its income came from the MTI and Phare. The publishers of *d-Test* magazine have been around since 1992 and have a very public editor, Ida Rozová, who combines the roles of lawyer and activist. Even then, the magazine, which follows international norms of rejecting advertising and not allowing commercial exploitation of its recommendations – can fund only about 35% of its costs from subscriptions, with the MTI underwriting the remaining 65% (Consumers International 2000: 36–7).[35]

By contrast, the consumer movement in Hungary "stands out as one of the strongest to have emerged in the countries of central and eastern Europe" (Pritchard 2000b: 226). Yet this does not mean that Hungarian consumer NGOs are sufficiently strong to play the role envisaged for them by the *acquis*. Indeed, the 2001 Commission report regrets a general dearth of Hungarian consumer advocacy groups (there were only nine as of the 2001 regular report). According to György Boda, there are five or six minor consumer protection NGOs that receive state funding and, in return, concern themselves with consumer education and assisting market controls (Boda interview). Unlike in the Czech case, the main Hungarian testing magazine (*TESZT*) does accept product advertising, so that while it is not eligible for acceptance in the international consumer movement, it is able to cover 73% of its costs from ads and sales, with the remainder coming from government grants (Consumers International 2000: 45–6). While European consumer organizations look down on accepting advertisements, the alternative is almost complete reliance on EU or state funding. So homesteading looks different here, with less reliance on the state than in the Czech case, but also with the willingness

---

[35] However, initial Czech policies precluded state support for *d-Test*, and several years passed before such support was provided (Trbojevic and Granson 2000a: 51).

to break with an important international norm in consumer protection in its willingness to take funds from advertisers.

This argument is potentially important because other observers have suggested that the importance of external actors has sometimes prevented the development of indigenous organizations.[36] In general, this evidence suggests that the homesteading claim is more plausible than the alternative images of either a nonexistent civil society or one that would have emerged more strongly but for the crowding-out effects of external civil-society promotion programs. Nevertheless, even in Hungary, where consumer organizations are more robust, it is likely true that "for the foreseeable future, no independent consumer organization providing professional services to consumers in its community . . . can expect, or be expected to, finance its operations from its own resources. All such organizations will continue to depend heavily on external funding . . ." (Consumers International 2000: 6). And for the policy area in general, it conforms to two predictions outlined earlier: sparse state and social actors in this policy sector have led to emulation mainly under EU pressure and mainly in ways that do little to adapt Western European practices to local conditions. It is too early to call these policy pioneers innovative, but also too early to conclude that they never can be.

This chapter has portrayed emulation as a tool of iterative and selective learning by a set of fairly well-established actors (e.g., health care) and as a tool for the expansion of a new subset of public law and the creation of a new set of state and nonstate actors to champion this law (e.g., consumer protection). Both cases have in common that the leverage wielded by the EU was fairly light – not so much that it could reach down inside national administrations and affect political coalitions, but it clearly could affect the legislative agenda in the consumer protection case. The next chapter deals with policy domains in which the EU has a great deal of leverage, both because it has a large *acquis* and because it spends a lot of money in them. In these political contexts, emulation appears both as an object of intense macro-political struggle and substantial domestic adjustment.

---

[36] An interesting example in the field of Czech environmental policy is Fagin and Jehlicka (2002).

3

Emulation Under Pressure

Regional Policy and Agriculture

> Each time an expert came to Hungary from a West European country, their
> influence was immediate, though it differed according to the country they
> came from. The French wanted us to centralize, then the Portuguese told
> us to emphasize sectors. Week by week, I could feel who was here.
>
> (Interview with Judit Rózsa, Hungarian regional policy official)

The majority of the EU's political influence comes through its ability to
regulate the behavior of states and firms. Unlike national governments,
it has relatively small fiscal resources that amount to just over 1% of the
GDP of the EU countries. That said, the EU does have two large pots of
money, and they are the subject of this chapter. The largest is also one
of the oldest of all the European integration projects, the CAP. Between
2000 and 2006, agricultural spending will average 42.5 billion euros per
year (in 1999 prices), of which about 38 billion will fall under the CAP
and the other 4.5 billion in rural development programs. About 35 euros
out of every 100 earned by EU farmers comes in some form of aid financed
by taxpayers or consumers. The second pot is almost as large, though it is
not nearly as old. The EU Structural and Cohesion Funds, often referred
to collectively as the structural funds, will receive over the same period
about 30.4 billion euros annually. Together, agriculture and the structural
funds combined will receive about 78% of the EU budget for this period
(Laffan and Shackleton 2000: 231).

    For CEE states, access to these programs was among the strongest in-
ducements they had to seek EU membership. In the end, the 2002 final
negotiations produced agriculture and the structural funds programs that
will account for around 90% of total EU expenditures in CEE between

2004 and 2006. Thus, these two programs will be even larger in relative terms than in current member states, though we will also see that the deal disappointed many CEE citizens and elites. Another oddity when compared to current member states is that spending for the structural and cohesion funds in CEE will significantly outstrip that for agriculture. Thus, total EU appropriations for the ten new member states will be just over 7 billion (2004), 8 billion (2005), and 10 billion euros (2006) for the structural and cohesion funds, but only 2 billion (2004), 3.6 billion (2005), and 4 billion (2006) for agriculture.[1] But access to these programs came with many strings attached, and the emulation required to get there was contentious, ambivalent, and, in many cases, reluctant. Indeed, when EU Commission President Romano Prodi announced at the European Parliament the impending close of negotiations in October 2002, he mentioned the "thousands of laws" that the CEE states had implemented. But he also gave specific warnings about continued shortcomings in "the institutions to manage and supervise agricultural policy" and "the departments in charge of managing and controlling structural funds" (2002).

REGIONAL POLICY: THE EU STRUCTURAL AND COHESION FUNDS

The CEE states are far poorer than the EU average, and this enlargement is the most ambitious ever in terms of integrating numerous poorer economies.[2] In each of the three previous EU enlargement waves, three new states joined and lowered total EU GDP per capita from 3 to 6 percentage points.[3] Based on 2000 GDP data, the "big bang" enlargement lowered average EU GDP per capita in purchasing power parity terms by 9% (13% had Bulgaria and Romania been included). As is well-known, however, the EU spends significant amounts to promote the economic development of the poorest regions of its member states. The EU's structural funds contribute financially to the member states' existing regional policies (RP), which vary substantially from state to state. CEE leaders have long anticipated help from the structural funds, since of a total population

---

[1] CEE states' total contributions to the EU are 3.4 billion euros for 2004, because they were members only as of May 1, and 5 billion euros for 2005 and 2006.

[2] On EU structural funds, see Hooghe (1996) and Allen (2000). For an overview of the link between macroeconomic stabilization, privatization, and regional policy, see Bachtler et al. (2000).

[3] Wave one was in 1973 (Denmark, Ireland, and the United Kingdom). Wave two was 1981 (Greece) and 1986 (Spain and Portugal). Wave three was 1995 (Austria, Sweden, and Finland).

in the then-candidate countries of 105 million, more than 98 million lived in regions with less than 75% of the EU's average GDP, the cutoff for so-called Objective 1 status.

Though the structural funds have been around since the mid-1970s, their importance came primarily with the 1986 Single European Act (SEA), which increased the funds as a means of securing the agreement of poorer member states to the increased economic competition that the SEA would bring.[4] The funds doubled within a few years. From 9% of the EU budget in 1987, the funds devoted to developing poorer regions came to comprise 25% of the 1992 budget and 37% of the 1998 budget (Allen 2000: 244). Major debates in the European integration literature turn on whether to see the funds as largely a function of intergovernmental bargaining (Pollack 1995; Peterson 1995) or as vehicles for influence on member state governments by either the European Commission, the subnational governments that implement the funds, or both (Peterson and Bomberg 1999; Bache 1998; Jeffrey 1997; Marks 1992). While the 1988 reforms sparked much discussion about "multilevel governance," the late 1990s have seen a partial renationalization, as member states generally have constrained both the Commission and their own subnational governments. As we shall see, however, the weak states of CEE were poorly situated to resist Commission pressures.

In terms of substantive policies, the EU structural funds underwent an ideological shift that corresponded roughly with the sharp rise in spending. Building on insights from endogenous growth theory, the theory of industrial districts, and flexible specialization, the Commission urged a reformulation of European regional policies away from a strict focus on inward investment for large, export-oriented firms and toward promotion of infrastructure and the better utilization of existing capacities, whether in the economy or the state.[5] The Commission has articulated four principles to guide the projects that it will support. There must be: a

---

4 "Structural funds" (see EC Regulation No. 1260/1999) is the common shorthand for the European Regional Development Fund (for ERDF, see No. 1261/1999), the European Social Fund (ESF, see No. 1784/1999), the Guidance Section of the European Agricultural Guidance and Guarantee Fund (EAGGF, see No. 1257/1999), the Cohesion Fund, and the Financial Instrument for Fisheries Guidance (FIFG). This section will focus primarily on the ERDF, Cohesion Fund, and the special programs designed to get CEE states ready for these two primary funds. The EAGGF will be treated in the section on agriculture.
5 For discussions of these theories, see Baudner (2003); Armstrong and Taylor (2000); Herrigel (1996); Leonardi and Nanetti (1994); Piore and Sabel (1984); Hooghe and Keating (1994); Locke (1995).

concentration of spending around priority objectives (see below); *partnership* between the Commission and the "appropriate authorities" at the "national, regional, and local level" and at every stage from preparation to implementation; *additionality* so that EU funds complement national funds rather than supplant them; and *programming*, in which multiannual and multitask efforts are favored over uncoordinated or ad hoc projects (Allen 2000: 254–60).

While the member states retain the responsibility to define their development priorities, the cofinancing role of the EU requires that individual projects respond to priorities set by the Commission: (1) promoting competitiveness in regions with low investment, poor infrastructure, or high unemployment; (2) revitalizing regions that face structural difficulties as a result of declining sectors; and (3) the sustainable development of urban areas (European Commission 1999e). Access to these funds also is predicated on planning competence and administrative mastery of complex procedures. Certain administrative competencies and the ability to follow a dense set of rules are a prerequisite for receiving structural funds. Thus, while the EU is reluctant to specify how nation states configure subnational units, both its functional demands and its administrative procedures generate a web of requirements and quasi-requirements that tend to require real administrative competence at the subnational level.

These expectations are in contrast to those that prevailed in CEE during the communist era. Then, many of the policy functions that would fall under the regional policy (RP) domain were instead addressed by sectoral promotion and income standardization. Such policies were highly centralized. Moreover, in the immediate postcommunist period, reformers focused their attention on macroeconomic policy and gave little, if any, attention to microeconomic issues besides privatization. Yet notwithstanding their relative novelty, CEE policy elites soon loaded down RP with a wide range of ambitions and expectations, including some that would likely be outside the bounds of even a richly endowed set of instruments. This is understandable since CEE national elites face much more widespread development problems than do current member states, while, at the same time, they generally are much less able to call upon assistance from either the regional or local levels of the state (Bachtler and Downes 1999: 801; Brusis 2001).

Given the newness of regional policy instruments in CEE states, there is some danger that the sums spent by the EU will cause economic distortions if not managed thoughtfully (see also Bachtler et al. 2002: 7). Table 7 indicates the main EU programs used in the areas of regional

TABLE 7. *Key Dimensions of the Preaccession Instruments for Regional Policy*

	Phare	**ISPA**	**SAPARD**
Parallel EU instrument	Structural funds (ERDF and ESF)	Cohesion fund	EAGGF and rural development
Year of introduction	1989 (regularly revised since then)	1999 (started 1 April 2000)	1999 (came into effect in 2000)
Value per year (2000 prices)	€1,587 million	€1,058 million	€529 million
Responsible EU DG	DG Enlargement	DG Regio	DG Agriculture
Aim	In Agenda 2000, Phare was refocused to concentrate its support on two priorities in the adoption of the *acquis*: institution building and investment support.	Contribution to the objectives in the Accession Partnership and to supporting national transport and environmental infrastructure programs.	To help candidate countries (CCs) to implement the *acquis* as it related to the common agricultural policy, and to facilitate sustainable agricultural and rural structural adjustment.
Scope	A range of national, multinational, and cross-border programs. Two foci: (1) institution building within the CCs to implement and enforce Community legislation; and (2) investment support to enable them to adapt enterprises and infrastructure to EU norms.	*Environment*: facilitate compliance with EC environmental legislation and principles. *Transport*: rehabilitate and construct new transport, linking with trans-European networks. *Technical assistance*: assistance for project quality and robust management.	Wide range of eligible measures to support agriculture and rural development, including: improving food process and marketing; rural diversification; land improvement; vocational training; and water resource management.
Funding	An agreed funding allocation cofinanced by CCs or international financial institutions.	CCs were allocated a range of funding rather than a specific sum, to provide an incentive and respond to change. Projects needed	As with Phare, an agreed sum of funding by the EU, cofinanced from partner countries and international

(continued)

TABLE 7 *(continued)*

	Phare	ISPA	SAPARD
		national contribution, including loan repayments.	financial institutions.
Comparison with parallel EU instrument	As with structural funds, program-based. Investment component supported economic development interventions similar to those in structural funds. Significant institution building element was distinctive.	Unlike the Cohesion Fund, it operated on a project, not a program, basis. The EC made an indicative allocation of resources between eligible countries. It only focused on environment and transport, but had similar monitoring and evaluation requirements.	It operated on a program basis, and programs must be consistent with CAP objectives. Overall, it was designed to be significantly similar to the rural development programs delivered through the EAGGF.

Source: Bachtler, Downes, McMaster, Raines, and Taylor 2002: 8. Used by permission.

policy. The EU created special instruments for CEE that "mirrored" the existing EU programs noted above. These programs generally followed the same objectives in CEE that they follow in member states: enhancing regional competitiveness, stemming structural decline, and promoting sustainable urban development. In addition, as Table 7 indicates, the EU has provided extra help for CEE modernization of environmental standards and transport and has made money available for "institution building" and the adoption of the *acquis*. The oldest program is Phare, which has been the main EU instrument for overall aid delivery to CEE since the onset of transition in 1989–90. Later, Phare also became the precursor to the structural funds (both the ERDF and ESF [see note 4]), and has run several pilot programs in each state since the mid-1990s. Beginning in 1999, the Commission also established two other instruments, and, like Phare, each of these mirrored an established EU instrument for its member states. (The Instrument for Structural Policies for Pre-accession [ISPA] mirrors the cohesion fund, and the Special Pre-accession Program for Agricultural and Regional Development [SAPARD] mirrors the EAGGF [see note 4] and rural development plans.) This chapter concentrates on the Phare/structural funds track.

Hungarian Regional and Cohesion Policy: A Brief Overview

Like much of the CEE region, Hungary suffers from two glaring patterns of economic disparity – an urban–rural divide and a West–East divide. For much of the 1990s, 75% of the country's foreign direct investment (FDI) went to Budapest, while unemployment in the eastern counties bordering Slovakia and Romania was from two to four times the rates in the western counties that bordered Austria, Slovenia, and Croatia.[6] Hungarian regional policy began well before the end of communism. From the early 1970s, Hungary had programs to promote the economic development of rural villages, while a 1985 parliamentary decree and subsequent ministerial resolution marked the first effort for systematic regional (as opposed to sectoral) development. This program, which was starved for resources and focused on only two eastern counties, had little lasting effect, but it did indicate some indigenous impulses to attack economic disparities in something other than sectoral terms. An important consequence of the mainly sectoral orientation of communist development policies was that the large industrial factories that were their hallmark were among the first to close after the onset of market liberalizations.

Further foundations of Hungarian RP were laid with the creation of the Ministry of Environment and Regional Policy (1990) and the Regional Development Fund (RDF) (1991). Trying to counteract growing regional disparities within Hungary between 1990 and 1995, the governments pursued further RP reform, including an initial legislative package in 1993. Though these reforms were plagued with both overcentralization and a dearth of funding, by 1995, about 17% of the Hungarian population lived in "assisted settlements" (Horváth 1998: 101–2; Horváth 2000). The RDF instrument was split in the mid-1990s into a program to coordinate the development programs of different sectoral ministries (TBARD) and another to pursue target objectives at the local government level (SEFA) (Bachtler and Downes 1999: 802).

As we shall see, however, a burst of activity in the mid and late 1990s left Hungarian RP much closer to the formally decentralized structures the Commission had been requesting since the mid-1990s. Hungary's first major step to address concerns over centralization and underfunding came in

---

[6] For detailed data on both issues, see Hungarian Ministry for Agriculture and Regional Development (MoARD) 1998. Barta (2002) shows that while FDI plays a huge role in the Hungarian economy, most of the big Western auto firms use almost no Hungarian subcontractors at all. Thus, FDI exacerbates regional differences in growth without transforming the "Hungarian" part of these economies.

1996 with the passage of the Law on Regional Development and Physical Planning (Act XXI). This law, to whose development Phare programs contributed significantly, served as the primary referent for screening Hungarian policy with EU directives. Act XXI's main principles are decentralization, subsidiarity, partnership, programming, additionality, transparency, and concentration, which already implies that these EU RP norms have reached a declaratory stage. Yet we will see that turning declared norms into behavioral changes has been more difficult (Hungarian Ministry of Agricultural and Regional Development 1998: 32–8; Horváth 1998: 16; Hughes and Sasse 2002).

Hungary also formed regional development councils (RDCs) and, as subsets of the councils, regional development agencies (RDAs). These bodies respond to EU demands to devolve decision making and management control to the regional level. By 1999, seven RDCs were set up at the so-called NUTS II level.[7] In a few cases, these RDCs had different boundaries and different competencies than when first set up on a voluntary basis. Even if they remain a weak link in the overall administrative structure (dominated by the central state and local government), these intermediate-level bodies still have been far more effective than in the Czech case (see the following sections).[8] EU involvement continued with the National Regional Development Concept (1998), National Programme for the Adoption of the Acquis (updated in 2001), and National Development Plan (2001). Negotiations finalized in late 2002 then set preliminary spending corridors for the period 2003–6.

Czech Regional and Cohesion Policy: A Brief Overview

Although Czechoslovakia was "the strictest follower of equalization policy among the former communist states," a mere five years after the end of communism, the traditional economic gradient separating more prosperous Bohemia in the west from less prosperous Moravia in the east had reappeared (Blažek 1996: 63). The vast majority of foreign investment flowed into Bohemian regions, while average income was nearly 50% higher and unemployment almost two points lower than in Moravia. As in Hungary, the capital city was by far the strongest economic core. Per

---

[7] The EU aggregates statistics over several levels, but the NUTS II level corresponds to the key policymaking bodies at the regional level in most of the member states.

[8] For an extensive discussion, see Downes (2000: 334–5).

capita GDP in Prague is actually well above the EU average (+21% in 2000), while every other region's GDP is below the Czech national average. Though income for Prague residents was only 6.4% above the Czech national average in 1989, by 1997 it was 31.5% higher (Červený and Andrle 2000: 89–95).

Czech RP got a later start than in Hungary. Though Czech privatization and transitional economic policies differed from Hungarian ones, both states faced the decline of state-owned heavy industry, the decline of the collectivized agricultural sector, the very low mobility of the workforce (due in part to lack of accessible housing), and pollution and environmental problems.[9] In the early 1990s, in the hardest-hit Czech regions, such as North Bohemia, some officials began to call for policies to address research and development, retraining, and restructuring. Rising unemployment figures revealed a growing cleavage between regions (Hampl 1999).

Through the early 1990s, overall Czech unemployment was remarkably low, but aggregate unemployment and regional disparities grew sharply throughout the second half of the 1990s. In July 2000, the unemployment rate had reached 9%, but in the worst-affected areas of North Bohemia, unemployment had reached 20.7% (Most District), and in North Moravia, it reached 18.4% (Karviná District) (Czech Republic 2000: 8). Early on, the Klaus government chose not to use regional policy to buck the unemployment trend. The Klaus government did focus on some industrial crisis points but neglected both interministerial coordination at the central level and coordination with actors at the regional and municipal levels. As such, early Czech regional policy tended more toward "bailouts" than development. Thus, while the Hungarian government did take an interest in broader European RP developments even prior to the Essen summit, the Czech government did not.

Dense Rules, Sparse Actors

There is no single EU RP model, and, indeed, a few states (Ireland and Portugal) distribute regional funds from a single central fund. But most EU member states, whether unitary or federal, have some form of political devolution to constituent units, and it was this notion that has occupied

[9] For a detailed case study of the EU influence on Czech regional policy, see Jacoby and Černoch (2002).

the Commission from the time of its initial 1997 opinions (Sasse and Hughes 2002). One of the main tasks in this policy sector has been to build up actors at regional levels who are competent enough to engage in the demanding tasks of planning and implementing RP. While the number of formal laws that must be transposed is actually small – RP is a policy area where "direct effects" dominate – the rules and norms around the EU structural and cohesion funds are many and strict (Brusis 2003). In this sense, the *acquis* – construed broadly – can be said to be fairly dense, while the actors needed have been, at least at the outset, quite sparse.[10] As noted, the EU has pushed the creation of new regional and local actors. The Czechs had more to build and less to start with because, unlike Hungary, there had been no efforts to regionalize politics in the waning years of communism.

The reform government of Petr Pithart abolished the regional communist party committees in 1990, although the seven regions lived on as territorial and statistical units. But the regions had no powers of self-government and were simply the (weakened) administrative arms of the central state (Innes 2002). The resulting lack of regional authority was apparent in comparison with that of many EU member states, even strongly unitary states. But this form of Czech exceptionalism hardly bothered Václav Klaus, whose Civic Democratic Party (ODS) emphasized the defense of the nation-state as the only source of identity and vigorously fought efforts to create strong Czech regions. The Czech Social Democratic Party (ČSSD) saw growing unemployment in structurally weak regions as a potential source of votes, however, and they responded with a stronger RP emphasis. In contrast to the ODS, pro-EU arguments began to appear in the ČSSD election campaigns and later found a prominent spot in the party program (ČSSD 1997).

An important lever for challenging central ODS control lay latent in the Czech Constitution of 1992, whose Article 99 foresaw the creation of a layer of self-administered regional governments (also called higher territorial administrative units) between the existing central and municipal levels. But the authors of the constitution left vague the provisions for regional governance (Blažek and Boekhout 2000: 309–10). The stalemate

---

[10] That said, the RP *acquis* is not nearly as dense as in agriculture, and member state RP is sometimes at odds with Commission preferences. For the cases of Germany and Britain, see Conzelmann (2003). In the terms Conzelmann introduces CEE states have both less ability and less motive to either "evade" or "resist" the EU. Thus, "adaptation" is their primary response.

dragged on throughout the entire first period covered in this paper. Despite the constitution's call for regional governments and the EU Commission's not so subtle warnings that some form of regional planning competence was required of all members, the Czechs made few changes. The EU paid a Czech regional planning group for three separate studies of foreign systems of regional policy formation, but ODS dominance continued to block the space for any form of emulation.

In addition, there were almost no established RP actors in the Czech case, and Czech privatization cut off and allowed to atrophy those networks that had existed (McDermott 2002). The Klaus government did bail out a few industrial crisis areas, but did little that could be called regional development. Only well after the ODS left the government did things shift. As a consequence of the lack of interest in regional policy by the ODS-led government, the Commission's initial 1997 assessment in this area was blunt: "Currently, the Czech Republic has no regional policy" (European Commission 1997b: 83). The Commission pointed at the functional necessity of authorities able to formulate regional development priorities. It also specified the need for a Czech partner able to develop and articulate such plans. The Commission noted that "Czech authorities have to determine the future legal basis of a Czech regional policy in order to provide the appropriate legal structure for the actions envisaged to counteract regional disparities and for financing structural policy expenditure" (European Commission 1997b: 84).

Phase 1: Voluntary Emulation

In the Czech Republic, the Klaus government allowed little space for any emulation of Western European RP practices during the period through the Essen summit. In Hungary, there is more of a story to tell. As noted, voluntary emulation of Western RP models began in Hungary even before 1989. The 1985 act, Long Term Tasks of Regional and Settlement Development, is, in fact, indebted to Western templates. Though Hungarian reformers were looking to the West for ideas, integration into the socialist bloc meant that direct copies were not acceptable.[11] The act aimed to approximate the following key Western elements: first, "cooperation between settlements instead of a hierarchical relations"; second, "wider use of local resources, together with the strengthening of local independence";

---

[11] The socialist government even established a parliamentary office in the late 1980s to check the compatibility of Hungarian legislation with EU law.

and third, "a new, decentralized financing system of settlements" (Lackó 1994: 151, 153–4). The act's modest scope, however, limited the effect of these steps.

With the collapse of state socialism in 1989, voluntary emulation of Western European models continued to play some role. Lawmakers slowly began to adapt the centralized, poorly funded communist-era RP. As in 1985, Hungarians used some templates to work through these reforms. Templates allowed the Hungarians to introduce more EU principles and ideas but also allowed them to mold the policies to their specific circumstances. One example is the government introduction of the Regional Development Fund in 1991. The fund used EU financing guidelines, but with the crucial difference that it retained management with the central government in Budapest rather than dispersing management authority. Here we see an echo of the Czech case: EU RP practices were appealing if they promised *techniques* (or *resources*) for dealing with growing unemployment. But those same practices were threatening if they seemed to erode central state *authority*.

Far more than the Czechs, the Hungarians made real use of the Phare instruments for regional policy – signing their first agreement in 1993 and following up with a second set of pilot projects in 1994 (Hungarian Ministry of Agriculture and Regional Development 1998: 61–8). While these projects were limited to certain areas, they also became a conduit for more general institutional reforms (Rózsa and Mólnár interviews). In the Czech case, we cannot point to any substantial and sustained use of templates during the period, though some Czech officials certainly took an interest in Western ways (Andrle interview). The first Czech pilot programs got off the ground only in 1998, long after those in Hungary had begun (Czech Republic 1999: 184).

Phase 2: The EU Grows Assertive

The EU set key RP thresholds for all CEE states. First, the EU presumes that states have in place formal regional actors who have the authority to formulate regional policy objectives. Second, the EU promotes the coordination of regional policy between the central government and the regions concerned. Third, the EU pushes the expectation that the allocation of structural funds will be based on competitiveness among regions. Fourth, the EU insists that states separate management and monitoring of regional policy. And fifth, the EU understands regional policy as an instrument of job creation and investment incentives, instead of a mere redistribution mechanism (European Commission 2000b: 60–2).

The EU began to use RP thresholds in earnest at the time of the first Commission report in 1997, and each subsequent regular report contained a multitude of such thresholds. For instance, in the 2001 regular report on Hungary, the Commission called for improvements in interministerial cooperation, technical preparation for fund management, partnership structures, and local participation in policy making, project evaluation, financial management, and regional statistics (European Commission 2001d: 74–5). Other thresholds were that budgeting must be multiannual, that expenditures concentrate on "priority objectives," and that EU spending not reduce member-state spending ("additionality"). The structural funds also contain a novel form of "area designation" that emphasizes areas of social and economic underdevelopment, industrial restructuring, and high unemployment as key objectives. Hungary's 1996 reforms moved from a very different form of area designation to explicitly embrace these categories (Downes 2000: 340). Though the EU insists states follow these guidelines, it recognizes that such thresholds can be met in a number of different ways.

Hungary has generally been more responsive to such suggestions than has the Czech Republic. By the time of its major 1996 RP reform, Hungary already had enshrined, in word if not yet in deed, the principles of decentralization, subsidiarity, partnership, programming, additionality, transparency, and concentration. When the Commission's 1999 regular report noted that Hungary needed to reform its mechanism for RP financing (1999a: 71), the Parliament's 2000 budget law introduced two new regional financing tools (2000b: 63). The Commission backed its thresholds by warning that if the regional financing system was not fixed, the Commission would not fund pilot programs. The Hungarians, in meeting this threshold, then chose a funding mechanism that follows the EU insistence that regional approaches take priority over sectoral ones.

One key feature of the Hungarian reforms – the most aggressively modeled on Western policies in all of CEE – is that the Hungarian political process was relatively open to the influence of Hungarian academics. These academics, in turn, had long nurtured contacts to Western Europe – contacts that were less available to Czech academics who, in any case, had less access to Czech decision making unless they were in the Klaus circle of economists. The Hungarian Law on Regional Development of 1996 was remarkably attuned to Western European developments, though it was also recognizably a product of Hungarian politics with any number of political compromises (Horváth 1998: 108–11).

EU pressures have also led to the heavy use of patches – faithful emulation of existing EU or member-state practices. Bachtler et al. report the use of new bookkeeping and payment procedures, control checklists, internal control systems, data systems, and evaluation methodologies (2002: 12, 22).[12] Because large-scale RP programs are unprecedented in these countries, the complex monitoring systems required have to be set up essentially de novo. To encourage CEE states to make these patches, the Commission earmarked a certain range of funds for ISPA, SAPARD, and Phare programs, so that better performance could be rewarded with spending at the high end of the range and lower performance with lower spending. In some cases, patches have been too specific to a particular member state, as implied in the epigraph to this chapter. The Commission's "Twinning" program places civil servants from member states inside the public administrations of CEE states. In RP, however, one result has been "a tendency for each involved member state to propose and implement its own country's solutions, leaving it up to the [CEE state] to harmonize the various, not always compatible results" (Bachtler et al. 2002: 25). These authors go on to call for a focus on "principles" rather than "context-specific details of practice" (25). As we have seen above, however, the political coalitions that drove the more voluntary use of emulation in other policy cases were not as apparent in the case of RP.

Hungary's Act XXI classified regions precisely as mandated by the EU (using multicounty regions equal to EU dimensions), and set up an EU-mandated National Regional Development Conception, National Regional Development Programme, and National Regional Development Plan (EU terms not used in Hungary prior to the act). Also, the act stipulated that the Parliament must organize and legislate the decentralization

---

[12] On the other hand, some parts of the Phare programs were not closely correlated with the structural fund regulations, in part because Phare regulations changed so often; also, some actors became disillusioned with the EU's refusal to reward their institutional changes with real responsibility, a situation some liken to "learning to swim without water" (quoted in Bachtler et al. 2002: 30). Later Commission concerns about generating opportunities for more corruption led to less emphasis on administrative decentralization (Leigh interview; Drevet 2000: 348). O'Dwyer (2002) argues that the Czech reluctance to promote administrative decentralization may have prevented the widespread party nepotism that followed in both Slovakia and Poland.

of Hungary's regional policy making and implementation, something Parliament had avoided to that point. Also introduced in this act were requirements for the regional development plan to take "spatial ordering" and environmental factors into consideration, and to construct a new regional information system. In many cases, Hungary dealt with EU thresholds not by innovating on existing institutions or policies, but by quickly adopting Euroconform patches learned about through screening or through the vetting of draft regular reports.[13] Some experts worry that "the theoretical basis [of Hungarian RP development] was 'imported' and used without the necessary adjustment to given conditions" (Lackó 1994: 151, 153–4).

As Hungary was implementing Act XXI, the Commission was looking in vain for appropriate partners in the Czech administration to implement Phare projects to prepare the ground for RP reform. When the Klaus government fell, the Tošovský government unblocked the RP issue and paved the way for future reforms. Most importantly, in late 1997, the Constitutional Act on the Formation of the Higher Territorial Administrative Units was passed by both chambers of the parliament. This represented the first major step toward fulfilling the provisions of Article 99 of the constitution. The Social Democratic minority government that emerged from the April 1998 elections eventually adopted "The Principles of the Government on Regional Policy," a document that at least discursively reflected the principles of the regional policy of the EU.[14] It used EU parlance to identify two types of problem regions according to the classification of structural funds: economically weak regions (what the EU calls objective 5b regions) and structurally weak regions (objective 2). While the former are marked by low levels of economic activity, the latter face specific structural (industrial, urban, or rural) problems contributing to high unemployment. The new government hewed closely to EU norms on its definitions of these regions (Blažek and Boekhout 2000: 302–3). In the Commission's eyes, these moves constituted real progress – the first they had seen.

In response, the Commission started a Phare-financed pilot project for North Bohemia. This project was run by the Ministry for Regional

---

[13] The Commission allowed the candidate countries to have drafts of the reports some months in advance and in many cases would soften the final language if convinced the candidate was ready to make more progress in a specific area. Obviously, what I am calling patches could be quite beneficial in these circumstances.

[14] Innes (2002) shows that the ČSSD initially continued the ODS policies.

Development (MRD), which now began to develop a regional policy according to the EU framework. The ministry's First Regional Operational Program involved not just the central government, but also actors from the regional and municipal levels. Before the creation of the higher territorial units in January 2000, these regional actors were mainly mayors and representatives of regional development agencies, some of whom were also set up with Phare financial support. In 1999 the regional actors formed special regional coordination committees (RCCs), which also included representatives of the state administration. These committees assumed the de facto role of informal, nonelected governments on the subnational level. With regional elections in fall 2000 leading to the establishment of the higher territorial units on January 1, 2001, the regions then incorporated the RCC into their administrative structures. Thus did Commission thresholds, Phare seed money, a latent constitutional provision, and a change of government produce new momentum for Czech RP (Marek and Baun 2002).

Would there have been Czech regional devolution even without the EU? After all, the constitution called for devolution. Yet it seems that the Czech Senate was a concession Klaus made as the price for the dissolution of the federation. It is not clear that this clause alone was sufficient to spark decentralization. After all, in Italy there were almost thirty years between such a provision and its realization (Putnam 1993). It is also true that Czech municipalities were quite fragmented and that devolution helped aggregate local government (see Innes 2002). Yet, again, lots of countries suffer such fragmentation yet cannot conduct such reforms. For many years, France had thousands more municipalities than were efficient, yet was unable to pass a general reform until very recently (Levy 1999). Finally, the ODS did submit a bill in 1994 to decentralize the Czech state, yet it seems unlikely that the ODS ever intended this bill to pass. Rather, it was meant primarily to appease its Christian Democratic coalition partners, who had their stronghold in Moravia. Thus, while it would be wrong to assert that the devolution was exclusively the product of EU pressures, it seems unlikely to have occurred in this time and manner absent those pressures.

In short, while indigenous reform dynamics matter a great deal, the EU has had a real effect. This finding is consistent with recent work on the EU's effect on the RP policies of even such strong member states as France and Germany (Le Galès 2001; Conzelmann 1998). A regional political layer of government is emerging in the Czech Republic in a way that is difficult to imagine without the EU's influence. Even in Hungary, where EU pressure met fewer vetoes, the EU practices, norms, and administrative rules played a decisive role. Both screening and negotiations have been instrumental in establishing a reform agenda and timetable in the candidate countries. In its regular reports, the Commission assessed the progress of each country in meeting the norms and institutional requirements it had laid out. Besides mere explication of the *acquis* in this highly structured process, the EU made substantial funds available to support the development of necessary administrative structures for a successful implementation of EU policies and also to start concrete work by financing pilot projects to promote infrastructure. In both states, emulation took the forms of approximation by responding to thresholds and faithfully emulating some very specific patches.

Summary: Emulation as Scaffolding

CEE residents often talk of the desire to "return to Europe," often invoking the metaphor of a "common European home." Pursuing this metaphor, we might think of EU regional policies as an external scaffolding from which elites can renovate the national edifice. But scaffolding is normally used to modernize existing structures, in this case the traditional regional policies of individual member states. In the Hungarian case and especially in the Czech case, given the paucity of such structures, the scaffolding has served not just as an external platform, but also as the framework of the new building. New actors have coalesced around its structures. Its improvised platforms have been transformed into a foundation, and its poles have been turned into the spindly pillars of a new building. The whole thing is unmistakably improvised, but it is just as unmistakably there.

The scaffolding still functions best in cases where the EU did not have to start from scratch. Hungarian CDCs build on historical administrative competence at the county level. This was a benefit even though the county level has been neglected in the postcommunist period. The Phare program was crucial in first funding the pilot project (1993–6) that resulted in the first two county development councils (CDCs). When those seemed fruitful even in the relative associational wastelands in Hungary's east and north, the model was generalized throughout the country. These CDCs received relatively clear mandates, as related by one longtime observer: "The coordination of development ideas from central and local governments and other actors; the socio-economic evaluation of the county and proposals for medium- and long-term development; participation in decision-making on the allocation of local government support and other funds; and the determination of evaluation guidelines from programs" (Downes 2000: 338). The RDCs are less well established, though they have become conduits for considerable government spending. In the Czech case, the scaffolding claim has to be limited in the sense that the established parties made it illegal for independent parties to run in the elections for the newly created regional governments – a point consistent with the notion that entrenched interests often seek to "capture" the institutions that result from emulation.

As in health care, the scaffolding in CEE has not been an exact replica of that used in current member states. Unlike in health care, however, the attenuation came as much from Western officials as from CEE ones. Although the Commission pushed hard for the Czech Republic and Hungary to create regional political authorities – and arguably were a necessary condition for their creation in the Czech case – their concerns about administrative efficiency led them to use top-down administrative procedures that often bypassed the actors they had helped create. When Czech regions clashed with the MRD over who had the lead in approving programs, the Commission clearly (and decisively) sided with the ministry in favor of more centralization (Marek and Baun 2002: 910–13; Keating 2002). Hungarian RDCs have more competence and authority than in the Czech case, but even there one observes a disjuncture between the Commission's ideal of decentralized programming and the reality of its policies (cf. Hughes, Sasse, and Gordon 2001; Bruszt and Stark 2003; Brusis 2001; Grabbe 2001a). Bachter et al. (2002: 16) show that while EU member states have decentralized program generation, in CEE the Commission retains responsibility for program selection. In broader comparative perspective, the CEE regions, unlike those Börzel contrasts in Germany and Spain, simply do not have the political or economic resources to "choose" cooperative or confrontational strategies vis-à-vis their own governments (2002). Other policy areas that show a substantial IO *acquis* and weakly constituted actors will likely display other variations of the basic scaffolding theme.

AGRICULTURE: STRATEGY AND STRUGGLE

Agriculture is a case where CEE states have well-established actors, the EU has a huge *acquis*, and yet until the end of the 1990s comparatively little emulation had resulted. This is a puzzle. In the previous case with well-established actors (health care), those actors used Western templates very extensively even though EU leverage was very slight. In the two cases where the EU did have leverage, it used it to oblige other forms of emulation, especially thresholds and patches. Yet if the regional policy *acquis* and technical standards made substantial demands on CEE states, agriculture is a policy area in which the sheer weight of EU demands is greater still, for the *acquis* is both older and much larger in agriculture than it is in regional policy. Of the 9,399 pieces of secondary legislation passed by the Community between 1958–96, a remarkable 52.7% (4,950 pieces) concerned agriculture (Fligstein and Stone Sweet 2001: 45).[15] Yet this section will show that emulation in agriculture was rare and that most of it came very late in the process compared to other policy sectors.

The puzzle's answer, worked out over the course of this chapter, is this: From a rational perspective, politicians could win few votes by anticipating the institutional reforms that CAP would require. These reforms, as we shall see, would have been extraordinarily expensive and benefited a rather narrow constituency in both states. Put differently, the reforms made sense only if their costs could be externalized – by achieving membership in the CAP. Thus, CEE elites pursued membership, but without being eager to anticipate the required intuitional changes by using emulation extensively in advance of membership.[16]

An important sociological factor also moderated incentives to emulate. Though agriculture has a huge and detailed *acquis*, the vast majority of the CAP *acquis* has direct affects. This institutional environment generated little need for the CEE states to transpose directives into national legislation and less call for emulation that met the demands for transposition.[17] Of course, significant legislative action was still required for other aspects of the *acquis* – especially for building administrative capacity to monitor and implement the complex CAP programs. But since CEE states could not then actually know what kind of CAP – if any at all – they ultimately would receive, emulating implementation mechanisms for payment systems that might never arrive would have been putting the cart before the

---

[15] The literature on the CAP is huge. Good overviews are Grant (1997); Piccinini and Loseby (2001); Moyer and Josling (2001); Milward (2000); Keeler (1987).

[16] Complementary to this interest constellation was an institutional factor: The CEE states had GATT/WTO commitments that would not allow them to pursue CAP-like policies while nonmembers. I thank Peter Weingarten for this point.

[17] The primary exceptions are the veterinary and phytosanitary categories.

horse. In historical institutionalist terms, both the structure of farms and of agricultural markets that emerged from communism also constrained the ability of the CEE elites to offer their own version of CAP-like supports while giving them incentives to seek such funds if provided by other parties. These latter features thus account for the important sources of cross-national variation.

The EU's Common Agricultural Policy

The CAP is built on four pillars: free movement of agricultural products within Europe, trade preferences for goods within the European Union over those from outside (Community preference), Community funding of guaranteed price levels, and, since 1992, direct income support for farmers. A combination of exploding costs and international pressure drove CAP changes since the early 1990s. The 1992 MacSharry reforms partially transformed the system towards more income support and partially away from price supports (Rieger 2000). This matters for CEE states because the new programs increased the burden on national state administration.[18] While price supports required relatively few verification mechanisms, income supports required a series of new market surveillance institutions, including computerized control systems for payments, land, and animals, as well as a huge new investment in aerial photography for verification purposes.

Why would CEE states want to join what the *Economist* has called "the single most idiotic system of economic mis-management that the rich Western countries have ever devised"? (quoted in Rieger 2000: 182).[19] The simple answer is that the CAP provides access to the EU's single largest pot of money – money that has traditionally been used to support agricultural prices (and store surpluses), but that has increasingly been available for the direct support of farmers' incomes. In addition to the financial incentives, there are political ones. The CAP offers national elites extraordinary tools for cushioning the agricultural sector from both "the internal threat of the industrial society and the external threat of American trade competition" (Rieger 2000: 183; see also Knudsen 2002). As many studies demonstrate, the CAP fulfills a number of important functions: it extends the welfare state into the agricultural sector, insulates the

---

[18] Though they also tend to diminish consumer prices, *ceteris paribus*.
[19] For an excellent overview of EU agricultural objectives in CEE, see Asbeek-Brusse (2002).

sector from international liberalization pressures, frees national governments from dealing with heterogeneous interests among farmers, and yet
provides national elites with key tools to buy targeted support within the
sector.

If the prospect of CAP subsidies created incentives for policy adaptation for some CEE actors, Western models also made demands. Some
of those demands – such as the introduction of strict phytosanitary and
veterinary standards – were fairly certain to affect CEE states as members (and were a condition for better trade access) and thus created some
incentives for emulation once some kind of enlargement seemed likely.
Others – such as the administrative capacities to implement systems of
payment – were dependent upon political grand bargains that lay well in
the future. For most of the 1990s, the size and shape of the CAP programs
to be extended to CEE – if, indeed, any at all – was a topic of endless speculation.[20] The 1999 Berlin reform outlined future CAP spending to the
CEEs for the 2000–6 period and assumed they would receive no direct
payments at all. This proposal was hotly contested by the CEE states. The
EU initially argued that CEE farmers should not receive direct payments
since these had been a compensation for lowering old price support levels –
price supports that the CEE farmers had never enjoyed. CEE agricultural
interests reacted angrily, calling the proposal one for "second class membership" and fearing a long-term competitive disadvantage due to lower
supports.

In 2002, the EU then agreed that CEE farmers would be phased into
the direct-payments portion of the CAP between 2004 and 2013. These
payments amount to 25% of EU–15 levels in 2004 and will rise gradually
(between 5–10% per year) until reaching 100% in 2013. The CEE states
will have some ability to "top-up" these payments by up to an additional
30% using redirected EU rural development funds or their own resources.
The Commission primarily defended these lower initial direct payments –
despite CEE demands for full payments – by arguing that full funding
would halt structural change: "If direct aids are introduced too quickly
in the candidate countries, their short-term positive effects on farm income would be outweighed by their negative impact on restructuring.

[20] The EU commissioned several studies on CEE agriculture. See Nallet and Van Stolk
(1994); Buckwell et al. (1995); Tarditi and Marsh (1995); Tangermann and Josling
(1994). More recent reports include Pouliquen (2001); Frohberg et al. (2002); Frohberg
and Weber (2002); Frohberg and Weingarten (1999).

TABLE 8. *EU Agriculture Expenditures by Country and Category*

	Estimated Direct Payments	Market Support Expenditures	Rural Development Commitments
Czech Republic			
2004	NA	45	148
2005	169	109	162
2006	204	111	172
SUBTOTAL	373	265	482
Hungary			
2004	NA	64	164
2005	265	152	179
2006	316	152	191
SUBTOTAL	581	368	534
Poland			
2004	NA	135	781
2005	557	350	854
2006	675	377	908
SUBTOTAL	1,232	862	2,543

Note: All prices in millions of euros (1999 prices).
Source: Author compilations from data in Commission 2002a: 4.

There is a significant risk that necessary restructuring would be slowed or even stopped, creating a durable vicious circle of low productivity, low standards and high hidden unemployment" (European Commission Directorate General for Agriculture 2001).

The 2002 deal also included additional rural development aid for CEE states, distributed to them quotas for several major commodities, and gave transitional periods for improving food safety to food processors in the Czech Republic (52 producers), Hungary (44), and Poland (485).[21] This chapter focuses on direct payments and market price supports. SAPARD will be mentioned more briefly, as regional development is already a prominent theme in the first part of this chapter.[22] Projected expenditures for all three categories are shown in Table 8, which

[21] http://europa.eu.int/comm/enlargement/negotiations/chapters/chap7/index.htm. See also Fehér (2002).
[22] SAPARD (EC No. 1268/1999) helped CEE candidate countries prepare for the CAP and the Single Market. It had two major objectives: first, to implement the *acquis*, and, second, to solve priority problems in the field of agriculture and rural development. For extensive data on rural development programs in both countries, see Chaplin (2001a, 2001b); Ratinger (2001); Ratinger et al. (2003).

also includes Poland for comparative purposes.[23] If the shape of the EU's immediate financial commitment is clear, the competitiveness of Czech and Hungarian agricultural products is debatable.[24] When measured against world prices, one meta-study of CEE agriculture indicated that in 1994–6, Hungarian and Czech producers enjoyed a competitive edge – measured strictly in terms of prices and not product quality – only in crops such as wheat, corn, barley, and sunflowers.[25] In all categories of dairy and meat production, however, CEE prices were above world prices, in part because postcommunist fragmentation of herds had reached amazing proportions such that the average dairy "herd" size in Romania and Bulgaria in 1996 was 1.8 and 1.4 cows, respectively (Gorton and Davidova 2001: 192–4).[26] Though labor costs in the region are generally low, farmers often pay above world market levels for seeds and fertilizers.[27] In both Hungary and the Czech Republic, crop farms of over 50 hectares are more competitive than farms under 50 hectares, and farming companies and co-ops are more competitive than even the larger individual farms (Gorton and Davidova 2001: 196).[28] For all these reasons, CEE farm groups are correct to anticipate that CAP direct payments often will make the difference between losses and profits (Gorton and Davidova 2001: 198; *Transitions Online*, May 17, 2002).

[23] The Polish case is covered more extensively in chapter 8.

[24] The econometric studies I cite in this paragraph provide a somewhat more pessimistic view than did official EU reports, which looked strictly at current prices and emphasized lower prices in Hungary and the Czech Republic for most commodities relative to EU prices (European Commission, Directorate General for Agriculture 2002a, 2002b: 13–15). The bottom line, however, remains that CEE prices are rising toward EU prices (well above world levels) at a time when productivity trends are not markedly improving.

[25] For some commodities, quality differences are likely to be substantial. The 2002 Commission report on Hungarian agriculture noted, "The average quality of beef and pork meat in Hungary is still substantially below average EU levels" (European Commission, Directorate General for Agriculture 2002b: 14).

[26] Poland, the largest agricultural producer in the region, had no crops at all that were price competitive. Of all CEE countries, Bulgaria was most price competitive (Gorton and Davidova 2001: 192–3).

[27] This fact has broader implications in that the subsequent lower use of fertilizers and pesticides – while consistent with one EU priority – means that current crop yields may be produced by overworking soils and thus may be unsustainable (Gorton and Davidova 2001: 194).

[28] Average EU farm size is 18 hectares (compared to 207 hectares for the United States). See http://europa.eu.int/comm/agriculture/external/wto/ usfarmbill/qa28.htm.

TABLE 9. *Predicted Percentage Changes in Producer Prices of Major Crops and Livestock Products Above FAPRI Baseline Prices*

	Wheat	Corn	Barley	Beef	Pork	Poultry	Cheese	Butter	NFD
EU–15									
2004/05	−3.9	−4.9	−2.7	−0.6	0.5	−0.1	−0.6	0.0	0.0
2009/10	4.4	−5.8	−2.5	2.8	0.3	−0.8	−2.7	−1.8	−4.2
Czech Republic									
2004/05	−36.2	−26.9	−35.2	−33.2	−28.5	−13.7	107.5	63.5	92.5
2009/10	−41.4	−34.2	−45.9	−34.1	−24.6	−21.5	88.2	44.2	55.1
Hungary									
2004/05	51.9	81.6	56.9	70.7	4.3	29.8	48.3	45.0	43.0
2009/10	59.1	77.5	33.9	63.0	2.4	28.3	34.5	24.8	20.4
Poland									
2004/05	6.7	28.3	−0.1	11.6	1.6	−11.5	57.5	43.5	58.4
2009/10	11.9	35.5	−8.3	−9.7	−3.8	−8.5	43.6	27.5	26.8

Source: Fuller et al. 2002: 418 (Scenario 2, with direct payments). Used by permission.

Table 9 indicates a further projection of the effects on prices (and, by extension, on trade patterns) of CAP membership in a scenario with phased-in direct payments. Table 9 uses a multimarket, world agricultural price model developed by the Food and Agriculture Policy Research Institute (FAPRI) at Iowa State University. The model uses both macroeconomic and trade and agricultural policy indicators to specify a predicted baseline for agriculture production and prices in all European countries. It then predicts the effect of direct payments to CEE farmers on these prices and production levels. Overall, the model predicts that most EU commodity prices are likely to fall moderately as a result of increased CEE production. For CEE, however, commodity prices should jump significantly in many cases (though prices for several Czech grains should fall). The expectation is that higher prices will spark higher CEE production, less domestic consumption, and, by extension, less trade to third countries but more trade to the EU–15 (Fuller et al. 2002).[29] With these macropolitical and market characteristics in mind, the next section sketches the main indicators of rural life in both states, their recent policies, current structural issues, EU evaluations, and rural development challenges.

[29] On the other hand, the less well-developed infrastructure (especially in first-stage food processing), inadequate access to capital, and lower productivity will limit these gains. I thank Wyn Grant for this point.

Hungarian Agriculture: A Brief Description

Fine soil and climate and abundant water have made agriculture – and rural life in general – a very important feature of Hungarian society.[30] Hungarian agriculture is comprised of about 60% crops (overwhelmingly wheat and maize) and 40% livestock. The importance of agriculture to the Hungarian economy is manifest in a number of indicators. The share of the rural population (though only a minority works in agriculture) in Hungary has been up to 3.5 times higher than in current EU member states (Baukó and Gurzó 2001: 362). Hungary also has the highest share of arable land in all of CEE – 63% (EU average, 41%). While it has shrunk in the postcommunist period, agriculture has stabilized after 1996 at a level of production of about 75% of the 1989–91 average (European Commission, Directorate General for Agriculture 2002b: 6–8).[31] Agriculture accounted for 4.3% of gross value added in 2001 and 6.1% of total employment (just above the EU average of 5%). As workers left the farms in the 1990s, average labor productivity in the sector rose sharply and now stands just above the EU-15 average (and well ahead of Poland and several member states) (New Zealand Ministry of Foreign Affairs and Trade 2001: 13). Finally, though food prices are low relative to EU prices, they are high relative to modest Hungarian incomes. Hungarians spent about 27% of their income on food in 2002, compared to 17% for the EU as a whole.

Unlike the Czech Republic, Hungary is a net agricultural exporter to the EU. Agri-food exports account for 9% of total exports, and Hungary's food sector has been quite successful in attracting foreign direct investment. In the early 1990s, Hungary joined the export-oriented Cairns Group, which generally argues for agricultural liberalization. It left the group in January 1998 as it began to align its policies with those of the EU, though its long-term interest may still lie with a CAP that is more liberal than the current one. Since full integration into EU agricultural markets will lead to a significant rise in producer prices for most Hungarian grain, meat, and dairy products, both domestic consumers and export competitiveness will likely suffer (Fuller et al. 2002: 418). Hungarian agriculture spending – focusing primarily on price supports – has increased in the run up to accession, as it has undertaken a host of tasks in building up

---

[30] English-language sources include Janos (1982, 2000); Crumley (2003); Szelényi (1998); Lampland (1995); Meurs (2001); Agócs and Agócs (1994).

[31] Total agricultural production was 4.4 billion euros in 1998 (European Commission 2002e: 10).

administrative capacity.[32] On the other hand, the EU did not require Hungary or the Czech Republic to harmonize their import duties or export subsidies until they actually joined the EU.[33]

Hungarian farms are smaller than in the Czech Republic, though not so fragmented as in Poland. A series of privatization measures in the early 1990s contributed to the proliferation of small holdings (Crumley 2003: 210–11). In 2000, Hungary's 1 million private holdings averaged a mere 4 hectares,[34] but they accounted for 60% of cultivated land.[35] Using an average landholding of 312 hectares (European Commission 2002e: 8), 8,382 corporate farms made up the other 40% of cultivation. The EU worries that fragmentation will make the sector too inefficient and administration of the CAP too complicated (2002e: 71). The 2002 Commission report remained very stern in the chapter on agriculture, concluding that "considerable further efforts are needed" in this policy sector (2002e: 69). The report went on to threaten that Hungary might well be unable to take full benefit of CAP programs or may even have to repay EU funds already received. The negative tone of the report was due mostly to lagging administrative capacity – to thresholds not met – rather than to the legislative basis of Hungarian agriculture.

Rural development remains a huge challenge in Hungary, as the microregions are quite heterogeneous. In localities where farmers are in a relatively good position – for example, Oroshaza – farmers wish to continue planting crops the EU already has in ample supply, and they resist cutbacks that would cost them current income. They also have little desire or opportunity to take up relatively minor EU SAPARD incentives to grow exotic or specialized "Hungarian" crops (like Kalocsa paprika), switch to organic farming, or plant woodlots. Experience under state socialism has left them committed to Fordist practices, especially given land patterns that generally favor such practices. In the poorest regions – for example, Sarkad – it is much easier to use SAPARD funds to coax farmers into new practices. But given the need for cofinancing such projects, a

[32] The 2002 Hungarian agricultural budget was 744 million euros (European Commission 2002e: 65).

[33] To do so would have obliged these states to violate WTO commitments.

[34] A hectare is about 2.5 acres. If the Hungarian government increased its minimum requirement for farms to one hectare, as in several EU member states, the number of individual farms would then fall from 958,000 to 270,000.

[35] Extensive research on the large second economy in Hungarian agriculture under communism suggests that it provides an uncertain foundation for private farming since so many people depended on the state system for the time, inputs, and marketing mechanisms provided by the state (Lampland 1995: 341–50).

disproportionate amount of SAPARD support will go to the best-endowed farms, further polarizing an already striking imbalance in rural incomes (Baukó and Gurzó 2001: 365–6). Thus history shapes what is locally rational: where investment and farming practices in the past have produced larger farms in stable rural regions, external inducements are of secondary value. Yet, despite the fact that such inducements are far more persuasive in poor regions, their cofinancing requirements may lead to further polarization. Tailoring programs to local needs is vital, but, as in the case of Sarkad, doing so may undercut the objective of promoting larger and more efficient units.

Czech Agriculture: A Brief Description

The Czech agricultural sector accounted for 4.2% of GDP and 4.6% of total employment in 2001.[36] The 2002 state agricultural budget was 420 million euros, about 1.8% of state spending (European Commission 2002d: 67). After the 2000 "double-zero agreement" to liberalize agricultural trade between the EU and CEE, both imports from and exports to the EU jumped about 12%, but the EU maintained a trade surplus vis-à-vis the Czech Republic of 667 million euros. Agriculture accounts for about 4.4% of Czech exports and 5.7% of total imports, and while production has shrunk in the postcommunist period, it also has stabilized since 1994 at about 75% of the 1989–91 average (European Commission, Directorate General for Agriculture 2002a: 6).[37]

Czech commodity prices are higher than in Hungary and, indeed, are above EU averages in both grains and meats, though below in dairy (Fuller et al. 2002). Full integration into EU agricultural markets likely will lead to a significant drop in producer prices for grain and meat producers and to increases for dairy (Fuller et al. 2002: 418). Falling prices in some sectors means the Czechs may actually move from importing to exporting some commodities (e.g., livestock). Where consumer prices rise – like the Hungarians, the Czechs spent about 27% of their income on food in 2002 – consumption will decline but supply will increase because of CAP purchasing guarantees. This is likely to lead to increased exports but, again because of rising prices, probably a diversion of exports to

---

[36] Defined as economically active persons who gain a significant part of their income from agriculture.

[37] Total agricultural production was just under 3 billion euros in 1998; see European Commission, Directorate General for Agriculture (2002a: 10); Csaki, Debatisse, and Honisch (1999).

third countries and into the EU instead (Fuller et al. 2002: 426–7). CEE states could contribute to worsening gluts of certain commodities (e.g., milk), and thus the EU has had an incentive to constrain their quotas.

As in Hungary, policy adaptation was driven by the need to create economically sustainable agriculture with limited access to protected EU markets. Yet Czech hopes of joining the EU and the CAP also required costly investments in production facilities to meet higher standards of food quality and safety. In contrast with other postcommunist countries, which chose a more gradual reform, Czech policy makers preferred rapid privatization. As Dr. Tomáš Ratinger from the Czech Research Institute of Agricultural Economy explains:

> After 1990, swift transformation to private ownership became more important than economic effectiveness. The agricultural crisis that accompanied the price liberalization in 1991 forced policy-makers to look for functioning models. This was logically the EU and the CAP. Czech agricultural policies were then gradually modeled according to CAP rules, but with opposite intentions. While the EU was interested in limiting agricultural production, Czech policy makers looked to make Czech agriculture economically sustainable. (Ratinger interview)

The agricultural sector is characterized by the clustering of agricultural land into larger production units as a result of the expropriation and collectivization efforts in the 1950s. In 2000, the average Czech individual farm had 18 hectares (exactly the EU average), 5.9 cattle, and 7.2 pigs. The average workforce was 0.5 persons for whom farming was their primary occupation and a further 1.4 persons for whom farming was a temporary or seasonal occupation. By contrast, the average institutional holding had 886 hectares, 446 cattle, and 1,017 pigs. It employed forty-three persons on a permanent basis and ten more on a seasonal or temporary basis (European Commission, Directorate General for Agriculture 2002a: 8). Thus, average Czech farms were four times larger than Hungarian ones, and institutional holdings were almost three times larger than their Hungarian counterparts.

The 2002 Commission opinion on Czech agriculture was far more positive than was the one on Hungary. The Czechs were praised for relatively steady progress in agriculture, with the report concluding that "the overall level of preparation in the agricultural sector is good, except as regards veterinary legislation" (73). Though some legislative deficiencies in the veterinary fields were noted (patches were required in the form of an overall framework law and various pieces of technical legislation), the report's main concern was the administrative capacity to undertake all that had been promised. Some Czech experts are less sanguine. Doucha notes that 500,000 hectares remain unprivatized, "three generations" of debt load exist on current holdings, producers rely very heavily on unstable year-to-year rental agreements (likely to channel much EU aid to investors rather than farmers), and Czech farmers are politically fragmented (*Transitions Online*, May 17, 2002).

The EU has been displeased with Czech rural development, however, which has reflected the same reluctant decentralization we saw in Czech regional policy. Since 1999, the EU has been prepared to contribute through SAPARD 23 million euros annually to the Czechs, with 60% for measures to support the adoption of EU standards and the rest for cofinancing agricultural investments, improving the processing and marketing of agricultural products, and strengthening administrative capacity in quality control and consumer protection. Despite the available funds, administrative adaptation to the implementation of these funds has been slow, and SAPARD began to operate in the Czech Republic only in April 2002.

With these brief national sketches in mind, the next two sections cover voluntary and less voluntary forms of emulation. As in the health care case, the focus will be on two main organizing principles that have been shaped by emulation, namely, agricultural price supports (including quotas) and direct payment mechanisms. Chronologically, the CEE states built greatly attenuated price support mechanisms earlier in the transition. Direct income support has been mainly a matter of high politics during the negotiations with the EU, though again, it has required the CEE states to build administrative capacity in order to implement these high-level bargains. Together, both trends explain why a huge and detailed *acquis* did not generate emulation until very late in the 1990s.

Phase 1: Voluntary Emulation – CAP-Like or CAP-Lite?

All agricultural reforms after 1989 happened against the backdrop of overall economic reform and privatization of state-owned property.[38] Mayhew identifies two distinct early phases. The first phase involved extensive liberalization of foreign agricultural trade, tariffs, and prices, and

---

[38] This chapter focuses on EU-oriented adjustments, but obviously, CEE agriculture had to be responsive to the GATT Uruguay Round and, later, to WTO concerns as well as those of the EU.

the significant reduction of subsidies. Though these policies contributed to the overall macroeconomic liberalization of the region, they combined with falling consumer demand for CEE food products and higher input prices (e.g., the loss of fertilizer and fuel subsidies) to seriously undermine agricultural profitability and farm incomes (1998: 243–5). By the mid-1990s, farm production had fallen by about one-fourth to one-half, depending on the sector.

The second phase, beginning with the one-sided Europe Agreements in 1991, took account of the flood of imports from the EU and moved to both protect and support domestic agriculture. Though resisted by liberals, farm lobbies and many other elites in both the Czech Republic and Hungary began to look "to the CAP of the Community as an example to follow" (Mayhew 1998: 251). Both states introduced price support mechanisms (though Bulgaria and Romania, for instance, did not). The Czech Republic instituted a milk quota, and its agricultural budget soon mirrored the main spending categories of the EU: price support, income support, and investment support. Hungary's main price support instrument was the new Office for Agricultural Market Regime (Hartell and Swinnen 2000: 194–5).

Given the budget constraints, however, these "CAP-like" policies were actually "CAP-lite" policies, with far fewer subsidies than were available in the member states. The prices that CEE governments were able to guarantee were far below the EU's intervention prices. For example, Hungary's 1994 wheat support prices were 51% of the EU's, while the Czech prices were at 67% of the EU's. Comparable figures for beef were 44% (Hungary) and 43% (Czech Republic), and for milk, 65% (Hungary) and 55% (Czech Republic) (Mayhew 1998: 253). Even then, relatively high world commodity prices meant that both governments rarely had to make good on such support floors. At the time, Tangermann and Josling (1994) noted that price supports approaching EU levels would have had almost unthinkable consequences for CEE consumers and for public deficits.

Overall, 1989–95 saw unsystematic agricultural reform that emphasized rapid land privatization and served individual political clienteles. The new political class generally lacked experience with farming under market conditions and lacked ideas on designing agricultural reforms beyond creating private ownership. This neglect had a political function: With job losses in industrialized sectors mounting rapidly, few elites had any interest in modernizing agriculture simultaneously. In this context, emulation of Western models began to play a more significant role only after the privatization process was advanced and the market for agricultural products began to settle. Even then, widespread uncertainty about whether enlargement would happen no doubt dampened enthusiasm for emulation. Given the combination of high potential rewards but high uncertainty about those rewards, both states' modest investment in new policy regimes makes sense; they implemented price support mechanisms that would be a foundation for future benefits but attenuated them in ways that fit their current budgetary priorities.

The year 1995 ushered in a new phase in domestic agricultural reform, a phase that began to emphasize EU membership (Grant 1999). New concepts and requirements began to affect reform, especially when the EU began to demand compliance with strict food and sanitary standards in connection with (gradual) opening of its markets to the CEE countries. The Association agreements with the EU, effective in February 1995, brought closer ties between the CEE states and the EU.[39]

Phase 2: Less-Voluntary Emulation

More than in any other policy area discussed here, institutional changes in agriculture presupposed some level of certainty that enlargement was going to happen. To take the opposite extreme, changes in consumer protection law did not commit CEE states to reforms whose costs could not be borne if the EU ultimately decided not to let them join. Nor could adjustment come through the increasingly noted "soft" approach to integration. Ritchie (2003) shows that in fisheries (also a policy area in the primary sector of the economy and with multiple and entrenched interests), hard EU rules based on regulations and directives are extraordinarily difficult to monitor and enforce, and soft rules that are less interventionist – and often generated by fisherman – prevail. Agriculture does not make much use of soft law (though its provisions are also devilishly hard to enforce). Indeed, in many ways, it is the last bastion of hard rules. Thus, only after the momentum for enlargement seemed likely irreversible did CEE elites move to emulate EU policies.

After 1998, when negotiations for EU accession began, CEE negotiators quickly understood that the final phase would be about financial compensation for their agricultural sectors. Thus, they had strong incentives to develop similar subsidy structures in order to maximize the returns from these negotiations. An example was the quota for grazing beef (suckler

[39] In 1995 the Czechs and Hungarians also joined the WTO.

cow premium). Here, even though the final figure negotiated by the Czechs in Copenhagen (90,300) was far below the originally demanded figures, Czech chief negotiator Pavel Telička noted that this was still far above the actual number of suckler cows in the Czech Republic. As it became clear that accession would bring CAP funding, Czech farmers began to invest in suckler cows and reduce reliance on mechanical hay cutting, a shift nicely captured in a phrase used in some rural areas: "Cows belong on the mountains; they cut better than tractors."[40]

A similar situation existed with milk quotas. The Czech quota of 2,737,931 tons again exceeded current Czech capacities by a significant margin.[41] This outcome (with its premise that Czech capacity will grow) would have been impossible without previous adaptation to CAP-like structures. While in EU member states milk production capacities are higher due to the effects of long-term price support and investment in production facilities (itself often a result of CAP spending), the underfinanced Czech dairy sector will use the higher milk prices under the quota to stimulate production and guarantee income to farmers. Introduced only in 2000, the quota had not yet been reached by Czech farmers by 2004, though agricultural experts expect that with CAP subsidies now in place, it soon would be.

The basic pattern that resulted during this period was that the EU increased pressure to adopt specific legislative patches, especially but not exclusively in the areas of veterinary and phytosanitary, while articulating a range of administrative thresholds in other areas of the agricultural *acquis*. Three thresholds stand out: (1) an agency to implement the EAGGF (footnote 4); (2) an organization that the EU calls an Integrated Administration and Control System (IACS); and (3) a functioning food-quality policy.

The EAGGF was established in 1962 as the Community's substitute for supporting agriculture through individual national structures. Though each member state has an EAGGF agency, the EU does not mandate one way to construct such an organization, which combines the very different functions of rural development (guidance) and price supports (guarantee). In May 2002, the Czechs decided to split CAP administration between two different agencies: the State Agricultural Intervention Fund (SAIF) and the SAPARD administration. The 2002 report noted, however, that "the SAIF

---

[40] "*Krávy patří na hory, sečou líp než traktory.*"
[41] Source of figures: European Commission; figures were also published in *Uniting Europe*, no. 213 (December 23, 2002: 10).

is not fully equivalent to intervention agencies in the EU, and needs to be upgraded in order to cover all the specific instruments of Community market regulation" (European Commission 2002d: 70). The Hungarians took a different path, choosing to establish only one agency for CAP administration. To do so, it took an existing agency, the Agricultural Intervention Center (AIK), and mandated it to be the EAGGF lead agency. Then, in August 2002, the Agriculture Ministry announced that from July 2003, the SAPARD agency (the tenth and last to be approved by the EU in CEE) would be merged with the AIK (2002e: 65–7). The AIK, for its part, remains unaccredited by the EU and does not yet have a coherent definition of tasks.

Agricultural subsidies have jumped in concert with these administrative changes. The most widely used measure of agricultural subsidies is the Producer Support Estimate (PSE). This figure, often expressed as the ratio of support to gross farm receipts (e.g., value of production plus farm support), averaged 32% in the OECD and 34% in the EU-15 in 2000 (OECD 2002: 158–60).[42] Czech and Hungarian PSE levels fluctuated wildly during the postcommunist period, indicating policy instability.[43] The Hungarian PSE fell from 39% in 1986–8 to a low of 6% in 1997 and was 12% in 2001, the most recent year for which data are available (OECD 2002). Czech PSEs averaged 60% between 1986 and 1988 and also fell precipitously to about 7% in 1997 before rising to 17% in 2001 (OECD 2002; see also Bauer 2001: 3–4). Two points stand out: First, the large initial differences between Czech and Hungarian PSEs have narrowed considerably by 2001; second, PSEs in both countries showed a sharp rise after 1997, a pattern we have seen in other policy sectors influenced by EU rules.[44]

A second important administrative threshold is the IACS system, which has a role in the oversight of direct payments. One interesting result of the December 2002 final agreement was that CEE states would enjoy several years in which they could choose a simplified version of the direct payment system. The main idea was to decouple payments from production and tie them instead to area payments. This was clearly an effort by the EU to

---

[42] It is possible to have a negative PSE, which means that farmers subsidize consumers and taxpayers. Bulgarian farmers in the postcommunist period have consistently had a negative PSE (Sharman 2003).

[43] About half of the support is in the form of market price supports with the rest a combination of input support, export support, and credit concessions. PSEs vary by product as well. Poultry, sugar, and milk are highly subsidized in both states.

[44] For comparison, Poland's PSE went from 22 to 25 between 1997 and 1999.

lower the administrative threshold of what is, even for member states, a very demanding set of controls.[45] Another purpose of the IACS system is to provide on-demand identification of livestock, especially in the event of disease outbreaks. Individual plots of land also require tracking systems. The Czechs are relatively advanced here, having completed digitization of aerial photographs that cover the entire country (European Commission, Directorate General for Agriculture 2002a: 68). On the other hand, the opinion notes that the Czech system is not yet complete (70). Here, too, Hungary seems behind. The 2002 opinion lamented that Hungary remained at the level of a feasibility study and concluded, "Very serious efforts are urgently needed in order for Hungary to be able to build up an operational IACS by accession. The necessary decisions must be taken immediately and the related funding put in place without delay if Hungary is to be in a position to administer and control efficiently the aid-schemes of the CAP as of accession" (2002e: 69).

A third threshold is a functioning food-quality policy, which the EU insists must be able to determine geographic origin and provide other forms of certification. Such measures are of high profile since the BSE ("mad cow") outbreak cost European farmers tens of millions of dollars in the mid-1990s. In April 2002, the Czech government established the Czech Agricultural and Foodstuff Inspection (CAFI) to secure these controls (European Commission 2002d: 68). In Hungary, the difference between an agency on paper and an agency that can function comes into sharp relief in this area. An agency was established in 1998 that, in principle, met all EU requirements. Yet not until 2001 were even the first five agricultural product names even registered by the new agency (European Commission 2002e: 66). Antal Németh, chief of the animal health and food control department at the Hungarian Ministry of Agriculture and Regional Development, admits that "regulations exist on paper, but what can be enforced in practice is another thing" (quoted in *Transitions Online*, March 7, 2002).

In terms of legislative approximation, the 2002 report praised Czech progress in the phytosanitary field but noted that "little legislative progress has been noted in the veterinary field over the past year ... " (European Commission 2002d: 69). In general, the phytosanitary area, which guards against harmful organisms, requires little investment compared to the much more demanding areas of food safety and veterinary standards. Nor

---

[45] For details on the agreement, see European Commission (2002a).

are these fields the only ones where the Commission demanded patches. There was also a set of administrative demands that did not require the Czechs to set up their own agencies so much as integrate with existing EU monitoring programs. Examples include the EUROPHY system or ongoing efforts to test for BSE (European Commission 2002d: 72). Hungary, on the other hand, quickly adopted the veterinary framework legislation, and it promulgated nineteen separate government decrees during 2001 designed to implement the EU rules (European Commission 2002e: 68). As we will see, emulation of specific practices can proceed even as the struggle over other institutions plays out at higher political levels.

Summary: Emulation and Struggle

The agriculture case also underscores the struggle associated with emulation. It would be wrong to suggest that struggle is only evident in this case, and indeed, it will be prominent in military reform as well. But struggle is more prominent here, perhaps because it happened at so many levels and because there were so many pressures for CEE states to simply conform to EU demands.[46]

At the *international level*, if emulation was a state tool to capture subsidies, then it was hardly guaranteed success in doing so. Indeed, it long was almost axiomatic that CEE agriculture would have a second-class status, as observers continually noted that extension of the basic CAP would be exorbitantly expensive. Struggle was fueled by the basic dilemma that, without subsidies, huge numbers of CEE farms would likely become insolvent (see Pouliquen 2001), while with full subsidies, farm incomes would jump well above other rural (and indeed urban) incomes while removing many incentives for needed modernization. CEE states continued to frame the debate around "second class membership," arguing that anything less than the full CAP was unfair. Both governments and agricultural interest groups lobbied hard for a generous deal.

But struggle does not guarantee success, and their results were mixed at best. While the EU's *Agenda 2000* foresaw no direct payments for CEE, by January 2002, the EU did offer phased-in payments. Though the CEE states were not able to increase these phased-in payments in the final deal, they did increase the ceilings on what they could spend to "top-up" these subsidies and also improved both their assigned quotas and the

---

[46] More generally, see Mair (2003); Gryzmała-Busse and Innes (2003); Holmes (2003).

"reference yields" that will help determine their productive potential.[47] Yet even these gains cannot be definitively attributed to CEE bargaining efforts or interest group agitation. The October 2002 Brussels European Council meeting had promised that new members would not be worse off financially after accession than they were as candidate countries. Yet given projections in fall 2002, "worse-off" scenarios were possible (and even likely) in four of the candidates (Czech Republic, Slovenia, Malta, and Cyprus). The options for avoiding this scenario were either a rebate of their payments to the EU or an increase in funds available through EU programs. In Copenhagen, the EU chose the latter course, agreeing both to higher direct payments for CEE farmers and for structural funds that would flow directly into the budgets of the CEE states. And struggles between the Commission and national governments continued right up to the eve of enlargement. Just six weeks before the May 1, 2004 enlargement, the Commission notified the Czech government of "serious consequences" if it failed to set up a proper disbursement agency for agriculture payments (Radio Prague, March 2004).

At the *domestic level*, the politics of emulation were hotly contested by domestic interest groups. Domestic agricultural interests in both states fought constant battles against their own governments, often in response to steps the EU had obliged the governments to undertake. Hungarian ultranationalist leader Istvan Csurka claimed that Western agents were behind the Hungarian "pig plague," a tactic that allowed foreign investors to snap up Hungarian meat processors cheaply (*Financial Times*, January 22, 1993). Later, Hungarian cooperative members, private farmers, and joint-stock-company workers demonstrated against higher monitoring and safety standards that many feared they would be unable to meet. In addition, they pushed the Hungarian government to defend laws passed early in the transition that prohibited foreign purchases of Hungarian land. Critics even framed foreign land purchases as a "Second Trianon," in reference to the post-WWI treaty under which Hungary lost two-thirds of its territory (*BBC Monitoring/Hungarian Radio*, December 15, 2002).

At the same time, many Hungarians used so-called pocket contracts to illegally sell their land to foreign investors, and Viktor Orbán speculated that up to 25% of five western counties was owned by Austrians (Crumley 2003: 213–15). The Czech Ministry of Agriculture (MoA) made headlines in early 1998 by slapping a 95% import duty on apple

---

[47] The EU also made some support conditional upon farmers' guarantees that the funds be used for investment rather than consumption.

imports from the EU after Czech farmers had threatened to block roads and border crossings in response to a tripling of EU apple exports to the Czech Republic since 1994 (*International Herald Tribune*, March 30, 1998). The EU immediately responded by putting import restrictions on pork from the Czech Republic. After five months, the Czechs dropped the duty in exchange for EU assistance in improving Czech fruit marketing practices.

Despite the fact that agriculture represents a small segment of most CEE economies (if not always small in employment terms), discussions about quotas, payments, and other forms of agricultural compensation dominated the final phase of the negotiations at the Copenhagen summit, in December 2002.[48] Classically, volatile markets and unpredictable weather have been crucial arguments for national subsidies to farmers. In CEE, however, the subsidies themselves were an added source of volatility. Subsidy systems changed continually, and farmers found it exceedingly difficult to engage in even medium-term planning. Low information flow between the countries' MoAs and farmers on EU priorities exacerbated uncertainty and disinformation. At bottom were fears that CEE farmers would be exposed to heavily subsidized competitors from the EU without any effective support or protection. Their experience with the one-sided Europe Agreements made such fears understandable.[49]

Farmer protests against the final CAP agreement in Copenhagen, however, partly reflected broader grievances that no deal there could have solved. Yet in the weeks after the deal, protests rapidly waned. In the Czech Republic, once the MoA guaranteed that it would use the right to "top up" direct payments by 30% to a total of 55% of the EU levels in 2004, the Agrarian Chamber dropped its opposition to enlargement. Other Czech agricultural groups quickly followed suit, including the Czech–Moravian Association of Agricultural Entrepreneurs, Association of Private Farmers, Chamber of Food Producers, Union of Agricultural Workers, and Association of Marginal Communities, which represents rural entrepreneurs from mountainous regions. The farmer associations even decided to launch their own pro-EU campaign to convince the rural voters. The chairman of the Union of Agricultural Workers, Bohumír

---

[48] At both the international and domestic levels, the Polish case was obviously very important, as demonstrated in chapter 8.

[49] Even the 2000 "double-zero" agreement eliminated all tariff barriers to imports from the EU but failed to eliminate a variety of nontariff barriers in product labeling, import licensing, and veterinary and phytosanitary areas that continued to keep many CEE agricultural products out of their largest potential market.

Dufek, explained the sudden change of opinion: "We mainly wanted to create pressure on Brussels, so that they would offer us better conditions. That worked out" (interview; see also Doucha 1999).

This aspect of the struggle thus had clear limits. Keeler (1999) has noted the EU's extreme difficulties in encouraging structural reform in agriculture in Greece, Portugal, and Spain. He argues that strong states would be required to resist pressures for protection and subsidy in CEE. Yet despite the weakness of these states, we should also remember that their interest organizations are, if anything, even weaker. Though we saw that contestation likely raised agricultural benefits somewhat, PSEs in CEE (even in Poland) remain about half those in the EU–15. For the present at least, agricultural policies in the East are not yet a mirror image of those in the West.

Finally, there is also an *intrasectoral struggle* over the terms of emulation. This is perhaps most clear in the Czech case. The battle line for EU funding runs between the old state farms and the individual farmers. While the CAP tends to benefit large farms in current member states, it seems that private Czech farmers have adapted best to the new conditions and will benefit most from exporting to the EU. Larger ones have restructured more, and many small ones do not rely exclusively on agricultural income. Former state farms actually have adapted much less and are most in need of subsidies to survive. Many cooperative farm managers worry that more open competition with EU farmers who get more CAP subsidies will make them even worse off. Cooperative farms are represented politically by the Agrarian Chamber, whose chairman, Václav Hlaváček, denounced the Copenhagen agreement at every opportunity and stressed that his members' prices for fuel and seed were already comparable to EU prices while ignoring their cheap labor and the fact that their land rents have been around 10% of EU levels (Kosc 2002).

Many of the battles, of course, lie in the future, and open questions abound. At the international level, given their budgetary constraints, will the CEE states embrace the full CAP funding that will be available to them by 2013 (and repress the knowledge that they are taking on a deeply troubled system), or will they press for CAP reform and try to rein in farm subsidies? This question will come up during the debate over the 2007–13 budget with the CEE states as full members. The path they take may well turn on whether to ally with France (minimal reform) or with Germany (more significant reform). At the domestic level, it is clear that the CAP incentives are not always healthy ones. In some areas (e.g., the Czech beef case mentioned above), CAP incentives will likely lead to surging capacity at the same time that EU-mandated environmental measures may reduce the land available for grazing. In other cases, when direct payments approach 100% of the EU level, farmers' incentives to increase productivity may well fall off. Finally, the structure of the agricultural economy is such that much of the money meant for income support for farmers will flow out of the sector in the form of higher rents (Ratinger et al. 2003: 2–3). With such questions still open, it is perhaps unsurprising that Western models often function as Rorschach tests upon which CEE states project their hopes and fears.

4

The Struggle for Civilian Control of the Military

American advisors have conducted top-to-bottom assessments of the armed forces of Lithuania, Latvia, Estonia, Bulgaria, and Romania and have written blueprints for their remodeling. In the Czech Republic, Poland, Hungary, Romania, and Slovenia, they are revamping command-and-control systems... American advisors have drafted military codes of justice and tactical war-fighting doctrines... Poland is allowing an eight-man U.S. military team to help reshuffle its insular general staff, which has resisted transferring control over troops to civilian authorities. The Americans say they will help Poland create a Nato-style joint staff tied to an interagency political process like that in the United States.

(*Washington Post*, Dec. 14, 1998: A1)

This chapter and the next take up the issue of emulation, both voluntary and under pressure, in the military realm. If this front-page story quoted from the *Washington Post* in 1998 seemed a little breathless about the ability of the United States to remake CEE societies, chapters 2 and 3 have hopefully suggested that the process is not quite so straightforward. The epigraph is typical of one unrealistic way of thinking about external influence – namely, that it is essentially a teaching/consulting process. But there is another even more misleading approach, which is to assume that external models play no role at all and that domestic factors fully explain institutional change in CEE.

During 1990 and 1991, CEE elites at the highest levels began calling for NATO and EU membership at roughly the same time, yet NATO decided to enlarge in 1997, five and half years prior to the EU decision. Because NATO membership came so much faster, there was less time for purely voluntary emulation. And because actual enlargement came sooner (1999 versus 2004), we have a much better opportunity to look at implementation after membership. This is important because a great deal of reform remained undone when NATO enlarged and because the new members have faced two crisis moments – the bombing of Serbia during the Kosovo conflict and the much longer "war on terrorism."

This chapter covers reforms of civil–military relations, which were initially voluntary but then increasingly under the influence of NATO thresholds.[1] This case corresponds to the book's "high rule density" scenario because, as we will see, NATO made constant (if vague) demands for improvement of civilian control institutions. The predicted dominant mode of emulation is an intense struggle over these thresholds, similar to the case of agriculture. This outcome should follow in a policy area with dense rules and well-established actors left over from the communist period.

Chapter 5 discusses efforts to promote military professionalism in the wake of membership and in the midst of two wars.[2] One war (Kosovo) was the first that NATO ever fought, and the other war (against Islamic terrorists) is the first in which it has activated Article 5, calling on all members to come to the aid of a member who had been attacked – the United States. Because NATO members have loose and diverse standards for what constitutes military professionalism, this case is much more one of "low density" of IO demands. Here, the dominant mode of emulation is the more voluntary use of templates, especially around the issue of an all-volunteer force, which NATO has not insisted upon but which the Czechs and Hungarians have nonetheless embraced. Chapter 5 also discusses patches. Since the militaries are well-established, we would expect the voluntary use of exact copies to be rare, and that is, in fact, the case.

The starting point for this chapter can be summarized by severe CEE difficulties on two defense fronts. First, some key institutional legacies of the Warsaw Pact were plainly incompatible with NATO membership. Second, since the Czech and Hungarian publics were ambivalent, at best, about their national militaries, mass and elite support for defense spending

---

[1] While this chapter focuses on NATO and its member states, other entities like the EU, Western European Union (WEU), and the Organization for Security and Cooperation in Europe (OSCE) were also active. For an inventory of external promotion of "security sector reform," see Forster (2002).

[2] This distinction between civilian control and military professionalism is developed in Ulrich (1999) and Cottey, Edmunds, and Forster (2002b).

was very low. As in the EU chapters, I do not discuss all reforms in the sector, but rather narrow in on those that can be fairly characterized as processes of emulating prevalent Western organizations and practices. That said, there can be no doubt in these cases that intervention by NATO and its member states was crucial.[3] Jeffrey Simon's (2004c) and Rachel Epstein's (2004) accounts of Poland show that even there, where national military traditions were much more deeply anchored than in the Czech Republic and Hungary, NATO influence was very significant.

The focus on emulation is in keeping with the central question of the book about what outsiders can offer to help foreign societies reform. The main NATO response was to use thresholds for these two difficulties. The two thresholds were for proper structures for civilian control of the military and for budget floors to guarantee a certain financial commitment to military spending. This chapter focuses on the much more interesting institutional threshold of civilian control.

While the story is broadly similar in both states, two historical institutional legacies of the late communist period provide some variation. The first is that the Hungarian military posed no threat of intervention during the transition, while the Czech military did (see Sarvaš 1999: 103–4). The second is that the Hungarian Communist Party made a key institutional change in late 1989 by distancing the Ministry of Defense (MoD) from government control. This change did not occur in the Czech case. When combined, these two factors resulted in less political urgency and more military insulation and so have slowed real civilian control institutions in the Hungarian case even more than in the Czech case. In the end, however, the rational and sociological factors that account for similarity are as interesting as the historical factors that best account for differences.

COMPARING THE EU AND NATO: SIX KEY DIFFERENCES

This book compares the experiences of the same countries with two different IOs. It highlights the importance of three factors: (1) the historically determined policy baseline in different issue areas, (2) the robustness of state and social actors in those domains, and (3) the character of IO demands in those issue areas. Of these three factors, only the last hints at the major differences between the EU and NATO. It is time to spell out six of those differences explicitly.

---

[3] An alternative view is Reiter (2000).

Americans

In both international organizations, the CEE states wanted membership early on but had to wait for the IOs to embrace them. Yet NATO enlargement preceded EU expansion by about five years. This happened primarily because NATO enlargement caught the imagination of the United States, which made enlargement a priority, built on latent German support, and overcame significant resistance from France and Russia. While American models are of low appeal to CEE states in areas like agriculture and health care, they play a significant role in defense reforms.

Uncertainty

Communism's collapse obliged both institutions to face the challenge of fundamental reform, but NATO's challenge was literally existential. NATO's principle reason for existing – containing the Soviet Union – disappeared. Even if Western Europe continued to worry about the possibility of a "Weimar Russia," the alliance's raison d'etre was widely questioned (Wallander 2001). The EU, by contrast, often seemed more relevant than ever, at least if judged by its institutional growth through Maastricht, Amsterdam, and monetary union.

Demands

The EU has a well-developed and explicit *acquis*. NATO, as a general rule, shows much more deference to the institutional traditions of its member states. And what can reasonably be called the NATO *acquis* was more modest and much more informal, though the challenge of incorporating CEE states has clearly "thickened" this set of rules over time, as exemplified, for example, by the Membership Action Plans of the second round of NATO enlargement.[4]

Bureaucracy

The EU's institutions are significantly more extensive than NATO's. Its Commission has the personnel to engage in extensive programming and monitoring (though these tasks did admittedly stretch the Commission very thin at times). NATO works bilaterally, and it has far fewer personnel

---

[4] I owe the term "NATO *acquis*" to Jeffrey Simon.

than does the EU (in many cases, only one reform specialist per CEE country in NATO headquarters).[5] Because NATO efforts to promote reform are understaffed, NATO was much more of a blunt instrument, able to set thresholds but hard-pressed to conduct detailed renovations of national capabilities.

Incentives

The EU has lubricated institutional change with significant amounts of money, while NATO has had far fewer resources with which to induce change. Most financial support for CEE military reform has come through bilateral aid from individual NATO members to individual CEE states. Also, EU assistance for regional growth or agricultural reforms grew as membership neared, while the primary NATO funds were cut off as soon as the CEE states achieved membership.

Manipulation

The member states of each IO largely determined the institutional requirements for membership. The reluctance of major European powers to enlarge the EU quickly led them to insist on high standards for membership. In some cases, they even raised the bar above that for current member states. The raised bar issue was not a significant factor in the NATO case, and in some cases, the bar was even lowered.

THE HIGH POLITICS OF NATO ENLARGEMENT: A BRIEF OVERVIEW

Most of this chapter and the next are concerned with the institutional adaptations of CEE militaries, but those reforms took place in a diplomatic context that was convoluted and opaque.[6] CEE elites began public discussion of NATO membership even prior to the 1991 dissolution of the Warsaw Pact. By May 1992, five months after the collapse of the USSR, Presidents Havel (Czechoslovakia), Wałesa (Poland), and Antall (Hungary) declared together that their goal was full-fledged membership

---

[5] NATO headquarters employs about 3,150 people, including about 1,400 who are actually members of national delegations (North Atlantic Treaty Organization 2001b: 219). The EU Commission has about 19,000 employees.

[6] This section follows Asmus's detailed reconstruction of that process (2002); see also Goldgeier (1999); Grayson (1999); Kay (1998); Yost (1998).

in NATO. The Clinton administration had come to office with a keen desire to put the United States relationship with Russia on a better footing, and its top officials were initially not disposed to accept a NATO enlargement that might antagonize Russia (Asmus 2002: 99–109; Goldgeier 1999: 51–65). At the December 1993 NATO summit, the United States responded to CEE calls for membership by introducing a new program called Partnership for Peace, which bought the administration more time. By then, a combination of factors had begun to erode the consensus against enlargement: mounting Western frustration at the inability to prevent the carnage in Bosnia; direct appeals of CEE leaders to President Clinton during the dedication of the Holocaust Museum in Washington in April 1993; episodic support for enlargement from the German government; persistent appeals of leaders of U.S. ethnic communities, including the 10 million-strong Polish community; and the desire to defuse growing pressure from the Republican Party to support enlargement.

After the 1994 "Contract with America" raised enlargement as a centerpiece of the Republican foreign policy program, the administration accelerated its push for enlargement. In doing so, it encountered ambivalent allies in Europe and an implacable opponent in Russia.[7] With France generally opposed to enlargement and Britain generally in favor, the Germans played a crucial role. Germany's chancellor, Helmut Kohl, was generally supportive of enlargement, although Germany made consideration for Russia's security concerns and domestic political balance a prerequisite. These concerns were shared by the Clinton administration, which sought to enlarge NATO without antagonizing Russia. This proved impossible. Though Boris Yeltsin apparently indicated to both the Poles and Czechs in late 1993 that he could tolerate an enlarged NATO, the Russian debate quickly produced an absolute consensus that NATO enlargement was intolerable (Asmus 2002: 37–41). Russian opposition was sustained and determined, often returning again and again to issues the Clinton administration thought had been settled. In late 1994, NATO finally announced that it would begin to study how enlargement could occur – a decision embraced warmly in CEE and bitterly denounced in Moscow (Asmus 2002: 92–5).

Two subsequent decisions in Washington and one in Moscow contributed to the ultimate breakthrough in which Russia grudgingly

---

[7] The George H. W. Bush administration apparently promised then–Soviet General Secretary Gorbachev during discussions on integrating the former GDR into NATO that NATO would not enlarge.

acquiesced to the reality of enlargement. First, the United States proposed that alongside enlargement, NATO and Russia should establish a separate pact that guaranteed significant new Russian prerogatives to observe, though not directly influence, NATO decision making. In doing this, the U.S. administration had to guard against Republican Party fears that Russia was to acquire "veto power" over NATO. The deal finally was reached for a permanent joint council between NATO and Russia in early 1997. Second, the administration acknowledged the tremendous unpopularity of NATO enlargement in Russian elite opinion, and in deference to Yeltsin's reelection chances, pledged not to raise any concrete plans for enlargement until after the 1996 presidential election. When Yeltsin narrowly won that election, and Clinton, several months later, won his own reelection, enlargement emerged as an immediate priority in the beginning of 1997. Yeltsin made some moves to acknowledge the imminence of enlargement in early 1997, though he and his advisors maneuvered to avoid or limit enlargement all the way up to its announcement at the NATO Council in Madrid in July 1997. At Madrid, U.S. support for a small first round of enlargement to just Poland, the Czech Republic, and Hungary prevailed over desires to add Romania (led by France) and Slovenia (led by Italy). (Asmus 2002: 238–44). After a major public relations campaign and a difficult ratification debate, the U.S. Senate ratified the enlargement treaty by a vote of 80–19 in April 1998. The three new members officially became members of NATO on March 12, 1999. Twelve days later, they were at war with Serbia.

WHY IS THE MILITARY POLICY AREA INTERESTING?

Though hardly unprecedented, suggesting to other countries how to run their militaries is a relatively rare and risky proposition. Voluntary emulation is, however, less rare, given the intense competition that can prevail (Rosen 1991: 185–220; Goldman and Andres 1999). The military is traditionally an area where European states guard their own sovereignty. The EU has had virtually no influence over national militaries, and even NATO has made very little effort over the years to tell member states how to shape their defense institutions. And in recent memory, there has been a checkered history of military-to-military programs – especially those in Latin America – that culminated in human rights abuses perpetrated by U.S.-trained officers. Finally, voluntary emulation in this policy area has been particularly difficult for the CEE states because of the great diversity of Western military models (Donnelly 2001). In spite of such long-standing patterns, the Czech and Hungarian elites have clearly tried to replicate some key military institutions of existing NATO members.

Civilian control institutions are particularly interesting, because with few exceptions (Barany 1997; Taylor 2001) they are a strand of democratic reforms that are often relegated to the narrower specialty journals in the academic discussions of CEE democratization. Yet civilian control was a key NATO demand. Having come onto the formal agenda with the founding meeting of the North Atlantic Cooperation Council in late 1991,[8] civilian control was underscored again with the advent of the Partnership for Peace (PfP) in 1993,[9] was one of the five "Perry Principles" of U.S. Secretary of Defense William Perry,[10] and appeared again in the 1995 *Study on Enlargement*, which called for "encouraging and supporting democratic reforms, including civilian and democratic control" (North Atlantic Treaty Organization 1995: 1). Yet none of these documents tried to define civilian control. NATO member states vary significantly in their own instruments of such control, and Turkey has seen several military interventions during the period of its NATO membership. But if there is no "NATO model," there was clearly an interest within NATO to coax CEE states toward better mechanisms of civil–military relations.[11]

What is civilian control? The argument here follows the framework outlined by one of the leading experts on CEE civil–military relations, Jeffrey Simon of the U.S. National Defense University. Simon's framework has two core virtues. First, it is detailed enough to rule out certain kinds of institutions (including many of those present in 1989) but without prescribing a blueprint that must be followed by all states. It is, in other words, primarily a functional model and not an exact recipe. Second, Simon was intimately engaged in the promotion of these policies to CEE states. Thus, the functional demands reflect many actual NATO priorities, though they are more detailed than NATO's own official pronouncements.[12] Simon's model posits four necessary conditions for effective

---

[8] See North Atlantic Cooperation Council declaration, December 20, 1991, para. 4–5.

[9] See North Atlantic Cooperation Council declaration, January 11, 1994, para. 14.

[10] Along with democracy, market economies, settled borders, and progress toward compatibility of the armed forces.

[11] I return below to the fact that NATO was often slow to issue detailed requirements.

[12] On the significance of functional versus exact forms of borrowing, see Jacoby (2000: chapter 2). On functional imperatives, Dunay notes that "although various individual Western states – and particularly the UK and the U.S. – influenced Hungarian reforms, differentiation between different Western models of civil–military relations did not play an important role in the process" (2002b: 65).

democratic oversight, and the claim that this is an area of dense demands turns on the complexity of these criteria:

1. A clear division of authority in the constitution or public law between the president and the government (prime minister and defense minister)
2. Parliamentary oversight of the military through control of the defense budget
3. Peacetime government oversight of General Staffs and military commanders through civilian defense ministries
4. Restoration of military prestige, trustworthiness, and accountability for the armed forces to be effective. (Simon 1996: 26–8)[13]

In addition to NATO pronouncements, CEE states received a lot of specific advice from British, German, and U.S. defense experts (Forster 2002). In Hungary alone, for example, Gutierrez notes that the British MoD conducted in-depth studies in 1995 (on civilian control) and 1998 (on defense planning). The German MoD, at the request of the Hungarian General Staff, also sent a team in 1995 to "provide NATO and German expertise in military–political, strategic, operational, and tactical matters to the Hungarian military." And the United States has had two defense consulting companies on contract in Hungary advising the government, MoD, and General Staff on how to "design and implement the reforms necessary to create a NATO-compatible military" (Gutierrez 2002: 5).

THE STARTING POINT: HISTORY, LEGITIMACY, MONEY

In order to later apply HI, SI, and RI hypotheses to this case, we need a short inventory of the factors each body of theory underscores. Subsequent discussions then employ various combinations of these factors to explain where emulation has made a difference and where it has flopped.

---

[13] Even in the specialized literature on CEE, such frameworks have proliferated. For a similar framework, see Cottey, Edmunds, and Forster (2002b: 7). Longer lists are in Barany (1999) and Busza (1996). Frameworks that encompass broader views of both the military and civilian sides in CEE are Nelson (2001) and Szemerkényi (1996). More broadly, the classic literature begins with Huntington (1959); Finer (1988); and Stepan (1988).

Historical Legacies

In 1989, both Czechoslovakia and Hungary had a long way to go to meet Simon's four conditions. We begin with their common experience as Warsaw Pact members. Since the Communist Party in both states was at least in part imposed, it saw in the military a potential adversary. From the start, the party sought to control the military and to make it subservient. While the institutions for doing so varied by name across all Warsaw Pact countries, there were three common themes (Barany 1995: 102–5; Sarvaš 1999). First, the party had its own political bodies, called variously the Defense Council or Military Committee, which were staffed by party members but which existed inside the military organization as a way of monitoring military loyalty. Second, each military itself had an organization, often called the main political administration, responsible for indoctrinating officers. Party membership among officers was extraordinarily high, averaging 75% across all Warsaw Pact states. Thus, while CEE militaries were not used to democratic controls, most were certainly used to accepting political authority, and this no doubt diminished the chance that they would intervene directly in politics (Dunay 2002b: 68). Third, the Soviet Union maintained direct controls over the national militaries of each country and kept about 60,000 troops and advisors in both Hungary and Czechoslovakia. Because much of the Czech and Hungarian publics came to see their own national militaries as agents of foreign domination, acceptance of them shrank during the Warsaw Pact period.

Yet communist-era civilian leadership in Czechoslovakia and Hungary also left their militaries with almost complete autonomy over operational matters as long as their political loyalty was assured. For example, while the communist systems did have ministries of defense, these were entirely the domain of the military itself. Rather than being staffed by civilians, they were staffed by officers, though ones who generally had expertise only in operational issues and not in matters of strategic doctrine. Thus, a combination quite toxic to future reforms resulted: Very few civilians had any expertise in defense policies, while the militaries were almost completely incompetent to join in the development of military doctrine and strategy or to jockey for limited resources in a democratic system.[14] On the other hand, they deeply distrusted and resented civilian intrusion into

---

[14] Gutierrez shows that none of the Hungarian officer training institutions "provided strategic planning or doctrinal development," but focused only on implementing Soviet strategies (2002: 58). On the potential role of civic groups in Hungarian security debates, see Szabó (2003).

what they regarded as their sphere of expertise, especially in the context of severe budget cuts (Gutierrez 2002: 22–6, 58–62). Historically, the "soft budget constraints" of communism had been even softer when it came to the military, which often paid in exchange vouchers rather than cash and which had ample scope to raise its own resources (Kornai 1986). As a result, the CEE militaries did not share much of the Western militaries' experience with explicit trade-offs, open negotiation with political leadership over major priorities, or even fixed values for currencies (Donnelly 2001; Woodruff 1999). More than just adopting formal structures, both CEE militaries have had to learn these skills.

Of course, there were important national peculiarities. Historically, the military in Czechoslovakia has usually been associated since the seventeenth century with a foreign power – first Austria, then briefly Germany, and then, since 1948, the Soviet Union. Moreover, the Czech military had not been called upon to defend the state since the Thirty Years War. In the twentieth century, the Czech military sat out several potential confrontations (in 1938–9 against Nazi Germany, in 1948 against the communist coup, in 1968 during the Prague Spring). For much of the public, the Czech military was worse than useless, since the military had also assisted the party in crackdowns during strikes in 1953 and once again in putting down demonstrations on the one-year anniversary of the Prague Spring.[15] With the post-1948 and 1968 purges of the military, the popular perception was that remaining officers were simply the stooges of foreign powers. Against this legacy, episodes like the bravery of émigré Czech pilots who flew out of Britain during World War II were mostly footnotes in the popular imagination. As a result, in 1991, 25% of the Czechoslovak population did not see any reason to have the armed forces at all.

The Hungarian military legacy was only marginally prouder. For the period prior to the twentieth century, it was possible to argue that the Hungarian military had sometimes been "the most highly regarded stratum of Hungarian society" and that "the swash-buckling Hussar, usually the son of a noble family, fulfilled a highly visible and extremely well-regarded social–political function throughout Hungarian history" (Volgyes 1978: 147). Yet where the Czech army did not fight, the Hungarian army did not

---

[15] In August 1993, General Nekvasil, then Chief of the General Staff, publicly apologized for the army's role in quelling the August 1969 demonstrations in which nearly 20,000 soldiers were mobilized and four people killed: "It [the army] was presented as a means of political power of the Czechoslovak Communist Party to suppress internal resistance by violent means" (*Independent*, August 21, 1993).

win, at least not since occupying Vienna in 1487. And unlike the Czech military, the Hungarian military has a twentieth-century tradition of intervention in politics under the regency of Admiral Miklós Horthy. The two countries did share the legacy of foreign domination; as Barany notes, with the exception of the interwar period, "foreign troops have been stationed on Hungarian territory since 1526" (1998a: 14).

The national cases also vary in the role their militaries played in the transition itself. Barany shows that in the long protracted transitions in Hungary, the military played a very small role. In places where the transition was abrupt – for example, Bulgaria and Romania – the military played a significant role. And in the intermediate cases, a small minority of party and military leaders made threats about "potential military and/or militia suppression of the ongoing demonstrations" in East Germany and Czechoslovakia (Barany 1995: 105). Thus while neither military either participated very directly in policy making or was heavily co-opted into the state administration – as opposed to, say, the Polish army – there remains a difference in their role in the actual transition, with the Czech case being the more ominous.[16]

In 1989, both states had large national militaries. The problem with both, however, was that they were bloated, unpopular, and pointed west.[17] Both states sought to reform these structures, downsize the military, and ultimately join NATO. But both countries spent the first years just trying to cut these militaries, so institutional reforms were secondary. The primary concerns were the overlarge militaries, irrelevant strategic concepts, and outdated equipment.

If the common motive of the Czech and Hungarian states was to join NATO, this was expressed more forcefully and consistently in Hungary. Hungary was both the first state to raise the possibility of leaving the Warsaw Pact and the first state to call for its dissolution in June 1990. Hungary was also the first to speculate publicly about becoming a NATO member (in February 1990 by Gyula Horn, the last communist foreign minister). When the Warsaw Pact was dissolved in July 1991 and the Soviets began to pull out of Hungary, it left the Hungarians without the manpower to defend the country, but also without major weapon systems. Air defense

---

[16] That said, by spring 1990, only 14% of Czech respondents feared possible military action, compared to 21% for the police and 38% for the secret service (Vlachová and Sarvaš 2002: 60).

[17] The Czech and Hungarian cases thus differ from those in the Baltics and much of the Balkans, where some countries have had to build their armies from scratch.

was lost entirely, and this at a time when Serbian aircraft often violated Hungarian airspace (Barany 1998a: 12). After a fairly short, but intensive, discussion about the possibility of neutrality, a consensus developed around Hungary joining the NATO alliance.

A look at the map suggests Hungary's anxiety makes some sense, for it bordered on all three of the disintegrating multinational states (the USSR, Yugoslavia, and Czechoslovakia). This "front line" status was a real shift. In Warsaw Pact planning, the Hungarian army would have been almost fully integrated into Soviet command structures in the event of a war. Its location in the southern tier of Soviet forces meant that it was not called upon to practice independent strategic planning, but rather was subordinate to Soviet armies in a variety of operational matters.

If Hungary went from being a backwater state to a potential front-line state, Czechoslovakia went from being a potential front-line state to a relative backwater. Its security problems were significantly less than those of the Hungarians during the entire period of transition. This meant the country with the marginally better-prepared army was least challenged by security problems, while the country with the less-prepared army was most challenged by turmoil on its borders.

In the last days of Hungarian communism, the party made a crucial decision in advance of the elections of spring 1990. The party expected that the opposition would control the new parliament but that the popular reform communist Imre Pozsgay would become the first president. The party then divided the armed forces between an administrative arm under MoD control and an operational arm under the direct command of the president (Pecze 1998: 15). While the new MoD – responsible to Parliament – received only 125 staff members from the old unified MoD, the new army command received the remaining 1,100 staff (Gutierrez 2002: 96). As it turned out, József Antall, not Pozsgay, became the first president, but the damage was done: Dividing the armed forces this way would give the army a powerful organizational base. This, in turn, would long allow the military to resist civilian encroachments into its operational autonomy, and it prevented the establishment of a unified chain of command under the control of the defense minister (Simon 1996: 140–42; 2004a). Early and sustained political attention could have solved this concern, but as we will see, Hungarian elites have been alternately indifferent to or opportunistic about this split.

This "original sin" of defense reform in Hungary did not occur in the Czech Republic, where the communists went more quietly, and it has cast a shadow over every subsequent effort to promote civilian control. Before moving to these specific battles, it is important to look at two more issues common across the two cases: the low popular support for the militaries and the fiscal meltdown of the defense budget.

The Societal Legitimacy of CEE Militaries

Lost wars, complicity or inaction in the face of foreign intervention against their own populations, and the mistreatment of conscripts has left both militaries with very low standing in the eyes of their own people. Cynicism about the military is widespread. A 1989 exposé of the armed forces, written by a forty-one-year veteran of the Hungarian army and entitled "Petty Tyrants in Uniform," received widespread attention for its charges that army officials under the communist regime had, for years, misused conscript labor for personal purposes (including building a huge private wildlife preserve) and had falsified military exercises (Barany 1989: 3). In the Czech Republic, the image of the incompetent Good Soldier Schweik encapsulated the image of the military for much of the population. The 1918 creation of Czech novelist Jaroslav Hašek, the fictional Schweik, served in the old Austro-Hungarian army, but his reluctance about all things military came to stand for Czech attitudes toward the military even after independence from Austria.

Another indicator of popular perception of the military is the extent to which members of the military are treated reasonably well, and since the end of communism, military personnel have been treated abysmally. Neither country has given priority to salaries, so the earnings of military personnel are quite low. The situation in CEE is, to be sure, not as bad as in Russia, where Brian Taylor reports that the MoD "issued instructions on foraging for food in the forest, and some units were supplied with dog food" (2001: 935). Yet in 1993, 46% of Hungarian noncommissioned officers (NCOs), 17% of officers and 57% of civilian employees of the army (HDF) were earning wages that put them under the officially established poverty line (Barany 1998a: 23).[18] The central point is that the catastrophic conditions in the CEE militaries today are not merely a reflection of the poor equipment, doctrine, and personnel of the Warsaw Pact years. Rather, in several important ways, the militaries have deteriorated very badly since 1989, so that in certain respects they are now much worse than under communism. This means that all institutional reforms, including

---

[18] Following national conventions, this paper refers to the two militaries as the Hungarian Defense Forces (HDF) and the Army of the Czech Republic (ACR).

those that rely on emulation of Western institutions, are conducted against a backdrop of frustration and distrust on the part of the military. Though one internal Czech military poll in 1998 reportedly ranked the military profession above only the street cleaners (Nečas interview), official Czech army data from April 1999 showed the combined "strong" and "moderate" support for the following institutions was the following:

Central Bank	67%	NATO	56%
Constitutional Court	63%	Municipalities	56%
Accounting office	62%	Army	47%
IMF	60%	Police	37%
EU	59%	Parliament	34%
President	58%	Senate	16%

The 47% support for the army (ACR) looks reasonable at first glance, until we see that it lumps together strong and moderate support (Vlachová 2002). "Strong" support for the military was only 3%. On the other hand, the military has seen its support rise after the disastrous floods of 1998 and 2002, when it rendered some invaluable service. And media reports on Czech peacekeepers were more positive in the wake of Kosovo than they were in the wake of Bosnia (Vlachová and Sarváš 2002: 50). While these negative perceptions are constraints, they do not mean that CEE militaries can never enjoy popular support. Indeed, Slovakians, who share many of the Czech legacies previously noted, have consistently ranked the military as the most trustworthy institution in the country (Ulrich 2002a: 404; Szayna 1999: 131).

Badly Funded Armies

The low legitimacy of the military gives CEE elites and many (though not all) military officers an interest in Western ways of organizing the military. Low legitimacy also means, however, that the funds for military reform are likely to be harder to come by than for an institution held in relatively high esteem. Unlike actors in the policy areas investigated in chapters 2 and 3, the communist-era militaries had their own means of generating financial resources. This ability did not immediately disappear in 1989, so for several years, the precipitous decline of the defense sector could be masked by the military itself. Still, the defense spending data in the following charts confirms that while nominal defense spending has risen, military budgets have declined sharply in both countries in both real and GDP terms. With CEE inflation running at fairly high levels, defense budgets were rapidly eaten up by inflation. Already in 1995, inflation had devalued the Hungarian defense budget by 40% vis-à-vis 1990 (Gutierrez 2002: 156).

GRAPH 1. Military Expenditure in Millions of 1995 Constant U.S. Dollars, 1989–2001.

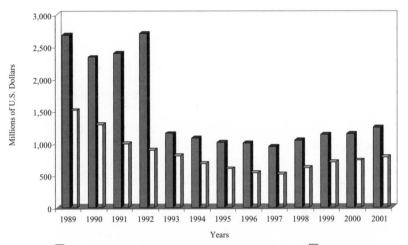

Source: *SIPRI Yearbook, 1999*, Table 7A3: 312; *SIPRI Yearbook, 2002*, Table 6A4: 286.

Stockholm International Peace Research Institute (SIPRI) data outlines the basic budgetary picture for the 1990s. Graph shows spending in constant U.S. dollars, and shows that the Czech Republic, with a similar population size, but larger GDP, is outspending Hungary on defense by a wide margin. Table 10 indicates that the Czechs spend a larger portion of their larger GDP on defense, while Table 11 shows that, while Hungary lags the Czech Republic in defense spending by about 25% when using market exchange rates, it provides less than half the Czech defense budget

TABLE 10. *Military Expenditure as a Percentage of GDP, 1989–2000*

	1989	1990	1991	1992	1993	1994	1995	1996	1997	1998	1999	2000
Czech Republic	Na	Na	Na	Na	2.3	2.1	1.8	1.7	1.6	1.8	2.0	2.0
Hungary	2.8	2.5	2.2	2.1	1.9	1.6	1.4	1.2	1.1	1.3	1.5	1.5

Source: *SIPRI Yearbook, 1999*, Table 7.4: 320; *SIPRI Yearbook, 2002*, Table 6A4: 286.

TABLE 11. *1995 Military Expenditure by Market Exchange Rates and Purchasing Power Parity Rates*

	ME Rate[a]	PPP Rate[a]	Deviation Index (Column 2/3)	Military Expenditure in MER Terms	Military Expenditure in PPP Terms
Czech Republic	26.54	10.51	2.5	$901 million	$2,118 million
Hungary	125.7	80.78	1.6	$612 million	$952 million

[a] Local currency/U.S. dollars.
Source: *SIPRI Yearbook, 1999,* Table 7C1: 332.

when using PPP measures. Thus, by any of these measures, the Czechs have spent more on defense than has Hungary.

A primary motivation of both the Czech and Hungarian parliaments has been to save as much money on defense as possible. With pressing social and economic investment needs in a variety of other policy domains – as seen in the EU chapters – the governments of the two states have been in no mood to spend on defense. Indeed, in some cases, NATO enlargement was pushed precisely because it might be cheaper than going it alone. For example, the Czech MoD, in announcing its 1996 budget of 30 billion Czech crowns (Kcs), suggested that in order to plan for its own defense outside NATO, it would have to have Kcs 45 billion (Simon 1996: 236). Once inside NATO, however, pressure to spend more on military modernization was frequently met with the argument that, given the gravity of the choices, the current government, uncertain of its grip on power, would have to defer reform until after the next election (Gutierrez 2002: 38–39).[19]

Of course, all European democracies spend significantly less on the military than does the United States. But the combination of small budgets and old equipment sometimes makes the actual military contribution almost vanishingly small. For example, in 1999, Poland spent more per capita on defense (about $88 per year per person) than either the Czechs or Hungarians.[20] Yet this figure was just barely above the cost of moving one of the army's older T-55M battle tanks 1 kilometer during a training exercise – provided that none of its weapons were fired (Yaniszewski

[19] As Dunay notes, this reluctance to spend on military modernization characterized Hungary during the communist period as well. The USSR tried, often in vain, to get the "goulash Communists" to divert spending from butter to guns (2002b: 66–7).
[20] This compares to $253 for Canada, $327 for Belgium, $414 for Germany, $568 for the UK, and $1,004 for the United States. The global average is $137 per capita (SIPRI 2002: 234).

2002: 393, 401). As one Czech defense expert in NATO headquarters put it, "We repress the military side of NATO. Whenever we talk about NATO, we sell it as a political alliance, but this is now backfiring because it does not help convince the public to support higher levels of defense spending" (Luňák interview).[21]

THE ROLE OF WESTERN CONTACT IN WEAKENING THE OLD MODEL

CEE countries did not need NATO to tell them that the institutional connections between the military and the state stood in need of reform in the postcommunist period. The new democracies moved to wrest control of the military from the Communist Party and establish some sort of democratic controls, and initially these were not necessarily oriented on any prevailing Western models. As noted earlier, the Czechoslovak People's Army (CSPA) had made plans during November 1989 for the possible use of force against opponents of the socialist regime. Though these plans were never enacted, the new Czechoslovak leaders moved quickly to reorder control of military forces. President Havel reorganized the Czechoslovak State Defense Council and subordinated it to his office so that the Communist Party would enjoy much less control over the military. A new inspectorate general was established in 1990 to further limit party influence, and the new civilian Minister of Defense, Lubos Dubrovský, also dissolved the old military counterintelligence section (Simon 1996: 198–200).

As is well-known, however, by mid-1992, elections had paved the way for the "velvet divorce," which resulted by January 1993 in the separate states of the Czech Republic and Slovakia. The new Czech constitution greatly reduced presidential power and subordinated the MoD to the prime minister's office, though there remained some ambiguity about the president's emergency powers vis-à-vis the military. The new Czech Republic's first Minister of Defense, Antonín Baudyš, pushed through a modest defense reform in 1993. Yet neither Baudyš's reforms, nor those of his successor, Vilém Holan, in 1994–5, needed to make changes to the

---

[21] An illustration of the differential between West and East: Spain has 40 million people and a GDP of $568 billion, and 1.27% of this GDP for defense equates to $7.2 billion to be spent on 143,450 soldiers. Poland has 39 million people, but its GDP is only $160 billion. Even a 2.06% commitment of its GDP results in only $3.3 billion, and this is spent on more soldiers (206,045). Thus, Spain spends about $50,000 per soldier and Poland about $16,000 (Cottey et al. 2002a: 2).

basic chain of command from prime minister through the MoD and to the Army General Staff (Simon 1996: 216). In other words, unlike in Hungary, the Czechs were able to establish fairly quickly a basic relationship between the military and the major political organs of the state.

In Hungary, it is also clear that some important steps prerequisite to institutional reforms did take place. As in the Czech case, a process of institutional destruction took place in which the Communist Party's constitutional leading role was abolished, as was its direct control over the armed forces. Party organs that carried out this control were abolished, and military oaths were rewritten (Barany 1995: 108–9).

Yet unlike the case of health care, where many actors saw Western models as useful templates for early reform, actors in the defense sector proposed few changes beyond rooting out the most obvious institutions of communism. The CEE militaries' autonomous sources of finance underscored this conservatism. Where the Bismarckian insurance model "conquered brains," it was left to a small minority of civilian and military officials to promote Western models of military organization. Of course, in both the Czech and Hungarian cases, returning exiles who worked as civilians in the new MoDs already had had exposure to Western ways, whether as academics, in NGOs, or as members of the press.[22] But there were far too few such exiles to restaff entire military organizations, and in any event they may not have been welcome in large numbers. NATO and its member states soon began exploring the idea of exposing CEE officers to foreign militaries, and they quickly developed a variety of programs designed to familiarize CEE officers with the practices of NATO members.[23]

Though both states have made ample use of these programs, Hungarians have probably outdone the Czechs in terms of top-level participation. By 2000, seven out of the top ten Hungarian military officials had been educated somewhere in the West since 1990. The Hungarian MoD claims that as early as 1998, over 1,000 Hungarian officers and NCOs had had some exposure to Western military educational institutions.[24] And by 1998, no general remained in the entire Hungarian defense forces that had received his promotion to general before 1989 (Barany 1998a: 20–7).

---

[22] A good example is Karel Kovanda, the longtime Czech ambassador to NATO.
[23] For a review of some of these European and U.S. programs, see Simon (1996) and Ulrich (1999).
[24] Vlachová and Sarvaš (2002: 56) report a similar number for the Czech case.

Clearly, however, exposure and familiarity are insufficient, in and of themselves, to hasten the shift to Western models of military organization. There are at least two key problems with these personnel programs. One problem is the inherited force structures, which, as in all Warsaw Pact armies, meant a very high ratio of officers to total personnel.[25] Thus, even when high-level officers genuinely internalize the reform imperative, officers at lower levels can make it very difficult for Western-trained personnel to implement the new ideas. The Western architects of these programs had few illusions that when such students returned to their units, they would be embraced for their newfound knowledge. But they were hardly prepared for the magnitude of difficulties. They worked, said one person intimately familiar with the programs, from the premise that "in the kingdom of the blind, the one-eyed man is king." This, he said, proved a "false hope," for "in the kingdom of the blind, the one-eyed man is a dangerous freak and a threat to the system." As a result, "in some CEE countries even as late as summer 2000, every single officer who had been sent abroad on training courses was, on return, either dismissed, demoted, or sent to serve in a dead-end job" (Donnelly 2001; see also Ulrich 1999).

Efforts to mark out a relatively clear career path for better-trained officers are complicated by the uncertainties of defense spending and the favoritism and cronyism that continue to characterize many personnel decisions (Fields and Jensen 1998: 147–9). These frustrations show up in the number of officers who seek out civilian careers. Of seventy-five Czech officers who spent time studying in Western military organizations since 1993, eleven had quit the army before it even entered into NATO (Gleick 1997: 36–7).[26]

In any event, Czech and Hungarian use of the personnel programs has tailed off markedly since those countries became members, in part because PfP funds that supported such visits have been redirected towards other applicants for membership (Gutierrez 2002: 142). Table 12 indicates this trend across all three first-wave members.

A second weakness of these personnel programs is resistance not from other officers but from the (sometimes nominally) civilian MoD. Again,

---

[25] Soviet military doctrine emphasized large numbers of officers, because in wartime they could function as "cadres" around whom masses of conscript and reserve forces could mobilize.

[26] On the other hand, Vlachová and Sarvaš report that over 1,000 Czech soldiers have studied in foreign military educational institutions, though it is not clear if that also includes Soviet ones (2002: 56).

TABLE 12. *Attendance at the George C. Marshall Center*

	Pre-NATO Attendance (13 Courses)	Post-NATO Attendance (8 Courses Through 2000)
Czech Republic		
TOTAL	47	19
Ave./Class	3.62	2.37
Hungary		
TOTAL	36	13
Ave./Class	2.77	1.62
Poland		
TOTAL	72	9
Ave./Class	5.54	1.13

Source: Gutierrez 2002: 130.

the problems are more extreme in Hungary, where the general staff has had a core of potential reformers at the top. Barany noted that in 1998, most MoD staff were either active or retired military officers (the latter classified as civilians).[27] He notes also that, "Among the eighteen department chiefs of the MoD, twelve were active officers and six were civilians (of whom four were retired officers and two were true civilians)" (1998a: 21–2). Of course, this data is not prima facie evidence that these programs have failed, but when one considers other successful efforts by international organizations to "co-opt" national officials, these have not been notably effective.[28]

THRESHOLDS: BORDERS, BUDGETS, AND CIVILIAN CONTROL INSTITUTIONS

The EU is an IO that makes its own laws, and we saw in chapters 2 and 3 that it used one of its normal legal instruments, the directive, to set

[27] The paucity of available civilian experts is a sociological dilemma, not a normative failing. There has been nothing inherently superior about civilian ministers in CEE. Nelson demonstrates convincingly that several CEE civilian ministers of defense have enriched themselves and generated few useful reforms (2002: 12–15).

[28] For a highly successful effort by the European Court of Justice (ECJ) to co-opt national judges and convince them to refer cases to the ECJ, see Alter (1998a, 1998b). Alter shows that the ECJ built its strategy around a recognition of the domestic impediments faced by their potential allies in the national judiciaries. Most of the personnel programs just noted failed to build any recognition of obstacles and resistance into the heart of the program.

functional thresholds in a variety of issues areas. NATO is not a lawmaking IO, but it was also able to set thresholds for membership. In time, CEE elites came to be quite aware of these thresholds, and, as one Hungarian official put it, "to figure out what was compatible with NATO and what other West European countries were doing." NATO officials saw their role as giving broad reform targets but without specifying any one blueprint. For example, Simon, an architect of some of the military to military personnel programs just discussed, observed that the CEE states have taken different paths to civilian controls. "That's fine," Simon argues, "they're sovereign states and can make their own decisions about how to get there, but they have to meet certain indicators; they have to be up to certain levels" (Simon interview).

CEE officials openly acknowledged the importance of these thresholds, and indeed they often wished for more explicit guidance from NATO.[29] Some early targets were in the PfP. After the Czechs joined the PfP, the MoD's Jaromír Novotný wrote, "Participation in the PfP has had a direct impact on the ongoing transformation of the Army of the Czech Republic. Our forces are being restructured according to the norms and practices of NATO nations" (1996: 25). But where the PfP gave only very general guidelines, the 1995 *NATO Study on Enlargement* set some specific expectations for the potential new member countries. Among other things, the report stated that prospective members would have to have:

- Demonstrated a commitment to and respect for OSCE norms and principles, including the resolution of ethnic disputes, external territorial disputes including irredentist claims or internal jurisdictional disputes by peaceful means...
- Undertaken a commitment to ensure that adequate resources are devoted to achieving the obligations...
- Established appropriate democratic and civilian control of their defense force. (North Atlantic Treaty Organization 1995: chapter 5)

Though this chapter concentrates on civilian control, NATO also pressed the demands for resolution of ethnic disputes and for adequate spending. NATO found it easiest to push these demands because they required fairly little detailed knowledge of CEE societies. The first threshold had to do with foreign policy, and it was most pressing in the Hungarian case since several million ethnic Hungarians live outside Hungary's

[29] For an extensive discussion of NATO's institutional reform tactics, see Epstein (2001, chapter 3: 7–14).

present borders. It is clear that the hope for integration into NATO provided an important stimulus for Hungary and Romania to reach accord on Transylvania, culminating in the Basic Treaty of September 1996 (Valki: 2002). The U.S. Ambassador to NATO, Robert Hunter, said the treaty with Romania was signed, "not because they liked each other," but because both governments were trying to convince NATO that their foreign policy problems had been solved (quoted in Barany 1999: 79). Hungary signed a similar bilateral treaty with Slovakia.[30] Meanwhile, though mutual Czech–German irritation over the post–World War II expulsion of the Sudeten Germans flares up often, it does not turn on contemporary border issues.

Another threshold was defense spending floors. During the accession talks with NATO, Hungary agreed to increase its defense spending by 0.1% of GDP per year until it reached 1.8%. At first, this threshold was met. After a decade of declining real budgets in Hungarian defense, the 1998 budget increased in real terms. Yet in 1999, the Fidesz government announced it would not meet its Social Democratic (MSzP) predecessor's commitment to NATO to raise defense spending to 1.8% of GDP. Instead, it would spend only 1.5% in 2000 and increase that to 1.6% by 2004 (Simon 2000b: 1–2).[31] The Hungarian government continues to acknowledge (if not meet) this threshold, but it also asserts that while NATO can set a threshold for overall spending, it cannot tell Hungary how it must spend that money. For example, in response to persistent NATO criticisms of the Hungarian military, former Prime Minister Viktor Orbán noted that, "our single main obligation is that this sum of money must be allocated from the central budget" (*Hungarian Radio/BBC Monitoring*, May 30, 2001). On the other hand, the Czechs did increase defense spending to 1.9% of GDP in 1999 and 2% in 2000. And 1998 spending increases came at a time when the budgets for all other ministries had been cut, a fairly strong indication that the agreement was affecting policy choices (Khol 2001: 153).[32]

---

[30] Later, under the Orbán government, Hungary claimed the right to speak for Hungarian coethnics in neighboring states – something it promised NATO officials it would not do (Wallander 2002: 6).

[31] In addition, Hungary counts part of its border guard costs as defense spending. NATO openly disapproves of this, and the amount is not trivial – about 0.2% of GDP (Dunay 2002b: 83).

[32] Obliging CEE states to spend on the military may well divert funding away from spending on other security organs, such as police forces (Nelson 2002).

If the first two thresholds required NATO to know little about Czech and Hungarian politics, that was not true of civilian control thresholds. That such thresholds might matter became most clear when the Polish application for NATO membership was threatened by ambiguity in whether the General Staff was under the command of the prime minister or the president.[33] The NATO Secretary General reportedly told Polish officials, "I'm not going to tell you how to write your constitution, but I can tell you that what happens concerns us." In the Poland–NATO report, released in September 1995, three conditions were underscored:

The military must realize that it is not the ultimate guardian of the state's social/political order, nor is it the exclusive definer of the national interest; second, the states must assign to the military a credible and honorable role in national defense and accomplishing state goals; and third, the states must prevent civilian politicians and military officers from misusing the military's monopoly of force to attain political goals or resolve partisan political disputes. (Fields and Jensen 1998: 139)

One immediate problem in all CEE states lay in finding adequate numbers of civilians who were reasonably well-informed about military affairs. In Hungary, the first Antall government managed to round up some token civilians, but almost none had military expertise, and the military perceived many of them as party political hacks. Indeed, his status as a civilian may well have been Lajos Für's *only* qualification to be the first postcommunist Minister of Defense. When the Social Democratic Party won the 1994 elections, it reversed the trend toward using civilians in the MoD. In what came to be called the "generals in suits" period, the military began to insulate itself even further from civilian intervention (Simon 1996; 2004a).[34] Table 13 details some of the key positions in which officers displaced civilians. Moreover, the new minister, György Keleti, announced his opposition to the rapid integration of the General Staff into the MoD. That these were more than merely organizational issues became clear when Keleti came under fire from Parliament for authorizing the purchase of 100 T-72 tanks from Belarus, selling government property to pay for defense purchases, and sending fighter aircraft to NATO live-fire exercises, all without parliamentary approval, and the latter in violation of the Hungarian constitution (Simon 1996: 160–5).

---

[33] For a thorough discussion of this conflict, see Simon (2004a), Epstein (2001), and Coughlan (1998).
[34] For a similar trend in the Czech case, see Ulrich (2002a: 408).

TABLE 13. *Remilitarization of the Socialist Ministry of Defense in Hungary*

Government Position	MDF Government (June 1994)	MSzP Government (August 1994)
Minister of defense	Civilian	Military
Political state secretary	Civilian	Civilian
Administrative state secretary	Civilian	Military
Department state secretary (press and social relations)	Non-existent	Military
Department state secretary (military affairs)	Military	Military
Department state secretary (economy/budget)	Civilian	Military
Department state secretary (international relations/defense policy)	Civilian	Civilian

Source: Gutierrez 2002: 104.

Thus, the personnel issue seemed merely one manifestation of large problems in civil–military relations.

Under the Orbán government, the generals-in-suits issue remained. Of the top five "civilian" MoD officials (the administrative state secretary and four deputy state secretaries), only one had no professional military background. Three of these were former generals, and one was a former colonel (Dunay 2000: 11; see also Vlachová and Sarvaš 2002: 54). Hungary has made only modest use of one of the best potential resources for upgrading civilian skills in military affairs, namely, the George Marshall Center in Garmisch-Partenkirchen, Germany. Hungary sent a total of fifty-one students to Garmisch between 1994 and 2000, but only seventeen were civilians. Of these, nearly half returned to positions not directly involving military issues (Gutierrez 2002: 142).

Like the Polish case, the Hungarian case involved a prolonged dispute about the chain of command, a central civilian-control issue. In the Social Democratic period, the military tried hard to assert its autonomy vis-à-vis the executive. But the Fidesz government tried to assert its control over the army by using party loyalists to circumvent the leadership vacuum at the MoD.

The problem, to recall, was the duplication of command structures that had grown up since 1989. These parallel structures sometimes took on comic proportions. Barany notes that in one case, "two separate Hungarian military delegations (one from the MoD and one from the command of the HDF) with the same purpose visited Sweden at the same time unbeknownst to each other" (1998a: 17). There had been several partial efforts to clarify the chain of command. Tension ran very high in October 1990 when President Árpád Göncz refused the Prime Minister's request to call the military into a transport strike. In September 1991, the Hungarian Constitutional Court ruled that the President, as commander in chief, could issue only guidelines, and not orders, to the military (Simon 1996: 148). While the ruling appeared to strengthen the MoD in its efforts to subordinate the HDF, the 1992 defense reform did remove the President from the normal chain of command, but did not bring the HDF Chief of General Staff under MoD control. The split remained, and a "siege mentality" prevailed on the part of many top officers (Gutierrez 2002: 98–103).

Meanwhile, Western officials frequently expressed their concern over the Hungarian arrangements. In 1996, a report by a visiting delegation from the British MoD confessed that, "When we started studying the structure of the Hungarian MoD and its relations with the HDF, it struck us that the MoD structure was not one that we were familiar with. It differs from known NATO MoDs in that it does not have a General Staff or a senior serving officer within it" (British MoD Study 810 1996: 31, quoted in Gutierrez 2002: 118). The study went on to express concern that the single MoD in fact masked two separate and often competing organizations, and it urged Hungary to truly integrate the General Staff into the MoD, in part because only then could the Hungarian Parliament justifiably hold the MoD responsible for the military's activities. A 1999 report by a U.S. consulting group (SAIC) underscored these recommendations, but it also added the concern that the Parliament and MoD often did attempt to reach too far down into matters that ought properly to be the domain of the army itself. Advice aside, after the British briefed their study to MoD and defense staff, one of the senior Hungarian military officers present was asked if the military was ready to implement the British recommendations. The response reportedly was simply, "Who said we want to implement this?" (Gutierrez 2002: 118–19).

Just as the split endured across the Hungarian Democratic Forum (MDF)–Hungarian Socialist Party (MSzP) transition, so too did it endure when the Association of Young Democrats (Fidesz) and the Smallholders (FKGP) formed a coalition after the 1998 election. Once again, the new Minister of Defense, János Szabó, had virtually no defense experience and was a weak politician from the junior coalition partner.

Szabó, it turned out, was not the key player at the MoD, but rather Tamás Wachsler, the administrative state secretary. Wachsler was a Fidesz loyalist and previously had been a longtime member of the parliamentary defense committee. Determined to bring the military officers more tightly under MoD control, Wachsler proposed a defense reform that would subject the chief of the General Staff directly to him (Gutierrez 2002: 101–2). For anyone familiar with the tensions of the past decade, the charges and countercharges were depressingly familiar: trespassing civilians and insubordinate officers. After months of tense standoff, which included Wachsler firing a series of questionable orders to the General Staff, the Chief of the General Staff, the well-regarded Ferenc Végh, resigned and was replaced by General Lajos Fodor (Simon interview; Gorka interview; Yaniszewski 2002: 389). But Fodor, too, was resistant to Wachsler's plans, and this time Wachsler was fired in September 2000.

The reform of Czech institutions of civilian control has been much less openly contentious, though there existed the similar problems of inadequate civilian expertise, military confusion over precise lines of authority, and the lack of a clear reform strategy (Ulrich 1999: 80–86). Though a series of political lightweights held the MoD position for the first several years of the Czechoslovak and then Czech states, most civil–military frustration remained under the public's radar. Under the short-lived caretaker government of Tošovsky, a certain level of trust was built between the military and the technocratic MoD Michal Lobkowitz. With the arrival of the ČSSD minority government, a former professor at the Brno military academy, Vladimír Vetchý, became minister. Vetchy's tenure, though short on fundamental reforms, at least did not add much more fuel to the fires of civil–military relations (Szayna 1999: 138–9).

NATO thresholds for civilian control obviously were blunt instruments. Where army and civilian disputes were very public and preceded membership (as in Poland), NATO could quietly suggest that the problems might prevent an invitation to join. Where constitutional clarifications had occurred and the state had formally adopted organizational features familiar from NATO member states (Hungary), NATO complained about remaining irregularities but did little beyond that. And where all the formal structures passed minimum standards (the Czech Republic), NATO had little comment.

The variation here turns significantly on historical institutionalist factors, since both material incentives from electoral politics (see below) and sociological incentives from NATO were roughly identical. One key difference between the Hungarian and Czech cases flows from the HDF's institutional insulation from Parliament. We have seen that the Communist Party utterly failed in efforts to retain control of the HDF, for the HDF removed the Communist Party's main institutions fairly quickly. But though the 1989 reform failed as a tool to perpetuate party control, it helped provide the military with a decade of insulation from executive control.

SELLING THE INSTITUTIONS: BUILDING PUBLIC SUPPORT

Rationalist approaches to institutional change are driven primarily by the reelection motives of politicians. Such politicians must take voter attitudes into account. This section makes three basic points. First, support for the military is quite similar in the two societies and thus provides little basis for differentiation. Second, support is so low that it can help explain why the political elite expends so little effort to clear NATO thresholds. Finally, given enough effort, the two societies do respond to political efforts to raise the profile of defense issues.

Support for NATO membership functions as an imperfect proxy for data on public support for emulating Western defense models.[35] No direct measures of the latter are available. But since there was little popular pressure for defense modernization, we at least need to know if NATO membership had broad support. In fact, public support for NATO membership in both countries has been modest. Moreover, as the diplomatic momentum for membership increased, public opinion lagged well behind. In one 1997 poll, only 36% of Czech respondents said they would vote for NATO membership if a referendum were held, while 21% were undecided and 22% were opposed. In Hungary, the numbers in early 1997 were somewhat higher: 47% for, 22% against, and 15% undecided. Hungarian military officers were also somewhat ambivalent, in a 1996 poll, in which 57% of officers favored joining NATO, though the number went to 69% after the Madrid conference in the summer of 1997 resulted in an official invitation for Hungary (Barany 1998a: 14–15; Törő 2001: 142–4). When USIA pollsters surveyed CEE citizens in 1996 and asked if they would be willing to spend more money on their military in order to meet NATO standards, large majorities said no: in Poland, by 74% to 16%, in Hungary, by 87% to 9%, and the Czech Republic by 84% to 11%.

---

35 Not all respondents would know that NATO membership required certain thresholds be attained, and respondents might judge the desirability of membership based on any of several factors.

At this same time in Poland, over 80% supported membership in NATO (Granville 1999: 165–70). The mass of voters does not support increased spending to meet NATO obligations. Given the large number of other demands on the budgets of these countries, this reluctance hardly seems surprising.

Yet neither are these low levels of support simply a given. For example, the November 1997 referendum in Hungary brought NATO to the public consciousness in an unprecedented way, and, indeed, 85% of those voting supported Hungarian accession to NATO.[36] In no small part, this was the result of a savvy media campaign combined with the fact that the opponents of membership had very little money given the party consensus in favor of joining Western organizations. The MSzP government of Gyula Horn took a very aggressive stance in promoting a yes vote. Horn needed the show of public support for NATO membership, in part, because he knew that his own party was divided on this question. The referendum required not only majority support of those voting, but it also had to do so with a turnout of at least 25% of the eligible population. If turnout fell below 25%, the referendum would not be binding and Parliament would make the final decision. There, the MSzP government would have to worry about its own backbenchers criticizing enlargement.

The government campaign was creative. The Ministry of Foreign Affairs convinced the producers of a popular Hungarian television sitcom called *Family Limited* to insert a new character, Major Zoltán Kardos.[37] Kardos did not simply mouth NATO propaganda. Rather, he was a consistently wise and forthright, problem-solving man, who, in the eyes of his sponsors in the foreign ministry, was meant to overcome public skepticism about the HDF's problem-solving ability. Beyond paying for Major Kardos's creation, the foreign ministry had HDF Lt. Colonel József Varga watch the show every week to make sure that the actor "got the ministry sentiments just right." The aim of the producer and Colonel Varga was to have the character "ooze comfort and make military restructuring palatable."

[36] Turnout was 49%, which means that about 42% of the nation's voters actively supported enlargement (Gyarmati 1999: 112).
[37] The source for the quotations in this paragraph is Spolar (*Washington Post*, November 6, 1997). In 2002, the Hungarian government ran another savvy media campaign to promote tolerance for the Romani minority. In one TV spot, Santa Claus strips off his beard to reveal a Romani man's face (*Transitions Online*, December 23, 2002).

The government also paid for an episode in a very popular radio soap opera in which the actors emphasized their enthusiasm for life under democracy. School libraries were supplied by the foreign ministry with a CD-ROM game for kids. This "free piece of slick-unabashedly, pro-NATO software" was paid for by McDonnell-Douglas, though distributed by the government. Western military corporations, including Saab, British Aerospace, Dassault Aviation, Lockheed-Martin, Boeing, and McDonnell-Douglas, gave more than 1 million dollars in 1997 to organizations that promoted NATO membership for Hungary. This occurred despite the fact that, "according to Hungary's media laws, foreigners are not allowed to support political programs financially" (Granville 1999: 167). By some estimates, the government and its supporters spent up to two million dollars in print and broadcast media to pay for positive stories about NATO membership.

Critics saw this as unabashed media manipulation. As the vote drew near and the government sent dozens of civil servants to drum up more interest among voters, critics of the government's media program began to protest. One group, Alba Kör (the Alba Circle), filed six complaints against the government strategy between May and November 1997. The state media complaint board sided with the peace advocacy group on two of the decisions and said that at minimum, the public should know who was paying for the promilitary sentiment in individual TV and radio programs. Having won the decision, however, Alba Kör was then faced with the dilemma that the producer of *Family Limited* refused to comply with this government body's decision and run the required disclosure. Said the leader of Alba Kör, Tamás Csapody, "We have to go to court now, to force them to abide by their own law" (Granville 1999).

Though the Czechs held no referendum, they also tried to build support for membership.[38] The MoD sponsored twenty different five-minute TV segments on what it called *NATO Myths*, with examples like "there will be nuclear weapons on Czech soil" or "there will be foreign military bases

---

[38] In opposition, most of the ČSSD had insisted on the need for a referendum on NATO membership, in part as a lever for increasing political access and in part because some opposed membership. Once in power, the ČSSD dropped its call for a referendum (see Khol 2001: 150). Remarkably, Foreign Minister Jan Kavan reportedly asked NATO's then–Secretary General Javier Solana if the Czechs could withdraw from NATO if they later held a referendum and it failed (*Neue Zürcher Zeitung*, April 15, 1998).

in the Czech Republic."[39] Support for NATO membership was pushed hard by certain NGOs as well, and the Czech Atlantic Council may have actually pushed the case harder than did the state itself (Khol 2001: 158–95). Sarvaš's detailed study of the Czech media suggests that, on balance, it made some modest contributions toward promoting public understanding of security issues and increasing the defense expertise of the Czech media (2000).

But if support for NATO can go up, it can also go down. After the 1999 Kosovo crisis, U.S. Information Agency (USIA) polls (see Table 14) indicated that in both the Czech Republic and Hungary (not in Poland), support for NATO membership softened (down seven and ten points, respectively, between 1998 and 2000). Of the four other categories, Hungarian support was slightly higher than Czech support in two (routine overflights and stationing NATO troops). On two other questions (sending troops to defend an ally and hosting routine exercises), Czech support was higher. While none of the recent downward trends fully reverse the increase in support since 1995–6, they do indicate both that Czech and Hungarian attitudes differ from those in Poland and that they seem to have responded negatively to initial experiences in the alliance. These data underscore again the main point of this section, which is that the primary "motor" for emulation from a rationalist perspective has been and remains a weak motor indeed.

A similar "enthusiasm gap" was prominent in what was ultimately a non-NATO military action in Iraq. In February 2003, even under the premise of a UN mandate, only 24% of Czechs supported the United States and its allies in preparations for war, while 62% were opposed. Without a mandate, support dropped to 13% and opposition rose to 76%. In Hungary, support for war even with a UN mandate was a mere 17% (*Transitions Online*, February 3, 2002).

IS MORE "CIVILIAN CONTROL" NEEDED?

This chapter has emphasized institutions of civilian control because this was NATO's most persistent threshold. This focus on control, which we saw in NATO's earliest pronouncements in CEE, reflects both the positive experiences of ultimate constitutional subordination of the military

---

[39] In fact, the guarantees the Czech government gave their voters were not ones that NATO was willing to grant to Russia. Both of these possibilities remain formally open.

TABLE 14. *USIA Poll Results on NATO Enlargement (All figures in percentages)*

	Hungary					Poland					Czech Republic				
	1995	1996	1997	1998	2000	1995	1996	1997	1998	2000	1995	1996	1997	1998	2000
NATO membership															
Support	58	57	55	76	67	81	72	83	76	81	59	51	60	68	61
Oppose	27	27	34			8	12	9			27	33	32		
Send troops to defend alliance partner															
Support	26	32	33	48	47	55	68	70	65	68	42	45	52	62	58
Oppose	69	60	63	49	47	35	24	23	27	23	50	48	44	33	37
Hosting routine NATO exercises															
Support	28	26	35	52	45	45	67	70	63	70	33	34	47	46	56
Oppose	67	67	60	47	49	45	25	43	28	20	60	61	48	40	39
Permit routine NATO/AC overflight															
Support	35	36	46	62	54	41	53	54	50	58	26	30	36	47	47
Oppose	58	57	50	36	40	47	37	37	42	32	67	63	60	47	50
Station NATO troops in country															
Support	34	44	38	53	53	56	52	55	56	60	30	31	29	37	38
Oppose	59	49	58	45	41	34	38	35	35	30	63	63	66	59	58

Source: USIA, U.S. Department of State; Gutierrez 2002: 155.

to democratic authorities in many NATO member states and the negative lessons from Latin American and African states, where militaries have perceived themselves as the protectors of the nation (Huntington 1992: 231–53).[40] Yet promoting control presumes a form of interventionism that is neither particularly common to the region nor likely for militaries held in such low esteem. Moreover, some Western experts, in their rush to promote control, have recognized neither the military's legitimate political role in formulating national security policies nor the civilian manipulation of the military that has been so prevalent in the past decade.

It is possible that civilian control has, at times, been taken too far in subsequent years and has been used as an inappropriate political lever. For example, there is some sense among careful observers of the Hungarian case that an overswinging of the pendulum has given civilians too much authority. The current constitution is relatively clear in identifying the roles of the military commanders and also those of the minister of defense, state secretaries, and deputy state secretaries. Moreover, a 1993 Constitutional Court decision confirmed certain strong powers of the uniformed military. A series of letters signed in 1998 and 1999 from administrative state secretary Tamás Wachsler ordered Chief of General Staff Végh to take some steps that were arguably in direct contradiction to the constitution and the 1993 court decision. If officers knowingly violate the constitution, even at someone else's direction, they are culpable. This put Végh in a lose–lose situation, for if he accepted the order, he could be prosecuted; yet if he rejected the order, he was liable to be seen as defying civilian control. In the end, Végh was fired, though this hardly resolved the more fundamental confrontation.

The Czech case contained none of these pyrotechnics. If one considers the Czech army, one sees that early in the transition period it faced cuts amounting to 50% of the defense budget. It then endured two humiliating rounds of vetting army officers that led to the departure of over half of the generals in the military. A quarter of the population saw no need

---

[40] One reason NATO chose not to be more specific in this threshold may be that some current members (e.g., Turkey) do not have robust civilian control. Under pressure to appoint more civilians to the National Security Council, Turkish Chief of General Staff Hüseyin Kivrikoglu noted, "If they want 100 civilians as members of the National Security Council, so be it. They asked us, and I told my friends, 'There will be no objections,' [...] In any case, MGK [NSC] decisions aren't taken through voting" (quoted in Schimmelfennig, Engert, and Knobel 2004: 19).

at all to have armed forces, while another quarter or more essentially held the army to be incompetent fools. Meanwhile, friction between the Czechs and the Slovaks spilled over into military affairs on more than one occasion. Yet in spite of all of these problems in the early 1990s, we see no move on the part of the military at all to challenge political authority.[41] Rather than continuing to focus on civilian control, it may be time to guarantee as well appropriate forms of military participation in politics (Colton 1979).

PARLIAMENTARY DEFENSE COMMITTEES

Healthy civil–military relations require more than a clear chain of command from the executive through the MoD and to the General Staff. In all Western democracies, parliaments have some degree of expertise in defense issues, usually concentrated in parliamentary defense committees (PDCs). Yet PDCs have been conspicuously weak in the two states (see also Forster 2002; Ulrich 1999: 91–8). On the other hand, both states have made use of technical NATO programs to enhance the capabilities of their PDCs.

When Hungary's Ferenc Juhász took over as MoD after the socialist victory in the 2002 elections, his ferocious criticism of the outgoing Fidesz–Smallholder government included the fascinating contention that his previous seat on the PDC had not allowed him access to budget figures: "I admit that despite the fact that as the vice chairman of the Parliamentary Committee on National Defense, I should have had detailed knowledge of the ministry's finances. I was confronted with the fact and magnitude of [unauthorized] withdrawals only as the Minister" (*Nepszave/BBC Monitoring*, September 14, 2002).

In the Czech Republic, the MoD has in recent years tried to get the PDC more engaged in the budgetary process, because its officials calculated that there was only one way to make the PDC more responsible: by making it list detailed spending priorities and denying it the ability to simply attack the ministry's priorities (Novotný interview). This effort to inject more responsibility into PDC work has paid some dividends, and the PDC and Parliament in general have become much more proficient in budgeting matters. Previously, Parliament would cut the defense budget by some set percent and then tell the MoD to choose the specific

---

[41] I am grateful to Thomas Szayna for this formulation of the Czech case.

cuts. In so doing, Parliament avoided political responsibility at the level of individual programs. The MoD's use of a specialized U.S. budgeting system – the PPPS – allowed it to force the PDC, and by extension the Parliament, to make choices about which programs to cut. This, along with lower turnover on the PDC, has led it to act more responsibly in recent years.

For a long time, the PDC in Hungary was nothing but a rubber stamp. Dunay reports that in 1999, the Smallholder PDC chair argued that "the main duty of the Defense Committee is to carry out the program of the government" (2002b: 75). Socialist MPs who supported the defense budget during the Fidesz years often got attacked by their own party (Rábai interview). Yet there has also been another side to the story. By 1996, an accountability faction was demanding weekly presentations from the military. This faction was pushing for transparency in the defense budget, but the members were also trying to use defense issues to raise their own profile.

Here too, the effort to build political accountability made use of foreign models. Hungarian officials looked specifically to the template of the U.S. Defense Resources Management System (DRMS), though they modified it significantly.[42] The DRMS is supposed to make long-term defense planning possible, but the Hungarian version is based upon its very different labor markets and weapons compared to those in the United States. These adaptations took about six months to puzzle through, but in the end DRMS became popular with the PDC because it allowed the military to answer the PDC's more-detailed questions (Szurgyi interview). That said, one of the key Hungarian participants noted that the HDF had trouble identifying and locating personnel for the DRMS system: "We couldn't get information on our own people from our own organization, but the experts in Monterey [California] came up with a list of the right people right away" (Deáki interview).

Yet a more competent PDC injects potential for new conflict. The Hungarian MoD has sought maximum budgetary flexibility and has tended to see parliamentary irresponsibility as its own best way of gaining flexibility.[43] As one official said in an interview, "The U.S. has a defense budget that looks like a book, and we have a few pages." For example, the 1998

---

[42] As then-U.S. Defense Attaché Arpad Szurgyi, who was deeply involved in this process, says, "cookie cutters are useless."

[43] Of course, flexibility can also be a euphemism for corruption, and the Hungarian MoD has been plagued by a series of high-profile scandals, some of which have required Supreme Court intervention. The MoD's very poor mechanisms of budget control likely

defense budget called for 164 billion forints of spending. It contained a mere ten pages of text laying out the general programs across the entire military, and then seventeen pages of charts with line items. That was it: twenty-seven pages of budget for the entire MoD. The cost of more pages – representing more parliamentary responsibility – would be a loss of MoD freedom to move line items around the budget.

SUMMARY

We have seen that the EU, with its codified body of law, gave CEE elites relatively clear targets to emulate. The EU also used its well-endowed bureaucracy to conceive and execute a detailed renovation of national laws well in advance of membership negotiations. NATO took roughly the opposite approach. On the basis of vague thresholds in its *Study on Enlargement* (which pointedly avoided discussion of the specific potential of new members), it extended invitations to three states in July 1997 and only then conducted a brief set of accession talks (in September and November 1997). Thus, only after the Madrid summit did NATO produce a detailed assessment of the two states' military needs and a list of tasks and time frames for the accomplishment of these tasks (Gutierrez 2002: 4–5; Dunay 2001: 258). Given the low priority of military reform for CEE governments – the Czechs did not even publish their first comprehensive outline of national security and military strategy until the defense "White Paper" of February 1999 – the lack of push from NATO meant that little systematic reform would occur in this period. Indeed, the Czech Parliament never approved any of the MoD's proposed strategic concepts during the early and mid-1990s. As a result, "only a general, four-page National Defense Strategy, hastily approved by the Parliament in March 1997 in order to satisfy NATO requirements just prior to the Madrid summit, existed as a guideline for military planning as of early 1999" (Szayna 1999: 134). In Hungary, the situation was different only insofar as it was worse – some major institutions of civil–military relations were not settled even on paper.

We have also seen that instead of asking how to maintain civilian control over the military, a better question might be, "What systematic dilemmas would civilians need to overcome in order to form an acceptable

diminish parliamentary readiness to support higher defense spending (see Barany 1999: 92).

relationship with CEE militaries?" There are, to sum up, at least three central dilemmas:

1. Though CEE civilians have little military expertise, their understanding of Western-sanctioned focus on civilian control emboldens many to make fairly authoritarian interventions into their militaries.[44] Although many of these civilians are not competent to dive deeply into military issues – for example, by being able to comment in detail on proposed budget lines – they are nevertheless often inclined to give orders whose execution would necessitate effects deep inside the military sphere. Significant civil–military discord has one of its roots here.

2. If the quality of civilian defense leadership is low, the best way to recruit better people may make the overall situation worse. This is because more effective politicians will only be drawn to defense in large numbers if discretionary spending there increases. But extra money will also invite more graft and corruption, and this would come on top of the already significant corruption that is "indigenous" to the defense sectors in both countries.[45]

3. In both CEE militaries, the steep downsizing of the past decade has generally reinforced the organizational conservatism of those officers who remain. In conjunction with their low respect for civilian expertise, this conservatism means that extra financial allocation often sustains the no-reform crowd. And because the personnel system is so unreliable, high-level reformers will have trouble identifying stable cohorts of officers with whom they might ally in efforts to promote long-term reorganization.[46] Donnelly notes the "almost total absence of an honest and open system for evaluating the abilities and qualifications of officers" and suggests that without such systems, CEE MoDs "will never be able to institutionalize

---

[44] On several occasions, the Hungarian civilian leadership has reacted to legitimate questions from the military by charging it with insubordination. Such interventions clearly happen in more mature systems of civilian control as well; see the discussion in Bland (1999 and 2001).

[45] See, for example, Ulrich 2002: 58–60; *Transitions Online*, July 25, 2003.

[46] This problem has deep roots. Goetz and Wollmann show that communist-era state administrations were underpoliticized in terms of policy-making capacity (e.g., weak executives) but overpoliticized in terms of personnel policy (e.g., politicized civil services) (2001: 865).

reform because they will not be able to identify officers with the qualities needed to create a new kind of army... " (2001: 33).[47]

When the Czech Republic and Hungary finally entered NATO as full members in March 1999, all three of these dilemmas were as thorny as ever. But now, they would have to be managed during wartime.

---

[47] The broader comparative literature on civil–military relations stresses the role of linking top reformers to networks of officers within the military. For the cases of Thailand, China, and Indonesia, see Heginbotham (2002).

5

Military Professionalization in War and Peace

> Paradoxically, the Kosovo crisis helped us let our problems be understood
> by the more important guys, by the Prime Minister. It has put the issue of
> military reform on the table.
>
> (Hungarian MoD State Secretary Tamás Wachsler,
> in Langenkamp 2000: 22)

This chapter shifts from a focus on civilian control to a focus on military
professionalism. It follows the definition of professionalism developed in
Forster, Edmunds, and Cottey, in which professionalism is "based around
the twin precepts of armed forces which accept that their role is to fulfill
the demands of the civilian government of the state and are capable of
undertaking military activities in an effective and efficient way" (2002:
6).[1] The chapter begins with a description of the Kosovo crisis because that
episode reveals clear evidence of limited professionalization in the Czech
Republic and Hungary. It then moves to specific efforts at emulation –
some under direct pressure from NATO but others motivated more by

[1] The use of the term *professionalism* should not be conflated to exclusively mean all-
volunteer armies as opposed to conscript armies, though that is one meaning of the term.
Taylor notes that the classic civil–military relations literature has offered conflicting definitions of professionalism (1998: 56–8). Most important, Huntington (1959) appears to
make it both the cause of and the measure of appropriate military behavior, leading to a
tautology at the center of the most influential work in the field. For that reason, Taylor
speaks of "the norm of civilian supremacy" rather than professionalism per se (2003).
As noted in chapter 4, however, CEE militaries generally have internalized such a norm
but may lack other aspects of professionalism. The aspects considered below – promoting
interagency coordination, building NCO corps, and moving toward all-volunteer forces –
are necessarily selective. For a longer list of features of military professionalism, see Forster
et al. (2002: 7–8).

domestic politics – that are aimed at promoting one or more aspects of military professionalization.

The three new members entered NATO in March 1999, less than two weeks before the first war in the fifty-year history of the alliance. If, as Corelli Barnett put it, war "audits" a nation's material resources, so too does it audit its political resources. Both the Czechs and Hungarians did most of what NATO asked them to do during Operation Allied Force (and after, in terms of peacekeeping). On the other hand, they were not asked to do much, especially in terms of combat missions. For example, Hungary's ability to even patrol its own airspace was quite limited, as it was able to patrol for about two hours per day, with other alliance members taking care of the other twenty-two hours.[2]

One major purpose of this chapter is to continue to track the thresholds introduced in chapter 4. The Hungarian chain-of-command problem described in the last chapter flared up continually in the period after the Kosovo crisis, indicating that once again civilian control issues in Hungary were far from fully settled. That said, because Hungary had a modest military exposure during the conflict, these concerns could stay under the surface much of the time. At the same time, the Czechs had to face questions during the war that exposed their own historically embedded fractures. Yet while NATO could and consistently did try to set thresholds for the integration of the Hungarian General Staff into the MoD, there were no reasonable institutional thresholds that might have addressed the Czech dilemma, for it ran deep in the parties and the political culture of the society.

A second major objective is to evaluate the extent to which Wachsler's claim in the epigraph above was correct. The bulk of the evidence suggests it was not. Nevertheless, actual membership and then participation in war did invigorate several efforts for institutional change in both countries; a third objective is to rejoin the discussion from chapters 2 and 3 about the voluntary use of national templates to address the remaining problems of military professionalism (in domains where NATO had few tools to promote changes and little right to demand them) and patches to deal with glaring problems of interoperability (where NATO officials felt eminently justified in making demands and inventing new tools to pursue targeted changes).

---

[2] During the Kosovo war, Hungarian MiG 29s could not patrol Hungarian airspace because they lacked NATO-compatible identification friend-or-foe (IFF) communication gear.

WELCOME TO NATO: THE BOMBING OF SERBIA

When violence between Kosovo Liberation Army irregulars and Serbian police and military escalated in March 1998, many Western observers feared the worst. As he had twice before, Serbian leader Slobodan Milošević seemed hell-bent on using force to improve the position of ethnic Serbs at the cost of other minorities. This time, however, since the territory was inside Serbia, Milošević's ability to cause human suffering was even greater than in the past. The United States and its allies responded to the violence by seeking a diplomatic solution that would increase the autonomy of the Kosovo region, whose population was overwhelmingly ethnic Albanian. When these efforts failed, NATO resorted to bombing in March 1999. As Daalder and O'Hanlon have shown, most NATO leaders' original expectations were that a short period of bombing would convince Milošević to end the attacks and accept increased Kosovar autonomy. But Milošević surprised NATO by intensifying his attacks, driving 1.3 million people from their homes and 800,000 from the country entirely (2000: vii). After eleven weeks of bombing (in which two-thirds as many sorties were flown as in the Gulf War) and under the growing threat of a ground invasion, Milošević finally capitulated (Clark 2002).

As the war dragged on, new scenarios and military needs arose, and the Czechs and Hungarians each faced some unexpected requests from NATO. Both the Czech and Hungarian governments faced difficulties in the first place in going to war against a country for whom many of their citizens had positive feelings. Three hundred thousand ethnic Hungarians live in the Vojvodina region of northern Serbia, while many Czechs still remember the diplomatic support of the non–Warsaw Pact Yugoslavs during the Prague Spring of 1968. This is not to deny that many citizens of both countries were deeply troubled by Serbian behavior over the course of the 1990s. Indeed, Hungarian foreign policy in the early 1990s was heavily tilted toward Croatia, and the country clandestinely delivered infantry weapons to the struggling Croatian army in 1991 (Barany 1999: 80). Yet it is one thing to disapprove of a foreign leader's policies and quite another to bomb his country. In both countries, the left struggled with this matter more than did the right. The left was in power in the Czech Republic (in a minority government) but in the opposition in Hungary.

Support for NATO *membership* (not for bombing) ranged significantly among the three new members during the bombing period and was lowest in the Czech Republic (45%, compared to 80% in Poland and 60% in

Hungary); (Vachudova 2001a: 208). On the other hand, neither Hungary nor the Czech Republic faced a large popular outcry over the bombing. In Hungary, Alba Kör and the green circle drew only about a hundred demonstrators to downtown Budapest for an initial demonstration that was very calm and ended after only about ten minutes (*English Service of the Hungarian News Agency* [*MTI*], April 3, 1999). Given the lack of large public protests, the government mostly worked to try to reassure Hungarians that it was committed to pursuing a diplomatic solution alongside the military one and that it took seriously the interests of ethnic Hungarians inside Serbia.

Foreign Minister János Martonyi emphasized into early April that, although it was in full agreement with NATO allies, Hungary was not participating in the military part of actions against Yugoslavia. He characterized Hungary's action as nothing that could be provocative vis-à-vis the Serbian government:

We can fully exclude the possibility of the Serbian leadership generating any sort of conflict with Hungary, as it would be accompanied by the most detrimental consequences for it both politically and militarily. If however, it does take some sort of completely senseless irrational action, then our membership in Nato implies our country is under the full protection of an alliance which has all the means necessary to protect against any sort of attack. (*MTI*, April 14, 1999)

In other words, Martonyi reassured the Hungarian population that Hungary was doing nothing provocative.[3] But if, in some irrational way it were seen as provocative, NATO would provide full protection.

During the Kosovo crisis, the twin foreign policy goals of deeper integration and protection of Hungarian minorities came into direct conflict, and Fidesz's policy was shaped by the reality of Hungarians living in Serbia. Its basic position "was that Hungary would support but not participate in the air strikes against the Yugoslav regime, and no NATO ground invasion could be launched from a Hungarian territory" (Vachudova 2001a: 214). Fidesz's backing of NATO bombing did expose it to domestic criticism. As Socialist defense expert János Gömbös noted, the Social Democratic Party essentially argued, "We accepted the bombing, but we couldn't accept the Hungarian Prime Minister calling, in his British visit,

---

[3] The Parliamentary Foreign Affairs Committee also argued that allowing NATO to use Hungarian airports was really a self-defense tactic to protect Hungarian airspace but was not, in fact, Hungarian participation in the NATO operation itself (*MTI*, March 28, 1999).

for an increase in bombing. That's too dangerous in the neighborhood we live in" (interview). The MSzP preferred Hungary's "silent participation," which meant "full logistical support, but not bombing from the Hungarian soil [because] when the Serbs identify NATO bombers as coming from Hungary, this changes the situation of Vojvodina completely" (Gömbös interview).[4]

MSzP ambivalence was manifest in other ways as well (Valki: 2002: 477–9). When Fidesz tried to pass a constitutional amendment to obviate the need for a specific parliamentary vote for any visit of foreign soldiers to Hungarian territory, the MSzP blocked the proposal. More importantly, the party's parliamentary group (VHSP) proposed to modify the parliamentary resolution that had given NATO unlimited access to Hungarian facilities and airspace. The motion would have limited NATO air offensives by not allowing them to be launched from Hungarian airports against targets in Yugoslavia. Orbán immediately denounced the proposal and claimed the socialists were backing out of the agreement, saying that "the VHSP exploits and makes the most of the fact that a sense of fear increases among people in the case of an armed conflict" (*MTI*, May 3, 1999). The motion was defeated, and no further high-profile breaks developed across the party lines.

In general, Hungary enjoyed the public respect of most of its new allies, who were clearly aware of the difficulties it faced. That said, German Chancellor Gerhard Schröder did tell the *Washington Post,* "We cannot be at war against a country and let a pipeline that runs through a NATO member country supply the adversary with fuel." All understood that he was talking about Hungary, and a representative of the Hungarian oil and gas company, MOL, quickly denied that it had delivered oil, either by pipeline, road, or water to Yugoslavia since the air raids were launched (*MTI*, April 23, 1999). At the NATO summit two days later, Orbán reiterated Schröder's warning and said that it was "unacceptable" to have Hungarian firms concluding oil deals with Yugoslavia (*MTI*, April 26, 1999).

Paradoxically, for some Hungarians, the Kosovo crisis signified the end of Hungary's exposure to instability. For example, Dunay concludes that "the Hungarian political parties generally share the view that the

---

[4] Hungary had made this distinction in February 1994, when it indicated it would close its airspace to AWACS in the event of Western bombing of Serbia. Despite this assertion, Hungarian-based AWACS were involved in the late February 1994 shooting down of four Serbian jets (*Financial Times*, March 3, 1994).

country's accession to the Atlantic Alliance has reduced both the scale and nature of threats to Hungarian security. In security terms, the transition era for Hungary came to an end with NATO accession, and Hungary's own perception of itself is of a 'security provider' rather than a 'security consumer'" (Dunay 2002a: 65). But if the results were diplomatically reassuring, they were troubling in a military sense. As a result of its poor performance in the Kosovo crisis, a major initiative was undertaken to reshape the Hungarian military between the years 2000–2013 (see below).

The Czech political elite was much more openly divided about NATO policy. The Czech left was in power, and its voters were more skeptical than the Hungarians. Up to 62% of the Czech population opposed the NATO campaign in Yugoslavia, and only 25% of Social Democratic voters supported NATO membership in the first place (*Prague Post*, July 7–13, 1999). Once the bombing began, Czech voters were subjected to a flurry of contending perspectives. Perhaps the most bizarre statement was when the Zeman government claimed in late March 1999 not to have been consulted on the air strikes against Kosovo but to have been presented with a fait accompli decided in the few days before their formal membership. The government condemned the air strikes. Within a few days it came out that in fact the Zeman government had approved the strikes in the NATO Council, and it had to retract its prior statement. The Vice Prime Minister, Egon Lánský, declared that Milosevic's ethnic cleansing of Kosovo was morally justified because of the NATO bombing, and a few ČSSD deputies traveled to Belgrade to express their support for Milosevic. On the other hand, in the actual vote on whether to allow NATO to use Czech air space on April 2, 1999, twelve of the sixteen ČSSD ministers voted yes, and four abstained. On April 21, the Parliament approved by a wide margin the use of Czech air facilities and roads for the transit of NATO forces (Vachudova 2001a: 219–21). In response, Zeman enlarged the State Security Council in April and thus strengthened its position vis-à-vis the cabinet (Ulrich 2002b: 74).

Four other decisions – by the Prime Minister, the ex–Prime Minister, the President, and the Foreign Minister – were noteworthy in the Czech case.[5] First, the ČSSD prime minister preemptively distanced the government from any kind of ground campaign. The Czech decision to take one option off the table before NATO had considered it formally was greeted with annoyance in several NATO capitals.

---

[5] For more on Czech policies during the bombing, see Znoj (1999) and Hendrickson (2000).

Second, Václav Klaus stunned many members of the Czech political establishment by denouncing the NATO bombing, and noting that the exodus of refugees from Kosovo rose significantly after NATO began bombing. Appealing to populist sentiments may particularly explain Klaus's move. On the other hand, Klaus's own clientele had typically been pro-NATO and were among the strongest Czech supporters of the bombing. In part, Klaus was trying to move his party, the ODS, and reshape his own image in a more nationalistic manner, a move that was also consistent with Klaus's constant criticism of the EU.

A third striking feature was that President Havel strongly and publicly supported the bombing, and in fact "regretted only that the military action had not started earlier." Havel did not merely support the bombing, but he justified the bombing with rhetorical flourishes such as the invocation of the Munich syndrome, and he constantly made reference to fears of appeasing a dictator.[6] It remains unclear whether to attribute the key role that Havel played to the underlying institutional prerogatives of the Czech presidency, which had lost much of its formal power under the 1993 constitution.

Finally, as the ČSSD government emphasized its efforts for a diplomatic settlement, Foreign Minister Jan Kavan pushed a joint Greek/Czech peace initiative that also increased NATO frustration toward Prague. Some Czechs tried to locate the initiative within an older Czech tradition of trying to build bridges between East and West in foreign policy. But the more proximate explanation is that the ČSSD was simply tending to its party clientele (as indeed was Green Foreign Minister Joschka Fischer in Germany, who launched a similar diplomatic initiative designed, in part, to shore up toleration on the German left for the bombing).

The perception of many observers of the Czech political scene was that the Kosovo crisis underscored the extent to which both the Czech political class and public opinion had been focused on the benefits of NATO membership, without really dwelling on its costs (cf. Ulrich 2002a; Hanley 1999; Stroehlein 1999). What, then, did NATO ask of the Czechs? First, NATO sought support for the air strikes. We have seen that such support was not immediately forthcoming, although the Zeman government did support the second wave of air strikes that began on March 30, 1999. Second, NATO asked for the use of Czech airspace, which it received from the Prime Minister. In terms of civilian control issues, this

---

[6] Even then, Havel's focus on the military during the Kosovo bombing should not obscure his relative indifference to the stalled reforms detailed in chapter 4 (Ulrich 2002a: 407).

was an executive decision, so the PDC was informed but did not need to give approval (Nečas interview). Third, NATO asked for the use of Czech air fields, and this required parliamentary approval, which was granted with no restrictions. Finally, NATO requested that the Czechs provide assistance to Albanian refugees. Again, this required parliamentary approval, and the Czechs responded with a field hospital. The Czech MoD found it very difficult, however, to find officers who spoke English and could thus work with others in the international force. Said Ivan Dvořák, Deputy Director of Strategic Planning, "That was not a success story. A great number of people had been studying at academies abroad, but the military lost these people because the military career system didn't work" (*Washington Post*, November 3, 2002).

Vachudova (2001a) and Hendrickson (2000) both emphasize the significant difference between strong Polish and, to a lesser extent, Hungarian political consensus and the Czechs' weak political consensus. While the Czech government met its basic procedural obligations during the Kosovo bombing, those obligations were relatively light given the Czechs' geographical position. Unlike the Czechs and Poles, the Hungarians were asked to do more significant things, and the Hungarians performed well politically if modest militarily.

The significant difference in the behavior of Czech and Hungarian elites cannot be linked solely to the greater Hungarian exposure to the geopolitical region where the problems lay. The other factor is the nature of the countries' left-wing parties (Vachudova 2001c). Where the Hungarian postcommunists had instituted thoroughgoing reforms that led to an embrace of a cross-party consensus on NATO membership, the ČSSD, though not a refoundation of the Communist Party, remained highly skeptical about NATO enlargement. The Hungarian socialist government under Gyula Horn recognized that leaving open contentious border issues in the name of protecting Hungarian minorities abroad was slowing down integration into Western organizations, and Horn's government reversed these policies, signing treaties with the Slovaks and Romanians. This generally put the country on a course toward deepening its integration in both the EU and NATO (Vachudova 2001b).

NEW FORMS OF EMULATION

Templates are used when state elites voluntarily approximate the features of existing foreign models. In chapters 2 and 3, the CEE states tended to do this before about 1997–8, when the imperative to respond to the *acquis communautaire* first appeared. After that point, the states faced much less voluntary (if often vague) thresholds, and they often responded to problems revealed during screening by "patching" the national legal code with quick fixes that were highly faithful to existing models in EU member states. The military dynamic has been different. Because real military modernization (as opposed to cuts without concepts) was a priority for neither the CEE politicians, the electorates, nor the armies, elites made very little use of foreign templates during the long period free from NATO pressures. We have seen in chapter 4 that NATO did then invoke some thresholds, and we have looked at one – civilian control institutions – in some detail. Yet even though NATO conducted no process fully analogous to the EU Commission's screening, it did ultimately pressure CEE states to patch some glaring holes in defense laws and practices. After they achieved membership, the CEE states – helped by consultants, but free of any obligation to do so – also have used specific national templates to reform other aspects of their armies. The next sections explore these two trends in detail and show that the Kosovo conflict lent some sense of urgency to these reforms, many of which had roots prior to the crisis itself.

TEMPLATES: COORDINATION, NCO CORPS, AND
ALL-VOLUNTEER ARMIES

We begin with an unsuccessful effort. The Hungarian effort to force interagency integration among the many players who have a role in the planning and execution of defense policy has, up to now, been a failure. The most auspicious effort was the so-called Secretariat for Security and Defense Coordination set up under the Fidesz government and using the basic design of the U.S. National Security Council. The Secretariat was to be headed by Dr. Béla Gyuricza, a retired general in the Hungarian military, and someone with good ties to the prime minister's office. The staff was to be around forty members, and the Secretariat was to have three major sections: a department for security and defense strategy, which would do long-term defense planning; a department for defense coordination, which would coordinate and prepare for civil emergencies; and a department for evaluation and analysis, which was meant to synthesize information from various sources and digest that information for the use of the prime minister and the cabinet.

Interviews with key officials inside the Secretariat suggest they paid close attention to Western models in designing the Secretariat. One official recalled that "in 1997–98, we recognized the lack of coordination, and we discussed functions first, and then we looked at foreign examples. We didn't copy anybody, but we looked at the American, British, and German models particularly closely" (Siklósi interview). After taking into consideration some of the unusual features of the Hungarian security situation (e.g., land borders to multiple troubled regions, located in very good tank country, Hungarian minorities living abroad, a military with a very low social status), simply copying other countries' national institutions would not have been realistic. Notwithstanding these significant adaptations, the Secretariat failed. Most important, the Secretariat played only a very minor role during the Kosovo bombing at a time when interagency coordination was desperately needed. It failed because adaptation to local circumstance must also take power relationships into account. In this case, neither the Smallholder-run MoD nor Fidesz's own Interior or Finance Ministries wanted to be coordinated by the prime minister's office.[7] When General Gyuricza died of cancer and the office lost his forceful personality, all chance of overcoming this resistance died with him.

For comparison, the Czech counterpart mechanism, the State Security Council (SSC), is not the result of emulation at all but rather a recent reinvigoration of a traditional Czech institution going back at least to the 1920s. When Czechoslovakia was dissolved in 1993, the Czech Republic did not include the SSC in the act of abolition that would have allowed its transfer to the new state. Informal (and often inadequate) interministerial coordination followed, and even after the SSC was revived in 1998, its role was uncertain. Yet the 1999 defense reform bill clarified the role of the SSC, and unlike in the Hungarian case, it was the site of serious discussion and deliberation during the Kosovo crisis and subsequently (Vlachová and Sarvaš 2002: 47–8). As was amply clear in that crisis, national security coordination in the Czech Republic remains a significant problem (Ulrich 2002a), but it does not suffer the institutional incoherence seen in Hungary.

The Hungarian Joint Staff is an example of a more enduring use of a Western template to promote coordination, albeit of a different kind. Hungary was the first (and for a long time the only) former Warsaw Pact country with a Western-style joint staff. One of its architects, Arpad Szurgyi, was U.S. Defense Attaché at the time. Said Szurgyi, "Development of the joint staff started over beer in my dining room. We mapped out

---

[7] For a case study of German and Danish efforts to convince the Polish military to use European norms to construct soldiers' unions, see Epstein (2001: 64–74). This effort failed for reasons similar to those outlined here.

our system and theirs on butcher paper to get started" (interview). Started over beer, but hardly finished over beer, the plan went through five further steps over the next two years. First, a series of seminars exposed the Hungarian military to the concept. Second, U.S. joint staff experts with various specialized responsibilities came to Hungary to consult with their Hungarian counterparts. Then, U.S. personnel left the Hungarians time to develop a Hungarian variant of the joint staff. Fourth, functional experts from different NATO countries came to vet each Hungarian proposal in each of the areas. Fifth, general officers from NATO's European command went over the refined version with their Hungarian counterparts before the organization emerged in 1997. Thus, intramilitary coordination functioned better than interagency coordination. If careful preparation ensured that emulation here was not hasty or superficial, there was one other key aspect. Faced with declining budgets, a joint staff allowed the military to better allocate the scarce resources accorded it by politicians. Using a gradual process and targeted incentives, some recalcitrants could be persuaded or bought off. And without the institutional power base of a ministry at their disposal, the remaining opponents could be defeated.

NCO Corps

Both Czech and Hungarian politicians have used Western templates to reform and expand their NCO corps, the "noncommissioned officers" who serve between commissioned officers and enlisted soldiers in the military chain of command. NATO did not push NCO corps as a condition of membership, but most NATO states do use NCO corps fairly heavily, and many bilateral programs, especially those run by the United States and Britain, have tried to build CEE NCO corps.

Most NATO militaries use "mission-type orders," which are quite different from the detailed directives top officers gave in Warsaw Pact armies (Fields and Jensen 1998: 124). To simplify, NATO-member officers tell their NCOs and enlisted men and women what to accomplish but do not tell them how to accomplish it, leaving them some discretion on questions of methods. In the Warsaw Pact, centralized control by officers meant that all significant decisions were carried out by other officers, often with detailed instructions from the top. The extreme case is the Russian military adage that "initiative is punishable." As British Air Commodore ES Williams has said of the Soviet military system, "everything depends upon the officers . . . if the backbone of the British army is the NCO, the backbone of the Soviet army is the officer . . . simple aircraft refueling and rearming is done by an officer. All tanks and APCs [armored personnel carriers] are commanded by officers and routine jobs about the ship are done by officers" (quoted in Fields and Jensen 1998: 124).

Soviet-style militaries did have NCO corps, but they tended to be very specialized, and there were relatively few of these NCOs. Rather, the party focused almost all military responsibility among officers, a high percentage of whom were party members. Thus the use of templates here is not a matter of building an NCO corps entirely from scratch, but of broadening their competencies and building their numbers.[8] This bodes well insofar as previous research suggest that institutional emulation works best when it builds on existing traditions and strengthens existing political constituencies (Jacoby 2000). Though the Hungarian NCO corps was purged by the Soviets after World War II, prior to the war it had been one of the best in Europe, certainly stronger than in the Czech case.

Both the PfP and the U.S. Joint Contact Team have been avenues for Hungarians to refurbish their NCO corps and raise their standards. In some cases, however, military officials have been quite unrealistic in their expectations. For example, as Arpad Szurgyi explained, "We've been talking about developing an NCO corps in Hungary and the Hungarian military said 'great we'll do it next year,' but we said that in order to get really qualified NCOs, you need fifteen years of training. You have to start somewhere, but don't expect the end product too quickly" (interview; see also Simon 2000b: 1–4).

In the meantime, the limited number of available NCOs – a sociological factor – radically limits the institutional reform options. Since Kosovo, the Hungarian MoD has been trying to change the NCO-to-officer ratio from the current 1:1 ratio to a 3:1 ratio (Langenkamp 2000: 23). To do so, it has established so-called contract NCOs, in which a soldier, after completing the conscription period, can sign an NCO contract for a minimum of two years. Upon doing so, the soldier receives further training and then serves as a professional NCO. A primary motivation for this change is to achieve short-term interoperability with NATO militaries that use NCOs extensively. The Hungarian MoD runs five secondary schools that train future NCOs (Barany 1998a: 28). In addition, the 1999 defense review resulted in a plan to build a central NCO training school (Dunay

---

[8] In comparison to NATO, CEE militaries also have far too few junior officers relative to field-grade officers.

2002a: 79). But the Hungarian military wants to recruit many more NCOs than it can attract with its current incentives. Dunay reports that about 9,700 NCOs left the Hungarian military between 1990–8, during which time only 7,800 new NCOs joined up, of which only 1,600 had actually attended the regular NCO school (2002a: 72). One interview partner suggested that the program actually attracts the most candidates in the fall because it offers many a chance to get off the streets for the winter (Rábai interview). Here we see again how institutional reforms inspired by a different social and political context pose unexpected challenges.[9]

In the Czech case, the current plans call for increasing the number of NCOs in the ACR from the current 9% to about 55%. At the same time, the officer share of the ACR is expected to drop from the current 60% to about 20% (Vlachová 2002: 47). Again, these are huge sociological shifts, and they are done on behalf of a constituency that does not yet exist and at the cost of one that does: current officers.

To be sure, not all Western experts support the rush to build up NCO corps. Christopher Donnelly, former Special Assistant for Central and Eastern Europe to the NATO General Secretary, notes the pattern in which CEE elites "look to Western militaries and see them doing well and conclude that they also need professional armies with large NCO corps. But then they completely underestimate the costs involved. The US and Britain did a lot of harm by promoting this rush to a particular model of professionalism. Other NATO states, like Norway, do fine without NCOs" (Donnelly 2001).

The NCO case suggests that emulation can be used to attempt to resurrect the fortunes of an older national institution. Now missing the occupational subclass that used to play a significant role in this institution (and indeed in Hungarian society), the Hungarians have had to remythologize their NCO corps to convince young people that there used to be such a thing in Hungary. Whether this history is an advantage or not is still unclear, for many worry that in trying to build a budget NCO corps, CEE armies might simply exchange their underfunded officers for underfunded NCOs with thin commitments to the military.

---

[9] That military reforms occur in a broader social context can also be underscored by a second benefit of a more robust NCO corps, namely, a reduction of the brutal hazing that takes place in East European militaries (Taylor 2001). Hazing feeds upon a hierarchy among the conscripts of time served, in which the newcomers service every whim of the "long-timers." One prerequisite is the scarcity of officers in the day-to-day existence of the recruits, and there is some hope that the presence of NCO corps will reduce hazing (Fields and Jensen 1998: 146).

The Electoral Logic of the Volunteer Army

The templates discussed so far have in common that they are matters for elites – politicians, high level officers, civil servants, and officials from NATO member states. Most citizens have no idea about these efforts, and most would not care if they did hear of them. There is one place, however, where West European templates and Central European votes intersect, and that is in the idea of an all-volunteer professional army that ends the traditional reliance on conscripts. Many citizens do care about this choice. Moreover, there is also evidence that moving toward an all-volunteer army is supported by a majority of officers.[10] All-volunteer forces are decidedly not a NATO threshold. Many NATO members continue to make use of conscription, though several others have gone to all-volunteer forces in recent years, including such smaller states as Belgium and the Netherlands.

The two CEE states have ultimately decided to take the same course and end conscription. The Czech Republic has announced that it will pursue an all-volunteer force by 2007, while Hungary intends to stop conscription around 2006 (Kominek 2001: 13). This move is often justified either by a generic Western norm or by reference to specific states, often the Netherlands, for example. Then-Czech MoD Jaroslav Tvrdík claimed, "All NATO members have professional armed forces, or are on their way to transforming their services into professional bodies; We would like to follow this trend" (Quoted in Kominek 2002: 1). This section shows that given the unpopularity of military service and the declining need for large numbers of conscripts, professional forces make short-term electoral sense for political elites. Indeed, Czech politicians tend to call for a professional army before every election because they know it helps them with young male voters. About 80% of those eligible for conscription favor an all-volunteer force (Vlachová 2002: 45).

But like the effort to build large NCO corps, all-volunteer forces are a double-edged sword. Though popular with voters, all-volunteer forces would remove the military even further from society and, therefore, might erode its legitimacy even more. In the Hungarian debate, some suggested that defense budgets would need to rise by half in order to pay for a full professional army, though it seems likely that the size of the HDF would shrink further before significant budget increases would be freed up (Dunay 2002a: 73; Barany 1999: 82). Some advocate a mixed force.

---

[10] Vlachová reports that internal ACR polls indicate that 70% of Czech officers support a move to all-volunteer forces (2002: 46).

For example, Hungarian MoD official Péter Siklósi argues, "We need a professional army for the new challenges, but we need to keep a small conscript army for old traditional military tasks" (interview; see also Vlachová 2002: 45).

The stampede to a fully professional army would have several drawbacks. First, the states would have no formal reserves; this would be a problem because it is politically unacceptable to NATO, and it is terribly inefficient to count on those who have left the military. A second concern, particularly in Hungary, which is close to geopolitical problem areas, is that there might be no preparation time before a conflict begins. As a result, the armies would require a higher (and more expensive) level of readiness. A third concern is that no CEE professional army could pay enough to keep talented people in the ranks, so they may well end up with less-educated forces in the long term. To be sure, CEE armies likely would be able to attract people for professional slots, but once they have trained them and increased their skill set, they likely would not be able to pay enough to keep them (Siklósi interview). For example, in 1996, the Hungarian government tried to attract extended-service contract soldiers. The plan was to hire 2,000 in 1996 and 1997 each and an additional 500 each year thereafter. But by March 1999, there was already a shortfall of 1,200 contract soldiers.

The Czech Republic also struggles with programs that develop warrant officers and recruit extended-service NCOs. In summer 2000, programs to do both of these things had been far from meeting their goals (Simon 2000b: 1–4). In 2001, the Czechs were only able to attract 1,400 contract soldiers of the 4,000 they had sought (Kominek 2002: 13; Ulrich 2002b: 68–9).

According to Czech PDC chair Petr Nečas, foreign models played an explicit role in Czech thinking about professional soldiers.[11] Specifically, the Belgians played a negative role and the Dutch a positive role. Both countries had made the switch to professional forces in light of the declining numbers of conscripts who were willing to report. In that sense, said Nečas, "their motives were the same as ours." These foreign models were also close to the size of the Czech military. In Nečas's view, however, the Belgians made a serious mistake by not cutting force levels right away. The Belgians were "too social." As he said in 1999, "We need to go to 38,000 in the long term, so we should go there right now. We should have

---

[11] Unlike in the Czech case, however, the PDC chair during much of the Hungarian conscription debate, Smallholder member Zsolt Lányi, opposed ending conscription.

a 50–50 professional–conscript mix to start, and then move up to 100% professional military within eight years" (Nečas interview).

Current Czech plans call for full professionalization of units allocated to NATO by 2005, followed within two additional years by full professionalization of the ACR. The ACR claims that the additional costs can be born if the Czech government spends 2.2% of GDP on the military and if personnel expenditures increase from the current 46% to about 50% of total military spending (Vlachová 2002: 44–7). Early returns, however, are not promising. In fall 2002, MoD Tvrdík noted that the Czech defense budget has been cut so drastically that "this will also strongly affect the conscripts, whose training will be winding down almost to zero" (*BBC Monitoring*, October 21, 2002).

Many of the popular forces that support the notion of an all-volunteer force are already voting with their feet and resisting conscription. Politicians have responded by shortening conscription periods. At the time of the collapse of communism, conscription lasted eighteen months in Hungary. By 1994, conscription was reduced to twelve months, in 1997 to nine months, and in 2002 to six months. A study of 11,000 Hungarian youth conscripted in 1997 showed further that fewer than 5% were college graduates, 25% had eight years of education or less, and nearly 40% had been unemployed before being conscripted by the military (Barany 1998a: 28).

Of course, reducing conscription time results in conscripts that are inadequately trained. In response, the HDF is considering a kind of "national guard" in which conscripts could get an additional six months of training to make them usable (Deáki interview). This fits a pattern of emulation first noted by Westney (1987) in her classic study of Meiji Japan: When state elites look once to a foreign model for institutional inspiration, they are likely to return later as new problems result from the first set of changes. That there is a cascade of subsequent adjustments to such a major shift is also clear to HDF leaders. HDF Chief of Staff Lajos Fodor noted that to make professionalization work, "our entire military enterprise must make a bold shift in everything from laws to daily unit routine" (quoted in *Armed Forces Communications and Electronics Association* 2002: 24). Given the HDF's track record on "bold shifts," this comment is hardly reassuring, but it accords well with the notion that emulation is not a simple act.

The turn away from conscription also has been strong in the Czech case. Czech politicians initially used partial professionalization to downsize their military, and many politicians also reached out to young male voters who wished to avoid conscription. The civilian MoD began to push professionalization under Antonín Baudyš, but the military itself was cautious, as were subsequent defense ministers. Only in 1997, in the run up to the Czech national election and with NATO membership on the horizon, did politicians begin to call for full professionalization. And once NATO membership both secured Czech borders and provided incentives for out-of-area operations, these factors also lent impetus to the politicians' calls for full all-volunteer forces. Skeptical or quiet up to then, respected voices such as Lobkowicz and Nečas began arguing publicly for full professionalization. The last conscripts were inducted in March 2004 for a mere eight months (*Radio Prague*, March 31, 2004).

All-volunteer forces have not meant that the U.S. model is the prime object of emulation. CEE politicians well understand that U.S. practices are supported by much larger defense budgets and higher levels of technological sophistication than they can aspire to. Instead, when confronted with a broad set of options for changing the military structure, Czech politicians have looked at specific national models in Western Europe – not just the Belgian and Dutch models mentioned above, but also the Portuguese and Danish models, two countries that are moving from semiprofessionalism to virtually full professionalism. Nečas has been very interested in the Scandinavian type of professional army too. All of these models involve national forces in activities that Czech youth find much more appealing than conscript life. Indeed, Vlachová and Sarvaš report that up to two-thirds of Czech youth consider as attractive professions serving in the Czech mission to NATO, in rapid reaction forces, as peacekeepers, or as pilots (2002: 61). While these are somewhat stylized occupational choices – after all, who spends a career on peacekeeping deployments? – the figures do suggest that the low esteem in which the soldierly life has been held does not mean the wholesale rejection of the military as a career path.

PATCHES: DPQ, TFG, DCI

The templates just discussed involve institutional choices that NATO has traditionally left to member states but where CEE states have chosen to use Western models to guide key aspects of their defense reforms. As we first saw in chapter 4, however, there have been junctures in which NATO articulated some broad thresholds for membership. These included the 1995 *Study on Enlargement* and the "intensified dialogue" with twelve hopeful new members during 1996 and 1997. In these talks, NATO was careful not to make institutional requirements too specific, especially since many countries engaged in the process were not strong candidates for early membership. NATO conducted studies of the readiness of the prospective new members in 1997, and, after three were invited at the Madrid summit to later join NATO, it conducted brief accession talks in September and November 1997. At the conclusion of these talks, each invitee sent a letter confirming its commitment to certain agreements (North Atlantic Treaty Organization 2001b: 63–4). Only with this last step do we begin to see the use of "patches" – specific institutional answers to specific IO demands. As we have seen in the EU cases, IOs sometimes shape requirements so that only fairly specific patches will do.

NATO has obliged far less use of such patches than has the EU, in part because it has more tolerance for institutional variation among its members. And yet there have been some moments where its demands on the Czechs and Hungarians have been quite specific. One such instance involved a modified version of NATO's annual Defense Planning Questionnaire (DPQ). This NATO instrument was not specifically designed for aspirant member states only (as was the EU's screening), but is something that each NATO member already completes every year. In the first year, however, a "mini-DPQ" was fashioned for prospective members to get them used to the process (Simon interview). CEE states then agreed to specific target force goals (TFG) that followed after the DPQ in 1997.

To be sure, not all of the thirty-one separate "compatibility goals" that the Czechs negotiated with NATO in 1999 can usefully be labeled "institutional." For example, some tasks included standardizing signs and maps and providing Western instrument-landing systems for their airports (Gleick 1997).[12] Reports indicate that they may have met as few as half of these more technical goals (Yaniszewski 2002: 394), but the interest here is in practices and structures, rather than pieces of technology per se. Certainly, the flurry of legislative activity in the run-up to membership is consistent with the concept of last-minute patches. In the Czech Republic, after years of legislative inaction, six fundamental defense reform bills passed in 1998 and 1999 (Vlachová and Sarvaš 2002: 49).[13]

---

[12] For an extended discussion of such military requirements as modernization of the arsenal, improvement in communication, interoperability reforms, military education, language capabilities, and reform of military doctrines, see Jones (1998) and Barany (1998a: 15).

[13] To be sure, some of the matters legislated in these bills are too big and make too little explicit reference to existing NATO-member-state practices to qualify as patches; some of these things – such as steps taken toward an all-volunteer army – have already been covered under templates.

Patches often rely on models from NATO member states for a wide variety of detailed provisions. A good example is the Czech Act on Professional Soldiers. Ironically, this act was necessary in the first place because of a peculiarity of Czech law – that the terms of employment for its soldiers were not, as is normally the case in NATO member states, already contained in the general civil service provisions of the state. But Czech civil service reform was so contentious that no civil service act was possible for many years. Marie Vlachová, head of the Czech MoD's research department, notes that the drafters of the law looked first to domestic considerations because they sought to make military compensation and personnel schemes consistent with those that prevailed in the area of Czech customs and police. Yet they also went far beyond the Czech border to look for more detailed models:

> the preparatory stage included an identification of areas which needed to be paid special attention in respect of laws in effect in other NATO countries. Especially important were retirement benefits, as the experience of various NATO armies shows that they play a significant role in respect of a person's decision to become a professional soldier and stay on active duty... The experience of foreign countries was also used in determining the restrictions of civil rights of soldiers, selecting the place of service, serving in multinational armed forces and peacekeeping missions abroad, participating in tasks where soldiers' lives and health are endangered, and conforming to military discipline. (Vlachová 2001: 16–17)

Still, in comparison to the EU, NATO was less likely to demand that all CEE institutional incompatibilities be fixed. A good example was the Hungarian prohibition against foreign deployment of its troops without an express authorization by Parliament. This rule, which had a constitutional basis, greatly complicated Hungarian participation in even routine NATO exercises. But while NATO wanted to see the rule change (and it was partially relaxed in June 2000), its officials waited patiently for the requisite two-thirds majority required for a constitutional change. It did not put undue pressure on Hungary to change something that it would not require of any of its other members (Dunay 2002b: 72; Yaniszewski 2002: 388). In early 2004, the change was accomplished.[14]

On the operational side, NATO began using a much less demanding form of screening only just before extending membership invitations. In

[14] On the other hand, the Czech government did achieve the changes necessary for the so-called blanket approval process in the wake of the Kosovo crisis. Cf. Act No. 310/1999 Coll. On Deployment of the Armed Forces of the Foreign Countries in the Territory of the Czech Republic.

response to its DPQ answers, the supreme allied commander of Europe sets TFGs for the new members. At first glance, the annual DPQ process seems to reveal a difference in the two countries' approaches, since Hungary has reportedly consistently signed up for more reform measures (40–45 annually) than the Czechs (20–25 annually). Yet, upon closer inspection, this turns out to be a distinction without a difference, as the Czechs apparently sign up for targets that they know in advance they can achieve, while Hungary tends to sign up for more ambitious plans but then often fails to meet several targets. In the end, the readiness to fulfill NATO responsibilities seems about the same (Gutierrez 2002: 31–3).

Reports in 2002 indicated that the Hungarian army made good on about one-quarter of the 100 points for army development that had been approved in talks with NATO officials. Moreover, the projects completed tended to be small-ticket items, such as upgrades in the equipment of peacekeeping units (*Nepszabadsag/BBC Monitoring*, August 9, 2002). At the same time, the Czechs adopted 52 TFGs to be met in three phases by all of their services with the first phase focused on the proposed NATO immediate reaction forces (Dolejsí 1999).[15]

With formal NATO membership approaching, civilian control issues took a back seat to interoperability (Ulrich 1999). The major driver of institutional change in this phase was NATO's new Defense Capabilities Initiative (DCI), launched in 1999 to ensure that all NATO member countries had compatible equipment, personnel, and training (*North Atlantic Treaty Organization* 2001b: 50–2; Valk: 2002: 482). While the DCI is a challenge to all members, it was especially so for the CEE states. Dunay argues, for example, that "*there was not a single area where the Hungarian Defense Forces had achieved compatibility with NATO* when the country joined the Alliance in 1999" (2002a: 77, emphasis in original).

NATO's High Level Steering Group oversees the implementation of the DCI, and it is comprised of representatives from all NATO countries. They meet each week to "review progress and guide the process." The DCI has five foci: mobility and deployability, sustainability, effective engagement, survivability, and interoperable communications (North Atlantic Treaty Organization 2001b: 52). Behind these awkward labels lies the broad goal of getting NATO forces quickly, legally, and efficiently

---

[15] The Czechs designated three units for the immediate reaction forces: (1) a chemical protection company, which was wholly professional; (2) a transportation platoon to provide logistical support to units that were to join the immediate reaction forces; and (3) a helicopter contingent of four MI-17s.

to out-of-area trouble spots, supporting them while there, and allowing them to use the latest technology as they fight in units that may include several nationalities (*American Forces Press Service*, Dec. 5, 2000).

The NATO summit in Prague in November 2002 was another opportunity for the new member states to reaffirm their commitment to NATO, and at least some of that reaffirmation came in the form of specific new pledges. Claiming that Hungary had met less than a third of its alliance commitments under the Orbán government, MoD Ferenc Juhász pledged that by 2005 Hungary would provide its own troops with protection against biological and chemical weapons, provide a rapid reaction battalion for NATO use and logistics for a second battalion, increase air transport (mostly by getting two NATO-compatible AN-70s from Russia), and upgrade its Russian-made MI-24 assault and transport helicopters.

As noted at the outset of this chapter, professionalism requires an effective military force. Though Hungary was first offered NATO membership nearly two years before the Kosovo crisis, its air force still had not been outfitted with communications systems that would help NATO air controllers distinguish its forces from those of Serbia. Indeed, Hungarian aircraft still did not have this ability even in 2002 (in part because planned upgrades were cancelled when the MoD had to bear all the costs of the Kosovo Force (KFOR) peacekeeping operation from its own budget) (Gutierrez 2002: 163).

These technical issues reveal a crucial point: Military deference to civilian priorities, while evidence of one aspect of professionalism, may allow the neglect of military effectiveness – which is another aspect of professionalism. Here, in the details of weapons systems, abstract concerns about civil–military relations assume concrete dimensions. By and large, CEE militaries continue to operate with equipment built to Soviet wartime standards, which meant crude and cheap, if also lethal. But Soviet doctrine also treated people as crude and cheap, and they made far lower investments in acquiring, training, and retaining personnel than did the Western militaries. Thus, sometimes the patches envisioned by NATO planners and CEE representatives try to bridge gaps that are simply too wide. It is one thing to call for interoperability, but, in the words of one close observer, "you simply can't integrate a MiG 29 into NATO" because the aircraft is built for a different task than are the NATO aircraft it would fly alongside. For example, in deference to democratic pressures, NATO exercises are conducted in remote areas far from bases. The preconditions for such exercises are long flight times to reach training areas and durable, low-maintenance equipment while "the pre-flight check for a MiG 29 is to walk around the airplane and look for oil leaks" (Donnelly 2001).

Raymond Millmen of the U.S. Army War College notes that "countries with Soviet equipment, especially aircraft, would have severe difficulties operating with NATO. Differences in communications, avionics and computerization would hamper interoperability. Soviet-made aircraft would not participate in a NATO air campaign because of the incompatibilities and the dangers of fratricide" (quoted in the *Guardian*, August 23, 2002). This danger was underscored during the Kosovo air campaign, in which the United States lost its first stealth aircraft in combat (after losing none despite hundreds more sorties in the Gulf War). Because the aircraft of some NATO members did not have appropriate identification systems, all NATO aircraft were obliged to fly in a preset formation. When Serb anti-aircraft batteries visually observed this pattern several days in a row, they were able to essentially ambush the stealth aircraft when it flew by at the customary time. On the other hand, Czech and Hungarian procurement plans to acquire Swedish Gripen fighters strike many as fanciful in light of current defense spending. When floods again hit the Czech Republic in summer 2002, the MoD quickly cancelled plans to purchase the Gripen. In short, while the concept of patches is meant to cover quick reforms done very late in the game, some of these patches cannot be done quickly at all and carry a price tag that may undermine other important reforms.

LEVERAGE LOST, LESSONS LEARNED

That NATO loses leverage once countries are inside is reminiscent of the famous "fear–greed" cycle among manufacturing subcontractors (Ahn et al. 2001; Forster 2002: 1). Though in CEE the cycle might more properly be called a "fear–indifference" cycle, the point remains that once the fear of exclusion is safely past, the will to please diminishes markedly. Hungary's longtime ambassador to NATO, András Simonyi, is scathing on this point, speaking of the time *since* 1999 as "three wasted years" and noting that "the problem is that, after getting into the club with considerable effort, we stopped caring" (2002: 56). Yet it is not the case that joining NATO means that all leverage is gone. In fact, a significant amount of crucial legislative work on civilian control did come as membership was being achieved. The legislative agenda in the Czech Republic for the 1998 and 1999 sessions was especially substantial, with nine different bills submitted to create a framework for the new military reforms. In other words, an enormous amount of the legislative base did not actually

precede NATO membership, but rather was being worked on as membership came to pass. This is a very significant difference from the EU, where
everything had to be in place in advance.

The second round of NATO enlargement, culminating in November
2002 with the offer of a new round of CEE enlargement, differed from
the first round in several ways, not least the use of "Membership Action
Plans" (MAPs) for the prospective members (see Simon 2001; Barany
2003). Indeed, a 2001 report of the NATO Parliamentary Assembly seemed to indicate that MAPs have taken on characteristics similar to EU
Commission screening. The report acknowledged that, in round one, "it
was generally understood that the new members would have to undergo
a transition period of several years before they meet the required level
of compliance with NATO military standards, primarily interoperability
with NATO weaponry and the ability to communicate in English" (*North
Atlantic Treaty Organization* 2001b: Section II, Para. 19). But, the report
said, this would change in round two:

MAP is more specific and goes farther than the 1995 *Study on NATO Enlargement*
in defining what applicant countries need to accomplish to meet the criteria for
eventual membership. It draws on the experience of the last enlargement round
and the Partnership for Peace. MAP is not, however, a checklist for applicant
countries to fulfill, nor could participation in the program guarantee an invitation
to be in accession talks. MAP is self differentiating, which means that it is up to
the participating countries themselves, why and how to match their participation
in the program with their national priorities. (*North Atlantic Treaty Organization*
2001b: Section II, Para. 24)

MAPs set up a system of annual national programs and yearly meetings with objectives and targets, individual country reports, feedback, and
guidance focused on the progress in the areas covered by the individual
national programs. Each applicant then reviewed the document at the annual spring meeting of the North Atlantic Council. This bore some resem-
blance to the annual reports on candidate countries by the Commission,
though admittedly with much less leverage and publicity. Like screening,
MAPs also had "chapters." Though there were five (instead of thirty-one
for screening), the much greater difference vis-à-vis screening was that
NATO had few personnel to devote to going over these chapters with
CEE personnel. MAPs also included a "focused feedback mechanism"
with workshops on specific problems and "clearinghouse meetings" with
individual countries. Unlike in EU screening, however, the countries did
not all meet in a big group at first, but met individually with representatives of all nineteen member states (plus Russia). NATO envisioned this

process as a way to help prospective members find a specific role that they could play and not as just an adoption of a kind of NATO *acquis*.

The major difference, then, remains that the EU insists on a higher level of uniformity in the screening process because, unlike NATO, it envisions no particular division of labor in a functional policy area like defense. It pursues minimum standards rather than a functioning division of labor. As in the EU, we do see an institutional "thickening" of NATO that, despite its obvious disadvantages in personnel and budgets, has made some adaptations since the first wave of enlargement. Evidence of this thickening lies in the proliferation of programs, including MAPs, the PfP, partnership goals, annual national plans, individual partnership programs, theater engagement plans, and bilateral security assistance and on-site evaluation visits from NATO member states (see *North Atlantic Treaty Organization* 2001b: Section II, Para. 32). Though some of these programs – such as the PfP – were also available to the Czech Republic and Hungary, NATO has devoted significantly more attention to them in the latest round. On the other hand, the terrorist attacks on September 11, 2001 ultimately were followed by a U.S. push for a "Big Bang" NATO enlargement. This meant that geopolitics softened these institutional demands almost as soon as they were made (Barany 2003).

SUMMARY

Historical legacies left bloated and ineffective CEE militaries that required major institutional transformation (especially in civilian control) and behavioral changes (professionalism). But neither state has nearly enough of the well-trained civilian and military personnel needed to drive such changes. Moreover, with the exception of the move to all-volunteer forces, there is no significant electoral incentive for politicians to devote themselves to modernization, either in terms of policy or in terms of gaining expertise. NATO incentives have also not been consistently effective. Even when the institutional environment has offered incentives for reform, the CEE legislatures or MoDs can simply pass "new" framework programs but then fail to implement them. It also turned out that Tamás Wachsler was wrong in the epigraph to this chapter: The Kosovo crisis did not really invigorate military reform, and the "more important guys" to whom he referred seem about as uninterested in defense as ever.

NATO has recognized this dilemma, as several implications attest. These implications are detailed in chapter 7 but can be sketched here: NATO has tried a new approach for the second round of enlargement (the

Membership Action Plans just noted); it has acquiesced as CEE states build two-tiered forces in which only the NATO-dedicated units meet professional standards; and it has allowed both the first- and second-wave states to develop particular specialty niches that can be of some use to multinational interventions out-of-area. But NATO's most important member state, the United States, has also drawn two other conclusions, namely, that NATO is no longer a serious military organization, and that, therefore, it makes more sense to ask its new members in CEE for fealty to American policy than to endlessly badger them to actually make their defense forces institutionally sound and militarily competent. This shift, in turn, poses the danger that the weak states of CEE may be caught between the competing demands of a distant superpower, which has nonetheless helped them greatly in hours of need, and of the medium-sized powers that dominate their immediate neighborhood.

6

Using Theory to Illuminate the Cases

> Although many recognize potential complementarities between [the] various institutionalisms, metatheoretical debate has often hindered theoretical dialogue and fruitful empirical work.
>
> (Jupille, Caporaso, and Checkel 2003: 8)

Chapters 2–5 described the variety of forms of emulation that have appeared in CEE over the past fifteen years. They traced the way various configurations of IO incentives and domestic considerations shaped elite use of four modes of emulation. The same chapters also explained the importance of the density of IO rules and the density of policy sector actors for four different kinds of outcomes of emulation. This chapter and the next connect that description to broader theoretical debates. This chapter assesses the cases in light of individual institutional theories. It does so by trying to sidestep the "metatheoretical debate" noted in the epigraph and noting the places where the three theory traditions are most helpful and where the lacunae in each lie. It begins with the NATO cases just explored and then returns to the EU cases discussed in chapters 2 and 3. Chapter 7 then employs limited syntheses of the three bodies of theory to mine the data for more insights about the overall postcommunist transformation.

DEFENSE REFORMS IN LIGHT OF THE THREE
THEORY TRADITIONS

Defense reform went through the same phases in each state. In a nutshell, the defense sector began the postcommunist period moribund and discredited in both states. Politicians eager to save on defense began making deep budget cuts, though these cuts were generally without any guiding concepts except to save money in the short term. Though each nation had a small military and a large minority that would have embraced neutrality, both states soon rejected that course and determined early on to seek NATO membership. Compared with the cost of building even a minimally competent national military, being in NATO made good fiscal sense, especially if states could later delay or evade some of their obligations. Membership also made strategic sense because it seemed likely to fill the regional security vacuum. After the mid-1990s, when NATO indicated that enlargement was on the agenda, both states passed a series of defense reforms geared to preparing for membership. Membership itself was coterminous with a major foreign policy crisis in Kosovo, and this challenged the government in both states. Yet after the crisis subsided, a sense of relaxation quickly returned. Today, ongoing efforts to improve professionalization are driven mostly by those alliance commitments hardest to shirk or by emphasizing those reforms that best respond to direct electoral incentives. Though doubts about NATO have lingered in public opinion, with the passage of time the party political consensus on NATO seems well established in both countries, though perhaps more so in Hungary.

This basic story, broadly similar in both countries, flows logically from the combination of historical, material, and sociological factors underscored throughout this book. Relative to the cases considered in chapters 2 and 3, military reform has all the cards stacked against it: a toxic past, significant entrenched interests, a weak institutional environment at the IO level, and thin material incentives at the national level. No other case had this many barriers to reform in general and to effective emulation in particular. Against this backdrop, the "cuts without concepts" outcome just described was overdetermined. Indeed, it is little wonder that the Czechs have only a formal veneer of military professionalization, and the Hungarians sometimes do not even have that.

There were also a few important differences between the two states. By Western standards, Hungary has had a significant institutional irregularity in the relationship between its MoD and general staff. Defense officials and private consultants from at least three NATO members (Great Britain, Germany, and the United States) have tried to coax the Hungarians to resolve this standoff, but progress was very slow. In the Kosovo crisis, on the other hand, Hungary showed loyalty to NATO *policy*, even at some domestic cost. The Czech Republic had a higher level of institutional conformity, but had a harder time supporting the NATO policy line during the Kosovo bombing. In part, Czech ambivalence followed from the Zeman government's indifferent efforts to explain the full ramifications of NATO membership to the Czech public.

The argument here provides a vocabulary for understanding the richness of emulation in CEE. It argues that emulation is not all one thing – not merely "IO imperialism" or CEE "dissembling," nor is this diversity captured by notions of mindless imitation or mechanical diffusion. Western models have sometimes been very helpful, and in some cases, CEE elites have taken them very seriously. Thus, the book's theoretical task is to explain the emergence and persistence of the empirical richness uncovered by this use of the concepts. Which of the theory traditions best helps us understand the pattern of stasis and change in defense reforms? The simple answer is that none is very satisfying on its own. To see why, it helps to return to the strengths and weaknesses of the heuristics in each theory, which were introduced in chapter 1.

Historical Institutionalism

The HI focus on the way each juncture shapes subsequent choices is consistent with the crude common phases noted above. Thus, NATO's initial arm's-length approach to prospective members helped ensure that the CEE countries got a very late start on real military reform. The brevity of the preparation period available once enlargement was imminent then led NATO to focus on highly visible thresholds like formal civilian control institutions, treaties resolving minority issues, and adequate spending levels. Poor military preparation helped ensure, in turn, poor military performance (or no performance) in the Kosovo conflict. As a result, NATO doubts about the new members grew in the wake of the crisis.

The HI approach also is consistent with the significant difficulties in promoting rapid institutional change. The evidence on patches especially revealed that the legacies of communist-era militaries are not subject to quick fixes, and would have been an imposing challenge to even a decade of dedicated and coherent reforms. And the HI approach usefully underscores at least three broad legacies of CEE militaries, namely, that they were bloated, unpopular, and pointed west. The latter was relatively easy to fix, and changes there helped accelerate rapid shrinkage of the huge military forces. The unpopularity has been very hard to reverse, though there are signs that the military is not permanently condemned in the court of public opinion. Moreover, the dysfunctional personnel systems in both states mean that reforms at the top face major barriers to bringing their organizations along with them – an illustration of the HI theme that gaps arise between the legacies of the past and the functional imperatives of the moment.[1]

Specific legacies also helped account for some variation in the national cases. Peculiarities in the 1989 transitional period in both states – the Czech army's preparations for intervention and the institutional isolation of the HDF – also provided key points of variation that the HI perspective can underscore. To be sure, however, these legacies also softened over time. The Czech intervention threat gave urgency to issues of civilian control at an important early moment, but it has played no enduring role. The Hungarian institutional peculiarity was longer lived and did impede a healthy civil-military balance, but unlike in Poland, NATO did not deem it bad enough to threaten to deny membership.

HI is not useful only for demonstrating the barriers to change. Its emphasis on existing capacity as a foundation for reform was useful in at least three ways. First, the very fact that Warsaw Pact militaries had been integrated into an alliance system both underscored their military vulnerability as national systems once the Soviets left and also gave them institutional experience in defense integration. This integration was involuntary and of a radically different nature than NATO integration, but the fact remains that neither officer corps had experience in running a truly national military establishment. Second, the HI perspective plausibly suggests that since Warsaw Pact armies had always been subject to political control (if not democratic control), they had an easier time accepting the basic institutional frameworks of deference to elected officials than might otherwise have been the case. Third, the HI approach is also consistent with less proximate historical factors, including the reinvigoration of older national traditions, such as the NCO corps in Hungary. The first two of these factors – multinational defense integration and traditions of deference to political leaders – reflect the sunk costs and increasing returns logics stressed by HI theorists. The third factor stresses the importance of historical antecedents that provide some local foundation for major institutional changes.

Yet the HI approach is clearly incomplete. During a period of significant change in CEE militaries, it can best account only for those that are new

---

[1] HI also underscores the possibility of gaps between member-state control and IO behavior. This has not been an important feature of the NATO case. Rather, a key problem has been that the IO is so dependent upon member-state resources that it lacks the levers to help drive much real military modernization of the CEE states.

variations of traditional structures. The important discontinuous changes in the cases are not easily explained by a theory tradition with such a weak motor. To find a more plausible motor of reform, we have to look at the other two theory traditions, RI and SI. In cases where NATO has set thresholds and/or obliged the two states to implement certain patches, SI is the preferable starting point because its concept of the institutional environment seems almost purpose-built for situations in which IOs have strong leverage over national states. Meanwhile, the RI, with its focus on the immediate electoral incentives of state officials, is a good starting point for looking at their much more voluntary use of templates.[2]

Rational Institutionalism

The RI concepts stressed here are the motive forces of electoral politics, the importance of external shocks in inducing movements toward new equilibria, the potential for national elites to gain material benefits through alliances with IO officials, and the position of various veto players inside the national arena.[3] We have already seen that the electoral force was quite weak, apart from the interesting exception of the all-volunteer force. There, CEE elites were drawn to various Western national templates as they came to recognize the widespread electoral appeal of ending their unpopular conscription programs. For the most part, however, a series of external shocks – especially the coup in the Soviet Union in August 1991 and the war in the Balkans – played key roles in raising the salience of defense issues and of focusing elite attention on security matters. We have also seen that, at least compared to the EU, NATO had very few financial inducements to lubricate CEE reforms, and it had few personnel who could increase the costs to CEE elites of shirking their responsibilities. Thus, promulgating a series of half-thought "strategic plans" without pursuing real implementation was an equilibrium outcome in many cases.

There were some intriguing veto points, for example, the fact that in the many coalition governments, the MoD was consistently in the junior partner's portfolio, far from the center of the government's agenda. Also, the 1989 Hungarian defense reform made it possible for the HDF

---

[2] While each of these theory traditions has clear comparative advantages, both the RI emphasis on the electoral incentives for politicians *and* the SI emphasis on the incentives emanating from IOs to reform defense provide little plausible source of variation between the national cases since elites faced essentially the same conditions in both states.

[3] As noted in the HI section, the focus on delegation does not reveal much in the NATO case, so it is ignored here.

to openly resist some civilian initiatives. Perhaps surprisingly, other institutional differences between the states seem not to have mattered very much. At the executive level, the stronger Czech presidency was rarely a factor, outside of the Kosovo crisis. At the legislative level, differences in the two states' electoral systems seem not to have mattered either in the broad desire to cut forces or the specific matter of all-volunteer forces. In the judicial sphere, the Hungarian Constitutional Court, despite its reputation of being overworked on domestic issues, has not played a decisive role in military reform (Sólyom and Brunner 2000). In short, the book's "most similar" case design intentionally minimized cross-national institutional differences, and of those that did exist, not all mattered for these policy areas.

The RI perspective also fits well with the observation that elections in the region have almost invariably ousted existing governments. In more than a decade since the collapse of communism, parties have very rarely remained in power across a national election.[4] Assuming that politicians are aware of this pattern, only short-term reforms provide them with electoral benefits. Institutional reforms with distant payoffs are likely to be of marginal interest. Certainly, this is not a bad first approximation of the way that Czech and Hungarian executives have treated their militaries. The electoral logic also fits the broad pattern in military procurement, which has comprised a very small part of defense spending in both states. For example, with an election looming in spring 2002, the Orbán government in Hungary put off procurement decisions until the period after 2006.[5] This meant that even had the Orbán government won another term (it did not), difficult procurement decisions would have waited beyond the horizon of its own complete second term. Clearly, the government wished to make procurement somebody else's problem.[6]

Finally, if one material logic connects elites and voters, another kind connects elites to certain policy areas. As we have seen in chapter 3, regional development and agriculture generate substantial discretionary

[4] In Hungary, like most of the rest of CEE, no government has won reelection. In the Czech Republic, Klaus's ODS won election in 1992 and reelection in 1996, but was soon toppled by scandal. The Czech Social Democrats won election in 1998 and reelection in 2002, but changed their Prime Minister at the election. On the virtues of party alternation for social learning, see Orenstein (2001).

[5] Specifically, the government proposed to focus on planning for "capability-based" forces in two phases up to 2008, before embarking on major procurement efforts (Dunay 2002b: 75–9). For an overview of Czech procurement, see Fiorenza (2001).

[6] And as a presumptive member of the EU at that point, procurement costs would weigh on the budget line covered in the Maastricht criteria.

spending. But the defense sector is neither an area of domestic political priority nor an area in which a well-endowed IO can distribute significant new resources. As a result, the defense sector has had difficulty drawing talented politicians at either the executive or legislative levels. We have already seen that the defense portfolio has consistently gone either to junior coalition partners or defense neophytes, or in some cases both at the same time. As one Hungarian official with close ties to NATO put it, "The best chance for getting a real political player to take the MoD position is to modernize equipment because then the availability of contracts and the opportunity to help out friends in the business community will ensure that a serious politician takes the job" (Rábai interview). With major procurement off the immediate agenda, this speculation may not be tested anytime soon.

As with HI, then, the RI approach better explains stasis than it explains change. To the extent that RI theorists might simply presume that it is "rational" for CEE elites to do whatever NATO asks of them in order to ensure membership, they would not only make the substance of elite interests completely exogenous, but also downplay the free-rider behaviors that are the bread and butter of the RI approach. Absent some mechanism for showing how elites can make trade-offs between the competing demands of electorates and IOs, it seems best to appreciate the insights an RI approach can elaborate without trying to stretch the theory past its breaking point.

Sociological Institutionalism

The SI perspective heavily emphasizes norms that prevail in the institutional environment. These specific norms have given concrete shape to the vague interest of producing more effective and professional militaries. As just noted, it might be rational for elites to respond to IO pressures to adopt certain norms, and this is fully consistent with the SI perspective (Meyer and Rowan 1991). On the other hand, SI scholars have taken a special interest in processes of persuasion, in which adopting favored norms comes to be seen as either the right thing or the smart thing to do. For reasons noted in chapter 1, the CEE cases are generally not well suited to trying to disentangle which motives – material or normative – carried more weight in any particular case of institutional reform. Rejoining Europe meant *both* a process of catching up to the institutional developments that had delivered freer and more prosperous societies in Western Europe *and* the prospect of having a better life as a result. What can be shown by the SI approach is simply that this desire to join Western Europe had very specific institutional contours. Each major IO generated a huge corpus of formal and informal practice that amounted to "how we do things." This corpus was not so imperialistic that it reshaped every aspect of national life, but there were few areas that it did not at least touch. Though NATO had a far smaller such corpus than did the EU, it was able to set certain broad thresholds prior to membership and oblige the CEE states to patch certain institutional holes after they joined.

SI scholars emphasize the potential for principled actors to institutionally codify their preferences and, if scope conditions are right, diffuse such preferences to others through formal or informal coalitions. Checkel's summary of scope conditions for "social learning," of which emulation is clearly one form, emphasizes common professional background, clear evidence of policy failure, repeated interaction, and insulation from political pressure.

As Checkel notes, some of these conditions are very hard to define ex ante (2001a: 26). Yet they do provide rough guidelines that can be evaluated against the evidence above. NATO tutelage occurred in a professionalized environment of military-to-military contact, and there was less overt political pressure on the CEE representatives than in the EU case, where a "failure to learn" might mean a postponement of membership. On the other hand, working against social learning was the tendency not to have iterative contacts with the same people, but rather to run lots of officers through different "familiarization" programs. As underscored repeatedly, NATO did not have the same structured contact with CEE representatives that the EU had. Moreover, it is not clear that the CEE militaries understood themselves to have clearly "failed" and thus be in need of learning lessons from the West. On the issue of civilian control, CEE militaries could rightly claim not to have intervened in politics despite many developments prejudicial to their corporate interests. Thus, from an SI perspective, these cases were moderately propitious for social learning.

Finally, the SI approach does more than provide the clearest account of the motor of emulation. It also provides the most persuasive account of how CEE elites manage the urgency of the IO demands with the bedrock political and material realities of their societies. The key concept is organizational dualism. Again, the central idea, as articulated by Meyer and Rowan (1991), is that since many organizations depend on external support for their existence and prosperity, they often develop formal structures that are favored by others in their broader institutional environment. The theory suggests it can be highly profitable to an organization to develop a dual nature in which an exterior "ceremonial" structure "buffers" its "actual work activities" (41). The military organizations most susceptible to such external pressures are the MoDs, general staffs, and the PDCs, though such pressure also affects other defense entities. With a premium on passing muster at the NATO level and a deficit of resources to devote to reform, defense elites in the region sometimes channel efforts from getting better into looking better.

THE NONDEFENSE POLICY SECTORS IN LIGHT OF THE THREE THEORY TRADITIONS

Historical Institutionalism

As in the NATO cases, there is substantial evidence that history shapes choices and outcomes in ways broadly consistent with the HI approach. Every case study contains examples that show the effect of path dependency on reform. Many others could be added. Take an important agricultural example from the Czech Republic: While differences in profitability explain access to credit among *corporate farms*, no such pattern prevails among *de novo family farms*. A variety of statistical methods reveals the cause: In the uncertain business environment, bankers make initial loan decisions based upon prior membership in communist-era financial networks, which generally include corporate farm managers but far less often include the farmers who bought privatized land. Profitability criteria help decide which of the insiders get credit and which are refused, but private farmers do not even get a fair hearing, and indeed have become much less likely to even ask for credit (Bezemer 2003: 29–34; see also McDermott 2002). The individual bankers' calculations are the proximate cause of this lending behavior, but the structure that creates these calculations – which, again, initially are *not* based upon profitability but on networks – has a hard-to-change historical anchor. Other examples have been seen throughout the health and regional policy cases. Even where the historical basis was thinnest – in consumer protection – several existing laws had to be gathered together from widely dispersed places in the Czech and Hungarian civil codes in order to comply with EU directives, affecting the way that courts apply the "old" parts of CEE consumer protection law.

The book's EU data gives some leverage for extending key HI insights in new ways. For example, HI approaches have underscored how time inconsistency problems sometimes allow agents to partially escape principal control (Pierson 1996). In CEE, however, the nominal agent, the European Commission, has often been able to set the agenda for the governments of the Czech Republic and Hungary, who will soon become members of its own collective principal. The Commission has used formal agenda-setting power by turning the harmonograms into legislative agendas. In some cases – see the data on the explosion of consumer protection legislation in 1997–8 – it essentially has been able to turn the national parliaments into statute laundering operations by setting the thresholds and watching as the governments quickly adopt Euroconform patches. It also has used informal agenda-setting power by stretching the *acquis* by giving hard interpretations to matters that are open and contentious among current member states.[7] None of these oddities count as falsification of agency theory. But where RI approaches tend to see agency slack as the residual price of a relationship designed by principals and for principals, the HI perspective has much more room for robust agents like the Commission, whose resources may long make it a formidable taskmaster for its nominal bosses.

We can also extend HI insights by noting the articulation of *national* institutional trajectories – where HI approaches are most well developed – with *international* institutional trends (see also Aspinwall and Schneider 2001: 12). The regional policy case offers a fascinating illustration: The premise of the EU structural funds is that states already have an existing national policy instrument for aiding poor regions. The EU instrument is intended to augment that national instrument and pursue certain priorities that might get lost at the national level in some member states, for example, promoting small- and medium-sized firms or vocational training. As we saw, however, what was meant as an EU scaffolding became, in fact, the main building in both CEE cases discussed in chapter 3. This edifice then had to compete with the traditional importance of counties as a locus of regional planning in Hungary and the episodic resistance of the national state in the Czech Republic. The mismatch between internationally sanctioned structures and the domestic politics has, in each case, left the resulting structures attenuated and the main actors ambivalent.

Rational Institutionalism

Reelection motives play prominent roles in most RI theory, and winning reelection has been rare for CEE governments. Thus, public criticism from the EU has been widely feared by elites. In an environment where time

---

[7] See Grabbe 1999b for several examples. On the Commission's ability to use informal tools to make formal policies, see Héritier (2001a); Schmidt (2001).

horizons were short, the Commission's annual reports became quite significant. They were discussed endlessly in the local media and used as a proxy measure of how well the government was performing (and how the country was faring) with the EU (Böröcz 2000). These responses were important because they gave texture to the public's broad support for EU membership for their nation. For unlike in current member states, there are few well-developed interest groups to push the state toward certain EU policies and away from others.

We saw that the electoral motor for EU reforms varied significantly across the cases. Electoral incentives can be dismissed in the consumer protection case. It was not a priority for Czech or Hungarian voters, and chapter 2 provided ample evidence that, without the EU, elites would have done very little in this policy sector.[8] By contrast, in the health care case, the EU's leverage was light, and domestic incentives were by far the dominant force. In part, we saw that there were electoral incentives for stabilizing health care spending as the states confronted growing fiscal crises. Even so, these incentives were not overwhelming, and the targeted benefits to health care workers and the increased budgets of MoH officials explained more of the reform impetus than did pure vote chasing. Electoral considerations may, however, explain the significant attenuation of the provider payment systems. Elites do seem to have calculated that it was a vote-losing proposition to ask voters accustomed to free and universal health care to make copayments or face consumption limits.

Electoral incentives are harder to gauge in regional policy. EU efforts raised the profile of this policy area, which CEE politicians on their own would not have attended to with the same intensity, let alone the same set of priorities. That said, regional policies potentially affect very large constituencies, especially given the large income disparities between capital cities and the rest of their respective countries. In a purely national context, politicians would be faced with a zero-sum game in which resources to poor regions would be financed from richer ones. The EU offered a way around this dilemma, at least in part. Yet CEE voters (and even regional politicians) understood the EU regional policy programs very poorly (Hughes and Sasse 2002). It seems likely that in this information

---

[8] RI approaches would suggest that low electoral salience would lead to low levels of reform. The point then is not that an area with a weak motor and no reform constitutes a problem for RI. The problem is rather that we see reform *despite* low electoral salience. SI approaches seem most helpful in explaining this puzzle, as EU demands essentially substitute for domestic demand that does not exist.

wasteland, the apparent promise of substantial EU funding made it possible for politicians to promise benefits to poor regions while plausibly reassuring richer regions that they would not be worse off. And the more underdeveloped the national systems of regional policy remained, the more persuasive this implicit promise appeared. This combination may help account for the scaffolding pattern previously emphasized in which EU programs became far more the foundation of national programs rather than a mere supplement. A similar logic held in agricultural funding, with the caveat that in preparation for the CAP, transfers from consumers and taxpayers to agricultural interests rose from less than 10% of farm income to well over 20% in just a few years, with most of these monies coming from the Czech and Hungarian national budgets.

RI theories also underscore the need for potential reformers to overcome collective action problems. CEE elites do have a collective action problem in that there seem to be many different (often mutually exclusive) ways to renovate their national institutions, but the effort expended to make painful reforms in one area may not be flanked with necessary reforms in related policy domains.[9] Thus, cabinet ministers especially have had incentives to free ride by letting other ministries bear the burdens of institutional modernization. The ministerial politics of communist governments were strongly compartmentalized, and pervasive shortages and power asymmetries gave ministries strong incentives for self-sufficiency. Duplication and waste were substantial, but all of this provided insurance against being held up by a lack of cooperation from others. A variant of this dilemma endures today, as we have seen in cases as different as military reform and regional policy, where interministerial coordination problems remain substantial. The EU's *acquis*, especially as interpreted by the Commission during screening and negotiations, has been a "focal point" that gave CEE elites an agenda, provided local rewards in the form of targeted aid programs for certain deficiencies, and provided a certain insurance that if they had to bear many of the costs of modernization, so too would other policy sectors.[10]

The RI approach shares with HI an interest in veto positions, though it tends to stress the institutional advantages that national rules give certain

---

[9] Of course, subnational actors have collective action problems too. Recall the crucial importance of outside money in the solvency of the Czech and (somewhat less so) Hungarian civic organizations devoted to consumer protection. In agriculture, after the initial public "disappointment" with the 2002 Copenhagen bargain, interest groups are now learning to use increased funding to help build their own organizations (Ratinger interviews).

[10] On focal points, see Garrett and Weingast (1993).

actors over the HI emphasis on resources and legitimacy embedded in particular organizations. The RI version of the veto position story is somewhat less useful simply because in the case at hand, the rules of the game have been so malleable, so uncertain, and so often broken during a period of enormous flux. It is much easier to read outcomes off of rules when those rules remain relatively stable; the point, however, has been to change the rules so that they accord better with what is acceptable to the EU.

Still, some interesting insights emerge from the cases. For example, against West European experiences it seems astonishing that no producer interests took an active role in shaping, let alone opposing, the hastily constructed consumer protection corpus (Trumbull 2002). In regional policy, the dog also didn't bark. The Hungarian counties were far too weak politically to block the new EU-inspired regime that, in any event, had some role for those counties to play.[11] In agriculture, we saw that the substantial interest groups of the policy sector were not trying to veto the CAP at all, but were trying to guard against a second-class CAP. But because the CAP *acquis* has direct effects, reluctant interest groups could only complain loudly or drag their feet in setting up the payment systems that would provide their financial benefits. They did the former with gusto, but to have done the latter would have been to cut off their nose in order to spite their face.

RI approaches to international organizations emphasize the principal–agent relationship, and these cases brought some novelties. In the EU, as noted, the member states make up a collective principal that often acts through the Council of Ministers to direct its agent, the Commission.[12] The Commission's powerful levers vis-à-vis future members of its own collective principal represent an unusual outcome for a theory that tends to stress principal dominance, though this outcome is not incompatible with principal–agent theory (Pollack 2003). At times, Commission assertiveness was what the Council expressly wished for. In that sense, the agent was acting at its current principal's behest or was, at most, exploiting discretion that the principal fully expected it to enjoy. In other cases, the Commission was able to take advantage of the preference heterogeneity of the members of the collective principal to carve out even more discretion.

---

[11] It is an open question how long this tacit support will endure, but chances seem good that it will since there is no obvious alternative basis that enjoys both legitimacy and resources that could fund poor areas.

[12] The Commission, in turn, is answerable to more than one principal since its president and commissioners are also responsible to the European Parliament (Pollack 2003; Hix 1999). On the concept of collective principals, see Nielson and Tierney (2003).

For example, since member-state regional policies vary considerably, the Commission has, in practice, had substantial latitude in its recommendations to CEE states. In the Czech case, after several years of pushing decentralization, the Commission actually intervened in a way that centralized de facto decision making. Such course changes seemed to be within the broad realm of discretion given to the Commission. Overall, the Commission has born a heavy load during the long preparations for enlargement (and indeed before). Unlike the market economy setting, where principal–agent theory was developed, agents are rare, and principals are highly constrained in trying to find agents to work on their behalf. This situation may leave such agents with significant amounts of discretion and may help explain cases in which "gaps" appear in member-state efforts to control such agents (Hawkins and Jacoby 2003; Pierson 1996).

Sociological Institutionalism

SI approaches also lend heuristics that illuminate the CEE politics of EU enlargement. While we could not simply read outcomes off of the *acquis* alone, both the size of the job and the kind of *acquis* mattered. The institutional environment's rule density varied widely, from high (agriculture) to moderate (regional policy), to low (consumer protection) to very low (health care). Moreover, in some cases, the *acquis* was composed largely of EU directives, which require the national legislature to adopt laws that fit the directives' framework but which can be tailored to national preferences and practices. By contrast, EU regulations have direct effects and require no such legislative action. This distinction helps explain why the huge *acquis* associated with the CAP generated so little legislative activity until very late in the accession process, when payment and monitoring systems finally had to be erected. One finding, then, is that density alone is not the only factor explaining the choice of modes of emulation, but that both the specificity of the rules and the burdens imposed by the rules also matter.

   Scope conditions for learning include the common professional background of participants, repeated interaction, clear and acknowledged evidence of policy failure, and insulation from political pressure. The screening process ensured that the first two conditions generally held in all four policy areas: Representatives of CEE ministries met with Commission officials and member-state experts who shared with them a common professional background (though in health care, this provided less consensus given the great diversity of Western models). Screening also generated repeated interactions, though this was far more the case for agriculture, which took longer than any other policy area. Variation aside, then, both points broadly hold.

The evidence on acknowledgment of policy failure is ambivalent. In two areas, consumer protection and regional policy, there was little sense that there had been a coherent prior policy domain, let alone one that could be counted as "failed." In part, this reality is what this book tries to capture by describing the outcomes as scaffolding (regional policy) and homesteading (consumer protection). Yet the puzzle holds even in health, where the MoH in both the Czech Republic and Hungary found much to admire in Western systems of health care and did seem to genuinely learn from the West. It is not clear, however, that a pervasive sense of failure motivated this learning process. Far more, key MoH officials calculated that a postsocialist health care system could not depend for adequate funding on a state in a long-term fiscal crisis. They rejected their old institutions because they worried that state insolvency might render them inadequate anyway. Similarly, in agriculture, state and interest group elites alike seem to worry less that CEE systems of agricultural support failed than that the very preconditions for that system – especially guaranteed markets in the communist block – simply disappeared.

If these are failures – and perhaps they are – they still are not the kind of failures that the previous literature on policy borrowing has emphasized (see Bennett 1991; Muniak 1985). Indeed, the sense of failure that mattered most may have been the one that came when the CEE states tried to negotiate a trading regime with the EU. The EU drove a very hard bargain and granted very few concessions in the Europe Agreements of 1991, and these disappointing outcomes underscored for many elites that they might do far better in what could be called a "learning game" through the screening process than they would in a classic "bargaining game." The sociological, norm-based approach was far preferable if it was one the EU could be convinced to play (Schimmelfennig 2001).

The one scope condition of learning that was not met was political insulation. In retrospect, now that we know enlargement ultimately did occur, screening may appear as a technocratic process of getting the institutions right. But in the late 1990s when screening began, no such certainty about enlargement was possible. In that context, and well aware that some member states opposed enlargement, CEE officials faced a real dilemma in which the detailed revelation of their weaknesses was both a prerequisite for crucial help from Phare and a big potential risk. The risk was that if they gave detailed evidence of institutional dysfunction, opponents of EU enlargement might use the evidence against them. With each call from prominent West Europeans to put off accession, that dilemma was sharpened (Jacoby 1999). The Commission took great pains to reassure CEE representatives that their intentions were strictly to promote better institutional functioning. Yet those representatives worried that full disclosure might compromise later negotiating positions with the Council of Ministers. The EU tried to circumvent this dilemma by building two separate tracks for the disclosure-cum-assistance and negotiation processes. The preparations for membership, including Phare activities and the so-called Accession Partnerships, were run by the Commission's Directorate General 1A (external relations). Screening, on the other hand, was part of the Commission's contribution to negotiations – a process run by the member states through the Council of Ministers.

If one form of dualism ran between assistance programs and negotiations, another form of dualism divided many of the organizations being reformed. As noted earlier, SI approaches expect that organizations develop formal structures that are favored by others in their institutional environment and that organizations may attempt to avoid being monitored or, failing that, ceremonialize such monitoring.[13] The need to comply or appear to comply with EU law has indeed thickened the connections between organizations, in part as a way of controlling external monitoring. Indeed, in many cases, Phare hired the same member-state consulting companies to both help CEE states with institutional reform and evaluate the outcomes of these reform efforts (Martens interview). The Commission also prepared drafts of its feared annual reports and shared those drafts with each state as a way of spurring quick changes that could remove negative evaluations before the final (public) versions were prepared. Governments quickly learned to prioritize those changes that could remove the most damaging language from the public versions. In other ways, however, Commission monitoring has been highly intrusive, and the ability of CEE states to ceremonialize it has been limited. Indeed, as CEE states adopted highly faithful legislative patches, they made it easier for the EU to monitor them because the Commission can compare them both to member states using similar laws and to other candidate countries with the same basic patches. Thus, while organizational novelty and complexity

---

[13] Current member states are far from immune from these trends. If one sees many irregularities in the regional policy and agriculture cases when one digs down to the local levels in CEE, the same can be said for current members, some of whom have had to pay back monies that were misspent.

within CEE states initially made EU monitoring difficult, growing organizational homogeneity across the region made it less difficult.

As in the NATO case, then, all three theory traditions make important contributions, and many of the same limitations previously discussed could be reiterated here. These conclusions are neither surprising nor particularly worrisome. Unless one is convinced that one theory tradition is the Rosetta stone of political analysis, a perfect fit between theory and findings ought more often to be grounds for suspicion than for celebration. But if one task lies in using the individual theories to clarify key aspects of a complex transformation, a second task lies in pointing out trends that can best be understood in light of particular combinations of theory. The next chapter undertakes this task.

7

Synthesis and Sequence

Juxtaposing Theory Traditions

> The value in juxtaposing [different] approaches is that critical confrontations reveal the junctures where a school's lacunae are best addressed by the other schools.
>
> (Lichbach 1997: 263)

All analytical approaches to politics have lacunae. Any theory that includes all relevant factors will necessarily collapse of its own weight. My pragmatic approach to synthesis differs from competitive tests or having one theory tradition subsume another.[1] Rather, this chapter makes six broad generalizations about CEE politics by using different pairs of the three institutionalisms. The chapter also shows again that institutional theories add more by synthesis and juxtaposition than in isolation. Different combinations of tools work best on different aspects of a longer sequence.

I argued in chapter 1 that because rational choice theory conceptualizes institutions mainly as outcomes of iterated strategic behavior of self-interested actors, it is unlikely, in isolation, to be a reliable guide to the immediate postcommunist period. This is true not because there were not plenty of strategic and self-interested actors, but because these actors were working in an environment of enormous uncertainty and on the basis of prevailing institutions that, in 1989, were very far from a reflection of aggregate social preferences. For many key actors, the noise of rapid change drowned out many of the signals that might have guided

---

[1] As noted in chapter 1, I prefer to see synthesis and subsumption efforts proceed at the same time. Many SI claims could be restated as RI claims and vice versa, though the costs of doing so may not be trivial.

interest-maximizing behavior.[2] Two factors in particular constrained the rational calculations of CEE political elites: the dense web of legal and institutional norms that emanated from the IOs they sought to join, and historical possibilities for and constraints on policy change that lay within their own societies. I introduced the notion of "embedded rationality" in chapter 1, however, because the sociological and historical approaches also failed to provide a fully satisfying explanation of the pattern of stasis and change that emerged across different policy areas, states, and IOs. Most generally, the SI focus on the influence of IO norms potentially overstates the motor of change, while the HI focus on path dependency often overstates the strength of the brakes.

For some questions, juxtaposing two theory traditions takes us farther than overreliance on any one tradition alone. To illustrate, I focus next on three broad themes relevant to both the EU and NATO cases. Those themes are, first, that each CEE society had both the desire to reform and the possibility of reform independent of the two IOs' influences, so that we must always consider the counterfactual of purely indigenous change. If we remove for a moment the force of the IOs' institutional environments, which this book has treated as a factor most central to SI theory, we can use RI and HI mechanisms to speculate on that counterfactual. The second theme is that when one emphasizes the IO reform demands, which grow significantly after the late 1990s, one sees that in some cases important CEE interests are *unwilling* to do all that the IOs ask of them. Such interests then have to choose between open confrontation with the IOs and dissembling or trying to deceive them. RI and SI heuristics are of significant use in analyzing such choices. The third theme is that a combination of SI and HI approaches helps us see that CEE states also are sometimes simply *unable* to fully incorporate Western institutional models. As a result, in some cases, a major gap appears between changes on paper and those on the ground.

The RI–HI Synthesis: The Counterfactuals

In the midst of almost manic efforts to integrate 80,000 pages of *acquis communautaire*, it is easy to forget that institutional change is usually halting, uncertain, and incomplete. It is easy to forget that successful grand

---

[2] Nonrationalist and rationalist treatments of the constraints on actors' ability to design institutions for their own benefit during postcommunist transitions include Pickel and Wiesenthal (1997); Moser (2001); Jones Luong (2003); Elster, Offe, and Preuss (1998).

reforms are few and that, more often, incremental reforms pile up, making yesterday's designs tomorrow's constraints. What would these policy areas have looked like absent the elite consensus in both states that EU membership was their highest foreign policy goal? In other words, without a set of demands emanating from the EU – the institutional environment emphasized by the SI approach – what reforms would the combination of electoral incentives (RI) and historical starting points (HI) alone have delivered?

Health care presents the easiest case for such speculation, for there we have seen that the EU *acquis* was so small that it mattered only at the margins. Here, Western models were important independent of the explicit conditionality that attended them in other cases.[3] The combination of RI and HI factors nicely highlights the exceptionally tenuous nature of the health reforms brought through emulation. A strong initial impetus for reform came from health care workers themselves, who associated institutional changes with the opportunity for better material and technological conditions in their daily work (Figueras, McKee, and Lessof 2002). This aspect is crucial, for foreign models must provide some docking point for established interests (Jacoby 2000). The downside has been the difficulty of gaining the support of elected officials, most of whom understand that health reforms cost money now and take time to pay dividends.

State weakness has been a consideration in tracking emulation and would also have been a factor had no emulation occurred. Elite efforts to distance themselves from the communist state have often so diminished state capacities that the state cannot oversee reforms. In some cases, this was a result of personnel losses to the private sector, but in other cases administrative decentralization left the Ministry of Health (MoH) without authority or resources. Thus, states have been too weak or governments too temporary to carry out good reform designs. And the health care system is complex enough that individual reforms (even those that *are* well thought-out) can be neutralized elsewhere in the system by conservative actors (Orosz and Holló 2001: 25; Szilágyi 2001).

Like health, the consumer protection case would also not be so different without strong SI pressures than it is today. To be sure, it is unlikely that a few dozen directives would have found a place in Czech and Hungarian law absent the EU's insistence. But we have seen that each state did have

---

[3] Obviously, SI theorists also emphasize the normative power of certain institutional models. It is not possible to remove this SI motor entirely, only to look for clues where it is relatively weakest.

some provisions for consumers, though they were not understood as a coherent and separate body of law and were widely scattered throughout the civil code. A handful of fledgling actors – characterized as "homesteaders" in chapter 2 – would likely not exist, while others would be even more starved for funds and less secure as official players in state economic policy making. But it is not as if the EU has really made them powerful. After all, the agricultural reforms we have seen in chapter 3 will be devastating to CEE consumer interests, and yet the formal consumer protection law and actors have played virtually no role at all in the discussion of policies that will radically increase CEE food prices.[4] The biggest difference we might see in the counterfactual is that a combination of RI and HI factors alone would never have placed such weak actors so quickly into any policy-making role at all. The EU has given them a chance where none would otherwise have existed; what they make of that chance will be up to them.

For several years, the agricultural counterfactual was arguably also not so very different. Here, the CEE states long made little use of emulation. That pattern flowed from two factors: the limited electoral incentives to provide CAP-like supports from national budgets and the predominance of direct effects in CAP regulations that obviated the need for substantial legislative transposition. Thus, the HI and RI factors, if left alone, would likely have produced much of what we see today in CEE agriculture, where a combination of path dependency and clientelism is evident in so many ways.

Yet the CAP has had three very significant effects on CEE agricultural sectors. First, we saw that aggregate support levels of agriculture had dropped very far (PSEs below 10%) in the mid-1990s, but rose sharply as states maneuvered to prepare for CAP programs and stimulate production that later would be used to calculate quotas. Second, there has been a large investment in food safety and quality that seems unlikely on this scale absent EU pressure (see Brosig and Hartmann 2001). Third, as the outlines of a CAP deal slowly emerged, a number of purpose-built administrative mechanisms appeared in each state (e.g., an EAGGF agency, an IACS body, a EUROPHY body). Thus, if many features of this policy sector can be explained by indigenous factors, removing SI factors emanating from the EU would significantly skew the picture. Over time, these factors

---

[4] Similarly, Sissenich (2003) has shown that while the EU has obliged CEE states to consult with nonstate actors (NSA) in developing their social policies, these NSAs have had only superficial effects on actual policy.

also will likely spur more intensive agricultural production in CEE as they have in every state that has previously joined the CAP.

Regional policy is another case where the counterfactual reveals that RI and HI forces alone likely would not have produced an outcome at all similar to the one that we see.[5] Rather, in Hungary, the traditional strength of the counties might well have provided the foundation for a regional policy of sorts, though it would have been more local than regional, and it likely would not have had the kind of funding that would bring together such a variety of different actors. In all likelihood, the Ministry of Interior's lock over local governments combined with severe fiscal limitations would have been a major barrier to any kind of coherent regional development policy (see below). In the Czech case, the situation would likely have been even more distant from current outcomes. No doubt, Social Democratic governance would eventually have drifted away from ODS policy, which saw the outright rejection of regional policy in favor of ad hoc bailouts along with a few programs to promote small- and medium-sized enterprises. A center-left government would have found some mechanism to slow the release of labor from heavy industry and agriculture. And perhaps some form of administrative devolution would have occurred absent the EU's constant threats, pleas, and inducements (Brusis 2003). But whatever form that was, it would hardly have had the boundaries and competencies of the current regions. In sum, the RI–HI combination underscores the considerable dynamism and the considerable constraints that are available from indigenous forces in CEE. But in at least some cases, no coherent account of reform can be offered absent a consideration of EU policies.

We can glimpse the defense counterfactual by the behaviors of CEE states in the period after the Soviet collapse. American and Western European foreign policy was focused on avoiding antagonizing Russia, and NATO enlargement was not yet on the table. Three trends might have been affected had NATO membership remained beyond reach of these states. First, CEE states made deep reductions in military expenditures, but they did so without any positive political consensus about what kind of military the state would need. Thus, "cuts without concepts" may well have continued throughout the 1990s if NATO membership had not occurred. Without NATO commitments there is little reason to expect that CEE states would have halted and even partially reversed this downward

---

[5] The policy area has been much less important for CEE governments than macroeconomic and sectoral reforms. Even while waiting for the agreed-upon structural funds to arrive, Czech and Hungarian regional policies have been inauspicious.

trajectory as the decade progressed. Second, the cuts may have exacerbated civil–military tensions that grew out of the peculiar traditions of Warsaw Pact militaries. We saw that while such militaries have generally not laid claim to direct power in the state's highest organs – and here Poland is the outstanding exception – they have enjoyed a host of prerogatives in budgeting, access to manpower, and even control of industrial capacity and real estate that would likely have brought them into direct conflict with the democratizing states. The aspiration to join NATO could not eliminate these conflicts, but it likely obliged their resolution somewhat faster than would otherwise have been possible. Third, absent a solid hope for NATO membership, the weak CEE militaries would have had to plan to bear the full burden of their own national defense. This would have generated calls for more reliance on territorial defense.

But NATO membership did come, and we saw that the CEE states struggled to keep pace with the full range of modernization demands. Accordingly, the CEE states have moved toward what might be called niche forces as a backup plan. Niche forces can be understood as the result of the collision between the soft public support for defense reforms (RI) and vestigial competencies left over from the Warsaw Pact era (HI). The upshot is that CEE states try to find some useful niche that they can fill to help in NATO missions and avoid the label of security free riders. To do so, they often try to build on competencies already present in some form. Accordingly, former NATO Secretary General Lord Robertson argues, "The new NATO is going to be about countries who do different things, and do each of them well" (quoted in the *Washington Post*, November 3, 2002). As Štefan Füle, Czech First Deputy MoD put it in 2002, "We are pushing for specialization among all NATO members, especially the Europeans since no one can compete with the USA in terms of budget size. In order to accomplish this, we will require a NATO umbrella. A new army must defend national interests abroad and not at home. It must be an army capable of responding to situations that do not fall under Article 5" (2002: 32). Hungary's Ambassador to NATO, András Simonyi, puts the point even more explicitly:

We must realize that it is nonsense to build smaller replicas of large countries' armies. Why should small countries field cripplingly expensive fighter aircraft, when the alliance has overcapacity in this area? Instead, we must look at areas of specialization. In Hungary's case, this might include engineers and troops for point defense, military intelligence, special forces, search and rescue and gendarmerie. (Simonyi 2002: 56)

In this context, the NATO Rapid Reaction Force – envisioned as 5,000–20,000 soldiers raised in 7–30 days and sustainable for 1 month – also contains an explicit division of labor. Germany is to provide airlift with C-17s, Norway will focus on special operations, the Dutch will emphasize smart weapons, the Romanians are to provide a mountain battalion, and the Czechs are to specialize in weapons of mass destruction (WMD) defenses. Moreover, the Czech Republic's expertise in defense against WMD attacks is a legacy of specialization that it undertook during the Warsaw Pact (*Washington Post*, November 3, 2002). Jozsef Bali, Deputy State Secretary in the Hungarian MoD, suggested that Hungary could focus on technical units like army health care or WMD defense (*Nepszabadsag/ BBC Monitoring*, August 9, 2002). Minister of Defense, Ferenc Juhász has also suggested WMD defense, along with combat engineering and special forces (Barnett 2002: 6).

Two ironies result. One irony is that the legacy of Warsaw Pact military integration (with highly homogenous units and no independent national defense planning abilities) has left CEE states capable only of a new kind of military integration in which there is quite an extreme division of labor.

The other irony is that such niche strategies may actually make good sense. NATO has encouraged the CEE militaries to prepare for World War III for far too long, and niche strategies as part of a broader alliance are hardly unprecedented – the Japanese military performs minesweeping functions that are vital to U.S. Navy operations in the Pacific. And niche strategies may provide reassurance both to those in CEE who worry about the military becoming too large and assertive and those who worry that, on the contrary, it will simply wither away. The first group might be reassured by the constraints on the military that come with being embedded in an alliance of democracies and the way that the modest forces of any individual CEE states soften the security dilemma for those on its borders (Jervis 1978). The second group might be reassured that no matter how thin the social commitment to the military, alliance obligations will ensure a certain minimum level of military competence, though for those who worry that the military is continually neglected, the evidence in chapters 4, 5, and 6 point to the difficulty the alliance has in holding CEE states to their agreements.

The SI–RI Synthesis: Political Barriers to Emulation

The EU occasionally asks things of CEE states that would impose significant costs on politicians or their clientele. In such cases, politicians must navigate between incentives from the institutional environment (SI) and those from powerful domestic interests and/or voters (RI). Given long traditions of "dissembling" in the face of ostensibly nonnegotiable Soviet demands (Jowitt 1978; 1992), how do CEE elites choose when to comply, when to openly resist EU demands, and when to simply agree on paper while shirking them in practice?

The broad pattern suggests that timing matters more than other kinds of variation. Once EU conditionality grew explicit in the late 1990s, we saw a general willingness of CEE representatives to agree, in principle, to almost everything that the EU demanded. Earlier, some nationalist regimes in CEE (e.g., Bulgaria and Romania) had largely ignored the EU *acquis*, while others (e.g., Slovakia) were undemocratic but surprisingly advanced in internalizing the *acquis*. But Czech and Hungarian elites, as front-runners in an accession process that was clearly some years away, had little incentive to openly resist the EU since promises cost them little. None of this prevented the Czech center right under Klaus and the Hungarian center right under Orbán from arguing that their now liberal societies feared that Brussels would reimpose soft forms of socialism and that national states needed to assert themselves and not assent to all demands. But during the screening of Czech and Hungarian laws, each state made remarkably few requests for derogations (temporary exceptions).

In many policy areas, elites found EU rules problematic or costly, but simply swallowed hard and assumed the Commission's position was nonnegotiable. Occasionally, attempts were made to adapt the *acquis* more fully to CEE conditions. We saw one such effort in consumer protection and the product liability standard. This standard protects producers from nuisance claims whose value is less than 500 euros. Hungarian Ministry of Economics officials argued that consumer protection laws might interest more Hungarian citizens if they contained a more realistic range of prices. They attempted to set a floor of 50 euros and hoped to request a derogation period of five years for the economy and living standards to rise high enough for the 500-euro threshold to become a meaningful one. However, the Hungarians withdrew their request when Commission officials warned them that such a change would be resisted by producer interests in the member states.

But some confrontations have occurred. The regional policy case noted the resistance of the Klaus government (continued for a time by the Social Democratic minority government) to the political decentralization demanded by the Commission. This was part of a larger pattern in which Klaus's "resistance against the political aspects of European integration became the foundation of officially sanctioned Euroskepticism. This two-sided approach consisted of intensive criticism of the EU as well as a perpetual presentation of the Czech Republic as the best prepared candidate for membership" (Neumayer 2000: 21). Similarly, the ODS vice chairman, Petr Nečas, has warned against sacrificing Czech national interests and national identity for "cheap pseudoeuropeanism."[6] And conflict erupted over the regional governments' attempts to create an "association of Czech regions," which presumably would give them a stronger voice in the Committee of Regions in Brussels. Klaus remarked, "We follow with bewilderment the efforts to create an Association of Czech Regions. We tried to explain to the governors that the association of Czech regions *is* the Czech Republic." Klaus argued further that "the representation of the regions of the Czech Republic in Brussels is in reality the Ministry of Foreign Affairs and the Czech Embassy. In no way is it the Association of Czech Regions."

As membership became more certain (or at least less dependent upon the appearance of institutional conformity), both states grew more assertive in the high-stakes final phase of negotiations. While the deal on regional policy was settled without major confrontations, this was not the case in agriculture. CEE states denounced Commission plans for phased-in direct payments and also the quotas that it had proposed for them. As we saw in chapter 3, the states gained modest improvement over the terms of Agenda 2000 (set in 1997), but not much more over the course of the final phase of negotiations. By and large, the outcomes reflected the weak bargaining hand held by the CEE states. Historically, new entrants have been able to "bargain up" on CAP entitlements once inside the EC.[7] This pattern will be hard for CEE states to continue, however. The main proponents of CAP reform – Germany, the Netherlands, Britain, and Sweden – were also the states most skeptical about extending direct payments to CEE. These states feared that such a move would solidify direct payments, which they wished to reduce. For these reasons, France and Spain were proponents of extending direct payments to CEE. To the extent that future CAP reforms push financing burdens back onto states, the fiscally strapped CEE states will be in a particularly difficult situation.

---

[6] Quotations in this paragraph are from *BBC Monitoring/ČTK* February 16, 2001. See also Yoder (2003).

[7] Historically, *all* new members have seen farm production rise after entering the CAP, though more-developed agricultural sectors have been stimulated more and faster than less-developed ones (Griffiths 2002).

In the defense sector, absent some clear geopolitical threat or some societal impulse for change from the inside, the only demand for reform has been one that was "simulated" by NATO. Yet once the CEE states were allowed to join, even this set of demands lost much of its force. The combination of weak electoral incentives (RI) and episodic demands from the institutional environment (SI) has opened the door for CEE states to develop two-tiered forces, in which showcase units are developed for any NATO contingency while other units starve for funds. The trend is especially clear in out-of-area peacekeeping missions, where the new NATO members have had to add some capabilities to contribute to NATO missions. Both the Czech Republic and Hungary have conserved on defense spending by singling out units earmarked for NATO operations for priority treatment (Barany 1998a: 13; Szayna and Larrabee 1995).

To be sure, two-tiered forces are present among existing NATO members. For example, Portugal is a longtime NATO member. Because its population is 9.9 million, both Czech and Hungarian officials often imply their contribution is comparable to that of Portugal. Like these states, Portugal, too, is in the process of abolishing conscription. Yet in terms of military spending and readiness, the Portuguese military is significantly ahead of Hungary and the Czech Republic. Its defense budget is $2.7 billion, which represents about 2.2% of its GDP and is much closer to Poland's expenditure than to the Czech Republic's (just over $1 billion), let alone Hungary's ($600 million). Nevertheless, Portugal's first airborne brigade, formed in 1994 as an elite unit, is NATO designated and has the latest equipment and training. Reserve units are indeed equipped with older, less capable weapons and training. Thus, it is not the *mere fact* of two-tiered forces in CEE, but their *extent* that is striking. Gutierrez reports that Hungary has divided one MiG-29 squadron of forty pilots into a group of twelve, who were designated as NATO qualified, though only two of them were qualified for both day and night missions (2002: 162). The remaining twenty-eight were designated part of the air defense system. The top Hungarian pilot flew 63 hours in 1997 and was scheduled for 45 in 1998. These figures compare to a NATO average of 160–180 hours per year for fighter pilots (see also Simon 1999; Dunay 2002b: 81; Barany 1999: 86).

It is also clear that engagement with NATO has driven CEE militaries to think much more in terms of power projection and to deemphasize territorial defense of their national borders (Forster, Edmunds, and Cottey 2002: 247–8). Dunay is blunt about the resulting danger, which is that "the Hungarian government ends up with the worst of both worlds – a defense force incapable of defending Hungarian airspace and territory, based on low-quality, poorly trained personnel and a small rapid reaction force capable of working with NATO, but adding little military capability to that force" (2002: 64). In the Czech case, Vlachová chronicles a "growing awareness in the MoD and the armed forces [that] the deployment of troops abroad is siphoning off too many personnel, is too expensive and is at the cost of a reduction of the fighting effectiveness of the ACR..." (2002: 42). Moreover, this is occurring at a time when only one-third of Czechs polled support Czech participation in foreign missions (Vlachová 2002: 41). In short, we see here states that face external demands that accord poorly with the wishes of their voters are doing the minimum necessary to meet these external demands.

The SI–HI Synthesis: Historical Barriers to Emulation

While it may be "rational" for elites to do whatever the EU asks of them, we would quickly face analytical problems if we supposed that CEE preferences are entirely externally driven. For example, it becomes difficult to explain why elites devote so much attention to some EU demands and so little to others. As the Czech regional policy case (and the whole previous section) demonstrated, this effort can hardly be read off of the intensity of the EU's external demands alone. Often, HI insights are crucial complements to the SI demands emanating from the institutional environment of the IOs. Above all, each case can help us see the ways in which CEE elites can sometimes promise reforms that historical constraints keep them from fulfilling. The pragmatic juxtaposition of SI and HI is thus the third broad theme.

Regional policy is a case in point, for the states vary. Hungary has a far more robust history of spatial planning than do the Czech lands, and prior to 1990 it already had an embryonic system for helping weak areas (Bachtler and Downes 1999: 804). It has been the most aggressive CEE country in developing a regional policy system that is EU compatible and capable of affecting regional disparities. On the other hand, the newer EU-driven administrative borders have not always matched the old voluntaristic agglomerations of counties. Some countries joined more than one regional development council and some joined none (Dieringer and Moisa 2001: 545). Thus the EU-driven pattern is not wholly consistent with the traditional administrative pattern. Moreover, Hungary did not integrate its RP apparatus into state administrative structures. Instead it built it much more around NGOs and ad hoc local organizations that some observers worry might be too "artificial" and degenerate into "political bargaining" (Dieringer and Moisa 2001: 554–5). Even so, Hungarian RDCs seem significantly more competent than their Czech counterparts (Downes 2000: 336). Thus, the Hungarian state can already off-load certain tasks that the Czech state cannot.[8]

In agriculture, path dependency in the face of stiff external demands is also ubiquitous. Take the crucial case of improving food quality, which demonstrates again the ways in which inherited farm structures condition the implementation of EU rules. In Hungary, the costs of complying with the *acquis* in dairy quality are much more difficult for small producers to bear than for large producers. Overall, 78% of Hungarian milk met EU quality standards in 1999, and this was up from only 28% in 1991. But the vast majority of this improvement has taken place in large enterprises and co-ops. Small farms, often with less than five cows, provide almost one-third of Hungarian milk production, yet pose two serious dilemmas. First, and contrary to EU rules, they often have no quality sampling system on site. Rather, milk quality is typically sampled only at collection centers (Kiss and Weingarten 2002: 9). Second, many small farms need new investment to attain EU standards. While large farms already in "good" compliance would need to invest only 0.8% of their 2000 average gate receipts for milk (which averaged 24 cents per liter), farms with less than five cows and in "bad" compliance would have to invest 13–18% of their receipts to achieve adequate modernization (14). Along with the earlier data about access to credit in the Czech case, the anecdote underscores the point that history constrains the ability of certain classes of actors to conform to demands underscored by SI theory.

The consumer protection case offers a different illustration. Consumers are notoriously difficult to organize, and CEE consumer protection organizations started slowly. Some Czech MTI officials argue that this is because "bad experience with organizations during communism has soured people on working in voluntary organizations" (Kočová interview; Tržický interview). As late as 2000, "no formal consultation procedures [exist] whereby consumer representatives are able to express their views on consumer law and policy relevant to state bodies" (Pritchard

---

[8] On the other hand, both states share the legacy that communist ministries were *sectoral* fiefdoms, so *regional* authority is hard to pry away from existing ministries. Many ministries retain control of "ancillary" activities that have huge spatial implications. See Downes (2000: 337–8). Also, when national offices for central planning were eliminated, plan organizations embedded in individual ministries survived. By 1993 in Hungary, there were twenty-six different funds being operated by ten different ministries (Horváth 1998: 100).

2000a: 43). But if history constrains, it does not determine. The weakness of Czech consumer organizations cannot be explained only by the communist past since, in Slovakia, a similar history has not prevented the rise of a consumer movement in the early 1990s. While there is still no single national organization for Czech consumers, EU influences have strengthened those that do exist. For example, Czech consumer associations were not allowed to take actions to court under the old civil code. At the EU's urging, the Czech state amended that code in January 2003 (Luhanová interview). In Hungary, reform communism allowed space for groups that did not exist in Czechoslovakia. The Hungarian National Consumer Council (OFE), formed in 1982, is one of the oldest consumer groups in the entire region.[9] It functions today as an umbrella organization – which the Czechs do not have – and itself helps fund many of the country's fledgling consumer organizations.

The new norms versus old patterns dilemma is least difficult in health care, where the SI factors arrive through the voluntary embrace of Western practices. There is no consensus at all on what constitutes modernity or best practices in this policy domain, and Western health care systems are characterized by significant heterogeneity. But historical factors have still been constraining. The universalism of socialist health care has made it difficult to later inject fiscal considerations into policy deliberations about health reforms (Kornai and Eggleston 2001). We saw that elite reluctance to ask citizens to make out-of-pocket payments to their providers has persistently attenuated the provider payment systems and contributed to insolvency and overuse of services. Socialist overinvestment in hospital care has stalled efforts to develop greater reliance on (generally less expensive) primary care. "Missing capacity" matters too; where advanced capitalist economies saw positive spillovers into health care from organizational innovations in industrial production and customer service, neither the industrial nor service sectors in CEE states have lent such dynamism to their social sectors (Figueras, McKee, and Lessof 2002: 6–16). In short, the role of history is ubiquitous but not easily predictable in the nondefense sectors: it refracts, delays, or blocks outright some external impulses, and is reinforced by others.

In the defense sector, we also see CEE responses to external demands heavily mediated by the peculiarities of their histories. The NATO *Study*

---

[9] This body was reorganized in 1991 as the National Association for Consumer Protection in Hungary (known by its Hungarian acronym of OFE).

on Enlargement, a key agenda-setting document in terms of how NATO would approach enlargement, was, in retrospect, written on the cusp of a new era. Though longer in its gestation, that era began in the spring and summer in 1995. In May, Serbian forces captured and held hostage seventy-two French UN soldiers, paving the way for a shift in French policy led by new president Jacques Chirac. In July, Serb forces under Ratko Mladic massacred as many as 7,000 Bosnian boys and men from the UN "safe area" of Srebrenica, and again, the UN soldiers had been sent by a NATO member (the Netherlands). Together, these events roused NATO to military action, first in 1995 to lift the siege of Sarajevo and then in 1999 over Serbian pressures on Kosovo. These combat experiences underscored for key NATO members (above all, Britain and the United States) that each member had both a diplomatic and a military role in the conflict. Ideally, each state would support the NATO common position in both ways.

Thus, while NATO has made many institutional demands on its new members, they were also subject to an expectation of policy discipline. Early on, Czech and Hungarian elites hoped to meet both sets of expectations by being good peacekeepers (Gorka 1995; Szayna 1999). For example, both Törő and Blinken show that debates in the Hungarian parliament in late 1995 suggested that rapid participation in Implementation Force (IFOR) might help Hungary curry favor with NATO (Törő 2001: 140–1; Blinken 1999). But this approach had limits for both states. The Czechs, with a population of 10 million, have 700 peacekeepers abroad, compared to Belgium, with a similar population, but over twice as many peacekeepers (1,500) in the field (Cottey, Edmunds, and Forster 2002a: 3).

As NATO members came to see the full measure of the Czech and Hungarian defense establishments, they grew less inclined to expect a real military contribution. At the same time, they did ask for diplomatic support and policy loyalty. Thus, NATO's recognition of the HI factors blocking real defense reform led it to refashion its key demands (SI) to stress the policy loyalty of CEE states. Because NATO works by consensus, at the end of the day, every policy has formal "unanimous" support. But the CEE states felt it imperative to get on board before the consensus was fully formed. As we saw above, in their first big test in Kosovo, one state essentially passed – providing helpful air access and diplomatic support – while the other was considered a political liability by many member states. Access to bases remains a key consideration, and the

Hungarian's main contribution during Kosovo was the provision of Taszar air base. Czech facilities, while not as valuable as Taszar, may prove helpful in a variety of future military contingencies (Szayna 1999: 142–43).

The demands for policy loyalty have gotten stronger in the wake of September 11th as the Bush administration in the United States has downplayed the institutional criteria for membership. CEE states have been responsive, as they were quick to support NATO's extension of Article 5 to the United States, showing none of the reluctance of a few older members (e.g., Belgium). This dynamic extended even beyond the three new members, as Bulgaria and Slovakia essentially pledged to act as if they were supporting Article 5 on behalf of the United States, even though they were not then members of NATO. Moreover, all three new members in CEE joined Britain, Spain, Italy, Portugal, and Denmark in publishing an open letter in support of U.S. President George W. Bush's policy toward Iraq (*Christian Science Monitor*, January 31, 2003).[10] The Polish Foreign Minister had indicated by late January that Poland would take part in a war with Iraq even without a UN Resolution, and Bulgaria, the only CEE state then on the UN Security Council, indicated very early on that it would support the U.S. position at the UN. Meanwhile, the Czech Republic, in keeping with the niche forces doctrine, had agreed to send a 400-person anti–chemical warfare unit, as well as open its air space to U.S. forces. And Hungary granted, albeit reluctantly, the U.S. access to Taszar once again, this time to train 3,000 Iraqi exiles (*Guardian*, January 24, 2003).[11]

Of course, CEE states did not direct these latter gestures of support at NATO as a whole but rather at the United States and Great Britain. NATO, after all, was deeply divided on the Iraq issue. France and Germany led the resistance to U.S. and British policy on Iraq, and they interpreted several of the CEE gestures as contrary to what they characterized as the European and, indeed, the EU line, even though the EU developed no official "common position." German officials grumbled about the damage to European solidarity, but French President Jacques Chirac went farther, fuming that the CEE states "could hardly have found a better way" of "[diminishing] their chances of entering Europe" (*Transitions*

---

[10] For example, Hungarian Foreign Minister Ferenc Juhász said that if the United States finalized a plan for missile defense, Hungary would participate in it (*Interfax Hungary Business News Service*, January 2003: 14).

[11] As it turned out, far fewer Iraqi volunteers materialized, and the camp graduated less than 150 trainees before being dismantled, to the obvious relief of the Medgyessy government (*Transitions Online*, April 10, 2003).

Online, February 24, 2003). CEE leaders and media reacted strongly, with Latvian President Vaira Vike-Freiberga noting that "we have not heard of any accession criterion that we can be seen but not heard" (*Transitions Online*, February 24, 2003). British Prime Minister Tony Blair and EU Commissioner for Enlargement Günther Verheugen (of Germany) both publicly underscored the CEE states' right to speak their mind within the EU.

In part, CEE states understood solidarity with the United States as an opportunity to improve their image with the United States in the wake of the events of the Kosovo crisis. But it was also notable how ambivalent was Czech and Hungarian support for U.S. policy. In the Czech Republic, President Václav Havel signed the letter of support for U.S. policy, giving Prime Minister Vladimír Špidla the chance to play it both ways by having the Czech Republic (but not the government) as a signatory. Havel's term expired within a week of signing the letter, and the Foreign Minister, Cyril Svoboda, simply noted that it was within "the president's powers" to sign the letter (*Transitions Online*, February 3, 2003). The Hungarian right (Fidesz) criticized Péter Medgyessy's socialist government for signing the letter without informing the parliamentary Foreign Affairs Committee and implied that this omission made the letter merely the Prime Minster's personal opinion.

Unlike the EU, where the *acquis* was manipulated by member states and the Commission but was concrete and highly institutional, NATO demands are much more fluid and have, in recent years, reflected demands for policy loyalty more than for military competence. The benefits to CEE states of the more exclusive emphasis on policy loyalty is that states like Bulgaria are invited to join NATO even though their military readiness is below even what was evident in the Czech Republic and Hungary. But the CEE states still face a stiff challenge given the deep divides between Europe and the United States on issues such as the International Criminal Court and NATO policy toward Iraq. If NATO falls apart or drifts farther toward irrelevance, the CEE states may be forced to choose even more often between their distant patrons in the United States and their local patrons within Europe.[12]

---

[12] In July 2003, all EU CEE candidate countries except Romania refused to sign nonextradition treaties with the United States exempting U.S. military personnel from prosecution before the controversial International Criminal Court. In response, the Bush administration cut military aid to thirty-five states by a total of $50 million.

INSTITUTIONAL THEORY: SUPPLY, REASON, SYNTHESIS

The argument that institutional change comes when its motors are stronger than its brakes cannot help us adjudicate which form of institutionalism comes closest to a meta-theory of politics. Instead, my purpose has been to show that emulation has many facets and that it cannot be reduced to IO imperialism, CEE dissembling, mindless imitation, or the mechanical spread of best practices.

This book has primarily used institutional theory to illuminate its cases, but there are also ways in which the cases at hand illuminate the theories. Most theories of institutions are demand-side theories, stressing the desires and designs of political actors. Such theories need not be explicitly functionalist or claim that institutions are merely the design of the powerful. But a focus on the demand for institutions, however subtle and rich the account, is likely to be incomplete. We have seen the importance of institutional supply as a major determinant of institutions in CEE. The availability of institutional templates – some ready-made and some in need of adaptation – has not made demand factors irrelevant. But it has given direction to many inchoate demands, strengthened weak demands, and occasionally mobilized largely new demands.

The book's core argument is built around a rationalist approach to institutional change – emphasizing those aspects of SI and HI that focus on the incentives of elites. It differs from an RI account of institutional formation, however, in that one key RI premise is that institutions reflect the aggregate micro-motives of individual actors (often through interaction with other actors). In these cases, that claim has been treated as broadly plausible, but hopelessly abstract. Given elite desires to get credit for helping their country into the EU and NATO, they have agreed to almost any reforms the IOs have demanded. But these reforms are too numerous and specific to be driven by any plausible projection of domestic interests. When all the items on a menu are largely unfamiliar, one cannot really choose in the same way one can with a menu of familiar items. To be sure, such choices are not hollow, but we have seen how significantly those choices are constrained and how detailed are the constraints.

The result is that rationality is embedded. It is embedded sociologically in that specific norms come to fill in the details of institutional reform that has no real indigenous motor (or which often runs up against actors that have different ideas). Rationality is also embedded historically in the sense that CEE elites sometimes agree to steps that are too bold for their histories. The case selection has shown us both cases in which the thinness of precedent leaves the emulated structures with no indigenous foundation, as well as cases in which the thickness of history poses a stiff challenge to the emulated rules and organizations. The purpose of the book is to explain what happens when each of these situations arises. A key claim is that in both situations, the generation of elite reason is highly contingent, and the pursuit of reason is highly constrained.

This chapter has sought to demonstrate the utility of various combinations of the three theories. It did so not by matching the facts of the case to the factors identified by any one complete theory tradition. Rather, it used truncated and lean versions of the theories in particular configurations with one another. This chapter concludes with three broader and briefer conclusions expressed in a similar format. These three conclusions are the indigenous capacity for change, the mismatch between organizational complexity and citizen demand, and the gap between commitments and implementation. Together, they help us see larger common patterns in the often very different EU and NATO dynamics.

The HI–RI Synthesis: CEE Capacities for Indigenous Change

One great danger of a book about emulation is that it could leave the impression that CEE states cannot reform without outside help. That impression would be wrong. And yet we would not see these particular changes, with this commitment of resources, and this level of coordination absent the interventions of these two major IOs. The SI heuristic of the institutional environment has helped describe the imperatives that come from the IOs. But we saw that some reform would have happened without such imperatives. In the NATO case, for example, the combination of RI and HI factors alone helped generate niche military forces. These were a second-best outcome; RI veto positions made full commitment to NATO norms impossible, but HI capacities did give a foundation for some contribution to collective security, though modest. This outcome was acceptable to NATO both because it seemed to have little other choice and because many of NATO's tasks can indeed be filled by a division of labor among different national militaries. In fact, the planned NATO Rapid Reaction Force envisions just such a division of labor.

In the EU, however, states cannot easily avoid their obligations by making a small contribution to some supranational division of labor. They have to catch up somehow. In all of the policy areas where CEE states had significant existing capacity – health, defense, and agriculture – we do see emulation occurring. While these areas could have functioned (and reformed) without emulation, they were also capable – once the decision was taken – of animating the new structures in ways that seem impossible in either consumer protection or regional policy.

The SI–RI Synthesis: Gap Between Organizational Complexity and Citizen Demand

The IO demands have created a gap between the organizational complexity of CEE states and the political demands of their citizens. As far as Czech and Hungarian citizens are concerned, few feel they have asked for many of the changes that occupy their politicians. The result is doubly worrisome. From the perspective of the IOs, some of the institutions seem inauthentic. From the CEE perspective, the greater worry is that it hollows out democratic institutions. Here, no institution has suffered like the parliaments, whose work has been severely distorted in the run-up to membership. In each state, parliament has lost substantial control of its agenda to actors outside its own government. Both the EU and NATO (though to a lesser extent) have been able to influence the legislative agenda and, mainly through thresholds, have significant leverage over the resulting legislation. In both states, we have seen a decline in delegation to committees and lost opportunities to promote specialization and expertise among parliamentarians. At times, floor debate has shrunk to remarkable levels. In 1999, with NATO membership just around the corner, the Czech parliament debated its new security strategy for all of five minutes. The hope now is that democratic traditions built in the several years before EU and NATO demands arose will regain strength in the early years of IO membership (Vachudova 2004).

The HI–SI Synthesis: Gap Between Commitments and Implementation

History constrains CEE states' ability to keep their promises. Just as the democratization literature spawned subsequent work on consolidation, so too will the emulation literature require work on implementation. The EU has tried to use screening and negotiations to prevent CEE commitments that cannot or will not be kept. In its second round of enlargement, NATO realized its mistake in round one and used the Membership Action Plans to conduct a variant of the screening process, though absent both the personnel and budget to do so adequately. In conducting implementation research, scholars would do well to remember that current member states do not keep all their promises either, and that Eastern and

Western European differences are likely to be of degree rather than of kind (Iankova and Katzenstein 2003).

If both IOs have long fretted about the potential implementation gap, that gap is only partially responsive to the will and skill of CEE officials. In the NATO case, we saw that the combination of external demands and historical constraints had resulted in CEE policy loyalty as a fallback position to the broader defense modernization that NATO initially demanded. The fundamentally different nature of the EU and its insistence that the *acquis* be implemented fully made such a fallback position impossible for it to accept. In some cases, EU negotiations produced derogations that will allow CEE states to move gradually toward EU standards. Such concessions were very important in the environmental *acquis*, for example. From an HI perspective, however, competent public administration might be the single most important factor differentiating cases where public officials engage in careful adjustment of Western models or lurch haphazardly from one quick fix to the next (Locke 1995: 15–25; Dorf and Sabel 1998). Here, the quality of public administration seems to vary cross-nationally more than by policy domains within a given nation (Nunberg 1999; O'Dwyer 2002). Notwithstanding the common challenges of low pay, constant personnel turnover, and inadequate interministerial coordination, some public administrations seem much more likely to be able to implement the *acquis* than others (Meyer-Sahling 2002; Jacoby 2002b: 146–7).[13] Meanwhile, across policy areas, the concern is that we see the most aggressive use of emulation – especially through patches – in those areas where states are least likely to be able to implement it.

---

[13] The most worrisome constant is the low esteem in which CEE citizens hold their national administrations. Eurobarometer data shows that CEE citizens "tend to trust" the EU at much higher levels than do citizens of member states. But they trust their own administrations much less. This is worrisome because EU rules are implemented by national governments. If citizens distrust them, these governments may be further disadvantaged in trying to implement the *acquis*.

8

Extensions and Conclusions

> The desire to achieve the standards of Western Europe, or in more general
> terms to modernize society along the lines pioneered by Western civilization,
> has been the chief motivating force in the history of modern Bulgaria.
>
> (Black 1957: 7)

Whether or not this epigraph remains plausible nearly a half century after
it was written, it is clear that the postcommunist Czechs and Hungarians are hardly novel in their approximations of Western practices and
structures. In a region long characterized by "backwardness," Western
European states have often appeared as models for reform (Janos 2000).

But we have seen that emulation is both hard to do and hard to describe. It is hard to do because elites must do more than simply copy best
practices. Rather, they must understand how attractive foreign models
actually work, agree with other actors on the desirability of emulating
them, and be able to execute their plans (Jacoby 2000). All of these are
challenges. It is easy to misperceive how foreign models actually work –
to see only their virtues and miss their vices. Actors must overcome political disagreements about the desirability and appropriateness of particular foreign models for their society. And actors must persevere through
difficulties in implementing foreign-inspired practices and designs. Unfortunately, the major macrosociological and political science research
tradition – that of diffusion – has a markedly difficult time with these
complexities since it blends out uncertainty and disagreement in favor of
tracking the spread of highly stylized models and generally ignores the
implementation phase altogether.

Emulation is hard to describe because it is difficult to isolate from other influences on institutions. Three problems stand out. The first is one of institutional antecedents. When examining the impact of Western models, we have had to disentangle their effects from those of indigenous models and from the Soviet institutional legacies and even the Austro-German designs that have also left their mark in the region. The second issue is of diffuse contributions. With multiple actors at the scene of institutional creation – both under late-communist-era roundtables and postcommunist pluralism – we have had to show the relative importance of Western models while acknowledging the importance of other factors' influence on choices and outcomes. The third difficulty is that we must distinguish between paper changes and real effects. To have emphasized only formal structural similarities could have led to an exaggeration of the importance of Western models.[1]

For all these reasons, emulation makes a better dependent variable than it does an independent variable. For some of the same reasons, it also is not fruitful to set up "external pressures" or "international imperatives" as *alternative explanations* of economic and political change in CEE. Some efforts to contrast external pressures to the weight of "Leninist legacies" eventually abandon the claim that these are real alternatives (Crawford and Lijphart 1995: 194–6; Stark and Bruszt 1998: 5–8). For example, Crawford and Lijphart conclude that ideological, sociological, and institutional legacies of the past are actually filtered by contemporary external pressures. This book has explored exactly that linkage between environmental pressures and national choices, but has abandoned at the outset the conceit that external pressures are best conceptualized as a freestanding alternative explanation to domestic reform processes.[2]

ORDERING FROM THE MENU: A SUMMARY OF THE CASES

Chapter 2 began with cases in which the EU made relatively light demands. The health case underscored that the West was often attractive in CEE independent of any inducements to promote emulation. To return to the book's initial menu analogy, CEE states tended to order à la carte in

---

[1] Conversely, emulation may occur down in the inner workings of an organization so that surface differences in organizational appearance – "national diversity" – mask a deeper organizational homogenization.
[2] In this, my approach is far closer to what Ira Katznelson (1997) has labeled "configurational" approaches to comparative politics.

health care, picking and choosing those individual items with appeal and not hesitating to make substitutions. We saw that a rough consensus developed early in the transition that CEE states should remove health care spending from the general fund and go "back to Bismarck" by setting up insurance-based funds found in much of Western Europe. Institutional learning was an iterative process here, in which initial emulation efforts were often followed up by protracted efforts at adaptation to local circumstance, especially in the various systems of provider payments. Absent external pressure, there was more adaptive learning in this case than in others considered.

The EU has a somewhat more substantial consumer-protection *acquis*, and this case developed the notion of CEE actors homesteading a new policy area. This policy area is not among the first rank in EU priorities – with the partial exception of food safety – and it has been even less so in CEE. Here, the menu items seemed exotic, expensive, and sometimes frivolous, but each CEE state ordered enough to satisfy the minimum table charge and generally avoided rousing the ire of the chef in doing so. The open question is what these states will do with what they have ordered. For now, CEE consumer-protection organizations have little influence over a wide range of problems that affect consumers.

In chapter 3, we saw policy areas that comprise the vast bulk of the EU budget – regional policies and agriculture. The major EU programs (structural funds and the CAP) are both administratively demanding. Regional policy, like consumer protection, had little indigenous architecture in the CEE states, yet because the EU was investing large sums of money in the programs, the result was not isolated homesteading with small outposts of activity. Rather, the EU programs and money provided structures around which local interests could and did congeal. It was an odd outcome – essentially one in which the EU programs, which were meant to be side dishes, instead became the main courses.

In agriculture, by contrast, actors were already well established in the policy sector. Despite a lot of talk about the implications of the CAP, remarkably little legislative or organizational emulation occurred until late in the decade. In part, this was because property structures were undergoing very significant changes during privatization, but it was also because the sectoral interests were able to pursue business as usual. CEE politicians had little reason to implement full CAP-like policies unless the EU was funding them. Only in the run-up to final negotiations have we seen a rush of activity to prepare for the CAP. The major CEE concern has been with limits that the EU would place on the CAP. Their prime fear was that CEE farmers would get more or less what they envisioned when they ordered, except that the portions would be far too small to satisfy them.

In chapter 4, we saw that the Western priority for civilian control of the military generated some significant resentments on the part of CEE militaries, who had to endure suspicion of their political behavior at a time when their budgets, quality of life, and levels of preparedness were falling precipitously. These resentments ultimately were managed in both states, though this was more difficult in Hungary. But both the de jure and de facto guarantees of military obedience fall far short of securing a healthy civil–military interaction in the two states. In civilian control, CEE states thought they were ordering an item long familiar to them from their own kitchens. But the dish has surprised them all with its real differences, and while some relevant actors have acquired a taste for it, others suffer from indigestion.

Chapter 5 then showed that the audit of war revealed a number of shortcomings in the area of military professionalism. It further showed that the CEE states continue to make heavy use of emulation even after becoming full members. Some of this emulation is responsive to electoral currents inside their societies (e.g., all-volunteer forces), and other examples continue to flow from NATO pressures (e.g., building NCO corps). The EU is a bizarre "you must eat everything" buffet. Compared to that, NATO is basically a Spanish tapas bar, where one makes (sometimes quite impulsive) selections from a long list of small snacks. Indeed, in response to postcommunist needs, NATO has developed a menu of scores of small programs to promote reform in one military field or another. CEE states pick among the long list of relatively minor potential reforms and see where their appetite and budget take them.[3]

EXTENSIONS I: MOVING BEYOND THE MOST SIMILAR AND MOST LIKELY CASES

We have seen remarkable variation across policy areas and relatively modest variation across states. In part, this pattern is an artifact of the largely homogenous demands placed on CEE states by the EU and NATO. But it is also an artifact of the book's research design, which focused on two front-running postcommunist states. The "most similar–most likely"

---

[3] Most of these programs are carried out by NATO-member states, and in some cases these states will cofinance the projects with CEE states.

design has the enormous benefit of allowing some semblance of control over many potential confounding variables (Collier and Adcock 2001; Jupille, Caporaso, and Checkel 2003; Snyder 2001; King, Keohane, and Verba 1994). The costs of this research strategy are that efforts to generalize the findings may be vulnerable to a series of important objections. In order to assess the generalizability of the model, this section explores four potential influences on the causal mechanisms already explored. Each influence is plausible, and we should look for it especially in cases where its effects are likely to be strongest and, hence, most visible. Each of these potential variables – size, distance, historical backwardness, and historical success – is well established in the theoretical literature on diffusion (Strang and Soule 1998).

Poland: How Much Does Size Matter?

The research design highlights variation across policy areas more than variation across states, yet it would be implausible to simply assert that the Czech and Hungarian findings translate directly to Poland as well. Though it was also a fairly consistent front-runner for EU and, especially, NATO membership, the Polish case differs along many dimensions. This section looks at just one of those differences, namely, that the Polish agriculture sector is far bigger, in both relative and absolute terms, than the Czech or Hungarian sectors.[4] In the budget allocations for the 2000–6 period, the Commission envisioned that fully 30–37% of total ISPA spending would go to Poland (and another 20–26% to Romania, the other populous CEE state).[5] SAPARD aid for 2000 in Poland was 169 million euros compared to 38 million for Hungary and 22 million for the Czech Republic (*Uniting Europe*, July 26, 1999: 2). This size difference increased the struggle over policy, but it did not, by and large, change the modes or outcomes of emulation.

Poland has almost four times the population of Hungary or the Czech Republic. Its agricultural sector is, in proportional terms, larger still, with 20–30% of the population being dependent upon agriculture.[6] How does this large size affect the prospects for emulation? Commission officials

---

[4] Poland's agricultural sector was never significantly collectivized, and enormous numbers of family farms remain, especially in the southern regions.

[5] The range is supposed to provide incentives for states to manage the funds properly.

[6] Yet agriculture accounts for less than 5% of Polish GDP, which is only slightly above the Czech and Hungarian levels noted in chapter 3.

have often acknowledged the effect of Poland's size on the enlargement. For example, Commissioner for Enlargement Günter Verheugen noted that Poland was the "key country" for agriculture and that it needed a firm and coherent policy for sectoral reform before the EU could even formulate its own proposals for the rest of CEE: "How can we [the EU] agree on solutions for the remaining candidates if we do not know whether it is compatible with the Polish situation? Therefore, we have an interest in trying to get Poland in the first wave of accession" (quoted in *Uniting Europe*, March 27, 2000: 2).

Yet for all the anxiety it provoked in Brussels, this size did not mean that emulation occurred in a different way. Indeed, the pattern of emulation in Polish agriculture is very similar to that in Hungary and the Czech Republic precisely because the same incentives held: The national state had little reason to emulate CAP programs in advance of membership because it would have been prohibitively expensive. For example, in the early 1990s, Polish farmers grew around 8.5 million hectares of grain annually at a time when low grain prices would have required the state to pay farmers "deficiency payments" of about 180 euros per acre *had the EU rules applied then*.[7] Even ignoring administrative costs, this would have required 1.5 billion euros for cereals alone during a period in which the total outlay for *all* Polish market support programs was well under one-third of this total (Johnson 1997: 51). Of course, like Hungary and the Czech Republic, Poland did need to prepare for the CAP by creating the organizations to apply the EU's direct effects policy instruments once membership was achieved.[8]

But if Poland faced exactly the same key EU thresholds in agriculture as the other CEE states – for example, sanitary standards, agricultural market regulations, and the environmental impact of agriculture – its size did affect the Polish governments' incentives to challenge the EU's agricultural regime more directly. The struggles noted in the earlier agriculture cases were, therefore, even more pronounced. For example, Poland had several high-profile trade disputes with the EU. In 1997 the EU briefly banned the import of Polish dairy products on the grounds that some dairy standards did not meet EU levels. In 1998, it cut off negotiations with Poland when

---

[7] A deficiency payment is a state compensation to farmers for market prices that are lower than some agreed-upon guarantee price. The lower the actual market price, the higher is the state payment to make up that "deficiency."

[8] For a fascinating account of the distributive effects of these apparently technical standards in Poland, see Dunn (2002).

the latter raised agricultural tariffs to WTO levels without notifying the EU as per the Europe Agreement. When Hungary and the Czech Republic concluded the "double-zero" negotiations with the EU in June 2000, the EU ceased its export subsidies for pork and milk products shipped to those countries. No agreement was reached with Poland, however, and the export subsidies remained in place (*Uniting Europe*, June 26, 2000: 11). This impasse was not broken until September 2000. Finally, in 2001, the EU Scientific Steering Committee named Poland a BSE ("mad cow") risk – ironically, because it had imported 100,000 tons of meat and bone meal from Germany just before several cases of BSE were discovered there (*Uniting Europe*, March 5, 2001: 10–11).

The sector's size allowed it to mobilize around agricultural issues in ways that went beyond the other two states considered. Indeed, Polish agriculture has been better represented in its own parliament than any other agricultural sector in CEE. Both the Peasant Party (PSL) and three relatively well-established agricultural trade unions (Farmers Solidarity, the National Union of Farmers, and the Union of Self-Defense) have played significant roles in public-policy formation. The PSL is one of only two parties to gain election to the lower house in each of the first three postcommunist elections and formed a part of the government (with the Democratic Left Alliance) from 1993–7 and 2001–3.[9] Pressure from farmers has produced significant state intervention and strong support for farmers in international negotiations (Sharman 2003: 15–16). Polish PSE levels have been positive – indicating a net transfer of resources from taxpayers and consumers to farmers – every year of the transition except 1990.[10]

One of the trade unions, Self-Defense (Samoobrona), rose to become the third strongest party in the Sejm by 2001. Its fiery populist leader Andrzej Lepper liked to argue that "the distance from Warsaw to Moscow is the same as to Brussels." Lepper asserted that "Moscow wanted us to produce a lot, and then they took everything from us. Brussels wants us to do the opposite: to import" (quoted in *Transitions Online*, December 21, 2001: 3). Demonstrations by various combinations of the three unions during the winter of 1998–9 led to clashes with police in which dozens were injured and, in March 1999, to the resignation of the Minister of

---

[9] In spring 2003, SLD Prime Minister Leszek Miller dismissed the Peasant Party from his coalition government only three months before the Polish referendum on the EU. The referendum later passed 77–23%, with a turnout of 59%.

[10] Polish PSE levels since the mid-1990s have ranged from 18 to 25, close to levels in both the Czech and Hungarian cases and in the EU overall.

Agriculture. These struggles extended both to internecine battles among the unions – especially between Lepper and National Union of Farmers leader Wladyslaw Serafin – and between the unions and the cabinet – with Lepper denouncing cabinet members as "idiots," "bandits," and "scum" (quoted in Sharman 2003: 16). For a time, it appeared that agricultural populists like Lepper would openly oppose the Copenhagen negotiations, but after a round of vitriolic denunciations, the major farm groups eventually assented to membership (Epstein 2004). It also appears that while such wrangling likely increased the Polish government's responsiveness to farmers (and led it to push back against the EU in ways noted above), in the end the mobilization did not bring a better deal from Brussels. About the only concession that Polish agriculture could point to after Copenhagen was a special agricultural fund for Polish farmers but which, crucially, was paid for out of funds previously allocated for Polish regional policy.[11] At best, this mobilization succeeded in shifting EU commitments from one area to another.

Even after Copenhagen, EU disputes with Poland over agriculture continue. Poland lags in the introduction of the IACS system described in chapter 3, along with systems to register both farmland and animals and improve veterinary standards, border controls, and animal welfare. The EU has threatened that if problems are not resolved, it may simply withhold payments to Polish farmers. Both Poland and the Czech Republic asked for transitional periods to set up the IACS, but the Commission denied these. Agriculture Commissioner Franz Fischler noted that the "IACS is non-negotiable. It has to be working before you can even think about implementing the policies" (*Uniting Europe*, July 2, 2001: 10).

In sum, size helps explain the particular difficulties of the Polish route to agricultural reform, and size made struggles over emulation much more visible. But it did not obviously change the outcomes of emulation. Size did not change either the entry conditions Poland faced, nor the timing and modes of emulations that we had observed in the Czech and Hungarian cases. Size mattered most in shaping the deal the EU offered. In particular, the phased-in direct payments were in no small part a response to the sheer costs of supporting so many Polish farmers. Of course, the size of the agricultural sector has had an enormous influence on domestic politics in Poland, but for all that influence (and for its vociferous protests against the

[11] Polish negotiators secured a special "cash flow facility" that provided Polish agriculture with 1 billion euros; the primary gain was not having to apply for the money in the future.

EU proposals), it seems to have had relatively little ability to generate more concessions from the EU. Thus, Poland's size likely shaped the conditions of accession for all entrants (in a negative way) much more than it shaped the character of emulation.

Bulgaria: Do Imperial Legacies Matter?

Does it matter for regional policy – which relies heavily on state administration – if a country was part of the Ottoman rather than Habsburg empire? The idea is certainly plausible. Clearly, the Ottomans practiced a novel form of state administration, especially the so-called millet system, in which each administrative unit ruled subjects who generally shared the same religion. The system helped produce long periods of peaceful coexistence among such bounded communities, though it often confronted religious minorities (who often were also ethnic minorities) with the options of assimilating or leaving. Bulgaria is a good case, since it was under Ottoman rule continuously from the fourteenth century until winning independence in 1878. Its population of just under 9 million makes it roughly comparable in size to both the Czech Republic and Hungary, and like them it is also a unitary state. Yet much more than the Czechs and Hungarians, Bulgarians have perceived themselves as outside of Western Europe and trying to get in, as noted in the epigraph to this chapter.

There are two major versions of the Ottoman legacies thesis. For most commentators, the Ottoman legacy is unambiguously negative. For example, Diamandouros and Larrabbee (2000) explicitly contrast a relatively modernized and enlightened Habsburg monarchy, whose power was checked by "powerful intermediate bodies" like the nobility, with the patrimonial and later "sultanic" forms of Ottoman rule. Where Ottoman patrimonialism was personalistic, it was at least legitimized and constrained by tradition. By the nineteenth century, however, the sultanic forms of rule threw off even the constraints of tradition so that personal rule was almost completely unchecked (2000: 30–1).

The result was a dual legacy: Nations that achieved their independence during this sultanistic period were essentially infected with similar "sultanistic logics concerning governance and administration," including regional and local ones (2000: 30). Moreover, the emphasis on "in-group solidarity," underscored by the millet system, led to a strong distrust of political division and a subsequent challenge to the development of pluralism. Diamandouros and Larrabbee deny that these legacies are "deterministic," immovable barriers to democratic reforms, but see them as constraints that any future reformers would have to confront (2000: 35). These legacies would be negative for the kind of regional policy that we have seen the EU promote in CEE, for this requires both subnational state administrations with reputations for planning competence and impartiality as well as engaged civic groups that can act in some sort of partnership role.

For other scholars, the Ottoman legacy is more mixed.[12] Meeker stresses that Ottoman rule was built on what he calls a "state-oriented provincial oligarchy." The Ottoman system encouraged (sometimes without explicitly meaning to do so) interpersonal networks built around local elites who were both "available and unavoidable" as agents of the central government (2002: 110; see also Barany 2002: 20–5). A key claim is that these networks, laid down primarily in the seventeenth century, set real limits on later modernizing reforms.[13] The constraints take two forms. First, these networks of local elites came to be endowed with significant enough power – to "tax commerce, raise armies, requisition supplies, impose labor, apprehend fugitives, and exact punishment" (Meeker 2002: xx) – that they often could defy the central state. Second, these interpersonal networks could accommodate themselves to modernizing reforms (including ones explicitly meant to weaken them). From this perspective, local competence is quite possible, though local elites also are adept at turning the modernizing agendas of higher levels of power to their own end.

Here we have a familiar HI dilemma: Which part of the legacy matters? Claims about the distorting affects of the Ottoman legacy would be more persuasive if Bulgaria had tried to implement regional policies but failed and for the kind of reasons noted above. Yet successive Bulgarian governments have barely attempted any regional policy, making such a test of the legacy claims premature. Little regional policy had existed during communist rule in Bulgaria. From 1957 to 1987, Bulgaria was divided into twenty-eight regions (*oblasti*), but these regions were administrative units with very little role in the economy. With the fall of communism came a long period in which the government showed little interest in

---

[12] A third possibility is, of course, that there is no Ottoman legacy. Crampton (1983) argues that postindependence Bulgaria devoted enormous energy to "dismantling" the Ottoman state, while Lewis (1961) suggests that the Ottoman empire's influence even in Turkey had significantly eroded by the mid-twentieth century.

[13] In its focus on the legacies of the deep past as an explanatory factor for current politics, Meeker's work bears resemblances to Putnam on Italy (1993). One important difference, however, is that the work is essentially both historical and ethnographic and so is in a position to document the transmission of these legacies in great detail.

regional policy even as GDP fell by one-third and regional disparities rose (Kamenova 2001; Giatzidis 2002; Drezov 2000; Spiridonova and Grigorov 2000). Pro-EU Bulgarians often refer to the "seven lost years" between 1990 and 1997, when inaction reigned in virtually every key policy arena regarding EU membership. The EU had little influence, and each new government made plans for administrative reforms but carried through almost none of them.

Regional policy was emblematic of this broader pattern. In 1998–9, after three earlier administrative reforms had been aborted, the new government reinstated the same 28 districts that had been used by the communist regime. As in the Czech case, the Commission pushed for a smaller number of districts to become the so-called NUTS II regions, and in 1999 Bulgaria formed six "macro-regions" for this purpose (European Commission 1999b: 47).[14] The government established the Ministry of Regional Development and Public Works in 1999 and made strides to establish the necessary infrastructure inside other ministries to effectively handle EU funds. Also in 1999, Bulgaria submitted to the EU a preliminary national development plan to guide regional policies up to 2006. Finally, the Law on Regional Development established a regional development board to coordinate the different national ministries whose policies have strong regional effects and created a board in each of the regions.

Bulgaria, of course, was not offered membership at the Copenhagen summit in 2002 and did not join the EU with the first wave in 2004.[15] Rather, the EU now expects both Bulgaria and Romania to be ready for membership sometime late in the decade. The 2003 Regular Report specifically notes that Bulgaria needs to make more progress in the development of regional policy instruments (18). Further legislation is required to distribute structural funds. More research, including careful case studies of different regions, would be needed to really pin down the Ottoman legacy thesis, but the initial evidence largely speaks against it.[16] Certainly,

---

[14] By comparison, Ottoman administration divided Bulgaria into eight territorial units, which were in turn divided into even smaller administrative units.

[15] Bulgarian President Peter Stoyanov argued in early 2001 for a preliminary EU "political membership," which would allow the EU to counter growing skepticism in CEE by offering a "big bang" enlargement in 2004, to be followed later by full membership. The proposal was quickly rejected by the Commission (*Uniting Europe*, February 5, 2001: 2–3).

[16] Gryzmaa-Busse (2002: 21) argues that imputing causal claims for postcommunist legacies requires demonstrating that they are clear, sustained, and have a mechanism of reproduction. The Ottoman legacy would seem to fail all three tests in Bulgaria.

the similarities between the Habsburg (Czech) case and the Ottoman (Bulgarian) case are hard to miss: thin legacies of formal regional policy, intense postcommunist struggles over the control of the state apparatus, long-standing indifference to EU suggestions and demands, the grudging revival of communist-era administrative units that would be too small to handle EU requirements, and, finally, the rushed and frantic effort to quickly patch a legislative domain long neglected but potentially important as a channel of outside revenue. If the Ottoman legacy thesis is to be validated in the case of Bulgarian regional policy, it will have to come in questions of the implementation of that policy and not in its initial formation.

Ukraine: Does Distance Matter?

If there is little evidence that either sheer size or imperial legacies had crucial implications for the modes or outcomes of emulation, there does seem to be evidence that distance matters. At one level, of course, distance is a wholly unsatisfying variable. Scholars of CEE transformations have come to the variable fairly recently and after exploring (and often rejecting) a host of more plausible sounding variables.[17] But granting that geographical distance from the current IO member states might simply be a proxy for some other relationship, there has long been a consensus within both the EU and NATO that postcommunist states far distant from current members would have a difficult time securing an invitation to join. The case of Ukraine and NATO reveals some of the reasons that geographical distance is often related to political distance.

During the later 1980s and into 1990–1, Ukrainian nationalist and democratic opposition groups at first and then the moderate Rukh opposition and national communists began to endorse the goal of independent Ukrainian armed forces. In July 1990, the Ukrainian Supreme Soviet's declaration of sovereignty included an assertion of the right to an independent army. However, until the failed Soviet coup of August 1991, there was no real movement toward this objective. After the coup, Ukraine moved quickly toward independence, which came after a popular referendum in December 1991 showed 90% in favor (Beissinger 2002: 190–8).

Initially, the emerging Ukrainian leadership nationalized the portion of the Soviet army within Ukrainian borders, instantly creating an

---

[17] For examples, see the discussion in chapter 1.

independent military with an army of over 725,000 – Europe's largest outside of Russia itself. In September, Soviet Major General Konstantin Morozov left his position as commander of the Soviet air force to become the Ukrainian Defense Minister. Officers refusing to take a new oath of allegiance were forced to retire or continue their military service outside of Ukraine.[18]

Since 1991, Ukraine has maintained a relatively stable structure of civilian control over the military, but unlike the Czech and Hungarian militaries, it has felt little compelling pressure to emulate Western structures. In 1991, President Leonid Kravchuk decreed that the president would be commander in chief of the armed forces. But this move "reflected the larger emerging Ukrainian political system, with the President playing the central role in appointing the Prime Minister and government and shaping many areas of policy." Further, "the absence of a pre-existing Ukrainian officer corps and General Staff with a strong corporate identity or any history of intervention in domestic politics meant that the military was relatively unlikely to become involved in domestic politics as a force in its own right" (Perepelitsa 2002: 238–9). A new constitution adopted in June 1996 consolidated the system of civilian political control. The President was confirmed as Commander in Chief and received the right to appoint key senior military commanders, appoint and lead the Cabinet of Ministers, head the Council of National Security and Defense, and declare war and martial law (with the approval of Parliament).

But Ukraine has maintained civilian control over the military for reasons other than Western emulation. Unlike the Czech Republic, Hungary, and Poland, Ukraine essentially nationalized part of an existing multinational military – a military the new state had ample incentives to watch closely.[19] Indeed, according to the secondary literature, Ukraine's engagement with NATO has had relatively little effect on its civilian control

---

[18] A CIS agreement allowing military personnel to choose where they would continue their service allowed many Ukrainians serving elsewhere to return to serve in the new Ukrainian army.

[19] Unlike the Czech and Hungarian cases, Ukraine's military is ethnically heterogeneous. In 1992, 45% of its officers were ethnic Ukrainians while 48% were ethnic Russians. By 1999, the figures were 55% and 39%. As of 2001, 81% of soldiers and sergeants and 67% of generals and admirals were Ukrainian, with ethnic Russians making up most of the rest (Pereplitsa 2002: 240–1). For the rich history of multinationalism in the Habsburg military, see Deák (1993).

structures, as it has been clear that it has not ever been a serious candidate for membership. In 1994, Ukraine became a founding member of NATO's Partnership for Peace. During the July 1997 Madrid summit, a NATO–Ukraine "Distinctive Partnership" was signed. Both of these steps were part of NATO's confidence-building measures vis-à-vis states that were not candidates for membership. Hence, it is unsurprising that they had little effect on Ukraine's domestic structures. More significant steps occurred in 2001, when Ukraine joined NATO's Planning and Review Process (Sherr 2002: 223). In 2002, President Leonid Kuchma then declared that Ukraine would seek formal NATO membership and announced Ukrainian hopes to begin EU entry negotiations by 2007. Even if these outcomes remain highly unlikely, they do indicate some change in Ukrainian positions towards western IOs. Thus, while the physical distance remains fixed, the political distance may be shrinking.

Ukrainian officials have begun to use emulation as part of the effort to shrink this distance. Both the 1999 and 2000 defense reforms proclaimed that a conscript-based force will not be adequate in the future and established a goal of an all-volunteer force by 2015. As in the Czech and Hungarian cases, there is good reason to be skeptical that all-volunteer forces will really address the deeper problems. It is especially unclear how Ukraine plans to transform its conscript force of 130,000 soldiers – which is cheap to maintain and pay – into a volunteer force with better wages and better training and facilities on a budget of about $500 million (Sherr 2002: 216). And as in the Czech and Hungarian cases, there is also a recent move towards building up NCO corps. In 2000, two new NCO academies were formed, and additional NCOs are being trained in U.S. facilities. Other areas in which the secondary literature indicates emulation might be used include the system of promotion. Among the middle-officer ranks, the promotion process is reasonably transparent, but higher-level officers have continued a Soviet tradition of choosing their own circles of deputies. This system has some positive features, but it also produces "clans in the armed forces" (Sherr 2002: 219). In short, the case of civilian control in the Ukrainian military underscores two points. First, it confirms that the findings from the Czech and Hungarian cases cannot easily be extended to countries that are physically distant from the EU and NATO's sphere of influence. But second, it shows that when such states attempt to shrink the political distance between themselves and Western IOs, the policy sector dynamics identified in the "most likely" cases play a role in the "least likely" ones as well.

Sweden: When Membership Requires Lower Standards
Rather Than Higher

The EU and NATO have challenged the CEE states to raise their institutional standards to some more demanding level widely attainted in those IOs' current member states. In some cases, of course, the starting point in CEE was not "low standards," but rather "no standards." We saw this pattern particularly in the area of consumer protection, in which some traditions of contract law aside, many of the specific EU directives had no Czech or Hungarian counterparts at all. The chapter developed the notion of institutional homesteading as a way of characterizing such relatively underdeveloped policy domains.

But what about cases in which acceding states actually have higher standards than what an IO requires? Consumer protection in the Scandinavian states that have sought EU membership is one such example. Sweden, which joined the EU in 1995, marks a particularly interesting case because of its long history of well-developed consumer standards. Consumer protection policy in Sweden developed ahead of and more fully than similar policy in much of the rest of Western Europe. Consumer policy in Sweden began growing in the 1940s and 1950s, marked by the creation of the Institute of Home Research (HFI) in 1944 by the Swedish Population Commission. Originally, the HFI was half funded by the business sector, with the rest coming from government grants. In subsequent years, as businesses decreased their contributions, the government nationalized the HFI and created from it two new public agencies: the Institute for Consumer Information and the National Council for Consumer Goods Research and Consumer Information. During the same period, the government established many other offices, including the Office of the Competition Ombudsman, the Competition Council, and the National Price and Cartel Office (Pestoff 1988).

By the 1980s and in more recent years, official consumer organizations funded by the Swedish government suffered substantial budget cuts and came under intense scrutiny from state officials. More recent developments in consumer policy have been characterized by policy decentralization and greater initiative by Swedish NGOs. But although the financing of Swedish consumer policy has changed, the basic strength of the consumer movement itself has remained intact.

With such long developments in consumer policy and other social policy in Scandinavia, it should come as no surprise that Sweden, along with Finland and Norway (though Norway eventually rejected membership), had little trouble meeting most related areas in the EU *acquis*. Indeed, as members of the European Free Trade Area (EFTA), these nations had much experience with the needed national and regional laws in areas such as consumer protection to guarantee the free movement of goods. Granell reports that eleven chapters for accession negotiations were already nearly covered by the European Economic Area (EEA), which the EFTA member countries negotiated with the Community in 1992, including consumer and health protection (1995: 122). But in some areas, Sweden and the other EFTA nations had higher consumer standards than the EU. This posed a curious problem in that the policy area was of considerable public interest and many feared that EU membership would require a lowering of national standards. Indeed, all four candidates for membership in 1995 requested derogations that would temporarily allow continuation of higher standards for certain environmental, health, and safety standards.

Particularly of note is environmental policy, an area closely related to consumer protection and which experienced a similar leading edge in Scandinavian politics (Kronsell 2002). Here, the applicant nations received four-year derogations to maintain national standards, during which time the EU would review and attempt to raise its own standards. By 1998, the EU managed to do so in most cases. However, EU failure to adopt more stringent restrictions for arsenic, pentachlorophenol (PCP), and cadmium necessitated another four-year extension of derogations until 2002, although the legality of this action was highly disputed (Molin and Wurzel 2000: 172). Because derogations cannot become permanent, Sweden (and Finland) have come under pressure to lower national standards to conform fully to the EU *acquis*. The Swedish case, then, is one of a few cases that demonstrate how EU accession can actually result in a lowering of standards for some nations in certain policy areas. And though this is certainly an unusual case, the aborted Hungarian efforts to develop a "higher" standard by providing a lower floor for defective product complaints suggests that the logic behind it is far from unique.[20]

These cases, though brief, perform an important role in the argument. A research strategy focused on policy sectors in the Czech Republic and Hungary can draw on controls that exclude a number of potential confounding variables (most similar cases) while looking at countries where the emulation dynamic is likely to be quite strong (most likely cases). But as noted earlier, the resulting clarity comes at the cost of generalizability.

[20] See chapter 2 for details on the Hungarian case referenced here.

Just as we already know there is wide variability in emulation dynamics across policy domains, so too is it likely that emulation in all of the post-communist world may differ from that in two relatively well-off front runners for EU and NATO membership.

Most obviously, the weakness of the emulation dynamic in Ukraine underscores the role of geographic and political distance cited in much earlier literature. Yet the other three cases suggest that the Czech and Hungarian cases are reasonable proxies for broader developments. The Swedish case underscores the EU's determination to push common rules despite domestic costs, even requiring a state to dismantle instruments that were "ahead" of the EU. The Polish case shows that even where size matters most – agriculture – it basically accentuates the trend already found in the Czech Republic and Hungary: that of an intense struggle over the implications of emulated structures.[21] In the Bulgarian case, despite theoretical grounds for supposing that the Ottoman legacy of state building might differ from the Habsburg legacy, we found no evidence of the importance of this factor even in a policy area where it would be quite likely to show up (regional policy).

The conclusion is not that national differences do not matter but that variations in processes of emulation are best tracked at the level of policy areas. This also helps explain why so much previous research cited in the introduction has found little explanatory power in variables such as foreign debt levels, GDP starting points, presidential versus parliamentary systems, and religion. These essentially national descriptors cannot explain reform outcomes as well as the sector-specific variables emphasized in this book, including the strength and configuration of state and societal interests in a given policy sector and the density of IO rules brought to bear in that sector.

EXTENSIONS II: WESTERN MODELS FOR DEMOCRATIZATION,
LIBERALIZATION, MEMBERSHIP

A second extension of the book's argument goes beyond geography. The book began with the question of the ways in which outsiders can assist processes of reform occurring in other countries. When this question is posed for forms of assistance such as trade access or FDI, it can be explored with widely known models (see Van Brabant 1996; Nicoll and Schoenberg

---

[21] A very similar story can be told about the struggles over Polish civil–military reforms (Simon 2004c).

1998; Stankovsky, Plasser, and Ulram 1998). Already with the question of foreign aid, however, the literature ratchets up the level of complexity required (Martens et al. 2002). With the emulation of institutions, the complexity is even more pronounced. The result is a stew of expectations, interests, and precedent. How, then, to simplify the story? One way is to link the influence of Western models to broader patterns of change. CEE reformers have, in the aggregate, made three huge commitments since the collapse of communism: They have committed their countries to constitutional democracy, economic liberalization, and membership in a new set of international organizations. Each choice required tearing down at least some of the old as a prerequisite for building the new. Western models played a role in all three sets of choices, but in very different ways.

In terms of constitutional democracy, the features of which generally change very slowly, the CEE states all had some usable past, and in some areas, such as the Czech lands, experience with interwar democracy had been substantial. In states where the interwar experience had been more deeply marred by undemocratic regimes, however, there may have been more sustained consideration of Western models of basic democratic organization. For example, Hungary's basic institutions bear a striking similarity to some in Germany: a weak presidency and strong prime minister (made even more chancellor-like under the Orbán government), a strong constitutional court, a constructive no-confidence provision, a 4% (later 5%) electoral threshold, and (initially) corporatist social insurance schemes. While Germany was no blueprint for reform – the fact that Hungary is not a federal state marks only one huge difference – a wide range of Hungarian roundtable participants had spent time in Germany during the reform socialist period and were intimately familiar with German structures and practices. Tőkés has shown that reform socialists were especially drawn to the German "social market" model, in part to draw on its legitimacy to buy more time for transition (2002: 121–2, 131–3; see also Schiemann (2002)). Similarly, the importance of French models (and historical connections) is widely noted in the Romanian case.

This book has generally not focused on constitutional issues, as these choices long preceded the campaigns for IO membership.[22] More research would be needed to substantiate the hypothesis that the perception of a usable past diminishes the incentives to emulate basic constitutional features of Western European states (Bernhard 2000; Dimitrova 2004: 21).

---

[22] The one case – civilian control – that did have clear constitutional implications turned out to be a focus of real concern only well into the transformation.

On such weighty matters, elites typically focus on particular institutional *functions* that they would like to reproduce – for example, government stability in a multiparty system – rather than the *exact designs* of foreign models per se (Jacoby 2000).

In matters of economic liberalization, it is easy to overstate the influence of Western models. Greskovits (1998) has shown that vibrant economic reform debates were indigenous to CEE for virtually the entire socialist period. Bockman and Eyal (2002) have shown how a transnational actor network of liberal economists dominated by American libertarians actually drew on both Eastern European data and Eastern European economists to extend an indictment of state intervention, an indictment that came to be known as neo-liberalism. If the Eastern European members of the network were little noticed, they were nevertheless deeply committed to extending the domain of markets. Indeed, by this account, shock therapy owed its radicalism less to naïve Western purveyors of one-size-fits-all market making (and their shock troops in the international financial institutions) than to the experience of CEE economists-cum-politicians. The latter insisted on radicalism because they had seen any number of half-hearted previous reforms swallowed up and neutralized by their countries' bureaucracies (2002: 339–45).

This argument about the indigenous roots of economic reform can be pushed too far – for example, Epstein (2004) shows extensive evidence of the "coaching" of Polish central bank authorities by international financial institutions – but it is essentially correct. My argument also shares with Bockman and Eyal the skepticism about the heuristic value of the diffusion concept – understood as the spread of wholly novel forms of institutions from one location to another – and it shares the insistence on the importance of transnational coalitions and the hybridity of CEE institutions.

But Bockman and Eyal's account works best in explaining the initial orientation of several important political figures who had worked as economists during the socialist period (e.g., Klaus, Jezek, Kornai, Nagy, Balcerowicz, Gaidar, and Yavlinsky). It would serve us less well as a guide to subsequent developments that shape institutional reforms in the course of joining IOs. For in analyzing institutional changes in the context of IO membership, CEE elites have faced both information problems and resource problems. Elites were uncertain (or divided) about what effects new institutions might have, and they lacked time and the means to experiment widely. IOs provided both a focal point (which means less meandering and wasted time) and some targeted financial assistance (to overcome resource problems). Both factors help explain why emulation has been an attractive option. But Western models have been attractive to

CEE elites for several other reasons as well. They minimized the search costs of harried elites, maximized the chances of harmonization with EU structures, and helped overcome the legitimacy deficits faced by all newly created institutions (Bönker 1994). These features were not so relevant to the case of economic liberalization, where search costs were low, the EU was not yet a factor, and the task seemed less to gain public acceptance of the reforms than to do them quickly before protests could derail them.

The key to explaining membership preparations, then, is that rather than viewing emulation as an alternative explanation to internal processes, we should view them as potentially complementary to domestic politics. In a previous book on emulation in Germany, I noted that "institutional transfer" that has succeeded on even the most basic terms, generally has done so when important domestic actors wanted it to succeed (Jacoby 2000). External manipulation alone, no matter how well backed by authority and money, was not enough. Transnational coalitions between outsiders and insiders do not guarantee success, but in their absence, most attempts quickly run into the sand. For this reason, when institutional creation processes are viewed in retrospect or at a distance, many cases of successful transfer may be hard to distinguish from apparently "indigenous" developments. For roughly the same reason, however, it is easy to overstate the role of diffusion when high-profile policy entrepreneurs advocate something that local actors are already doing with far less fanfare. My argument has tried to get that balance right and, in so doing, has shown that emulation varies by IO, country, and especially by policy area.

Can this variegated picture contribute to an understanding of the overall shape of postcommunist reform? It can. An early wave of postcommunist scholarship was pessimistic about the links between radical liberalization and democratization. Parts of that literature denounced the superficiality or the implausibility of successful imitation of Western practices, including neoliberalism (Elster, Offe, and Preuss 1998; Henderson 1998; Pickel and Wiesenthal 1997). Other parts underscored the way in which neoliberal policies also were indigenous to the region (Greskovits 1998).

More recent scholarship has been more optimistic that democracy and market reforms can be mutually reinforcing in CEE (Stark and Bruszt 1998; Khakee 2002). The causal linkages vary. Hellman argues that though the economic winners of reform – often ex-communist insiders – were much stronger politically than the losers of reform, successive elections have largely broken this grip (1998: 225–30). Orenstein, in a comparative study of Poland and the Czech Republic, argues that weak governments have been obliged to learn, listen, and compromise. In this view, electoral turnover does not so much break the strangleholds of privileged insiders as it creates constant obligations for parties to improve their policies (2001). Both accounts, along with that by Fish discussed in chapter 1, tend to deny any strong causal incompatibility between market reforms and democracy. The reforms discussed here do not all fit easily within the ambit of "market liberalization," and some of them (e.g., the CAP) do not fit at all. Nevertheless, since the EU is often understood primarily as a liberalizing force vis-à-vis the more restrictive forms of national regulation, it makes sense to investigate it in this light (Scharpf 1993).

The cases above provide grounds for both optimism and pessimism. On the optimistic side, many positive changes have been accelerated far beyond what would likely have occurred without EU and NATO pressures. Some of these reforms are ones that are very likely to benefit CEE states, including setting up a rudimentary system of regional policy during a period in which regional disparities are growing rapidly, partially decoupling health spending from fiscally strapped state central budgets, and clarifying the chain of military command. Many other improvements from other policy areas (for example, improving the efficiency of public administration, the accountability of the judiciary, and the transparency of state aids to industry) could be added to the list.[23] If some of the reforms strain both budgets and personnel, they also helped mobilize significant amounts of Western expertise and money to help ease the burden. Even when some of the changes appear to have relatively low intrinsic value to CEE states – as I argued was the case with some of the consumer protection statutes – the engagement they bring in broader European policy networks probably at least matches the modest efforts made to match European standards.

The pessimistic case, however, is that many of the reforms are purely elite-driven projects. The elite nature of the reforms has been at the center of the book, and data has been offered in several places to underscore how little the EU and NATO reforms are understood by the broad population and even by local and regional government officials. This picture dovetails with that won in other surveys of the region. Howard has convincingly documented the oft-rumored weakness of civil society in much of the

---

[23] Some of these examples include EU support for basic democratic institutions (see Schimmelfennig, Engert, and Knobel 2004; Vachudova 2004) or the EU's significant influence on CEE states' policies toward gypsies (see Barany 2002).

region (2003). Greskovits has described the "dual democratic regimes" of CEE, in which most are excluded from the major democratic institutions other than elections; that finding accords well with both the basic elite account offered here and the observation of the systematic downgrading of parliament in the institutional reform process (1998: 177). To Bartlett's argument that electoral democracy undercut the organizational basis of collective resistance (1997) can be added the finding here that even if such grievances had been systematically articulated, the EU's screening process is exquisitely tailored to ignore them (see also Mair 2003; Gryzmała-Busse and Innes 2003; Holmes 2003).

The pessimistic case also is further bolstered when one considers that some of the EU rules may just be bad ideas in CEE. The prevailing EU rules are the result of debates among current member states, all of whom are wealthier and have more recent democratic traditions than the CEE states. This issue is not easily captured in the question of whether the institutions will "fit" in CEE. Institutions that really matter rarely do fit; rather, because they formalize procedures that are not well calibrated to prevailing conditions, they force adjustments that lead to aggregate welfare gains. We saw in chapter 3 that one major worry is that the bloated CAP will not really have a modernizing function in CEE agricultural sectors. When institutions fit too well, they simply reinforce existing practices. But when they demand radical revisions without specifying intermediate steps or offering transitional aid, the destruction they cause may be creative of nothing but market exit and political resentment. EU and CEE officials are aware of that tension, but given the inflexibility of the *acquis* and the relative stinginess of the current member states, are little able to resolve it. In short, the glass is at least half full, but it is also very fragile.

IMPLICATIONS OF THE ARGUMENT

My findings have implications for three specific literatures. The first is the growing literature on external influences on both democratization and economic reform in CEE. The early almost exclusive focus on forces internal to the region has been augmented by a steadily growing interest in the external influences on the various political and economic transformations of the region (Carothers 1999; Bönker, Müller, and Pickel 2002; Linden 2002; Zielonka 2001; Dawisha 1997; Grey 1997). The political and economic wings of this literature tend to be disconnected from one another now, but they can and should be joined (Pridham, Herring, and Sanford 1997). Both wings respond to the initial descriptions and typologies about "transitions," which emphasized internal political considerations in accounting for institutional choices (What should the constitution look like? How should the central bank be established? etc.). But a focus on external influences is a growth area for good conceptual work only if it addresses the union of foreign and domestic influences. As noted, there is a trend toward setting up external influences as an alternative explanation to domestic considerations (Henderson 1998; Campbell 1993). This is exactly the wrong approach because external influences can almost never have any real purchase unless they are joined together with domestic ones. Casting them as an alternative is empirically wrong (for the reason just stated) and analytically unpromising (because we do not yet have real theories of external influence and are not likely to get them through this route).

The book also speaks to a second, more established, literature on conditionality. Notwithstanding predictions that the "era of conditionality" ushered in by the debt crisis of the 1980s had passed (Nelson 1995), aspirant IO members sometimes have been confronted with tough tests for joining (Schimmelfennig and Sedelmeier 2004). In the EU case, member states have manipulated the size and shape of the *acquis* in unprecedented ways (Grabbe 1999b). Those who heralded the end of the era of conditionality assumed that the decline of the acute phase of the debt crisis and the end of the Cold War robbed those who set conditions of both the leverage and motivation for doing so. But in these European cases, CEE aspirations to join IOs (not a factor in IMF–World Bank discussions) resulted in a new kind of leverage. The evidence above underscores the claim that small states are particularly vulnerable to such conditions (Stone 2002), but it also introduces the concept of thresholds to underscore that not all conditionality consists of detailed ex ante specifications of institutional or policy outcomes. Rather, in many cases we have seen the EU and, to a lesser extent, NATO invoke broad principles rather than specific forms.

The importance of conditionality underscores that it is not wholly convincing to speak of CEE as a mere testing ground for new ideas, as, for example, Deacon and Hulse (1997) do. It is undoubtedly true that different agencies and their different consultants give conflicting, often incommensurate advice. Yet the EU, by virtue of the desirability of membership that it controls, has had a weight far disproportionate to the other agencies. Since about 1998, the EU has also demonstrated a willingness to impose tough conditions on aspirant member states, and has not been shy about pointing to institutional deficiencies in various policy domains. In addition, the financial contribution that the EU, through its Phare program and now through the negotiated terms of membership, dwarfs any new spending coming out of the alternate agencies. Emphasis on the disproportionate weight of the EU does not mean that these other agencies have no effects or that the image of CEE as a testing ground for novel ideas is wholly wrong. Other agencies undoubtedly do look to the region as a potential testing ground (Mendelson and Glenn 2002), but they generally lack the leverage and resources to pitch their experiments as anything but complementary to the approximation of the *acquis* (Schwellnuss 2004).

NATO also was able to set conditions for entry, but it is much less capable of setting new obligations for states that have become members or, as we have seen in chapters 4 and 5, even of obliging members to keep their prior commitments. Wallander's call for a membership monitoring committee is representative of the frustration many NATO officials and observers feel. She notes, for example, that corruption problems in new members raise the specter of intelligence leaks: "How can NATO function if its members cannot trust one another with the sensitive information on vulnerabilities that must be shared to enable cooperation in preventing terrorist attacks?" (2002: 6). This perspective is consistent with evidence in chapter 7 that the U.S. currently sees NATO as a potential diplomatic asset more than a military one.

Third, there is a burgeoning literature on "Europeanization," a process in which states adopt EU rules to varying degrees.[24] One premise is that the EU is a system of multilevel governance in which "rule-making competencies are spread across different levels of governance, and the validity of rules may be limited to certain levels and territories" (Schimmelfennig and Sedelmeier 2004: 3). In other words, supranational rules confront national and subnational constraints. Yet there is a profound difference between Western Europe and CEE in terms of the EU's effects. In Western Europe, these national constraints seem far better anchored than in CEE (see also Morlino 2002; Dimitrova 2004). Even in agriculture, where struggle and resistance most characterized the CEE response to EU imperatives, all but a few of the harshest critics of the EU's offer on the CAP ultimately chose to accept the EU's take-it-or-leave-it deal in December 2002. Europeanization processes also differ substantially over those in Western Europe. Where scholars of Europeanization in the West emphasize the way that EU rules have often "differentially empowered" domestic

[24] Good overviews include Radaelli (2000); Héritier (2001b); Goetz (2000). There is no truly analogous literature on NATO and its effect on the defense sector.

actors, who then help call upon their national governments to embrace
EU rules, Europeanization in CEE has come much more through the classic intergovernmental bargaining route (Schimmelfennig and Sedelmeier
2004; Moravcsik and Vachudova 2003; Börzel and Risse 2000; Knill and
Lehmkuhl 1999).

That the EU has set so much of the legislative agenda in CEE runs
counter to the scholarship on the existing member states that locates decisions about institutional design much more squarely in the domestic
politics of each nation (e.g., Goetz 2000). We have seen that a particular
kind of Europeanization is occurring through emulation in CEE. That
process, to be sure, includes a good deal of hasty activity as a way of
satisfying the demands of an institutional environment in which the EU
is so dominant. We saw this pattern most clearly in consumer protection, but also in military professionalism and even in regional policy. In
other policy areas, more robust traditions and more organized interests
remained, so that the Europeanization process has been truly mediated,
as it is in current member states. In different ways, this was the case in
agriculture, health care, and civilian control of the military. Even within
policy sectors, small enclaves of officials may have dense contacts with EU
or NATO institutions, while all other officials remain ill-informed about
European initiatives.

OPEN QUESTIONS

This book highlights little-understood themes about institutional change
in CEE. In so doing, it raises crucial·questions for all three of these literatures for which it cannot, at present, provide convincing answers. For
example, external influences have generated many organizations absent
any demand for them inside CEE societies. Is there a "Says Law" of
institutions in which institutional supply eventually helps create its own
demand? If elites build it, will the people come? Or where Meyer and
Rowan argue that organizational dualism is a coping strategy that allows
mature organizations to serve multiple constituencies, will the imperative
of securing external support for new organizations in CEE appear cynical
or undercut the organization's practical work?

In terms of conditionality, NATO has reduced its demands for military competence and stepped up demands for policy loyalty. But given the
fractures within NATO, which member states will the CEE states obey?
In launching the Iraq invasion the United States had the upper hand. Will
that be true in the medium and long term? In the EU, will the strenuous

efforts to meet EU conditions provoke a backlash against the EU on the part of CEE voters? By and large, the significant potential for nationalist politics was held extraordinarily well in check in most of the states, especially in the latter stages of their long betrothal to the EU (Vachudová 2004). Will the EU's relatively weak levers over its own member states – as evidenced in the Austrian and Italian cases of far right parties joining the government – be strong enough to prevent nationalist and ethnic mobilization?[25]

In terms of Europeanization, the biggest open question is what kind of members the CEE states will be. Will they act as "CEE states" in a block that belies the modest policy coordination they have mustered during the 1990s? Will they join coalitions of other states to serve important constituencies within their societies – for example, a coalition of Poland, Spain, and France in favor of maintaining the current CAP? Alternatively, if budget constraints tighten further, will the CEE states, unlike all those who have joined before, be much less able to expand their own access to CAP and the structural and cohesion funds once inside the EU? In the event the EU begins to roll back some forms of supranational rule making – and both agriculture and regional policy are oft-mentioned candidates for partial renationalization – how would CEE states respond? When combined with CEE public ambivalence about membership in both IOs, must one anticipate an erosion of the "permissive consensus" that has allowed such substantial Europeanization in the run-up to membership? (see also Dyson and Goetz 2003).

Finally, to what extent can emulation help catalyze development and growth in a world in which there already are clear winners and losers? This question links the situation of the middle-income countries of CEE and that of truly poor countries. Emulation of the perceived leaders is a time-honored response of followers, as both Veblen and Marx recognized long ago. Yet given the current distributions of markets and the power to organize and protect those markets, the successful policies of the future are unlikely to simply retrace those of the current winners, even if their path could be reliably identified. Many citizens seem to perceive their countries as permanent losers in this struggle. Meanwhile, the winners, determined to stay on top, may be unaware of how much the current rules reflect their interests and capabilities.

The countries studied here are neither rich nor poor. Their hopes lie with the winners, their fears with the losers. What role will outsiders play

[25] Recent summaries include Howard (2002) and Minkenberg (2002).

in determining which is realized? As noted, this is an open question. One paradox that emerges from this book, however, is that organizations with low performance levels often seek to copy the attributes or structures of those with relatively high levels of performance. At its extreme, the aspiration is to go from "worst to first." For the individual organization, this sometimes is an insurmountable challenge. For the population of organizations, emulation homogenizes the pool and removes niche players. Both outcomes promote more direct competition and better potential cross-national policy coordination. On the other hand, they also make external monitoring easier and may reduce the range of adaptive strategies available in times of crisis. As new policy instruments spread from place to place in the context of globalization or regionalization, these advantages and disadvantages should be kept firmly in mind.

In closing, two things are plain to see. First, Eastern Europeans have looked West for inspiration and tried to emulate some of the things they saw. Second, social science techniques for understanding such complex process are underdeveloped. While I hope this book has made progress, I stress at its close that these techniques remain underdeveloped. I have attempted to provide a richer conceptual vocabulary for this process and to connect it to the major theories of institutionalism so that larger numbers of scholars will wish to join this debate. As the last section has again made clear, there is much left to do. My intention is that this book functions like the maps of early explorers. Even in places where it is wrong, I hope that it nevertheless remains helpful. When later and better maps are possible, I hope they show that this one got the contours right, reduced the size of the terra incognita, and let none of its users sail off the edge of the Earth.

Appendix: Selected List of Persons Interviewed

Ágh, Attila. Budapest University of Economics. Budapest.
Allgayer, Friedemann. European Commission, ISPA. Brussels.
Andor, László. Budapest University of Economics. Budapest.
Andrle, Alois. Terplan. Prague.
Bagge, Véronique. European Parliament. Brussels.
Balabán, Miloš. Czech Ministry of Defense. Prague.
Bertolissi, Paola. European Commission, Directorate General for
   Consumer Affairs. Brussels.
Blažek, Jiří. Charles University. Prague.
Boda, György. General Inspectorate of Consumer Protection.
   Budapest.
Boháč, Libor. Czech Ministry of Foreign Affairs. Prague.
Bojar, Martin. Czech Ministry of Health. Prague.
Bonacci, Giorgio. European Commission Task Force on Hungary.
   Brussels.
Bozóki, András. Political Science Department, Central European
   University. Budapest.
Briët, Lodewijk. European Commission Delegation to the U.S.
   Washington, DC.
Brusis, Martin. Center for Applied Policy Research. Munich.
Čapek, Aleš. Czech National Bank. Prague.
Carnovale, Marco. NATO Political Affairs Division. Brussels.
Černoch, Pavel. European Commission Delegation to the Czech
   Republic; Charles University. Prague.
Červený, Miloš. Terplan. Prague.

Csaba, Ivan. Central European University. Budapest.

Cziomer, Erhard. Krakow University. Krakow.

Danopoulos, Constantine. San Jose State University. San Jose.

Davidson, Jonathan. European Commission Delegation to the U.S. Washington, DC.

Deáki, Endre. NATO Headquarters, HDF Defense and Force Planning. Brussels.

Donnelly, Christopher. NATO Headquarters, Office of Central and Eastern Europe. Brussels.

Doyle, Bob. Hungarian Ministry of Defense. Budapest.

Dufek, Bohumír. 2002. Czech Union of Agricultural Workers, Prague.

Dunay, Pál. Geneva Centre for Security Policy. Geneva.

Dupal, Jaroslav. Terplan. Prague.

Enyedi, Zsolt. Central European University. Budapest.

Ficsor, Mihály. Hungarian Ministry of Justice, Legal and International Department. Budapest.

Filip, Cornelis. European Commission Task Force on Hungary. Brussels.

Franco, Marc. European Commission, Directorate General for External Relation, Unit for Czech Republic and Hungary. Brussels.

Gaudenzi, Francoise. European Commission Task Force on Poland. Brussels.

Gazdag, Ferenc. Institute for Strategic and Defense Studies. Budapest.

Gömbös, János. Center for Security and Defense Studies Foundation. Budapest.

Gorka, Sebestyén. Hungarian Ministry of Defense. Budapest.

Gregr, Petr. European Commission Delegation to the Czech Republic. Prague.

Halmai, Gábor. Human Rights Information Center. Budapest.

Illner, Michael. Czech Academy of Sciences. Prague.

Inotai, András. Institute for World Economics, Hungarian Academy of Sciences. Budapest.

Jakoš, Marjan. Slovenian Ministry of Defense. Ljubljana.

Javůrek, Leoš. European Commission Delegation to the Czech Republic. Prague.

Jetton, Michael. Center for Economic Research and Graduate Education, Charles University. Prague.

Karkoszka, Andrzej. Geneva Centre for the Democratic Control of Armed Forces. Geneva.

Kazocins, Janis. British Ministry of Defense. London.

Kenclová, Alena. Voice of America. Prague.

Kjer-Hansen, Eva. European Parliament, Budget Control Committee. Brussels.

Klener, Pavel. Charles University. Prague.

Klíma, Michal. Economics University. Prague.

Kočová, Irena. Czech Ministry of Industry and Trade, Consumer Protection Department. Prague.

Körnerová, Markéta. Czech Mission to the European Communities. Brussels.

Kotnik-Dvojmoč, Igor. Slovenian Ministry of Defense. Ljubljana.

Kovács, László. Hungarian Socialist Worker's Party. Budapest.

Kovanda, Karel. Czech Ambassador to NATO. Brussels.

Král, David. Europeum, Charles University. Prague.

Lake, Michael. European Commission, Directorate General for External Relations. Brussels.

Leigh, Michael. European Commission Task Force on the Czech Republic. Brussels.

Lobkowicz, Michal. Czech Chamber of Deputies. Prague.

Luhanová, Jana. Czech Association for Consumer Protection. Prague.

Luňák, Petr. Liaison Office of the Czech Republic at NATO Headquarters. Brussels.

Lunk, Tamás. Hungarian Ministry of Agriculture and Regional Development, Phare Regional Development Programme Management Unit, Budapest.

Magnant, Catherine. European Commission, Directorate General for External Relations. Brussels.

Martens, Bertin. European Commission, Directorate General for External Relations, Phare Evaluation Unit. Brussels.

Mejstřík, Michal. Center for Economic Research and Graduate Education, Charles University. Prague.

Mólnár, Annamária. European Commission Delegation to Hungary. Budapest.

Murmokaitė, Raimonda. Lithuanian Ministry of Foreign Affairs. Vilnius.

Nagy, Péter. Hungarian Ministry of Defense. Budapest.

Nečas, Petr. Czech Parliamentary Defense Committee. Prague.

Nelson, Daniel. George C. Marshall Center for Security Studies.
Garmisch-Partenkirchen, Germany.
Nimants, Didzis. Latvian Ministry of Defense. Riga.
Novotný, Jaromír. Czech Ministry of Defense. Prague.
Parker, Fred. NATO Political Affairs Division, Partnership and
Cooperation Section. Brussels.
Provazníková, Denisa. Czech Ministry of Industry and Trade, Consumer
Protection Department. Prague.
O'Shaughnessy, Fidelma. Phare Information Office. Brussels.
Rábai, Zsolt. Liaison Office of Hungary at Nato Headquarters. Brussels.
Ralph, Michael. European Commission, ISPA. Brussels.
Rath, David. Czech Medical Chamber. Prague.
Ratinger, Tomáš. Research Institute of Agricultural Economics.
Prague.
Reinišová, Jana. Czech Ministry of Foreign Affairs. Prague.
Roth, Michael. German Bundestag. Berlin.
Rovná, Lenka. Charles University. Prague.
Rózsa, Judit. European Commission Delegation to Hungary. Budapest.
Schultz, Volkmar. German Bundestag. Berlin.
Shea, Jamie. NATO Headquarters, Public Affairs Office. Brussels.
Siklósi, Péter. Hungarian Ministry of Defense. Budapest.
Simon, Jeffrey. National Defense University. Washington, DC.
Škaloud, Jan. Prague School of Economics. Prague.
Somssich, Réka. Hungarian Ministry of Justice, European Law
Department. Budapest.
Švec, Peter. Slovakian Army, General Staff. Bratislava.
Szücs, Tamás. European Commission Task Force on Hungary. Brussels.
Szurgyi, Arpad. Defense Attaché, U.S. Embassy in Hungary; Science
Applications International Corporation. Budapest.
Tapparo, Frank. Logistics Management Institute. Washington, DC.
Tatham, Allan. European Commission Delegation to Hungary.
Budapest.
Teleki, Zsuzsa. Hungarian Ministry of Justice, European Law
Department. Budapest.
Thompson, Gayden. Atlantic Council. Washington, DC.
Tóka, Gábor. Central European University. Budapest.
Tržický, Josef. Czech Ministry of Industry and Trade, Consumer
Protection Department. Prague.
Ulrich, Marybeth Peterson. U.S. Air Force Academy. Colorado Springs.
Valki, László. NATO Research and Information Centre. Budapest.

Van Gilst, Willem. NATO International Staff, Defense Planning and Operations Division. Brussels.

Vassikeri, Vlassia. European Commission Delegation to the U.S. Washington, DC.

Věrný, Arsène. University of Economics. Prague.

Volný, Jan. Czech Ministry of Justice, Department for Compatibility with EC Law. Prague.

Westlake, Martin. European Commission, Unit on Relations with Other Institutions. Brussels.

Works Cited

Adler, Emanuel. 1997. Seizing the Middle Ground: Constructivism in World Politics. *European Journal of International Relations* 2: 319–63.

Ágh, Attila. 1995. The Permanent "Constitutional Crisis" in the Democratic Transition: The Case of Hungary. In Joachim Jens Hesse and Nevil Johnson, eds. *Constitutional Policy and Change in Europe*. New York: Oxford University Press: 296–328.

Agócs, Peter, and Sándor Agócs. 1994. "The Change Was but an Unfulfilled Promise": Agriculture and the Rural Population in Postcommunist Hungary. *East European Politics and Societies* 8(1): 32–57.

Ahn, Toh-Kyeong, Elinor Ostrom, David Schmidt, Robert Shupp, and James Walker. 2001. Cooperation in PD Games: Fear, Greed, and History of Play. *Public Choice* 106(1/2): 137–55.

Allen, David. 2000. Cohesion and the Structural Funds. In Helen Wallace and William Wallace, eds. *Policy-Making in the European Union*, 4th ed. New York: Oxford University Press: 243–66.

Alter, Karen. 1998a. Explaining National Court Acceptance of European Court Jurisprudence: A Critical Evaluation of Theories of Legal Integration. In Anne-Marie Slaughter, Alec Stone Sweet, and J. H. H. Weiler, eds. *The European Court and the National Court – Doctrine and Jurisprudence: Legal Change in Its Social Context*. Oxford: Hart: 227–52.

Alter, Karen. 1998b. Who Are the Masters of the Treaty? European Governments and the European Court of Justice. *International Organization* 52(1): 121–48.

Armed Forces Communications and Electronics Association. 2002. Hungary's Military Deals with a Plethora of Changes. *Signal* 57(1): 23–6.

Armstrong, Harvey, and Jim Taylor. 2000. *Regional Economics and Policy*. 3rd ed. Oxford: Blackwell.

Armstrong, Kenneth, and Simon Bulmer. 1997. *The Governance of the Single European Market*. Manchester: Manchester University Press.

Asbeek-Brusse, Wendy. 2002. Facing the Fifth Enlargement: Dilemmas and Prospects for the Common Agricultural Policy. Council for European Studies Meetings, Chicago.

Asmus, Ronald. 2002. *Opening NATO's Door.* New York: Columbia University Press.

Aspinwall, Mark, and Gerald Schneider. 2001. Institutional Research on the European Union: Mapping the Field. In Gerald Schneider and Mark Aspinwall, eds. *The Rules of Integration: Institutionalist Approaches to the Study of Europe.* Manchester: Manchester University Press: 1–18.

Bache, Ian. 1998. *The Politics of European Union Regional Policy: Multi-Level Governance or Flexible Gatekeeping?* Sheffield: Sheffield Academic Press.

Bachtler, John, and Ruth Downes. 1999. Regional Policy in the Transition Countries: A Comparative Assessment. *European Planning Studies* 7(6): 793–808.

Bachtler, John, Ruth Downes, and Grzegorz Gorzelak. 2000. Transition, Cohesion and Regional Policy in Central and Eastern Europe: Conclusions. In John Bachtler, Ruth Downes, and Grzegorz Gorzelak, eds. *Transition, Cohesion and Regional Policy in Central and Eastern Europe.* Burlington, VT: Ashgate: 355–78.

Bachtler, John, Ruth Downes, Irene McMaster, Philip Raines, and Sandra Taylor. 2002. The Transfer of EU Regional Policy to the Countries of Central and Eastern Europe: Can One Size Fit All? Working Paper No. 10. European Policies Research Centre, Future Governance Series.

Bainbridge, Timothy. 2002. *The Penguin Companion to the European Union.* London: Penguin.

Barany, Zoltan. 1989. Military Higher Education in Hungary. *Armed Forces and Society* 15(3): 371–88.

Barany, Zoltan. 1995. The Military and Security Legacies of Communism. In Zoltan Barany and Iván Volgyes, eds. *The Legacies of Communism in Eastern Europe.* Baltimore: Johns Hopkins University Press: 101–17.

Barany, Zoltan. 1997. Democratic Consolidation and the Military Experience: The East European Experience. *Comparative Politics* 30(1): 21–43.

Barany, Zoltan. 1998a. Hungary: Appraising a New NATO Member. *Clausewitz-Studien* 1998: 3–31.

Barany, Zoltan. 1998b. The Hungarian Army Revealed: Colonel Bokor's Sensational Book. *Radio Free Europe Background Report* 221: 1–7.

Barany, Zoltan. 1999. An Outpost on the Troubled Periphery. In Andrew Michta, ed. *America's New Allies: Poland, Hungary, and the Czech Republic in NATO.* Seattle: University of Washington Press: 74–111.

Barany, Zoltan. 2002. *The East European Gypsies: Regime Change, Marginality, and Ethnopolitics.* New York: Cambridge University Press.

Barany, Zoltan. 2003. *The Future of NATO Expansion: Four Case Studies.* New York: Cambridge University Press.

Barnett, Neil. 2002. Hungary Reviews Defense to Mollify Critics. *Jane's Defence Weekly* (August 7): 6.

Barta, Györgyi. 2002. Strong Regional Competition – Weak Cooperation: Attempts at "Bottom Up" Co-operation and Contradictions in Governmental Efforts in Hungary. *European Spatial Research and Policy* 9(1): 5–20.

Bartlett, David. 1997. *The Political Economy of Dual Transitions: Market Reform and Democratization in Hungary.* Ann Arbor: University of Michigan Press.

Batt, Judy. 1997. The International Dimension of Democratisation in Hungary, Slovakia, and the Czech Republic. In Geoffrey Pridham, Eric Herring, and George Sanford, eds. *Building Democracy? The International Dimension of Democratisation in Eastern Europe.* London: Leicester University Press: 154–69.

Baudner, Joerg. 2003. The Impact of European Regional Policy – "Policy Learning" and Sociological Institutionalism. European Union Studies Association Conference, Nashville, TN.

Bauer, Kai. 2001. A Review of Agricultural Policies in Hungary 1998. Working Paper No. 1/2. Bonn: IDARA.

Baukó, Tamás, and Imre Gurzó. 2001. Dilemmas in Agricultural and Rural Development in Hungary: The EU Accession Partnership and the Sapard Programme. *European Urban and Regional Studies* 8(4): 361–9.

Baun, Michael. 2000. *A Wider Europe: The Process and Politics of European Union Enlargement.* Lanham, MD: Rowman & Littlefield.

Beissinger, Mark. 2002. *Nationalist Mobilization and the Collapse of the Soviet State.* New York: Cambridge University Press.

Békési, László, Pál Simon, István Loványi, and Dénes Kellner. 2001. Building the Basics of a Unified Healthcare Information System in Hungary. *Studies in Health Technology and Informatics* 84: 703.

Bennett, Colin. 1991. How States Utilize Foreign Evidence. *Journal of Public Policy* 11(1): 31–54.

Benoit, Kenneth, and John Schiemann. 2001. Institutional Choice in New Democracies: Bargaining over Hungary's 1989 Electoral Law. *Journal of Theoretical Politics* 13: 159–88.

Berend, Ivan. 1999. *Central and Eastern Europe 1944–1993: Detour from the Periphery to the Periphery.* Cambridge: Cambridge University Press.

Bergman, Torbjorn. 2000. The European Union as the Next Step of Delegation and Accountability. *European Journal of Political Research* (Special issue: Parliamentary Democracy and the Chain of Delegation) 37(3): 415–29.

Bernhard, Michael. 2000. Institutional Choice After Communism: A Critique of Theory-Building in an Empirical Wasteland. *East European Politics and Society* 14: 316–47.

Bernhard, Michael, Christopher Nordstrom, and Timothy Reenock. 2003. Economic Performance and Survival in New Democracies: Is There a Honeymoon Effect? *Comparative Political Studies* 36(4): 404–31.

Bezemer, Dirk. 2003. Credit Allocation and Farm Structures in the Czech Republic, 1993–1997. *Comparative Economic Studies* 45: 25–43.

Black, Cyril. 1957. Bulgaria in Historical Perspective. In L. A. D. Dellin, ed. *Bulgaria.* New York: Praeger: 1–25.

Bland, Douglas. 1999. Managing the Expert Problem in Civil-Military Relations. *European Security* 8(3): 25–43.

Bland, Douglas. 2001. Patterns in Liberal Democratic Civil-Military Relations. *Armed Forces and Society* 27(4): 525–40.

Blažek, Jiří. 1996. Regional Patterns of Economic Adaptability to the Transformation and Global Processes in the Czech Republic. *Geographica* 37: 61–70.

Blažek, Jiří, and Sjaak Boekhout. 2000. Regional Policy in the Czech Republic and the EU Accession. In John Bachtler, Ruth Downes, and Grzegorz Gorzelak, eds. *Transition, Cohesion and Regional Policy in Central and Eastern Europe.* Burlington, VT: Ashgate: 301–17.

Blinken, Donald. 1999. How Hungary Joined NATO. *European Security* 8(4): 109–29.

Blyth, Mark. 2002. *Great Transformations: Economic Ideas and Institutional Change in the Twentieth Century.* New York: Cambridge University Press.

Bockman, Johanna, and Gil Eyal. 2002. Eastern Knowledge as a Laboratory for Economic Knowledge: The Transnational Roots of Neoliberalism. *American Journal of Sociology* 108(2): 310–52.

Bönker, Frank. 1994. External Determinants of the Patterns and Outcomes of East European Transitions. *Emergo* 1(1): 34–54.

Bönker, Frank, Klaus Müller, and Andreas Pickel, eds. 2002. *Postcommunist Transformation and the Social Sciences: Cross-Disciplinary Approaches.* Boulder, CO: Rowman & Littlefield.

Böröcz, József. 2000. The Fox and the Raven: The European Union and Hungary Renegotiate the Margins of "Europe." *Comparative Studies in Society and History* 42(4): 847–75.

Börzel, Tanja. 1999. Towards Convergence in Europe? Institutional Adaptation to Europeanisation in Germany and Spain. *Journal of Common Market Studies* 37: 573–96.

Börzel, Tanja. 2001. Non-Compliance in the European Union: Pathology or Statistical Artifact? *Journal of European Public Policy* 8(5): 803–24.

Börzel, Tanja. 2002. *States and Regions in the European Union: Institutional Adaptation in Germany and Spain.* Cambridge: Cambridge University Press.

Börzel, Tanja, and Thomas Risse. 2000. When Europe Hits Home: Europeanization and Domestic Change. *European Integration Online Papers* 4(15). Accessed at <http://eiop.or.at/eiop>.

Börzel, Tanja, Tobias Hofmann, and Carina Sprungk. 2003. Why Do States Not Obey the Law? Lessons from the European Union. European Union Studies Association, Nashville, TN.

Boyer, Robert, Elsie Charron, Ulrich Juergens, and Steven Tolliday, eds. 1999. *Between Imitation and Innovation: The Transfer and Hybridization of Productive Models in the International Automobile Industry.* Oxford: Oxford University Press.

Brosig, Stephan, and Monika Hartmann, eds. 2001. *Analysis of Food Consumption in Central and Eastern Europe: Relevance and Empirical Methods.* Kiel: Wissenschaftsverlag Vauk.

Brusis, Martin. 2001. Institution Building for Regional Development: A Comparison of the Czech Republic, Estonia, Hungary, Poland, and Slovakia. In Jürgen Beyer, Jan Wielgohs, and Helmut Wiesenthal, eds. *Successful Transition: Political Factors of Socio-Economic Progress in Postsocialist Countries.* Baden-Baden: Nomos Verlag: 223–42.

Brusis, Martin. 2003. Instrumentalized Conditionality: Regionalization in the Czech Republic and Slovakia. Working Paper, Munich: Center for Applied Political Research.

Bruszt, László, and David Stark. 2003. Who Counts? Supranational Norms and Societal Needs. *East European Politics and Societies* 17(1): 74–82.

Buckwell, A., J. Haynes, S. Davidova, V. Courboin, and A. Kwiecinski. 1995. *Feasibility of Agricultural Strategy to Prepare Countries of Central and Eastern Europe for EU Accession.* Brussels: European Commission.

Bulmer, Simon, and Martin Burch. 2001. The "Europeanization" of Central Government: The U.K. and Germany in Historical Institutionalist Perspective. In Gerald Schneider and Mark Aspinwall, eds. *The Rules of Integration: Institutionalist Approaches to the Study of Europe.* Manchester: Manchester University Press: 73–96.

Bunce, Valerie. 1995. Should Transitologists Be Grounded? *Slavic Review* 54(1): 111–27.

Bunce, Valerie. 1997. Presidents and the Transition in Eastern Europe. In K. von Mettenheim, ed. *Presidential Institutions and Democratic Politics.* Baltimore: Johns Hopkins University Press: 161–76.

Bunce, Valerie. 1999. *Subversive Institutions: The Design and Destruction of Socialism and the State.* New York: Cambridge University Press.

Bunce, Valerie. 2003. Rethinking Recent Democratization: Lessons from the Post-Communist Experience. *World Politics* 55(2): 167–92.

Busse, Reinhard, Alena Petraková, and Roman Prymula. 2001. Implementing Hospital Reforms in the Czech Republic. *Eurohealth* 7(3): 29–31.

Busza, Eva. 1996. Transition and Civil–Military Relations in Poland and Russia. *Communist and Postcommunist Studies* 29(2): 167–84.

Calvert, Randall. 1995. The Rational Choice Theory of Social Institutions: Cooperation, Coordination, and Communication. In Jeffrey Banks and Eric Hanushek, eds. *Modern Political Economy: Old Topics, New Directions.* Cambridge: Cambridge University Press: 216–67.

Cameron, David. 2003. The Challenges of Accession. *East European Politics and Societies* 17(1): 24–41.

Campbell, John. 1993. Institutional Theory and the Influence of Foreign Actors on Reform in Capitalist and Post-Socialist Societies. In Jerzy Hausner, Bob Jessop, and Klaus Nielsen, eds. *Institutional Frameworks of Market Economies.* Aldershot: Avebury: 45–67.

Caporaso, James. 1997. Across the Great Divide: Integrating Comparative and International Politics. *International Studies Quarterly* 41(4): 563–92.

Caporaso, James. 2000. *The European Union: Dilemmas of Regional Integration.* Boulder: Westview.

Carothers, Thomas. 1996. *Assessing Democracy Assistance: The Case of Romania.* Washington, DC: Carnegie Endowment.

Carothers, Thomas. 1999. *Aiding Democracy Abroad: The Learning Curve.* Washington, DC: Brookings Institution.

Červený, Miloš, and Alois Andrle. 2000. Czech Republic. In John Bachtler, Ruth Downes, and Grzegorz Gorzelak, eds. *Transition, Cohesion and Regional Policy in Central and Eastern Europe.* Burlington, VT: Ashgate: 85–98.

Chaplin, Hannah. 2001a. Czech Republic: Review of Policies and Information Affecting Diversification. Working Paper. Wye: IDARA, January 2001.
Chaplin, Hannah. 2001b. Hungary: Review of Policies and Information Affecting Diversification. Working Paper. Wye: IDARA, January 2001.
Checkel, Jeffrey. 1999. Social Construction and Integration. *Journal of European Public Policy* 6(4): 545–60.
Checkel, Jeffrey. 2001a. Constructing European Institutions. In Gerald Schneider and Mark Aspinwall, eds. *The Rules of Integration: Institutionalist Approaches to the Study of Europe.* Manchester: Manchester University Press: 19–39.
Checkel, Jeffrey. 2001b. Why Comply? Social Learning and European Identity Change. *International Organization* 55(3): 553–88.
Checkel, Jeffrey. 2003. 'Going Native' in Europe? *Comparative Political Studies* 36(1/2): 209–32.
Checkel, Jeffrey. 2004. Social Constructivisms in Global and European Politics. Forthcoming in *Review of International Studies.*
Chenet, Laurent, Martin McKee, Naomi Fulop, Ferenc Bojan, Helmut Brand, Angela Hort, and Pawel Kalbarczyk. 1996. Changing Life Expectancy in Central Europe: Is There a Single Reason? *Journal of Public Health Medicine* 18: 329–36.
Cichowski, Rachel. 2000. Western Dreams, Eastern Realities. *Comparative Political Studies* 33(10): 1243–78.
Clark, Wesley. 2002. *Waging Modern War.* New York: Public Affairs.
Cohen, Joshua, and Charles Sabel. 1997. Directly Deliberative Polyarchy. *European Law Journal* 3(4): 313–58.
Collier, David, and Robert Adcock. 2001. Measurement Validity: A Shared Standard for Qualitative and Quantitative Research. *American Political Science Review* 95: 529–46.
Colomer, Josep. 1995. Strategies and Outcomes in Eastern Europe. *Journal of Democracy* 6: 74–85.
Colton, Timothy. 1979. *Commissars, Commanders, and Civilian Authority: The Structure of Soviet Military Politics.* Cambridge, MA: Harvard University Press.
Comisso, Ellen. 1991. Political Coalitions, Economic Choices. In György Szoboszlai, ed. *Democracy and Political Transformation: Theories and East-Central European Realties.* Budapest: Hungarian Political Science Association.
Consumers International. 2000. *Handbook: Consumer Policy and Consumer Organisations in Central and Eastern Europe.* Alastair Macgeorge, ed.
Conzelmann, Thomas. 1998. "Europeanisation" of Regional Development Policies? Linking the Multi-Level Governance Approach with Theories of Policy Leaning and Policy Change. *European Integration Online Papers* 2(4). Accessed at <http://eiop.or.at/eiop>.
Conzelmann, Thomas. 2003. Contested Spaces: Europeanised Regional Policy in Great Britain and Germany. Conference of European Union Studies Association, Nashville, TN.
Cottey, Andrew, Timothy Edmunds, and Anthony Forster. 2002a. Beyond Prague. *NATO Review* 3: 1–5.

Cottey, Andrew, Timothy Edmunds, and Anthony Forster. 2002b. The Challenge of Democratic Control of Armed Forces in Postcommunist Europe. In Andrew Cottey et al., eds. *Democratic Control of the Military in Postcommunist Europe.* New York: Palgrave: 1–20.

Cottey, Andrew, Timothy Edmunds, and Anthony Forster, eds. 2002c. *Democratic Control of the Military in Postcommunist Europe.* New York: Palgrave.

Coughlan, Elizabeth. 1998. Democratizing Civilian Control: The Polish Case. *Armed Forces and Society* 24(4): 519–33.

Cox, Robert. 1993. Creating Welfare States in Czechoslovakia and Hungary: Why Policymakers Borrow Ideas from the West. *Government and Policy* 11: 349–64.

Crampton, Richard. 1983. *Bulgaria 1878–1918: A History.* New York: Columbia University Press.

Crawford, Beverly, and Arend Lijphart. 1995. Explaining Political and Economic Change in Post-Communist Eastern Europe: Old Legacies, New Institutions, Hegmonic Norms, and International Pressures. *Comparative Political Studies* 28(2): 171–99.

Crombez, Christophe. 2001. The Treaty of Amsterdam and the Co-decision Procedure. In Gerald Schneider and Mark Aspinwall, eds. *The Rules of Integration: Institutionalist Approaches to the Study of Europe.* Manchester: Manchester University Press: 101–22.

Crumley, Michele. 2003. Agrarian Institutions and the State: Hungary and Slovakia in the Post-Communist Era. *East European Quarterly* 37(2): 195–230.

Csaki, Csaba, Michel Debatisse, and Oskar Honisch. 1999. Food and Agriculture in the Czech Republic: From a "Velvet" Transition to the Challenges of EU Accession. Technical Paper No. 47. Washington, DC: World Bank.

Czech Republic, Ministry of Foreign Affairs. 1999. *Position Paper of the Czech Republic on the Commission Opinion of 1998.* Prague.

Czech Republic, Ministry of Industry and Trade, Budget and Support to Business Division. 1999. *Conception of the Consumer Policy for the Years 1999–2000.* Prague.

Czech Republic, Ministry of Regional Development 2000. *Regional Development Strategy of the Czech Republic, Government Document 682/2000.* Prague.

Czech Social Democratic Party. 1997. *An Alternative for Our Country.* ČSSD Party Program, March 15, 1997, Chapter I.2., accessed at <www.socdem.cz>, March 13, 2001 (ČSSD, Návrh střednědobého programu, Alternativa Pro Naši Zemi, program schválený XXVIII. sjezdem ČSSD dne 15.3.1997).

Daalder, Ivo, and Michael O'Hanlon. 2000. *Winning Ugly: NATO's War to Save Kosovo.* Washington, DC: Brookings Institution.

Danopolous, Constantine, and Daniel Zirker, eds. 1996. *Civil Military Relations in the Soviet and Yugoslav Successor States.* Boulder: Westview.

Dawisha, Karen, ed. 1997. *The International Dimension of Postcommunist Transitions in Russia and the New States of Eurasia.* Armonk, NY: M. E. Sharpe.

Dawisha, Karen, and Bruce Parrot, eds. 1997. *The Consolidation of Democracy in East-Central Europe.* Cambridge: Cambridge University Press.

De Jong, Martin, Konstantinos Lalenis, and Virginie Mamadouh, eds. 2003. *The Theory and Practice of Institutional Transplantation: Experiences with the Transfer of Policy Institutions.* Dordrecht, the Netherlands: Kluwer.

De Nayer, Benoit, and Jens Karsten, eds. 2000. Distance Selling. In Jean-Paul Pritchard, ed. *Consumer Protection in Czech Republic.* Louvain, Belgium: Centre de Droit de la Consommation: 156–67.

Deacon, Bob, and Michelle Hulse. 1997. The Making of Postcommunist Social Policy: The Role of International Agencies. *Journal of Social Policy* 26(1).

Deák, István. 1993. *Beyond Nationalism: A Social and Political History of the Habsburg Officer Corps.* New York: Oxford University Press.

Diamandouros, P. Nikiforos, and F. Stephen Larrabbee. 2000. Democratization in South-East Europe: Theoretical Considerations and Evolving Trends. In Geoffrey Pridham and Tom Gallagher, eds. *Experimenting with Democracy: Regime Change in the Balkans.* London: Routledge: 24–64.

Dieringer, Jürgen, and Ionel-Sorin Moisa. 2001. Öffentliche Verwaltung versus Regionalpolitik? Die Europäisierung der Regionalstruktur Ungarns und Rumäniens. *Südosteuropa* 50(10–12): 537–60.

DiMaggio, Paul, and Walter Powell. 1991. The Iron Cage Revisited: Institutional Isomorphism and Collective Rationality in Organizational Fields. In Walter Powell and Paul DiMaggio, eds. *The New Institutionalism in Organizational Analysis.* Chicago: University of Chicago Press: 63–82.

Dimitrova, Antoaneta. 2004. Conditionality Meets Post-Communism: Europeanisation and Administrative Reform in Central and Eastern Europe. In Frank Schimmelfennig and Ulrich Sedelmeier, eds. *The Europeanization of Eastern Europe: Evaluating the Conditionality Model.* Ithaca: Cornell University Press: (in press).

Dolejší, Prokop. 1999. The Czech Republic as a Member of NATO: The Czech Military in the Malestrom of Changes. *Military Technology* 23(4): 9–16.

Dolowitz, David, and David Marsh. 1996. Who Learns What from Whom: A Review of Policy Transfer Literature. *Political Studies* 44(2): 343–57.

Dolowitz, David, and David Marsh. 2000. Learning from Abroad: The Role of Policy Transfer in Contemporary Policy-Making. *Governance* 13(1): 5–24.

Donnelly, Christopher. 1997a. Defense Transformation in the New Democracies: A Framework for Tackling the Problems. *NATO Review* 1: 15–19.

Donnelly, Christopher. 1997b. Developing a National Strategy for the Transformation of the Defense Establishment in Postcommunist States. *Central European Issues, Romanian Foreign Affairs Review* 3(2): 63–81.

Donnelly, Christopher. 2000. Shaping Soldiers for the 21st Century. *NATO Review* 48(2): 28–31.

Donnelly, Christopher. 2001. Reform Realities. *NATO Review* 49(3): 30–3.

Dorf, Michael, and Charles Sabel. 1998. A Constitution of Democratic Experimentalism. *Columbia Law Review* 98(2): 267–473.

Doucha, Tom. 1999. Main Political Forces and Interest Groups Influencing the Formation of Long-Term Agricultural Policy in the Czech Republic. In Klaus Frohberg and Peter Weingarten, eds. *The Significance of Politics and Institutions for the Design and Formation of Agricultural Policies.* Kiel: Wissenschaftsverlag Vauk: 234–7.

Douglas, Mary. 1986. *How Institutions Think.* Syracuse: Syracuse University Press.

Downes, Ruth. 2000. Regional Policy Evolution in Hungary. In John Bachtler, Ruth Downes, and Grzegorz Gorzelak, eds. *Transition, Cohesion and Regional Policy in Central and Eastern Europe*. Burlington, VT: Ashgate: 209–26.

Drevet, Jean-François. 2000. Regional Policy in Central and Eastern Europe: The EU Perspective. In John Bachtler, Ruth Downes, and Grzegorz Gorzelak, eds. *Transition, Cohesion and Regional Policy in Central and Eastern Europe*. Burlington, VT: Ashgate: 345–54.

Drezov, Kyril. 2000. Bulgaria: Transition Comes Full Circle, 1989–1997. In Geoffrey Pridham and Tom Gallagher, eds. *Experimenting with Democracy: Regime Change in the Balkans*. London: Routledge: 195–218.

Dunay, Pál. 2001. Hungary. In Hans Giessman and Gustav Gustenau, eds. *Security Handbook 2001*. Baden-Baden: Nomos Verlagsgesellschaft: 249–82.

Dunay, Pál. 2002a. Building Professional Competence in Hungary's Defence. In Anthony Forster, Timothy Edmunds, and Andrew Cottey, eds. *The Challenge of Military Reform in Postcommunist Europe: Building Professional Armed Forces*. New York: Palgrave Macmillan: 63–78.

Dunay, Pál. 2002b. Civil–Military Relations in Hungary: No Big Deal. In Andrew Cottey, Timothy Edmunds, and Anthony Forster, eds. *Democratic Control of the Military in Postcommunist Europe: Guarding the Guards*. London: Palgrave: 64–87.

Dunn, Elizabeth. 2002. Trojan Pig: Paradoxes of Food Safety Regulation. Unpublished Paper, Social Science Research Council, Prague.

Dyson, Kenneth. 1997. Policy Transfer in Regional Economic Development: The Case of SME Policy. *Regional Review* 7(1): 9–10.

Dyson, Kenneth, and Klaus Goetz. 2003. Europeanization Compared: The Shrinking Core and the Decline of "Soft Power." In Dyson and Goetz, eds. *Germany, Europe, and the Politics of Constraint*. Oxford: Oxford University Press: 349–76.

Ekiert, Grzegorz, and Jan Zielonka. 2003. Academic Boundaries and Path Dependencies Facing the EU's Eastward Enlargement. *East European Politics and Societies* 17(1): 7–23.

Ekiert, Grzegorz, and Jan Kubik. 1999. *Rebellious Civil Society: Popular Protest and Democratic Consolidation in Poland, 1989–1993*. Ann Arbor: University of Michigan Press.

Ellison, David, and Mustally Hussain. 2003. In the Face of Uncertainty: EU Membership and the Quest for Convergence. Conference of Midwest Political Science Association, Chicago.

Elster, Jon, Claus Offe, and Ulrich Preuss. 1998. *Institutional Design in Postcommunist Societies: Rebuilding the Ship at Sea*. Cambridge: Cambridge University Press.

Epstein, Rachel. 2001. International Institutions and Domestic Policy: Depoliticization and Denationalization in Postcommunist Poland. Ph.D. Dissertation, Cornell University.

Epstein, Rachel. 2004a. How NATO can Spread Democracy, But Not Just That: The Transformation of European Security. *Security Studies* (forthcoming).

Epstein, Rachel. 2004b. Rule Adoption in Postcommunist Poland: The Divergent Effects of Social Learning and Conditionality. In Frank Schimmelfennig and

Ulrich Sedelmeier, eds. *The Europeanization of Eastern Europe*. Ithaca: Cornell University Press (in press).

European Commission. 1997a. *Agenda 2000: For a Wider and Stronger Union*. Bulletin of the European Union, Supplement 5/97. Luxembourg: Official Publications of the European Communities (PEC).

European Commission. 1997b. *Opinion on the Czech Republic*. Luxembourg: PEC.

European Commission. 1997c. *Opinion on Hungary*. Luxembourg: PEC.

European Commission. 1998a. *Regular Report on the Czech Republic's Progress Towards Accession*. Luxembourg: PEC.

European Commission. 1998b. *Regular Report on Hungary's Progress Towards Accession*. Luxembourg: PEC.

European Commission. 1999a. *Enlarging the EU: A Historical Opportunity*. Luxembourg: PEC.

European Commission. 1999b. *Regular Report on Bulgaria's Progress Towards Accession*. Luxembourg: PEC.

European Commission. 1999c. *Regular Report on the Czech Republic's Progress Towards Accession*. Luxembourg: PEC.

European Commission. 1999d. *Regular Report on Hungary's Progress Towards Accession*. Luxembourg: PEC.

European Commission. 1999e. *The Structural Funds and Their Coordination with the Cohesion Fund, Guidelines for Programmes in the Period 2000–2006*. Luxembourg: PEC.

European Commission. 2000a. *Proposal for a Decision of the European Parliament and of the Council Adopting a Programme of Community Action in the Field of Public Health (2001–2006)*. Luxembourg: PEC.

European Commission. 2000b. *Regular Report on the Czech Republic's Progress Towards Accession*. Luxembourg: PEC.

European Commission. 2000c. *Regular Report on Hungary's Progress Towards Accession*. Luxembourg: PEC.

European Commission. 2001a. *Commission Staff Working Paper: Food Safety and Enlargement*. Luxembourg: PEC.

European Commission. 2001b. *Commission Staff Working Paper: Health and Enlargement*. Luxembourg: PEC.

European Commission. 2001c. *Regular Report on the Czech Republic's Progress Towards Accession*. Luxembourg: PEC.

European Commission. 2001d. *Regular Report on Hungary's Progress Towards Accession*. Luxembourg: PEC.

European Commission. 2002a. *Enlargement and Agriculture: A Fair and Tailor-Made Package Which Benefits Farmers in Accession Countries*. Memo/02/301, December 20, 2002.

European Commission. 2002b. *Enlargement and Agriculture: Successfully Integrating the New Member States into the CAP*. Issues Paper, Brussels, 30.1.2002, SEC(2002) 95.

European Commission. 2002c. *Regular Report on Bulgaria's Progress Towards Accession*. Luxembourg: PEC.

European Commission. 2002d. *Regular Report on the Czech Republic's Progress Towards Accession.* Luxembourg: PEC.

European Commission. 2002e. *Regular Report on Hungary's Progress Towards Accession.* Luxembourg: PEC.

European Commission, Directorate General for Agriculture. 2001. Questions and Answers: Commission Enlargement Proposals on Agriculture. Press release, January 30, 2001. Accessed at <http://europa.eu.int>.

European Commission, Directorate General for Agriculture. 2002a. *Agriculture Situation in the Candidate Countries: Country Report on the Czech Republic.* Luxembourg: PEC.

European Commission, Directorate General for Agriculture. 2002b. *Agriculture Situation in the Candidate Countries: Country Report on Hungary.* Luxembourg: PEC.

European Community Studies Association, ed. 1993. *The Legal, Economic and Administrative Adaptations of Central European Countries to the European Community.* Baden-Baden: Nomos Verlagsgesellschaft.

European Observatory on Health Care Systems. 1999. *Health Care Systems in Transition: Hungary.* Copenhagen: World Health Organization.

European Observatory on Health Care Systems. 2000. *Health Care Systems in Transition: Czech Republic.* Copenhagen: World Health Organization.

Eyal, Gil, Ivan Szelenyi, and Eleanor Townsley. 1999. *Making Capitalism without Capitalists: Class Formation and Elite Struggles in Postcommunist Central Europe.* London: Verso.

Fagin, Adam, and Petr Jehlicka. 2002. The Impact of EU Accession on the Czech Environmental Movement: Empowerement or Depoliticisation? European Consortium for Political Research Conference Paper, Turin, Italy.

Fallenbuchl, Zbigniew. 1991. Economic Reform and Changes in the Welfare System in Poland. In J. Adam, ed. *Economic Reforms and Welfare Systems in the USSR, Poland, and Hungary.* Basingstroke: Macmillan: 110–31.

Fehér, István. 2002. Meeting EU Standards in Eastern Europe: The Case of the Hungarian Agri-food Sector. *Food Control* 13: 93–6.

Fields, Frank, and Jack Jensen. 1998. Military Professionalism in Postcommunist Hungary and Poland: An Analysis and Assessment. *European Security* 7(1): 117–55.

Figueras, Josep, Martin McKee, and Suszy Lessof. 2002. Ten Years of Health Sector Reform in CEE and NIS: An Overview. *Ten Years of Health Systems Transition in Central and Eastern Europe and Eurasia.* Washington, DC: USAID Conference, July 29–31, 2002.

Finer, Samuel. 1988. *The Man on Horseback: The Role of the Military in Politics,* 2nd ed. Boulder, CO: Westview Press.

Finnemore, Martha. 1993. International Organizations as Teachers of Norms: The United Nations Educational, Scientific, and Cultural Organization and Science Policy. *International Organization* 47(4): 565–97.

Finnemore, Martha. 1996. Norms, Culture, and World Politics: Insights from Sociology's Institutionalism. *International Organization* 50(2): 325–47.

Finnemore, Martha, and Kathryn Sikkink. 1998. International Norm Dynamics and Political Change. *International Organization* 52(4): 887–917.

Fiorenza, Nicholas. 2001. Integration Challenges: Czech Republic Stretches Its Defense Budget to Meet NATO Standards. *Armed Forces Journal*: 16–19.

Fish, M. Steven. 1998a. Democratization's Requisites: The Postcommunist Experience. *Post-Soviet Affairs* 14(3): 212–47.

Fish, M. Steven. 1998b. The Determinants of Economic Reform in the Postcommunist World. *East European Politics and Societies* 12(1): 31–78.

Fligstein, Neil, and Alec Stone Sweet. 2001. Institutionalizing the Treaty of Rome. In Alec Stone Sweet, Wayne Sandholtz, and Neil Fligstein, eds. *The Institutionalization of Europe*: Oxford: Oxford University Press: 29–55.

Forster, Anthony. 2002. West Looking East: Civil-Military Relations Policy Transfer in Central and Eastern Europe. Working Paper Series No. 52. Geneva: Geneva Centre for the Democratic Control of Armed Forces.

Forster, Anthony, Timothy Edmunds, and Andrew Cottey. 2002. Introduction: The Professionalisation of Armed Forces in Postcommunist Europe. In Anthony Forster, Timothy Edmunds, and Andrew Cottey, eds. *The Challenge of Military Reform in Postcommunist Europe: Building Professional Armed Forces*. New York: Palgrave Macmillan: 1–16.

Franchino, Fabio. 2001. Delegation and Constraints in the National Execution of the EC Policies: A Longitudinal and Qualitative Analysis. *West European Politics* 24(4): 169–92.

Frohberg, Klaus, and Gerald Weber. 2002. *Auswirkungen der EU-Osterweiterung im Agrarbereich*. Halle, Germany: Institut für Agrarentwicklung Mittel- und Osteuropa.

Frohberg, Klaus, and Peter Weingarten, eds. 1999. *The Significance of Politics and Institutions for the Design and Formation of Agricultural Policies*. Kiel: Wissenschaftsverlag Vauk.

Frohberg, Klaus, Monika Hartmann, Peter Weingarten, and Etti Winter. 2002. Auswirkungen der EU-Osterweiterung auf die Beitrittsländer: Analyse unter Berücksichtigung bestehender bi- und multilateraler Verpflichtungen. In Martina Brockmeier, Folkhard Isermeyer, and Stephan von Cramon-Taubadel, eds. *Liberalisierung des Weltagrarhandels: Strategien und Konsequenzen*. Münster: Hiltrup: 183–93.

Frye, Timothy. 1997. A Politics of Institutional Choice: Postcommunist Presidencies. *Comparative Political Studies* 30(5): 523–52.

Füle, Štefan. 2002. Interview. *Jane's Defense Weekly* 38(8): 32.

Fuller, Frand, John Beghin, Jacinto Fabiosa, Samarendu Mohanty, Cheng Fang, and Phillip Kaus. 2002. Accession of the Czech Republic, Hungary and Poland to the European Union: Impacts on Agricultural Markets. *World Economy* 25(3): 407–28.

Gaddy, Charles. 1998. *The Price of the Past: Russia's Struggle With the Legacy of a Militarized Economy*. Washington, DC: Brookings.

Garrett, Geoffrey, and Barry Weingast. 1993. Ideas, Interests, and Institutions: Constructing the European Community's Internal Market. In Judith Goldstein and Robert Keohane, eds. *Ideas and Foreign Policy: Beliefs, Institutions, and Political Change*. Ithaca: Cornell University Press: 173–206.

Geddes, Barbara. 1995. A Comparative Perspective on the Leninist Legacy in Eastern Europe. *Comparative Political Studies* 28: 239–74.

General Inspectorate for Consumer Protection (Hungary). 2002. Consumer Protection in Hungary. Accessed at <http://www.fvf.hu/gicp.php3?page=ehist#today>. January 28, 2002.

Giatzidis, Emil. 2002. *An Introduction to post-Communist Bulgaria: Political, Economic, and Social Transformation.* Manchester: Manchester University Press.

Gleick, Elizabeth. 1997. Are They Up to It? A Promising Czech Soldier Says His Nation Is Not Ready for NATO. *Time* (December 15): 36–37.

Glenn, John. 2003. EU Enlargement. In Michelle Cini, ed. *European Union Politics.* Oxford: Oxford University Press: 211–28.

Goetz, Klaus. 2000. European Integration and National Executives: A Cause in Search of an Effect? *West European Politics* 23(4): 211–31.

Goetz, Klaus, and Harold Wollmann. 2001. Governmentalizing Central Executives in Post Communist Europe: A Four Country Comparison. *Journal of European Public Policy* 8(6): 864–87.

Goldgeier, James. 1999. *Not Whether but When: The U.S. Decision to Enlarge NATO.* Washington, DC: Brookings Institution.

Goldman, Emily, and Richard Andres. 1999. Systemic Effects of Military Innovation and Diffusion. *Security Studies* 8(4): 79–125.

Good, David, ed. 1994. *Economic Transformations in East and Central Europe: Legacies from the Past and Policies for the Future.* London: Routledge.

Gorka, Sebestyén. 1995. Hungarian Military Reform and Peacekeeping Efforts. *NATO Review* (November): 26–29.

Gorton, Matthew, and Sophia Davidova. 2001. The International Competitiveness of CEEC Agriculture. *World Economy* 24(2): 185–200.

Gorton, Matthew, Sophia Davidova, and Tomáš Ratinger. 2000. The Competitiveness of Agriculture in Bulgaria and the Czech Republic vis-à-vis the European Union. *Comparative Economic Studies* 42(1): 59–86.

Government of Hungary. 1990. *Programme for the Nation's Renewal.* Budapest: Government of Hungary.

Grabbe, Heather. 1999a: A Partnership for Accession? The Implications of EU Conditionality for the Central and East European Applicants. EUI Working Paper RSC No. 99/12. San Domenico: European University Institute.

Grabbe, Heather. 1999b. The Transfer of Policy Models from the EU to Central and Eastern Europe: Europeanisation by Design? Conference Paper. Birmingham, England: Institute for German Studies.

Grabbe, Heather. 2001a. How Does Europeanization Affect CEE Governance? Conditionality, Diffusion and Diversity. *Journal of European Public Policy* 8(6): 1013–31.

Grabbe, Heather. 2001b. *Profiting from EU Enlargement.* London: Centre for European Reform.

Grabbe, Heather. 2004. Free and Partly Free: The Europeanization of the Movement of People. In Frank Schimmelfennig and Ulrich Seddelmeier, eds. *The Europeanization of Eastern Europe*: Ithaca: Cornell University Press (in press).

Granell, Francisco. 1995. The European Union's Enlargement Negotiations with Austria, Finland, Norway and Sweden. *Journal of Common Market Studies* 33(1): 117–42.

Grant, Wyn. 1997. *The Common Agricultural Policy.* New York: St. Martin's Press.

Grant, Wyn. 1999. The International Dimension of the Transition Process in CEECs: How Does the International Framework Influence the Domestic Institution-Building Process? In Klaus Frohberg and Peter Weingarten, eds. *The Significance of Politics and Institutions for the Design and Formation of Agricultural Policies.* Kiel: Wissenschaftsverlag Vauk: 234–7.

Granville, Johanna. 1999. The Many Paradoxes of NATO Enlargement. *Current History* 98(April): 165–70.

Grayson, George. 1999. *Strange Bedfellows: NATO Marches East.* Lanham, MD: University Press of America.

Green Cowles, Maria, James Caporaso, and Thomas Risse. 2001. *Transforming Europe: Europeanization and Domestic Change.* Ithaca: Cornell University Press.

Greskovits, Béla. 1998. *The Political Economy of Protest and Patience: East European and Latin American Transformations Compared.* Budapest: Central European University Press.

Grey, Robert. 1997. The Impact of External Factors on the Future of Democracy in the FSU and Eastern Europe. In Robert Grey, ed. *Democratic Theory and Postcommunist Change.* Upper Saddle River, NJ: Prentice Hall: 248–66.

Griffiths, Richard. 2002. The Common Agricultural Policy and Earlier EU Enlargements. Council for European Studies Meetings, Chicago.

Grzymała-Busse, Anna. 2002. *Redeeming the Communist Past: The Regeneration of Communist Parties in East Central Europe.* Cambridge: Cambridge University Press.

Grzymała-Busse, Anna. 2003. Formal Demands, Informal Responses: The EU and State Reform in Candidate Countries. Conference on Eastern Enlargement of the European Union: Confronting New Unknowns? University of California, San Diego, May 22–24.

Grzymała-Busse, Anna. 2004. The New Dysfunctionalism? Paradoxes of EU Enlargement and the Postcommunist Candidate Countries. Conference of Council for European Studies, Chicago, March 12.

Grzymała-Busse, Anna, and Abby Innes. 2003. Great Expectations: The EU and Domestic Political Competition in East Central Europe. *East European Politics and Societies* 17(1): 64–73.

Grzymała-Busse, Anna, and Pauline Jones Luong. 2002. Reconceptualizing the State: Lessons from Post-Communism. *Politics and Society* 30(4): 529–54.

Guillén, Mauro. 2001. Is Globalization Civilizing, Destructive or Feeble? A Critique of Five Key Debates in the Social Science Literature. *Annual Review of Sociology* 27: 235–60.

Gutierrez, Brad. 2002. Defense Reform in Central Europe and the Challenges of NATO Membership: The Case of Hungary. Dissertation, Department of Political Science, University of California, San Diego.

Gyarmati, István. 1999. Hungary's Security and the Enlargement. In Anton Bebler, ed. *The Challenge of NATO Enlargement*. Westport, CT: Praeger: 110–15.

Hall, Peter. 1993. Policy Paradigms, Social Learning, and the State. The Case of Economic Policymaking in Britain. *Comparative Politics* 25(3): 275–96.

Hall, Peter, and Rosemary Taylor. 1996. Political Science and the Three New Institutionalisms. *Political Studies* 44: 936–57.

Hampl, Martin, et al. 1999. *Geography of Societal Transformation in the Czech Republic*. Prague: Charles University, Department of Social Geography and Regional Development.

Hanley, Sean. 1999. Pathetic Cowards? *Central Europe Review* 0(28). Accessed at <www.ce-review.org>.

Hanson, Stephen. 1998. Analyzing Postcommunist Economic Change. *East European Politics and Society* 12(1): 145–70.

Hartell, Jason, and Johan Swinnen, eds. 2000. *Agriculture and East–West European Integration: From Central Planning to the Common Agriculture Policy*. Aldershot: Ashgate.

Hartnell, Helen. 1997. Subregional Coalescence in European Regional Integration. *Wisconsin Law Journal* 16(1): 115–226.

Haverland, Marcus. 2000. National Adaptation to European Integration: The Importance of Institutional Veto Points. *Journal of Public Policy* 20: 83–103.

Hawkins, Darren, and Wade Jacoby. 2003. Why Agents Matter. Conference Paper, Weatherhead Center for International Affairs, Harvard University, December.

Hay, Colin, and Ben Rosamond. 2002. Globalization, European Integration, and the Discursive Construction of Economic Imperatives. *Journal of European Public Policy* 9(2): 147–67.

Hayek, Friedrich. 1989. *Order – With or Without Design?* London: Centre for Research into Communist Economies.

Heginbotham, Eric. 2002. The Fall and Rise of Navies in East Asia: Military Organizations, Domestic Politics, and Grand Strategy. *International Security* 27(2): 86–125.

Hellman, Joel. 1998. Winners Take All: The Politics of Partial Reform in Postcommunist Transition. *World Politics* 50(2): 203–34.

Henderson, Jeffrey, ed. 1998. *Industrial Transformation in Eastern Europe in Light of the East Asian Experience*. New York: St. Martin's.

Hendrickson, Ryan. 2000. NATO's Visegrad Allies: The First Test in Kosovo. *The Journal of Slavic Military Studies* 13(2): 25–38.

Héritier, Adrienne. 2001a. Covert and Overt Institutionalization in Europe. In Alec Stone Sweet, Wayne Sandholtz, and Neil Fligstein, eds. *The Institutionalization of Europe*. New York: Oxford University Press: 56–70.

Héritier, Adrienne. 2001b. Differential Europe: The European Union Impact on National Policymaking. In Adrienne Héritier et al., eds. *Differential Europe: The European Union Impact on National Policymaking*. Lanham, MD: Rowman & Littlefield: 1–23.

Herrigel, Gary. 1996. *Industrial Constructions: The Sources of German Industrial Power*. New York: Cambridge University Press.

Hix, Simon. 1999. *The Political System of the European Union*. London: Macmillan.

Hix, Simon, and Klaus Goetz. 2000. Introduction: European Integration and National Political Systems. *West European Politics* 23(4): 1–26.

Hoffmann, Stanley. 1963. Paradoxes of the French Political Community. In Stanley Hoffmann et al., eds. *In Search of France*. Cambridge: Harvard University Press: 1–117.

Hollis, Martin, and Steve Smith. 1991. Beware of Gurus: Structure and Action in International Relations. *Review of International Studies* 17: 392–410.

Holmes, Martin. 1996. *Review of Parliamentary Oversight of the Hungarian MOD and Democratic Control of the Hungarian Defense Forces*. London: Directorate of Management and Consultancy Services.

Holmes, Stephen. 1996. Cultural Legacies or State Collapse? Probing the Postcommunist Dilemma. In Michael Mandelbaum, ed. *Postcommunism: Four Perspectives*. New York: Council on Foreign Relations: 22–76.

Holmes, Stephen. 2003. A European Doppelstaat? *East European Politics and Societies* 17(1): 107–18.

Hooghe, Liesbet. 2001. Top Commission Officials on Capitalism: An Institutionalist Understanding of Preferences. In Gerald Schneider and Mark Aspinwall, eds. *The Rules of Integration: Institutionalist Approaches to the Study of Europe*. Manchester: Manchester University Press: 152–73.

Hooghe, Liesbet, ed. 1996. *Cohesion Policy and European Integration: Building Multi-Level Governance*. New York: Oxford University Press.

Hooghe, Liesbet, and Michael Keating. 1994. The Politics of European Union Regional Policy. *Journal of European Public Policy* 1: 367–93.

Horváth, Gyula. 1998. *Regional and Cohesion Policy in Hungary*. Pécs, Hungary: Centre for Regional Studies.

Horváth, Gyula. 2000. Hungary. In John Bachtler, Ruth Downes, and Grzegorz Gorzelak, eds. *Transition, Cohesion and Regional Policy in Central and Eastern Europe*. Burlington, VT: Ashgate: 115–30.

Howard, Marc Morjé. 2002. Can Populism Be Suppressed in a Democracy? Austria, Germany, and the European Union. *East European Politics and Societies* 14(2): 18–32.

Howard, Marc Morjé. 2003. *The Weakness of Civil Society in Post-Communist Europe*. Cambridge: Cambridge University Press.

Howells, Geraint, and Hans Micklitz. 2000. Sale of Consumer Goods and Associated Guarantees. In Jean-Paul Pritchard, ed. *Consumer Protection in Czech Republic*. Louvain, Belgium: Centre de Droit de la Consommation: 77–100.

Hughes, James, and Gwendolyn Sasse. 2002. The Ambivalence of Conditionality: Europeanization and Regionalization in Central and Eastern Europe. Conference of European Consortium for Political Research, Turin, Italy.

Hughes, James, Gwendolyn Sasse, and Claire Gordon. 2001. The Regional Deficit in Eastward Enlargement of the European Union: Top Down Policies and Bottom Up Reactions. Working Paper No. 29/01: University of Birmingham, Centre for Russian and East European Studies.

Hungarian Ministry of Agriculture and Regional Development. 1998. *Regional Development in Hungary*. Budapest.

Huntington, Samuel 1959. *The Soldier and the State: The Theory and Politics of Civil-Military Relations.* Cambridge, MA: Belknap Press of Harvard University Press.

Huntington, Samuel. 1992. *The Third Wave: Democratization in the Late Twentieth Century.* Norman: University of Oklahoma Press.

Huszay, Gábor. 2002. Conformity of Consumer Protection Legislation to EU Directives. Unpublished Ministry of Economics chart containing Hungarian legislation on consumer protection and relating EU directives.

Iankova, Elena, and Peter Katzenstein. 2003. European Enlargement and Institutional Hypocrisy. In Rachel Cichowski and Tanja Börzel, eds. *State of the European Union, Volume 6: Law, Politics and Society.* New York: Oxford University Press: 269–90.

Illner, Michael. 1997. The Territorial Dimensions of Public Administration Reforms in East Central Europe. Working Paper 97/7. Prague: Institute of Sociology, Academy of Sciences of the Czech Republic.

Immergut, Ellen. 1992. *Health Politics: Interests and Institutions in Western Europe.* Cambridge: Cambridge University Press.

Innes, Abby. 2002. The Changing Power of the State in Eastern Europe. Conference of European Consortium for Political Research, Turin, Italy.

Inotai, András. 1995. From Association Agreements to Full Membership? The Dynamics of Relations Between the Central and Eastern European Countries and the European Union. Working Paper No. 52. Budapest: Hungarian Academy of Sciences, Institute for World Economics.

Jachtenfuchs, Markus. 1995. Theoretical Perspectives on European Governance. *European Law Journal* 1(2): 115–33.

Jacoby, Wade. 1999. Priest and Penitent: The European Union as a Force in the Domestic Politics of Eastern Europe. *East European Constitutional Review* Winter/Spring: 62–7.

Jacoby, Wade. 2000. *Imitation and Politics: Redesigning Modern Germany.* Ithaca, NY: Cornell University Press.

Jacoby, Wade. 2001a. Das Wettrennen um die EU–Mitgliedschaft: Warum die Osterweiterung für Makroökonomen von Bedeutung ist. *WSI-Mitteilungen* May: 292–9.

Jacoby, Wade. 2001b. Tutors and Pupils: International Organizations, Central European Elites, and Western Models. *Governance* 14(2): 169–200.

Jacoby, Wade. 2002. Talking the Talk and Walking the Walk: The Cultural and Institutional Effects of Western Models. In Frank Bönker, Klaus Müller, and Andreas Pickel, eds. *Postcommunist Transformation and the Social Sciences: Cross-Disciplinary Approaches.* Boulder, CO: Rowman & Littlefield: 129–52.

Jacoby, Wade, and Pavel Černoch. 2002. The EU's Pivotal Role in the Creation of Czech Regional Policy. In Ronald Linden, ed. *Norms and Nannies: The Impact of International Organizations on the Central and East European States.* Lanham, MD: Rowman & Littlefield: 317–40.

Janos, Andrew. 1982. *The Politics of Backwardness in Hungary, 1825–1945.* Princeton: Princeton University Press.

Janos, Andrew. 2000. *East Central Europe in the Modern World: The Small States of the Borderlands from Pre- to Postcommunism.* Stanford: Stanford University Press.

Jeffrey, Charlie, ed. 1997. *The Regional Dimension of the European Union.* London: Frank Cass.

Jervis, Robert. 1978. Cooperation Under the Security Dilemma. *World Politics* 30(2): 167–214.

Johnson, D. Gale. 1997. Economies in Transition: Hungary and Poland. Working Paper 141. Rome: Food and Agriculture Organization of the United Nations.

Johnson, James. 1993. Is Talk Really Cheap? Promoting Conversation Between Critical Theory and Rational Choice. *American Political Science Review* 87: 74–86.

Johnston, Alistair Ian. 2001. Treating International Institutions as Social Environments. *International Studies Quarterly* 45(4): 487–515.

Jones, Christopher. 1998. NATO Enlargement: Brussels as the Heir of Moscow. *Problems of Post-Communism* 45(4): 44–55.

Jones Luong, Pauline. 2003. *Institutional Change and Political Continuity in Post-Soviet Central Asia.* New York: Cambridge University Press.

Joó, Rudolf. 1996. *The Democratic Control of Armed Forces: The Experience of Hungary.* Paris: Institute for Security Studies of the Western European Union.

Jowitt, Kenneth. 1978. *The Leninist Response to National Dependency.* Berkeley: Institute of International Studies, University of California Press.

Jowitt, Kenneth. 1992. *New World Disorder: The Leninist Extinction.* Berkeley: University of California Press.

Jupille, Joseph, James Caporaso, and Jeffrey Checkel. 2003. Integrating Institutions: Rationalism Constructivism, and the Study of the European Union. *Comparative Politic Studies* 36(1/2): 7–41.

Kahan, James, and László Gulácsi. 2000. Envisioning Health Care Quality in Hungary. *Eurohealth* 6(2): 2–4.

Kamenova, Tsveta. 2001. *Regional Policy and Regional Capacities in the Republic of Bulgaria.* Accessed on May 15, 2003, at <www.cap.uni-muenchen.de/download/2000/RPBulgaria.PDF>.

Karsten, Jens. 2000a. Unfair Contract Terms. In Jean-Paul Pritchard, ed. *Consumer Protection in Czech Republic.* Louvain, Belgium: Centre de Droit de la Consommation: 103–15.

Karsten, Jens. 2000b. Unfair Contract Terms. In Jean-Paul Pritchard, ed. *Consumer Protection in Hungary.* Louvain, Belgium: Centre de Droit de la Consommation: 101–14.

Katznelson, Ira. 1997. Structure and Configuration in Comparative Politics. In Mark Lichbach and Alan Zuckerman, eds. *Comparative Politics: Rationality, Culture, and Structure.* Cambridge: Cambridge University Press: 81–112.

Katzenstein, Peter, and Rudra Sil. 2004. Rethinking Asian Security: A Case for Analytical Eclecticism. In J. J. Suh, Peter Katzenstein, and Allen Carlson, eds. *Rethinking Asian Security in East Asia: Identity, Power and Efficiency.* Stanford: Stanford University Press.

Kay, Sean. 1998. *NATO and the Future of European Security.* New York: Rowman & Littlefield.

本

Keating, Michael. 2002. Regionalization in Central and Eastern Europe: The Diffusion of a Western Model. Conference Paper, Florence, Italy: European University Institute.

Keeler, John T. S. 1987. *The Politics of Neocorporatism in France: Farmers, the State, and Agricultural Policy-Making in the Fifth Republic.* New York: Oxford University Press.

Keeler, John T. S. 1999. The Limits of Agricultural Modernization in Eastern Europe: Farmers, the State, and Instutional Obstacles to Liberal Reform. In Klaus Frohberg and Peter Weingarten, eds. *Studies on the Agricultural and Food Sector in Central and Eastern Europe,* vol. 2. Kiel: Wissenschaftsverlag Vauk: 70–9.

Khakee, Anna. 2002. Democracy and Marketization in Central and Eastern Europe: Case Closed? *East European Politics and Society* 16(2): 599–615.

Khol, Radek. 2001. Czech Republic: A Pan-European Perspective. In Gale Mattox and Arthur Rachwald, eds. *Enlarging NATO: The National Debates.* Boulder, CO: Lynne Rienner: 147–68.

King, Gary, Robert Keohane, and Sidney Verba. 1994. *Designing Social Inquiry: Scientific Inference in Qualitative Research.* Princeton, NJ: Princeton University Press.

Kiss, Piroska, and Peter Weingarten. 2002. Cost of Compliance with the *Acquis Communautaire* in the Hungarian Dairy Sector. Halle, Germany: IAMO Working Paper.

Kitschelt, Herbert, Zdenka Mansfeldova, Radoslaw Markowski, and Gabor Tóka. 1999. *Postcommunist Party Systems: Competition, Representation, and Inter-Party Cooperation.* Cambridge: Cambridge University Press.

Knill, Christoph. 2001. *The Europeanisation of National Administrations: Patterns of Institutional Persistence and Change.* Cambridge: Cambridge University Press.

Knill, Christoph, and Dirk Lehmkuhl. 1999. How Europe Matters: Different Mechanisms of Europeanization. *European Integration Online Papers* 3(7). Accessed at <eiop.or.at/eiop>.

Knudsen, Ann-Christina. 2002. Why the EU has an Agricultural Dilemma. Conference of Council for European Studies Meetings, Chicago.

Kohler-Koch, Beate. 2000. Europäisierung: Plädoyer für eine Horizontalerweiterung. In Beate Kochler-Koch and Michele Knodt, eds. *Deutschland zwischen Europäisierung und Selbstbehauptung.* Frankfurt: Capmus: 11–31.

Kohler-Koch, Beate, and Rainer Eising, eds. 1999. *The Transformation of Governance in the European Union.* London: Routledge.

Kominek, Jiří. 2001. Czech Defense Minister Wants Professional Army. *Jane's Defense Weekly,* May 23, 2001: 10.

Kominek, Jiří. 2002. Czech Republic Approves Plan to Reform Army. *Jane's Defence Weekly,* May 8, 2002: 13.

Kopstein, Jeffrey, and David Reilly. 1999. Explaining the Why of the Why: A Comment on Fish's "Determinants of Economic Reform in the Postcommunist World." *East European Politics and Societies* 13(3): 613–24.

Kopstein, Jeffrey, and David Reilly. 2000. Geographic Diffusion and the Transformation of the Postcommunist World. *World Politics* 53(1): 1–37.

Kornai, János. 1980. "Hard" and "Soft" Budget Constraint. *Acta Oecoonomica* 25(3–4): 231–46.

Kornai, János. 1986. The Soft Budget Constraint. *Kyklos* 39(1): 3–30.

Kornai, János. 1990. *The Road to a Free Economy, Shifting from a Socialist System: The Example of Hungary.* New York and London: Norton.

Kornai, János. 2001. The Borderline Between the Spheres of Authority of the Citizen and the State: Recommendations for the Hungarian Health Reform. In János Kornai, Stephan Haggard, and Robert Kaufman, eds. *Reforming the State: Fiscal and Welfare Reform in Post-Socialist Countries.* Cambridge: Cambridge University Press: 181–209.

Kornai, János, and John McHale. 2000. Is Postcommunist Health Spending Unusual? A Comparison with Established Market Economies. *The Economics of Transition* 8: 369–99.

Kornai, János, and Karen Eggleston. 2001. *Welfare, Choice and Solidarity in Transition: Reforming the Health Sector in Eastern Europe.* Cambridge: Cambridge University Press.

Kosztolanyi, Gusztav. 1999. Operation Successful, Patient Dead. *Central Europe Review* 1(16). Accessed at <www.ce-review.org/99/16/csardas16.htm>.

Kronsell, Annica. 2002. Can Small States Influence EU Norms? Insights from Sweden's Participation in the Field of Environmental Politics. *Scandinavian Studies* 74(3): 287–304.

Krygier, Martin. 2002. Parables of Hope and Disappointment. *East European Constitutional Review* 11(3): 62–5.

Lackó, László. 1994. Settlement Development Processes and Policies in Hungary. In Zoltán Hajdú and Gyula Horváth, eds. *European Challenges and Hungarian Response in Regional Policy.* Pécs, Hungary: Centre for Regional Studies, Hungarian Academy of Sciences: 151–6.

Laffan, Brigid, and Michael Shackleton. 2000. The Budget. In Helen Wallace and William Wallace, eds. *Policy-Making in the European Union,* 4th ed. Oxford: Oxford University Press: 211–42.

Lampland, Martha. 1995. *The Object of Labor: Commodification in Socialist Hungary.* Chicago: University of Chicago Press.

Langenkamp, Daniel. 2000. Sweeping Changes. *Jane's Defense Weekly* 34(1): 22.

Lawson, Colin, and Juraj Nemec. 2003. The Political Economy of Slovak and Czech Health Policy, 1989–2000. *International Political Science Review* 24(2): 219–35.

Le Galès, Patrick. 2001. Est Maître Des Lieux Celui Qui Les Organise: When National and European Policy Domains Collide. In Alec Stone Sweet, Wayne Sandholtz, and Neil Fligstein, eds. *The Institutionalization of Europe.* New York: Oxford University Press: 137–54.

Leonardi, Robert, and Raffaella Nanetti, eds. 1994. *Regional Development in a Modern European Economy: The Case of Tuscany.* New York: Pinter.

Levi, Margaret. 1997. A Model, a Method, and a Map: Rational Choice in Comparative and Historical Analysis. In Mark Lichbach and Alan Zuckerman, eds. *Comparative Politics: Rationality, Culture, and Structure.* New York: Cambridge University Press: 19–41.

Levy, Jonah. 1999. *Tocqueville's Revenge: State, Society, and Economy in Contemporary France.* Cambridge, MA: Harvard University Press.

Lewis, Bernard. 1961. *The Emergence of Modern Turkey.* Oxford: Oxford University Press.

Lewis, Jeffrey. 2003. Institutional Environments and Everyday EU Decision Making: Rationalist or Constructivist? *Comparative Political Studies* 36(1/2): 97–124.

Lichbach, Mark. 1997. Social Theory and Comparative Politics. In Mark Lichbach and Alan Zuckerman, eds. *Comparative Politics: Rationality, Culture, and Structure.* New York: Cambridge University Press: 239–76.

Lieberman, Robert. 2002. Ideas, Institutions, and Political Order: Explaining Political Change. *American Political Science Review* 96(4): 697–712.

Lieven, Anatol, and Dmitri Trenin, eds. 2003. *Ambivalent Neighbors: The EU, NATO, and Price of Membership.* Washington, DC: Carnegie Endowment.

Linden, Ronald, ed. 2002. *Norms and Nannies: The Impact of International Organizations on the Central and East European States.* Lanham, MD: Rowman & Littlefield.

Locke, Richard. 1995. *Remaking the Italian Economy.* Ithaca: Cornell University Press.

Locke, Richard, and Kathleen Thelen. 1995. Apples and Oranges Revisited: Contextualized Comparisons and the Study of Comparative Labor Politics. *Politics and Society* 23(3): 337–67.

Lowi, Theodore. 1972. Four Systems of Policy, Politics, and Choice. *Public Administration Review* 32: 298–310.

Lupia, Arthur, Matthew McCubbins, and Samuel Popkin, eds. 2000. *Elements of Reason: Cognition, Choice, and the Bounds of Rationality.* New York: Cambridge University Press.

Mair, Peter. 2003. Popular Democracy and EU Enlargement. *East European Politics and Societies* 17(1): 58–63.

Majone, Giandomenico. 2001. Two Logics of Delegation: Agency and Fiduciary Relations in EU Governance. *European Union Politics* 2(1): 103–22.

Malová, Darina, and Tim Haughton. 2002. Making Institutions in Central and Eastern Europe and the Impact of Europe. *West European Politics* 25(2): 100–20.

Maniet, Françoise. 2000. General Product Safety. In Jean-Paul Pritchard, ed. *Consumer Protection in Czech Republic.* Louvain, Belgium: Centre de Droit de la Consommation: 61–76.

Marek, Dan, and Michael Baun. 2002. The EU as a Regional Actor: The Case of the Czech Republic. *Journal of Common Market Studies* 40(5): 895–919.

Marks, Gary. 1992. Structural Policy in the EC. In Alberta Sbragia, ed. *Europolitics: Institutions and Policy-making in the "New" European Community.* Washington, DC: Brookings Institution: 191–224.

Marrée, Jörgen, and Peter Groenewegen. 1997. *Back to Bismarck: Eastern European Health Care Systems in Transition.* Aldershot: Averbury, Ashgate Publishing.

Martens, Bertin, Uwe Mummert, Peter Murrell, and Paul Seabright. 2002. *The Institutional Economics of Foreign Aid.* Cambridge: Cambridge University Press.

Massaro, Thomas, Jiří Nemec, and Ivan Kalman. 1994. Health System Reform in the Czech Republic: Policy Lessons from the Initial Experience of the General Health Insurance Company. *Journal of the American Medical Association* 271(23): 1870–74.

Mattox, Gale, and Arthur Rachwald. 2001. *Enlarging NATO: The National Debates*. Boulder, CO: Lynne Rienner.

Mayhew, Alan. 1998. *Recreating Europe: The European Union's Policy Towards Central and Eastern Europe*. New York: Cambridge University Press.

McAdam, Doug, Sidney Tarrow, and Charles Tilly. 1997. Toward an Integrated Perspective on Social Movements. In Mark Lichbach and Alan Zuckerman, eds. *Comparative Politics: Rationality, Culture, and Structure*. New York: Cambridge University Press: 142–73.

McDermott, Gerald. 2002. *Embedded Politics: Industrial Networks and Institutional Change in Post Communism*. Ann Arbor: University of Michigan Press.

McKee, Martin, Elias Mossialos, and Rita Baeten, eds. 2002. *The Impact of EU Law on Health Care Systems*. Brussels: Peter Lang.

Meeker, Michael. 2002. *A Nation of Empire: The Ottoman Legacy of Turkish Modernity*. Berkeley: University of California Press.

Memmelaar, Ellen. 1990. East Europe Sees a Model for Banks in Credit Unions. *American Banker* (January): 6.

Mendelson, Sarah, and John Glenn, eds. 2002. *The Power and Limits of NGOs*. New York: Columbia University Press.

Meurs, Mieke. 2001. *The Evolution of Agrarian Institutions: A Comparative Study of Post-Socialist Hungary and Bulgaria*. Ann Arbor: University of Michigan Press.

Meyer, John, John Boli, George Thomas, and Francisco Ramirez. 1997. World Society and the Nation-State. *American Journal of Sociology* 103: 144–81.

Meyer, John, and Brian Rowan. 1991. Institutionalized Organizations: Formal Structure as Myth and Ceremony. In Walter Powell and Paul DiMaggio, eds. *The New Institutionalism in Organizational Analysis*. Chicago: University of Chicago Press: 41–62.

Meyer-Sahling, Jan-Hinrik. 2002. Personnel Policy Regimes, Political Discretion and Civil Service Reform in Central and Eastern Europe. Conference of European Consortium for Political Research, Turin, Italy.

Michta, Andrew, ed. 1999. *America's New Allies: Poland, Hungary, and the Czech Republic in NATO*. Seattle: University of Washington Press.

Mill, John Stuart. 1970. *Two Methods of Comparison* [1888] as reprinted in Amatai Etzioni and Frederic L. Du Bow, eds. *Comparative Perspectives: Theories and Methods*. Boston: Little, Brown: 205–13.

Milner, Helen. 1998. Rationalizing Politics: The Emerging Synthesis of Intertational, American, and Comparative Politics. *International Organization* 52: 759–86.

Milward, Alan. 2000. *The European Rescue of the Nation-State*, 2nd ed. London: Routledge.

Minkenberg, Michael. 2002. The Radical Right in Postsocialist Central and Eastern Europe: Comparative Observations and Interpretations. *East European Politics and Societies* 16(2): 335–63.

Molin, Katarina, and Rüdiger Wurzel. 2000. Swedish Environmental Policy. In Lee Miles, ed. *Sweden and the European Union Evaluated*. London: Continuum: 166–79.

Moravcsik, Andrew. 1998. *The Choice for Europe: Social Purpose and State Power from Messina to Maastricht*. Ithaca: Cornell University Press.

Moravcsik, Andrew, and Milada Vachudova. 2003. National Interests, State Power, and EU Enlargement. *East European Politics and Societies* 17(1): 42–57.

Morlino, Leonardo. 2002. What We Know and What We Should Know on Europeanization and the Reshaping of Representation in SE Democracies. Conference Paper. Berkeley: University of California.

Moser, Peter. 1997. A Theory of the Conditional Influence of the European Parliament in the Cooperation Procedure. *Public Choice* 91: 333–50.

Moser, Robert. 2001. *Unexpected Outcomes: Electoral Systems, Political Parties, and Representation in Russia*. Pittsburgh: University of Pittsburgh Press.

Mosher, James, and David Trubek. 2003. Alternative Approaches to Governance in the EU: EU Social Policy and the European Employment Strategy. *Journal of Common Market Studies* 41(1): 63–88.

Mossialos, Elizas, and Martin McKee. 2002. *EU Law and the Social Character of Health Care*. Brussels: Peter Lang.

Moyer, H. Wayne, and Timothy Josling. 2001. Agricutural Policy Reform in the US and the EU: The Impact of Shifting Paradigms. Conference Paper. European Communities Studies Association, Madison, Wisconsin.

Muniak, Dennis. 1985. Policies That Don't Fit. *Policy Studies Journal* 14: 1–19.

Nallet, H., and A. Van Stolk. 1994. *Relations Between the European Union and Central and Eastern European Countries in Matters Concerning Agriculture and Food Production*. Report to the European Commission Directorate General VI, Brussels.

Nelson, Daniel. 2002. Definition, Diagnosis, Therapy: A Civil–Military Critique. *Defense and Security Analysis* 18(2): 157–70.

Nelson, Joan, ed. 1994. *Intricate Links: Democratization and Market Reform in Latin America and Eastern Europe*. New Brunswick, NJ: Transaction Publishers.

Nelson, Joan. 1995. Is the Era of Conditionality Past? Working Paper No. 72. Madrid: Juan March Institute.

Nelson, Joan. 2001. The Politics of Pension and Health-Care Reforms in Hungary and Poland. In János Kornai, Stephan Hagggard, and Robert Kaufman, eds. *Reforming the State: Fiscal and Welfare Reforms in Post-Socialist Countries*. New York: Cambridge University Press: 235–66.

Neumayer, Laure. 2000. Political Parties and European Integration in Central Europe: Poland, Hungary, Czech Republic. *Integrace* (February 2000), 21.

New Zealand, Ministry of Foreign Affairs and Trade. 2001. Agriculture in Poland and Hungary and the Potential Effects on the EU's Agricultural Policies. Working Paper No. 16. NZ Trade Consortium.

Nicoll, William, and Richard Schoenberg, eds. 1998. *Europe Beyond 2000: The Enlargment of the European Union towards the East*. London: Whurr Publishers.

Nielson, Daniel. 2003. Supplying Trade Reform: Political Institutions and Trade Policy in Middle-Income Democracies. *American Journal of Political Science* 47(3): 470–91.

Nielson, Daniel, and Michael Tierney. 2003. Delegation to International Organizations: Agency Theory and World Bank Environmental Reform. *International Organization* 57(2): 241–76.

Nielson, Daniel, Michael Tierney, and Mona Lyne. 2003. A Problem of Principals: Common Agency and Social Lending at Multilateral Development Banks. Conference Paper, University of California, San Diego, September 18.

Nolte, Ellen, Rheinhard Scholz, Vladimir Shkolnikov, and Martin McKee. 2002. The Contribution of Medical Care to Changing Life Expectancy in Germany and Poland. *Social Science and Medicine* 55: 15–31.

North Atlantic Treaty Organization. 1995. *Study on NATO Enlargement*. Brussels: NATO Office of Information and Press.

North Atlantic Treaty Organization. 2001a. *NATO Enlargement: Draft Interim Report*. Brussels: NATO Office of Information and Press.

North Atlantic Treaty Organization. 2001b. *NATO Handbook*. Brussels: NATO Office of Information and Press.

North, Douglass. 1990. *Institutions, Institutional Change, and Economic Performance*. New York: Cambridge University Press.

Novotný, Jaromír. 1996. General Director of the Foreign Relations Section of the Ministry of Defence of the Czech Republic. *NATO Review* 44: 25–29.

Nunberg, Barbara, ed. 1999. *The State After Communism: Administrative Transitions in Central and Eastern Europe*. Washington, DC: The World Bank.

O'Dwyer, Conor. 2002. Civilizing the State Bureaucracy: The Unfilled Promise of Public Administration Reform in Poland, Slovakia, and the Czech Republic, 1990–2000. Working Paper. Berkeley Program in Soviet and Post-Soviet Studies.

O'Dwyer, Conor. 2003. Runaway State Building: How Parties Shape States in Post-Communist Poland, the Czech Republic, and Slovakia. Ph.D. Dissertation. University of California, Berkeley.

Offe, Claus. 1991. Capitalism by Democratic Design? Democratic Theory Facing the Triple Transition in East Central Europe. *Social Research* 58(4): 865–92.

Offe, Claus. 1997. *Varieties of Transition: The East European and East German Experience*. Cambridge: MIT Press.

Orenstein, Mitchell. 2001. *Out of the Red: Building Capitalism and Democracy in Postcommunist Europe*. Ann Arbor: University of Michigan Press.

Organisation for Economic Co-operation and Development. 2002. *Agricultural Policies in Transition Economies*. Paris: OECD.

Orosz, Éva, and Andrew Burns. 2000. The Healthcare System in Hungary. Working Paper No. 241. Organization for Economic Co-operation and Development. Economics Department.

Orosz, Éva, and Imre Holló. 2001. Hospitals in Hungary: The Story of Stalled Reforms. *Eurohealth* 7(3): 22–5.

Orosz, Éva, Guy Ellena, and Melitta Jakab. 1998. Reforming the Health Care System: The Unfinished Agenda. In Lajos Bokros and Jean-Jacques Dethier, eds. *Public Finance Reform During the Transition: The Experience of Hungary*. Washington, DC: World Bank: 221–53.

Ozcan, Yasar, and Ivan Gladkji. 1997. Development of a Graduate Healthcare Management Program at Palacky University, Czech Republic. *The Journal of Health Administration Education* 15: 182–9.

Pecze, Zoltán. 1998. *Civil–Military Relations in Hungary 1989–1996*. Groningen, the Netherlands: Centre for European Security Studies.

Perepelitsa, Grigoriy. 2002. The Development of Civil–Military Relations in Post-Soviet Ukraine. In Andrew Cottey, Timothy Edmunds, and Anthony Forster, eds. *Democratic Control of the Military in Postcommunist Europe*. New York: Palgrave Macmillan: 233–47.

Pestoff, Victor. 1988. Exit, Voice, and Collective Action in Swedish Consumer Policy. *Journal of Consumer Policy* 11: 11–27.

Peterson, John. 1995. Decision–Making in the European Union: Towards a Framework for Analysis. *Journal of European Public Policy* 21(1): 69–93.

Peterson, John, and Elizabeth Bomberg. 1999. *Decision-Making in the European Union*. London: Macmillan.

Piccinini, Antonio, and Margaret Loseby. 2001. *Agricultural Policies in Europe and the USA: Farmers Between Subsidies and Markets*. New York: Palgrave.

Pickel, Andreas. 1997. Neoliberalism, Gradualism, and Some Typical Ambiguities and Confusions in the Transformation Debate. *New Political Economy* 2(2): 221–35.

Pickel, Andreas, and Helmut Wiesenthal. 1997. *The Grand Experiment: Debating Shock Therapy, Transition Theory, and the East German Experience*. Boulder, CO: Westview Press.

Pierson, Paul. 1996. The Path to European Integration: A Historical Institutionalist Analysis. *Comparative Political Studies* 29(2): 123–163.

Pierson, Paul. 2000a. Increasing Returns, Path Dependence, and the Study of Politics. *American Political Science Review* 94(2): 251–67.

Pierson, Paul. 2000b. Not Just What but When: Timing and Sequence in Political Processes. *Studies in American Political Development* 14(Spring): 72–92.

Piore, Michael, and Charles Sabel. 1990. *The Second Industrial Divide: Possibilities for Prosperity*. New York: Basic Books.

Polanyi, Karl. 1946. *The Great Transformation: Origins of Our Time*. London: Victor Gollancz.

Pollack, Mark. 1995. Regional Actors in an Intergovernmental Play: The Making and Implementation of EC Structural Policy. In Carolyn Rhodes and Sonia Mazey, eds. *The State of the European Union, Vol. 3: Building a European Polity*. Boulder, CO: Lynne Reiner: 361–90.

Pollack, Mark. 1997. Delegation, Agency and Agenda Setting in the European Community. *International Organization* 51: 99–134.

Pollack, Mark. 2003. *The Engines of European Integration: Delegation, Agency, and Agenda Setting in the EU*. New York: Oxford University Press.

Pouliquen, Alain. 2001. *Competitiveness and Farm Incomes in the CEEC Agrifood Sectors: Implications Before and After Accession for EU Markets and Policies*. Brussels: Report to the European Commission, DG VI.

Powell, Walter, and Paul DiMaggio, eds. 1986. The *New Institutionalism in Organizational Analysis*. Chicago: University of Chicago Press.

Pravda, Alex, and Jan Zielonka, eds. 2001. *Democratic Consolidation in Eastern Europe*. Oxford: Oxford University Press.

Pridham, Geoffrey. 1997. The International Dimension of Democratization: Theory, Practice, and Inter-Regional Comparisons. In Pridham, Geoffrey, Eric Herring, and George Sanford, eds. *Building Democracy? The International Dimension of Democratisation in Eastern Europe*. London: Leicester University Press: 7–29.

Pridham, Geoffrey, Eric Herring, and George Sanford, eds. 1997. *Building Democracy? The International Dimension of Democratisation in Eastern Europe*. London: Leicester University Press.

Pritchard, Jean-Paul, ed. 2000a. *Consumer Protection in Czech Republic*. Louvain, Belgium: Centre de Droit de la Consommation.

Pritchard, Jean-Paul, ed. 2000b. *Consumer Protection in Hungary*. Louvain, Belgium: Centre de Droit de la Consommation.

Prodi, Romano. 2002. The Final Lap. Speech delivered to the European Parliament, Brussels, 9 October 2002. Available at <http://www.europa.eu.int>.

Prymula, Roman, Juri Pavlicek, and Alena Petrakova. 1997. University Partnership Project in Health Services Management Education: The Driving Force Behind the Czech Republic Educational Network. *The Journal of Health Administration Education* 15: 190–9.

Putnam, Robert. 1993. *Making Democracy Work: Civic Traditions in Modern Italy*. Princeton: Princeton University Press.

Radaelli, Claudio. 2000. Whither Europeanization? Concept Stretching and Substantive Change. *European Integration Online Papers* 4(8): 1–27. Accessed at <http://eiop.or.at/eiop>.

Ratinger, Tomáš. 1997. *The Competitiveness of Czech Agricultural Producers in an Integrated European Market*. Prague: EU ACE Programme on Agriculture and East-West Integration, Final Report.

Ratinger, Tomáš. 2001. Methodology for Assessing Determinants of Competitiveness of Czech, Hungarian, and Polish Farms. Working Paper. Wye: IDARA.

Ratinger, Tomáš, Ivan Foltyn, Ladislav Jelinek, Kamila Koutna, Frantisek Nohel, and Jaroslav Prazan. 2003. Integrated Strategy for Agricultural and Rural Development in the Czech Republic. Working Paper. Wye: IDARA.

Reiter, Dan. 2000. Why NATO Enlargement Does Not Spread Democracy. *International Security* 25(4): 41–67.

Rieger, Elmar. 2000. The Common Agriculture Policy. In Helen Wallace and William Wallace, eds. *Policy-Making in the European Union*. 4th ed. Oxford: Oxford University Press: 179–210.

Risse, Thomas, Maria Green Cowles, and James Caporaso. 2001. Europeanization and Domestic Change: Introduction. In Maria Green Cowles, Thomas Risse, and James Caporaso, eds. *Transforming Europe: Europeanization and Domestic Change*. Ithaca: Cornell University Press: 1–20.

Ritchie, Ella. 2003. Modes of Regulation in the Common Fisheries Policy: A Moveable Feast? European Union Studies Association, Nashville, TN.

Róna-Tas, Ákos. 1997. *The Great Surprise of Small Transformation: The Demise of Communism and the Rise of the Private Sector in Hungary*. Ann Arbor: University of Michigan Press.

Rosamond, Ben. 2000. *Theories of European Integration*. New York: Palgrave.

Rose, Richard. 1991. Lesson Drawing Across Nations. *Journal of Public Policy* 11(1): 3–30.

Rose, Richard. 1993. *Lesson-Drawing in Public Policy: A Guide to Learning Across Space and Time*. Chatham, NJ: Chatham House.

Rosen, Stephen. 1991. *Innovation and the Modern Military: Winning the Next War*. Ithaca: Cornell University Press.

Ruggie, John. 1998. *Constructing the World Polity: Essays on International Institutionalization*. Longdon: Routledge.

Sajo, András. 1997. Universal Rights, Missionaries and "Local Savages". *East European Constitutional Review* 6(Winter): 44–9.

Sandholtz, Wayne, and Alec Stone Sweet, eds. 1998. *European Integration and Supranational Governance*. New York: Oxford University Press.

Sarvaš, Štefan. 1999. Professional Soldiers and Politics: A Case of Central and Eastern Europe. *Armed Forces and Society* 26(1): 99–118.

Sarvaš, Štefan. 2000. The NATO Enlargement Debate in the Media and Civil–Military Relations in the Czech Republic and Slovakia. *European Security* 9(1): 113–26.

Scharpf, Fritz. 1985. Die Politikverflechtungsfalle – Europäische Integration und deutscher Föderalismus im Vergleich. *Politische Vierteljahresschrift* 26: 323–56.

Scharpf, Fritz. 1988. The Joint-Decision Trap: Lessons from German Federalism and European Integration. *Public Administration* 66: 239–78.

Scharpf, Fritz. 1993. Positive und Negative Koordination in Verhandlungssystemen. In Adrienne Héritier, ed. *Policy-Analyse: Kritik und Neuorientierung*. Opladen: Westdeutscher Verlag: 57–83.

Scheffler, Richard, and Franci Duitch. 2000. Health Care Privatisation in the Czech Republic: Ten Years of Reform. *Eurohealth* 6(2): 5–7.

Schiemann, John. 2002. The Negotiated Origins of the Electoral System. In András Bozóki, ed. *The Roundtable Talks of 1989: The Genesis of Hungarian Democracy*. Budapest: Central European University Press: 165–90.

Schimmelfennig, Frank. 2001. The Community Trap: Liberal Norms, Rhetorical Action, and the Eastern Enlargement of the European Union. *International Organization* 55(1): 47–80.

Schimmelfennig, Frank. 2004. *The EU, NATO and the Integration of Europe: Rules and Rhetoric*. New York: Cambridge University Press.

Schimmelfennig, Frank, Stefan Engert, and Heiko Knobel. 2004. Basic Europeanization: The Impact of EU Political Conditionality. In Frank Schimmelfennig and Ulrich Sedelmeier, eds. *The Europeanization of Eastern Europe*. Ithaca: Cornell University Press (in press).

Schimmelfennig, Frank, and Ulrich Sedelmeier, eds. 2004. *The Europeanization of Eastern Europe: Evaluating the Conditionality Model*. Ithaca: Cornell University Press.

Schmidt, Susanne. 2001. A Constrained Commission: Informal Practices of Agenda Setting in the Council. In Gerald Schneider and Mark Aspinwall, eds. *The Rules of Integration: Institutionalist Approaches to the Study of Europe*. Manchester: Manchester University Press: 125–46.

Schneider, Gerald. 1994. Getting Closer at Different Speeds: Strategic Interaction in Widening European Integration. In Pierre Allan and Christian Schmidt, eds. *Game Theory and International Relations*. Cheltenham: Edward Elgar: 121–5.

Schneider, Gerald. 1995. Agenda-Setting in European Integration: The Conflict between Voters, Governments and Supranational Institutions. In Finn Laursen, ed. *The Political Economy of European Integration*. Maastricht: European Institute of Public Administration: 31–61.

Schwellnuss, Guido. 2004. Conditionality and Its Misfits: Non-Discrimination and Minority Protection in the EU Enlargement Process. In Frank Schimmelfennig and Ulrich Sedelmeier, eds. *The Europeanization of Eastern Europe*. Ithaca: Cornell University Press.

Sharman, J. C. 2002. Agrarian Politics in Eastern Europe in the Shadow of EU Accession. *European Union Politics* 4(4): 447–71.

Sherr, James. 2002. Professionalisation of Armed Forces: The Case of Ukraine. In Anthony Forster, Timothy Edmunds, and Andrew Cottey, eds. *The Challenge of Military Reform in Postcommunist Europe: Building Professional Armed Forces*. New York: Palgrave Macmillan: 211–30.

Silvia, Stephen, and Aaron Beers Sampson. 2003. *Acquis Communautaire* and European Chauvinism: A Genealogy. Conference Paper. European Union Studies Association, Nashville, TN.

Simon, Jeffrey. 1996. *NATO Enlargement and Central Europe: A Study in Civil–Military Relations*. Washington, DC: National Defense University Press.

Simon, Jeffrey. 1999. Partnership for Peace: After the Washington Summit and Kosovo. *Strategic Forum* 167: 1–5.

Simon, Jeffrey. 2000a. The Next Round of NATO Enlargement. *Strategic Forum* 176: 1–4.

Simon, Jeffrey. 2000b. Transforming the Armed Forces of Central and Eastern Europe. *Strategic Forum* 172: 1–4.

Simon, Jeffrey. 2001. Roadmap to NATO Accession: Preparing for Membership. INSS Special Report. Washington, DC: National Defense University.

Simon, Jeffrey. 2004a. *Hungary and NATO: Problems in Civil-Military Relations*. Lanham, MD: Rowman and Littlefield.

Simon, Jeffrey. 2004b. *NATO and the Czech and Slovak Republics: A Comparative Study in Civil-Military Relations*. Lanham, MD: Rowman and Littlefield.

Simon, Jeffrey. 2004c. *Poland and NATO: A Study in Civil-Military Relations*. Lanham, MD: Rowman and Littlefield.

Simonyi, András. 2002. Interview. *Jane's Intelligence Review* 14(7): 56.

Sissenich, Beate. 2003. State-Building by a Nonstate: European Union Englarement and Social Policy Transfer to Poland and Hungary. Ph.D. Dissertation, Cornell University.

Smith, Steven, and Thomas Remington. 2001. *The Politics of Institutional Choice: The Formation of the Russian State Duma*. Princeton, Princeton University Press.

Snyder, Richard. 2001. Scaling Down: The Subnational Comparative Method. *Studies in Comparative International Development* 36(1): 93–110.

Sólyom, László, and Georg Brunner, eds. 2000. *Constitutional Judiciary in a New Democracy: The Hungarian Constitutional Court.* Ann Arbor: University of Michigan Press.

Spiridonova, Julia, and Nikolai Grigorov. 2000. Bulgaria. In John Bachtler, Ruth Downes, and Grzegorz Gorzelak, eds. *Transition, Cohesion and Regional Policy in Central and Eastern Europe.* Burlington, VT: Ashgate: 71–84.

Stallings, Barbara. 1992. International Influence on Economic Policy: Debt, Stabilization, and Structural Reform. In Stephan Haggard and Robert Kaufman, eds. *The Politics of Economic Adjustment: International Constraints, Distributive Conflicts and the State.* Princeton: Princeton University Press.

Stankovsky, Jan, Fritz Plasser, and Peter Ulram. 1998. *On the Eve of EU Enlargement: Economic Developments and Democratic Attitudes in East Central Europe.* Vienna: Zentrum für Angewandte Politikforschung.

Stark, David. 1996. Recombinant Property in East European Capitalism. *American Journal of Sociology* 101(4): 993–1027.

Stark, David, and László Bruszt. 1998. *Postsocialist Pathways: Transforming Politics and Property in East Central Europe.* New York: Cambridge University Press.

Steinmo, Sven, Kathleen Thelen, and Frank Longstreth, eds. 1992. *Structuring Politics: Historical Institutionalism in Comparative Politics.* New York: Cambridge University Press.

Stepan, Alfred. 1988. *Rethinking Military Politics: Brazil and the Southern Cone.* Princeton: Princeton University Press.

Steunenberg, Bernard. 1997. Codecision and its Reform: A Comparative Analysis of Decision Making Rules in the European Union. In Bernard Steunenberg and Frans van Vught, eds. *Political Institutions and Public Policy: Perspectives on European Decision Making.* Dordrecht: Kluwer: 205–25.

Stiles, Kendall. 2002. *Civil Society by Design: Donors, NGOs and Intermestic Development Circles in Bangladesh.* Westport, CT: Praeger Publishers.

Stokes, Gale. 1991. The Social Origins of East European Politics. In Daniel Chirot, ed. *The Origins of Backwardness in Eastern Europe.* Berkeley: University of California Press: 210–52.

Stockholm International Peace Research Institute. 1999. *SIPRI Yearbook 1999: Armaments, Disarmament, and International Security.* New York: Oxford University Press.

Stockholm International Peace Research Institute. 2002. *SIPRI Yearbook 2002: Armaments, Disarmament, and International Security.* New York: Oxford University Press.

Stone, Randall W. 2002. *Lending Credibility: The International Monetary Fund and the Post-Communist Transition.* Princeton, Princeton University Press.

Stone Sweet, Alec, Wayne Sandholtz, and Neil Fligstein, eds. 2001. *The Institutionalization of Europe.* New York: Oxford University Press.

Stone Sweet, Alec, Neil Fligstein, and Wayne Sandholtz. 2001. The Institutionalization of European Space. In Alec Stone Sweet, Wayne Sandholtz, and Neil Fligstein, eds. *The Institutionalization of Europe.* New York: Oxford University Press: 1–28.

Strang, David, and Sarah Soule. 1998. Diffusion in Organizations and Social Movements: From Hybrid Corn to Poision Pills. *Annual Review of Sociology* 24: 264–90.

Strnad, Ladislav, and Ivan Gladkij. 2001. Performance of the Health Care System in the Czech Republic as Compared to EU Countries and Other EU Candidate Countries. *Biomedical Papers* 145(2): 97–9.

Stroehlein, Andrew. 1999. Clear Land Corridors Bring Clearer Roles. *Central Europe Review* 0(31).

Swidler, Ann. 2001. *Talk of Love: How Culture Matters*. Chicago: University of Chicago Press.

Szabó, Máté. 2003. Civil Society and Security Reform in Hungary, 1989–2002. *Central European Political Science Review* 4(12): 6–34.

Szalai, Julia, and Éva Orosz. 1992. Social Policy in Hungary. In Bob Deacon, ed. *The New Eastern Europe*. London: Sage: 144–66.

Szayna, Thomas. 1999. A Small Contributor or a "Free Rider"? In Andrew Michta, ed. *America's New Allies: Poland, Hungary, and the Czech Republic in NATO*. Seattle: University of Washington Press: 112–48.

Szayna, Thomas, and F. Stephen Larrabee. 1995. *East European Military Reform After the Cold War: Implications for the United States*. Santa Monica: RAND Corp.

Szelényi, Iván. 1998. *Privatizing the Land: Rural Political Economy in Postcommunist Societies*. London: Routledge.

Szelényi, Szonja. 1998. *Equality by Design: The Grand Experiment in Destratification in Socialist Hungary*. Stanford: Stanford University Press.

Szemerkényi, Réka. 1996. *Central European Civil-Military Reforms at Risk*. Adelphi Paper 306. New York: Oxford University Press.

Szent-Miklósy, István. 1957. *Political Trends in the Hungarian Army, 1945–1956*. Santa Monica: RAND.

Szilágyi, Tibor. 2001. The Unwanted Child of Transition and Health Reform: Health Development in Hungary. *Health Promotion Journal of Australia* 11: 78–83.

Tangermann, Stefan, and Timothy Josling. 1994. *Pre-Accession Agricultural Policies for Central Europe and the European Union*. Study prepared for the DGI of the European Commission, Brussels.

Tarditi, Secondo, and John Marsh. 1995. *Agricultural Strategies for the Enlargement of the European Union to Central and Eastern European Countries*. Study prepared for the DGI of the European Commission, Brussels.

Tatham, Allan. 1997. European Community Law Harmonization in Hungary. *Maastricht Journal of European and Comparative Law* 4(3): 249–83.

Taylor, Brian. 1998. The Russian Military in Politics: Civilian Supremacy in Comparative and Historical Perspective. Ph.D. Dissertation, Massachusetts Institute of Technology.

Taylor, Brian. 2001. Russia's Passive Army: Rethinking Military Coups. *Comparative Political Studies* 34(8): 924–52.

Taylor, Brian. 2003. *Politics and the Russian Army: Civil–Military Relations, 1689–2000*. New York: Cambridge University Press.

Thelen, Kathleen. 1999. Historical Institutionalism and Comparative Politics. *Annual Review of Political Science* 2: 369–404.

Tökés, Rudolf. *Hungary's Negotiated Revolution: Economic Reform, Social Change, and Political Succession, 1957–1990*. New York: Cambridge University Press.

Tökés, Rudolf. 1999. A Tale of Three Constitutions: Elites, Institutions, and Democracy in Hungary. In Hans-Georg Heinrich, ed. *Institution Building in the New Democracies: Studies in Post-Communisms*. Budapest: Collegium Budapest.

Tökés, Rudolf. 2002. Institution Building in Hungary: Analytical Issues and Constitutional Models, 1989–90. In András Bozóki, ed. *The Roundtable Talks of 1989: The Genesis of Hungarian Democracy*. Budapest: Central European University Press: 107–36.

Törő, Csaba. 2001. Hungary: Building National Consensus. In Gale Mattox and Arthur Rachwald, eds. *Enlarging NATO: The National Debates*. Boulder, CO: Lynne Rienner: 129–46.

Trbojevic, Drago, and Alain Granson. 2000a. Non-Governmental Consumer Organisations. In Jean-Paul Pritchard, ed. *Consumer Protection in Czech Republic*. Louvain, Belgium: Centre de Droit de la Consommation: 47–57.

Trbojevic, Drago, and Alain Granson. 2000b. Non-Governmental Consumer Organisations. In Jean-Paul Pritchard, ed. *Consumer Protection in Hungary*. Louvain, Belgium: Centre de Droit de la Consommation: 49–58.

Trumbull, Gunnar. 2002. The Rise of Consumer Politics: Market Institutions and Product Choice in Postwar France and Germany. Working Paper Series, No. 03–054. Harvard Business School.

Tsebelis, George. 1994. The Power of the European Parliament as a Conditional Agenda Setter. *American Political Science Review* 88: 128–42.

Tsebelis, George. 2002. *Veto Players: How Political Institutions Work*. Princeton: Princeton University Press.

Ulrich, Marybeth Peterson. 1999. *Democratizing Communist Militaries: The Cases of the Czech and Russian Armed Forces*. Ann Arbor: University of Michigan Press.

Ulrich, Marybeth Peterson. 2002a. Developing Mature National Security Systems in Postcommunist States: The Czech Republic and Slovakia. *Armed Forces and Society* 28(3): 403–25.

Ulrich, Marybeth Peterson. 2002b. The Czech Republic: Negotiating Obstacles on the Way to Integration. In Daniel Nelson and Ustina Markus, eds. *Central and East European Security Yearbook, 2002 Edition*. Washington, DC: Brassey's: 57–84.

Vachudova, Milada. 2000. EU Enlargement: An Overview. *East European Constitutional Review* 9(4): 64–9.

Vachudova, Milada. 2001a. The Atlantic Alliance and the Kosovo Crisis: The Impact of Expansion and the Behavior of New Allies. In Pierre Martin and Mark Brawley, eds. *Alliance Politics, Kosovo, and NATO's War: Allied Force or Forced Allies?* New York: St. Martin's: 203–32.

Vachudova, Milada. 2001b. The Czech Republic: The Unexpected Force of Institutional Constraints. In Jan Zielonka and Alex Pravda, eds. *Democratic*

Consolidation in Eastern Europe. Oxford: Oxford University Press: 325–62.

Vachudova, Milada. 2001c. The Trump Card of Domestic Politics: Bargaining over EU Enlargement. *East European Constitutional Review* 10(2): 93–7.

Vachudova, Milada. 2003. Strategies for European Integration and Democratization in the Balkans. In Marise Cremona, ed. *The Enlargement of the European Union*. Oxford: Oxford University Press: 141–60.

Vachudova, Milada. 2004. *Europe Undivided: Democracy, Leverage, and Integration After 1989*. Oxford: Oxford University Press.

Valki, László. 2002. Hungary's Membership of NATO. *East European Monographs* (619): 461–84.

Van Brabant, Jozef. 1996. *Integrating Europe: The Transition Economies at Stake*. Boston: Kluwer.

Van Brabant, Jozef. 1998. *The Political Economy of Transition: Coming to Grips with History and Methodology*. London: Routledge.

Van Oudenaren, John. 2003. *The Changing Face of Europe: EU Enlargement and Implications for Transatlantic Relations*. Washington, DC: American Institute for Contemporary German Studies.

Vlachová, Marie. 2001. The State of Democratic Control of the Armed Forces in the Czech Republic. Conference at Geneva Centre for the Democratic Control of Armed Forces.

Vlachová, Marie. 2002. Professionalisation of the Army of the Czech Republic. In Anthony Forster, Timothy Edmunds and Andrew Cottey, eds. *The Challenge of Military Reform in Postcommunist Europe: Building Professional Armed Forces*. New York: Palgrave Macmillan: 34–48.

Vlachová, Marie, and Štefan Sarvaš. 2002. Democratic Control of Armed Forces in the Czech Republic: A Journey From Social Isolation. In Andrew Cottey, Timothy Edmunds, and Anthony Forster, eds. *Democratic Control of the Military in Postcommunist Europe*. New York: Palgrave: 44–63.

Volgyes, Ivan. 1978. The Military as an Agent of Political Socialization: The Case of Hungary. In Dale Herspring and Ivan Volgyes, eds. *Civil–Military Relations in Communist Systems*. Boulder: Westview Press: 145–64.

Výborná, Olga. 1995. The Reform of the Czech Health-Care System. *Eastern European Economics* 33(3): 80–94.

Walberg, Peter, Martin McKee, Vladimir Shkolnikov, Laurent Chenet, and David Leon. 1998. Economic Change, Crime, and Mortality Crisis in Russia: A Regional Anaylsis. *British Medical Association* 317: 312–18.

Walker, Jack. 1969. The Diffusion of Innovation Among the American States. *American Political Science Review* 63: 880–99.

Wallace, Helen, and William Wallace. 2000. *Policy-Making in the European Union*. 4th ed. Oxford: Oxford University Press.

Wallander, Celeste. 2000. Institutional Assets and Adaptability: NATO after the Cold War. *International Organization* 54(4): 705–36.

Wallander, Celeste. 2001. Lost and Found: Gorbachev's New Thinking. *Washington Quarterly* 25(1): 117–29.

Wallander, Celeste. 2002. NATO's Price: Shape Up or Ship Out. *Foreign Affairs*. 81(6): 2–8.

Weiler, J. H. H. 2000. *The Constitution of Europe: Do the New Clothes Have an Emporer? And Other Essays on European Integration.* Cambridge: Cambridge University Press.

Westney, Eleanor. 1987. *Imitation and Innovation: The Transfer of Western Organizational Patterns to Meiji Japan.* Cambridge, MA: Harvard University Press.

Williamson, John. 1990. Democracy and the "Washington Consensus." *World Development* 21(8): 1329–36.

Williamson, John. 1997. The Washington Consensus Revisited. In Louis Emmerij, ed. *Economic and Social Development Into the XXI Century.* Washington, DC: Inter-American Development Bank: 48–61.

Woodruff, David. 1999. *Money Unmade: Barter and the Fate of Russian Capitalism.* Ithaca: Cornell University Press.

World Bank. 1999. *Czech Republic: Toward EU Accession. Main Report.* Washington, DC: World Bank.

World Health Organization. 2000. *Highlights on Health in Hungary.* Copenhagen: World Health Organization.

World Health Organization. 2001. *Highlights on Health in Czech Republic.* Copenhagen: World Health Organization.

Yaniszewski, Mark. 2002. Postcommunist Civil–Military Reform in Poland and Hungary: Progress and Problems. *Armed Forces and Society* 28(3): 385–402.

Yoder, Jennifer. 2003. Decentralisation and Regionalisation after Communism: Administrative and Territorial Reform in Poland and the Czech Republic. *Europe-Asia Studies* 55(2): 263–86.

Yost, David. 1998. *NATO Transformed: The Alliance's New Roles in International Security.* Washington, DC: United States Institute of Peace Press.

Zielonka, Jan, ed. 2001. *Democratic Consolidation in Eastern Europe: Institutional Engineering.* New York: Oxford University Press.

Zielonka, Jan, and Peter Mair. 2002. Introduction: Diversity and Adaptation in the Enlarged European Union. *West European Politics* 25(2): 1–18.

Znoj, Milan. 1999. Czech Attitudes Toward the War. *East European Constitutional Review* 8(3): 47–50.

Index

agriculture policy, 17, 94–99
  in Czech Republic, 99–100, 103–105
  in Hungary, 99–103
  see also emulation in agriculture policy
Alba Kör (the Alba Circle), 145, 157
Alliance of Young Democrats (FIDESZ)
    (Hungary), 138, 140, 141,
    157–158, 211
Antall, Jozsef, 120, 128

Bali, Jozsef, 202
Barany, Zoltan, 127, 136, 140
Barnett, Corelli, 155
Baudys, Antonin, 133, 170
Belicza, Éva, 49
best practices, 41, 212, 216
Black, Cyril, 216
Blair, Tony, 211
Bockman, Johanna, 234
Boda, György, 75
Bojar, Martin, 54
Börzel, Tanja, 94
Bulgaria, 15, 224–227
Bulmer, Simon, 23
Bunce, Valeria, 14
Burch, Martin, 23

Checkel, Jeffrey, 186
Chirac, Jacques, 209, 210
Christian Democratic Union-Czech
    People's Party (KDU-ČSL),
    92

Civic Democratic Party (ODS) (Czech
    Republic), 86–87, 92, 160, 184
civil-military relations, 17–18, 117,
    123–124, 125–129
  in Czech Republic and Hungary,
    125–129, 133–143, 146–149
  in Poland, 227–229
  Parliamentary Defense Committees in
    Czech Republic and Hungary,
    149–151
  see also emulation in civil-military
    relations
Clinton, Bill, 12, 121, 122
Communism, legacies of
  in agriculture policy, 102–103
  in civil-military relations, 118, 125–129,
    181–182, 201–202
  in consumer protection policy, 67
  in health care policy, 52
  see also institutional theory, historical
    institutionalism
conditionality, 238–239, 240
conscription in Czech Republic and
    Hungary, 169–170, *see also*
    military professionalism
consumer protection policy, 16–17
  in Czech Republic, 64–68
  in Hungary, 64–66, 68–69
  in Sweden, 230–231
  see also emulation in consumer
    protection policy
Crawford, Beverly, 217
Csapody, Tamás, 145